written by
ROBERT JORDAN

adapted by
CHUCK DIXON

artwork by
ANDIE TONG

colors by
NICOLAS CHAPUIS

lettered by
BILL TORTOLINI

original series edited by
ERNST DABEL
RICH YOUNG

consultation
ERNST DABEL
LES DABEL

thematic consultants
MARIA SIMONS
BOB KLUTTZ
ALAN ROMANCZUK

Covers by Andie Tong
Collection edits by Rich Young
Collection design by Bill Tortolini

Dynamite Entertainment:

NICK BARRUCCI • PRESIDENT
JUAN COLLADO • CHIEF OPERATING OFFICER
JOSEPH RYBANDT • EDITOR
JOSH JOHNSON • CREATIVE DIRECTOR
RICH YOUNG • BUSINESS DEVELOPMENT
JASON ULLMEYER • GRAPHIC DESIGNER

www.dynamiteentertainment.com

D1211657

A Tor Book
Published by Tom Doherty Associates, LLC
175 Fifth Avenue
New York, NY 10010

www.tor-forge.com

Tor® is a registered trademark of Tom Doherty Associates, LLC.
ISBN 978-0-7653-3789-4
First Trade Paperback Edition: June 2015
Printed in the United States of America

Robert Jordan's the WHEEL of TIME

the EYE of the WORLD

Volume Four

TOR®

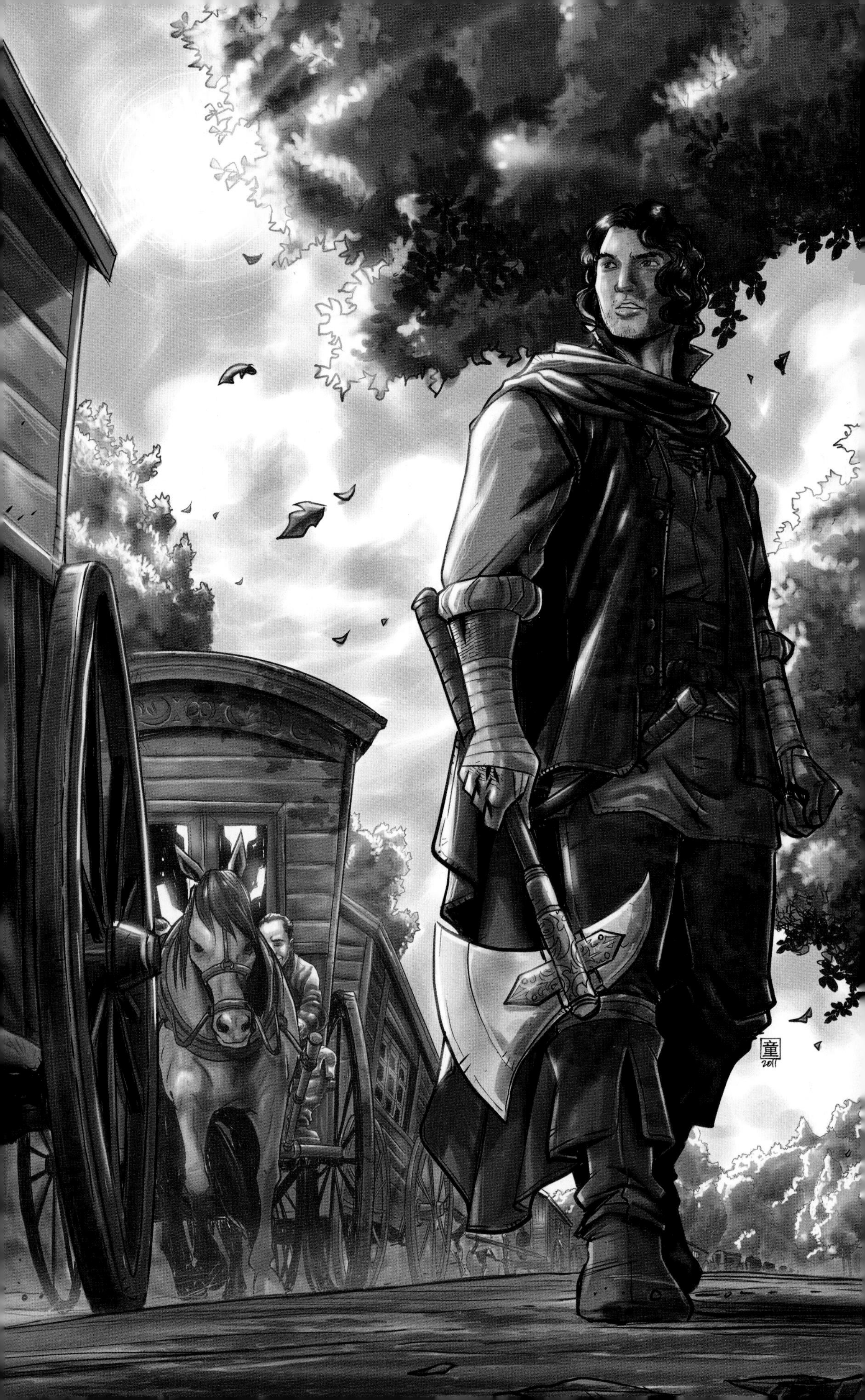

Table of Contents

What Came Before 8

Chapter One...11

Chapter Two 35

Chapter Three 59

Chapter Four 83

Chapter Five 107

Chapter Six 131

Bonus Materials

    Cover Gallery 155

    Biographies 169

WHAT CAME BEFORE...

On the run from the forces of Ba'alzamon, Moiraine leads the Emond's Fielders to the dead city of Aridhol, a place of sleeping evil so great that even the Trollocs fear to set foot inside its walls.

Believing themselves safe from danger, at least during the day, Rand, Mat, and Perrin decide to strike out from the group for a while to explore the city and search for treasure.

What they find is someone named Mordeth, a man of the shadows who does his best to trick the young men into bringing some of the city's vast treasure out past the city walls.

When temptation doesn't work, he reveals himself as the cursed thing that he is, sending the boys scrambling.

Against their will, the Trollocs have entered Aridhol—
also known as the cursed Shadar Logoth—to find their
prey. What they find instead is the mindless, seeping
evil of Mashadar, the foglike thing that devoured all
life in the city in the first place.

In their hurry to escape both the Trollocs and
Mashadar, the Emond's Fielders are separated. Perrin
and Egwene are washed across the river, where they
meet the enigmatic Elyas.

Thom Merrilin brings Rand and Mat to a river ship,
booking them all passage as gleemen.

Moiraine can sense that the others are heading in two
separate directions and must decide which one she, Lan,
and Nynaeve will follow....

chapter one

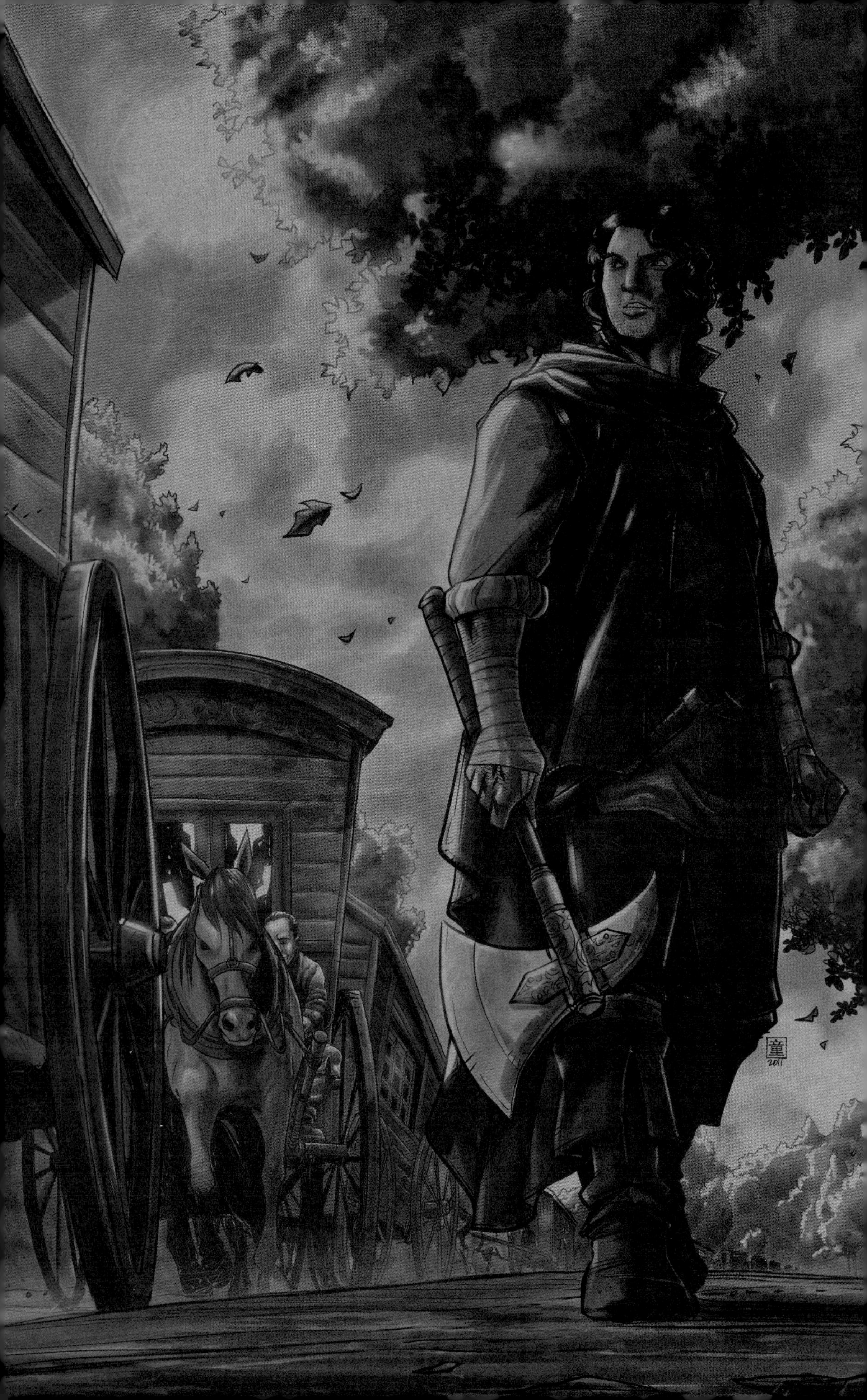

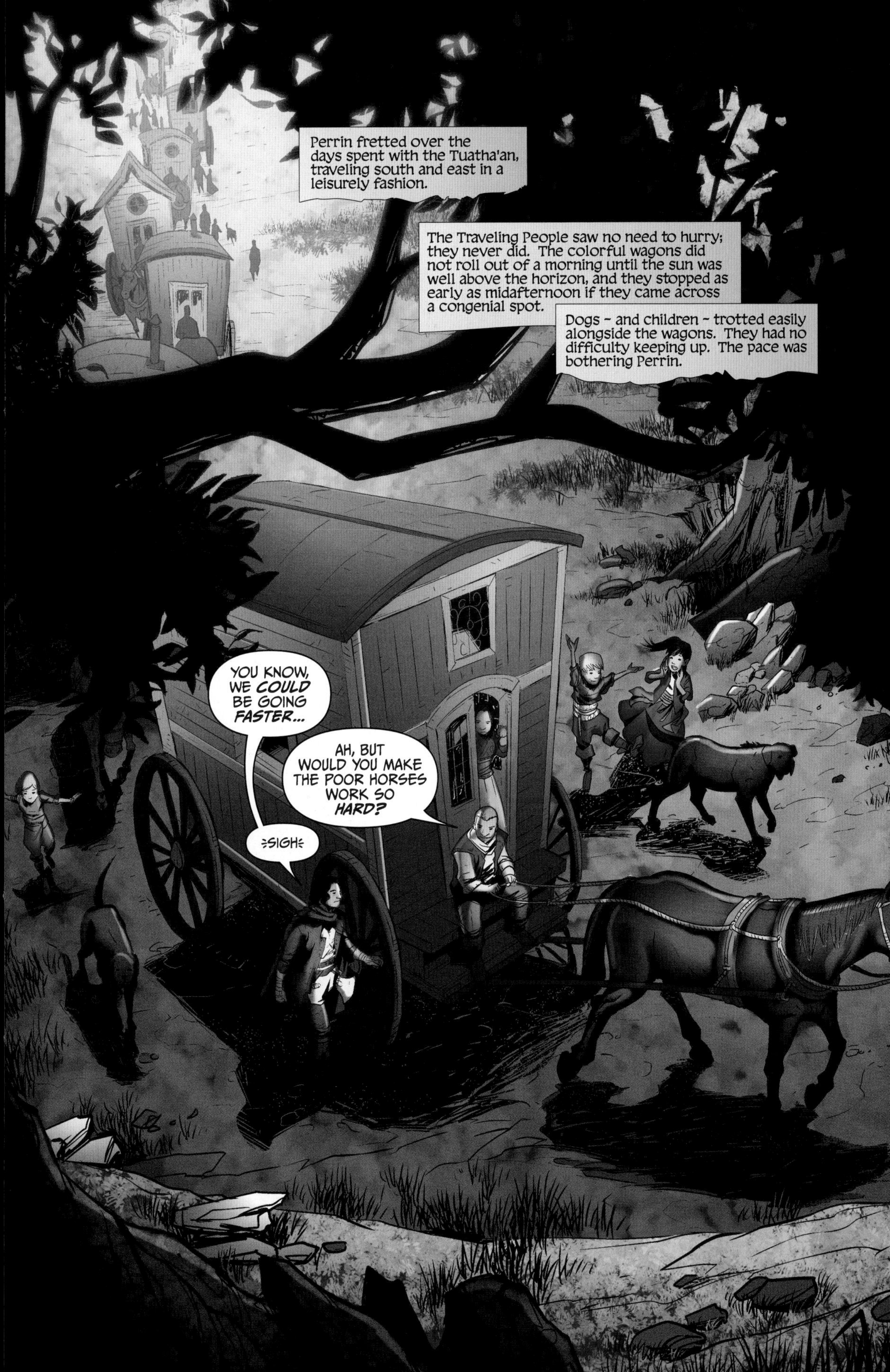
Perrin fretted over the days spent with the Tuatha'an, traveling south and east in a leisurely fashion.
The Traveling People saw no need to hurry; they never did. The colorful wagons did not roll out of a morning until the sun was well above the horizon, and they stopped as early as midafternoon if they came across a congenial spot.
Dogs ~ and children ~ trotted easily alongside the wagons. They had no difficulty keeping up. The pace was bothering Perrin.
YOU KNOW, WE *COULD* BE GOING *FASTER...*
AH, BUT WOULD YOU MAKE THE POOR HORSES WORK SO *HARD?*
SIGH

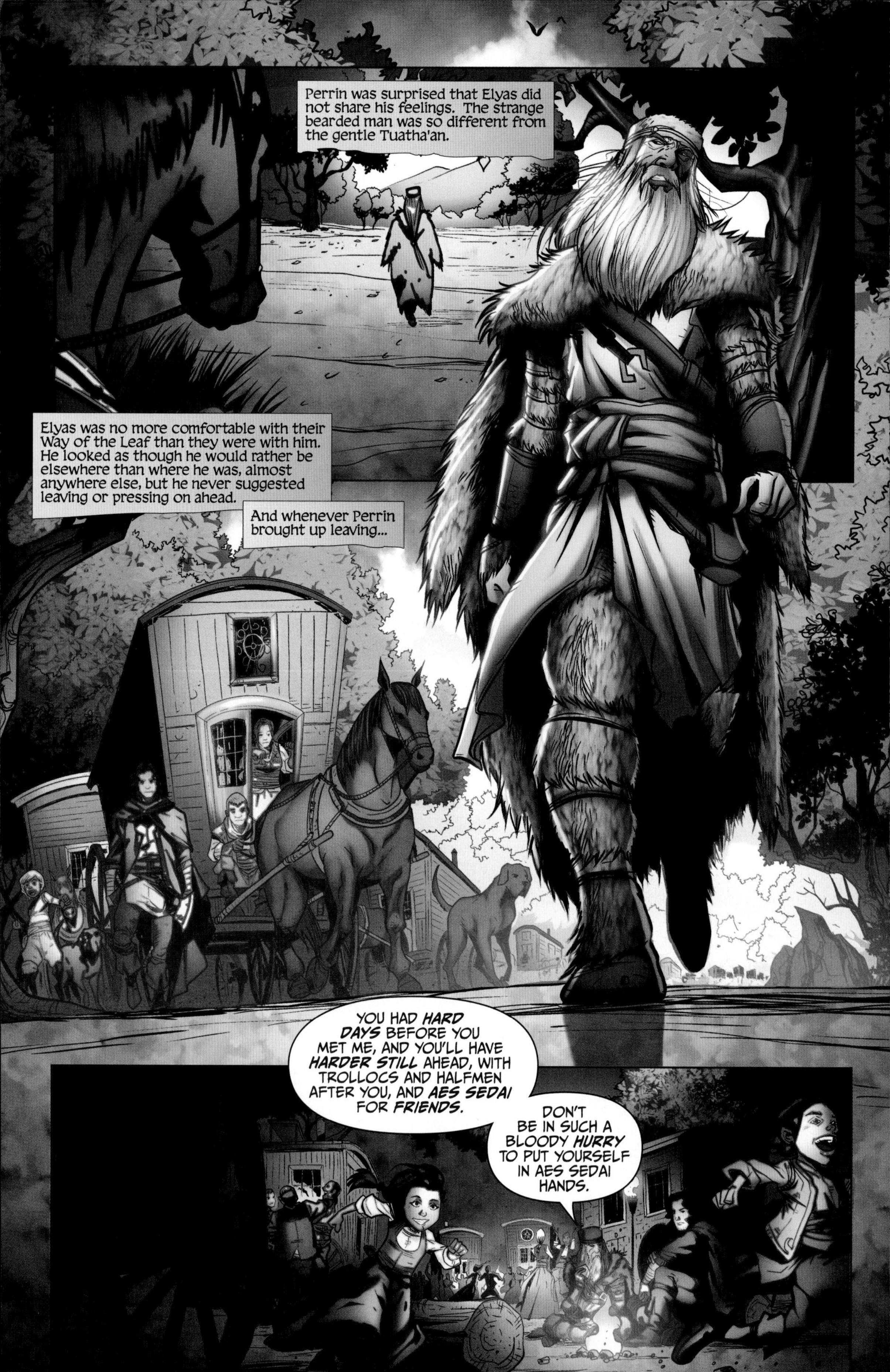
Perrin was surprised that Elyas did not share his feelings. The strange bearded man was so different from the gentle Tuatha'an.
Elyas was no more comfortable with their Way of the Leaf than they were with him. He looked as though he would rather be elsewhere than where he was, almost anywhere else, but he never suggested leaving or pressing on ahead.
And whenever Perrin brought up leaving...
YOU HAD HARD DAYS BEFORE YOU MET ME, AND YOU'LL HAVE HARDER STILL AHEAD, WITH TROLLOCS AND HALFMEN AFTER YOU, AND AES SEDAI FOR FRIENDS.
DON'T BE IN SUCH A BLOODY HURRY TO PUT YOURSELF IN AES SEDAI HANDS.

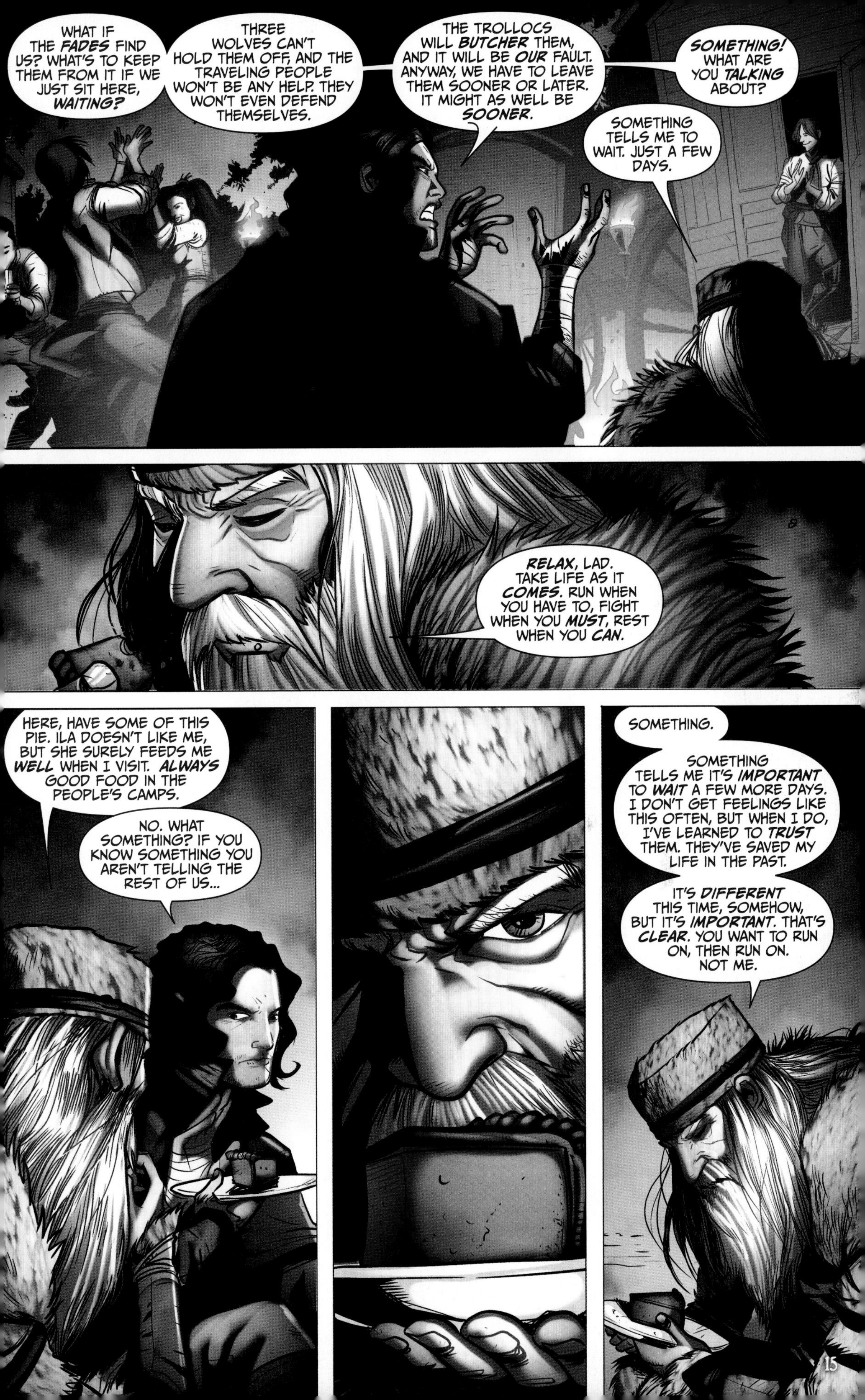
WHAT IF THE FADES FIND US? WHAT'S TO KEEP THEM FROM IT IF WE JUST SIT HERE, WAITING?
THREE WOLVES CAN'T HOLD THEM OFF, AND THE TRAVELING PEOPLE WON'T BE ANY HELP. THEY WON'T EVEN DEFEND THEMSELVES.
THE TROLLOCS WILL BUTCHER THEM, AND IT WILL BE OUR FAULT. ANYWAY, WE HAVE TO LEAVE THEM SOONER OR LATER. IT MIGHT AS WELL BE SOONER.
SOMETHING TELLS ME TO WAIT. JUST A FEW DAYS.
SOMETHING! WHAT ARE YOU TALKING ABOUT?
RELAX, LAD. TAKE LIFE AS IT COMES. RUN WHEN YOU HAVE TO, FIGHT WHEN YOU MUST, REST WHEN YOU CAN.
HERE, HAVE SOME OF THIS PIE. ILA DOESN'T LIKE ME, BUT SHE SURELY FEEDS ME WELL WHEN I VISIT. ALWAYS GOOD FOOD IN THE PEOPLE'S CAMPS.
NO. WHAT SOMETHING? IF YOU KNOW SOMETHING YOU AREN'T TELLING THE REST OF US...
SOMETHING.
SOMETHING TELLS ME IT'S IMPORTANT TO WAIT A FEW MORE DAYS. I DON'T GET FEELINGS LIKE THIS OFTEN, BUT WHEN I DO, I'VE LEARNED TO TRUST THEM. THEY'VE SAVED MY LIFE IN THE PAST.
IT'S DIFFERENT THIS TIME, SOMEHOW, BUT IT'S IMPORTANT. THAT'S CLEAR. YOU WANT TO RUN ON, THEN RUN ON. NOT ME.

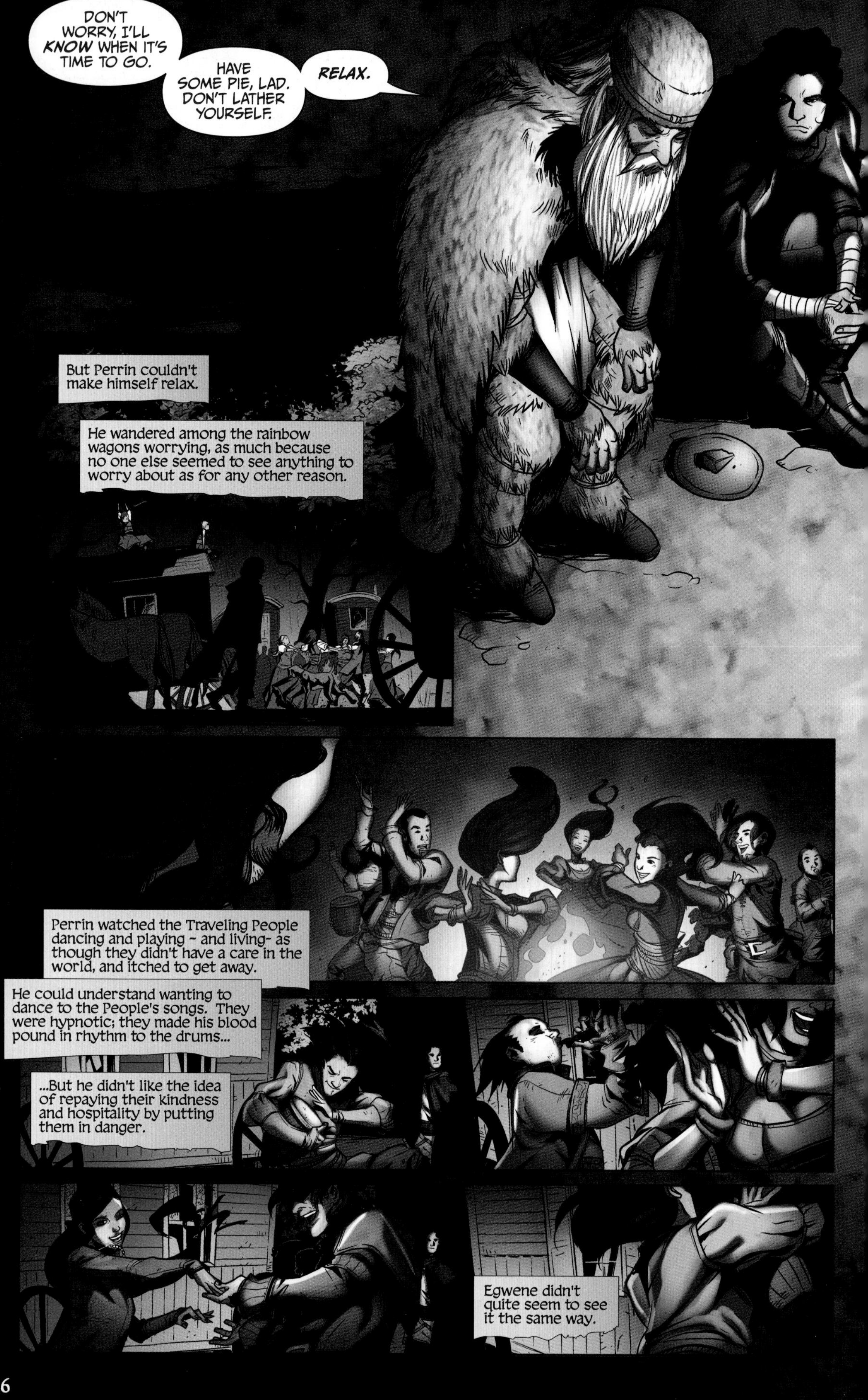
DON'T WORRY, I'LL KNOW WHEN IT'S TIME TO GO.
HAVE SOME PIE, LAD. DON'T LATHER YOURSELF.
RELAX.
But Perrin couldn't make himself relax.
He wandered among the rainbow wagons worrying, as much because no one else seemed to see anything to worry about as for any other reason.
Perrin watched the Traveling People dancing and playing ~ and living- as though they didn't have a care in the world, and itched to get away.
He could understand wanting to dance to the People's songs. They were hypnotic; they made his blood pound in rhythm to the drums...
...But he didn't like the idea of repaying their kindness and hospitality by putting them in danger.
Egwene didn't quite seem to see it the same way.

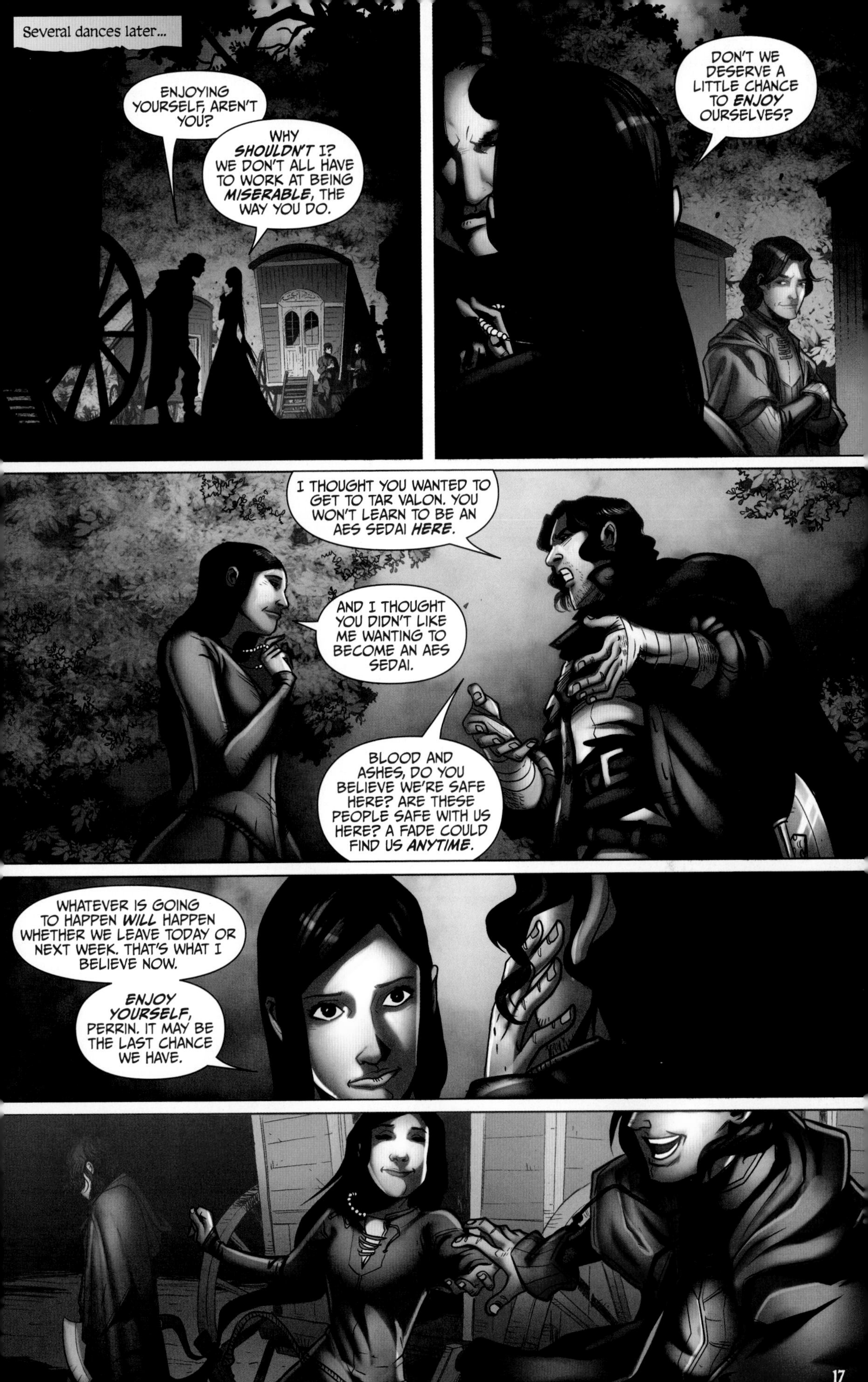
Several dances later...
ENJOYING YOURSELF, AREN'T YOU?
WHY *SHOULDN'T* I? WE DON'T ALL HAVE TO WORK AT BEING *MISERABLE*, THE WAY YOU DO.
DON'T WE DESERVE A LITTLE CHANCE TO *ENJOY* OURSELVES?
I THOUGHT YOU WANTED TO GET TO TAR VALON. YOU WON'T LEARN TO BE AN AES SEDAI *HERE*.
AND I THOUGHT YOU DIDN'T LIKE ME WANTING TO BECOME AN AES SEDAI.
BLOOD AND ASHES, DO YOU BELIEVE WE'RE SAFE HERE? ARE THESE PEOPLE SAFE WITH US HERE? A FADE COULD FIND US *ANYTIME*.
WHATEVER IS GOING TO HAPPEN *WILL* HAPPEN WHETHER WE LEAVE TODAY OR NEXT WEEK. THAT'S WHAT I BELIEVE NOW.
ENJOY YOURSELF, PERRIN. IT MAY BE THE LAST CHANCE WE HAVE.

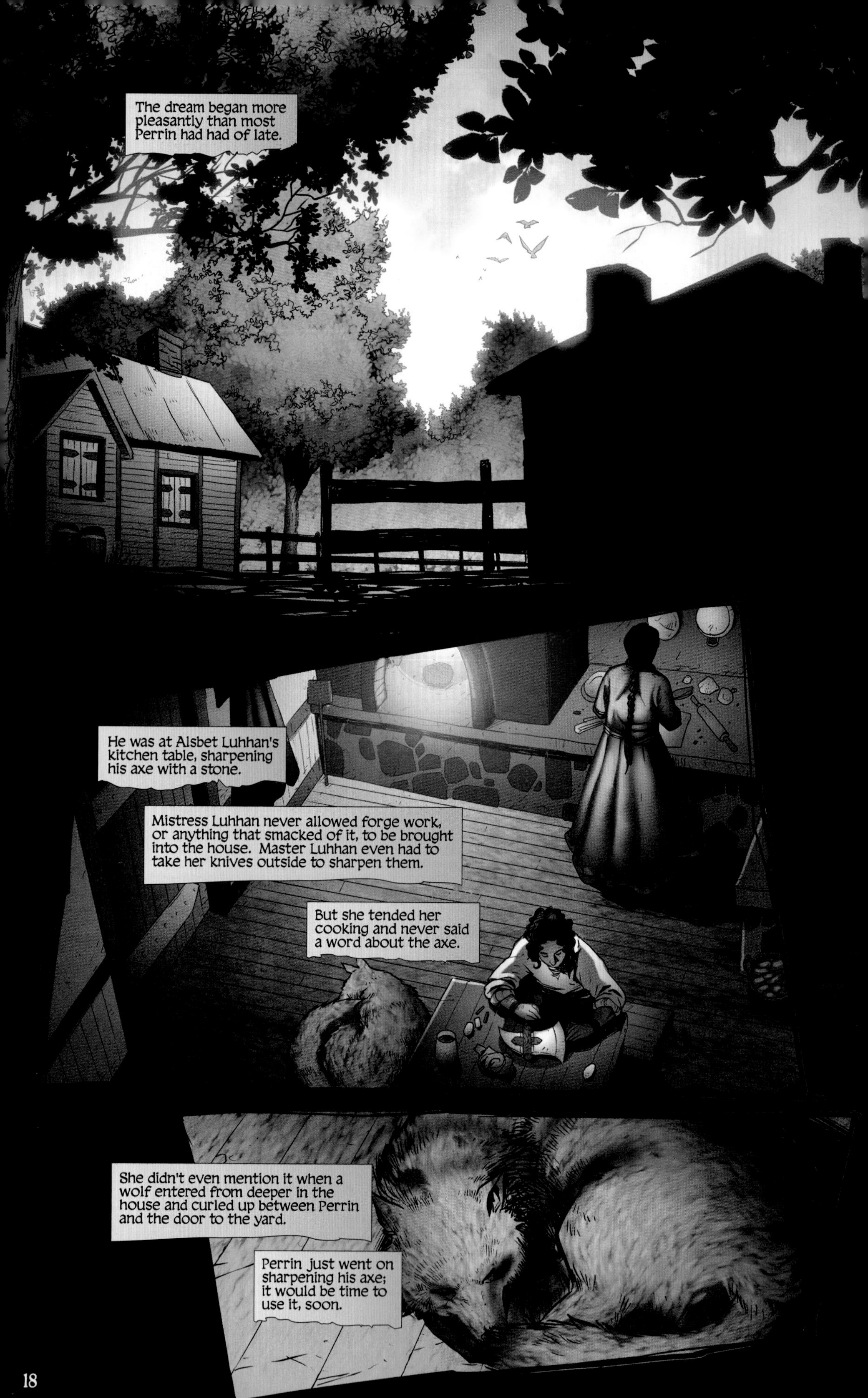

The dream began more pleasantly than most Perrin had had of late.
He was at Alsbet Luhhan's kitchen table, sharpening his axe with a stone.
Mistress Luhhan never allowed forge work, or anything that smacked of it, to be brought into the house. Master Luhhan even had to take her knives outside to sharpen them.
But she tended her cooking and never said a word about the axe.
She didn't even mention it when a wolf entered from deeper in the house and curled up between Perrin and the door to the yard.
Perrin just went on sharpening his axe; it would be time to use it, soon.

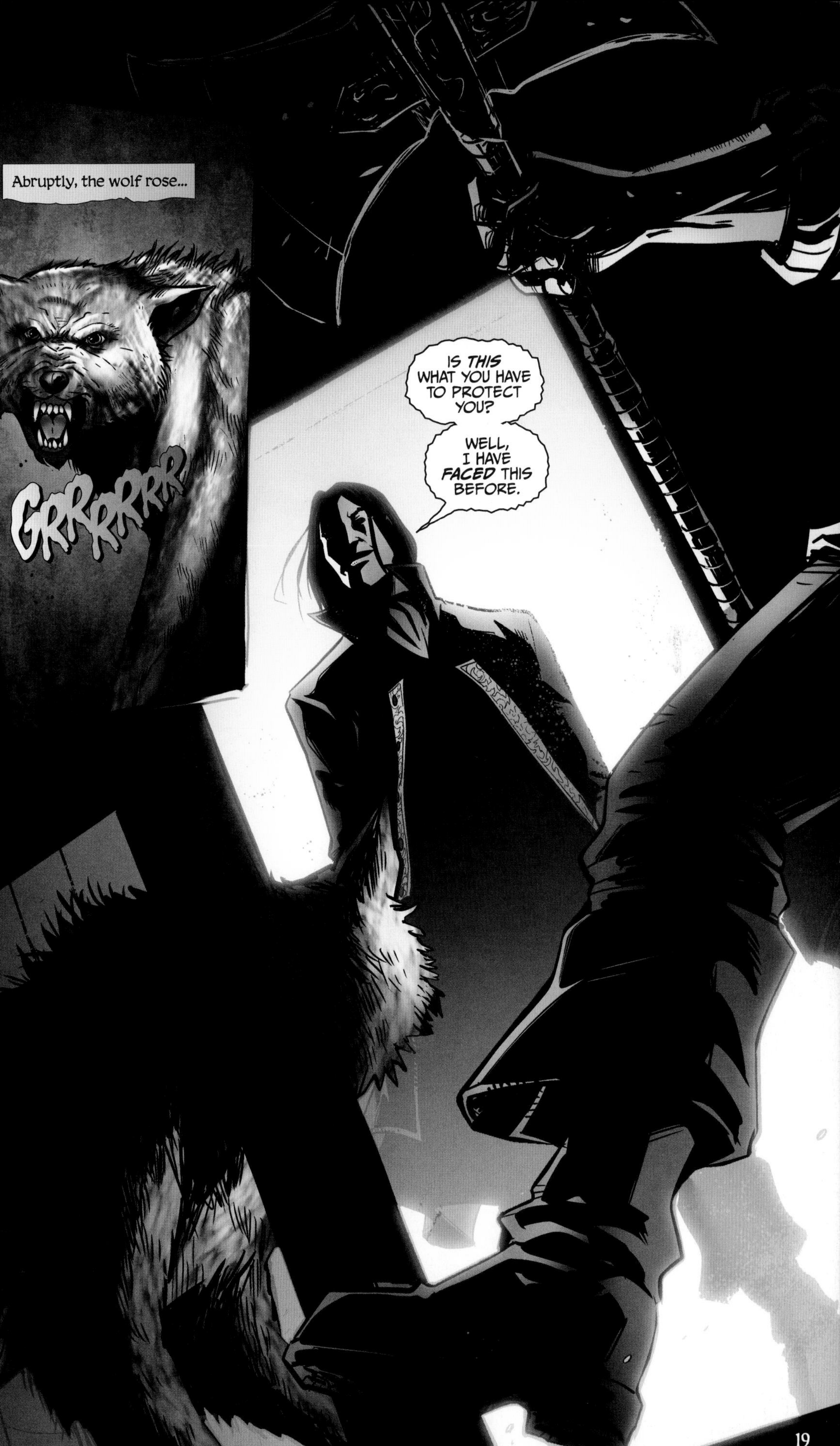
Abruptly, the wolf rose...
GRRRRRR
IS THIS WHAT YOU HAVE TO PROTECT YOU?
WELL, I HAVE FACED THIS BEFORE.

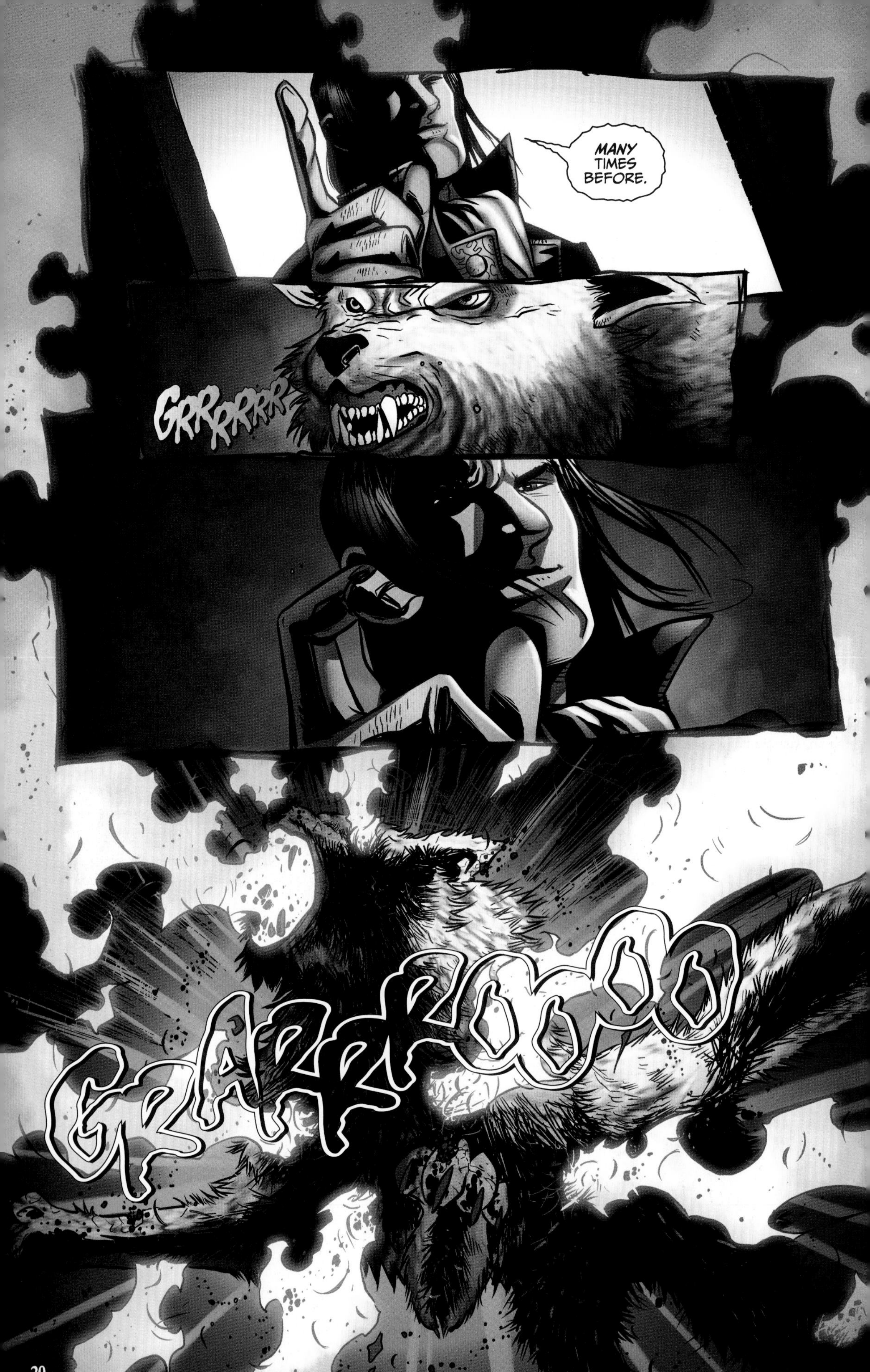
MANY TIMES BEFORE.
GRRRRRR
GRARROOOOO

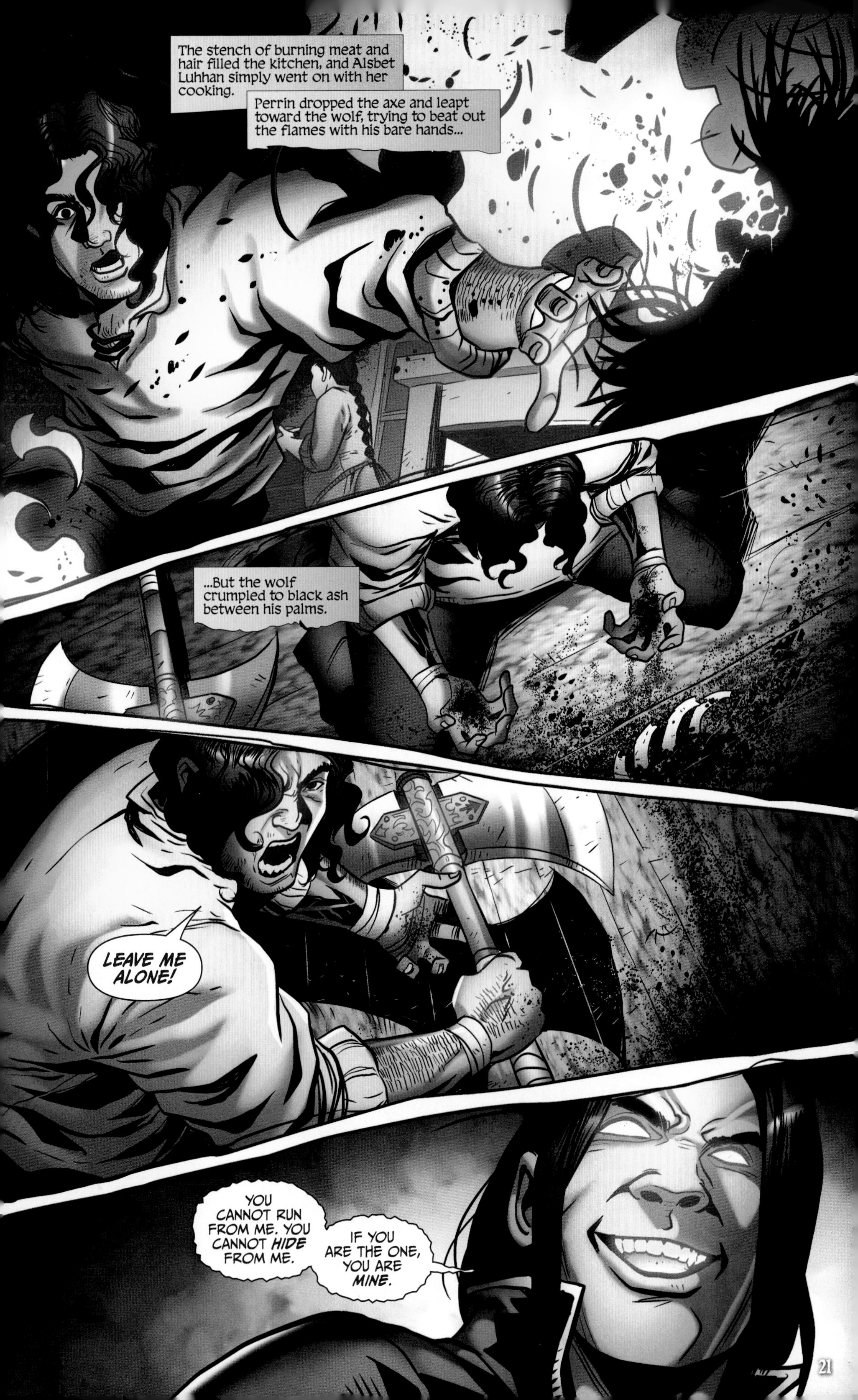
The stench of burning meat and hair filled the kitchen, and Alsbet Luhhan simply went on with her cooking.
Perrin dropped the axe and leapt toward the wolf, trying to beat out the flames with his bare hands...
...But the wolf crumpled to black ash between his palms.
LEAVE ME ALONE!
YOU CANNOT RUN FROM ME. YOU CANNOT HIDE FROM ME.
IF YOU ARE THE ONE, YOU ARE MINE.

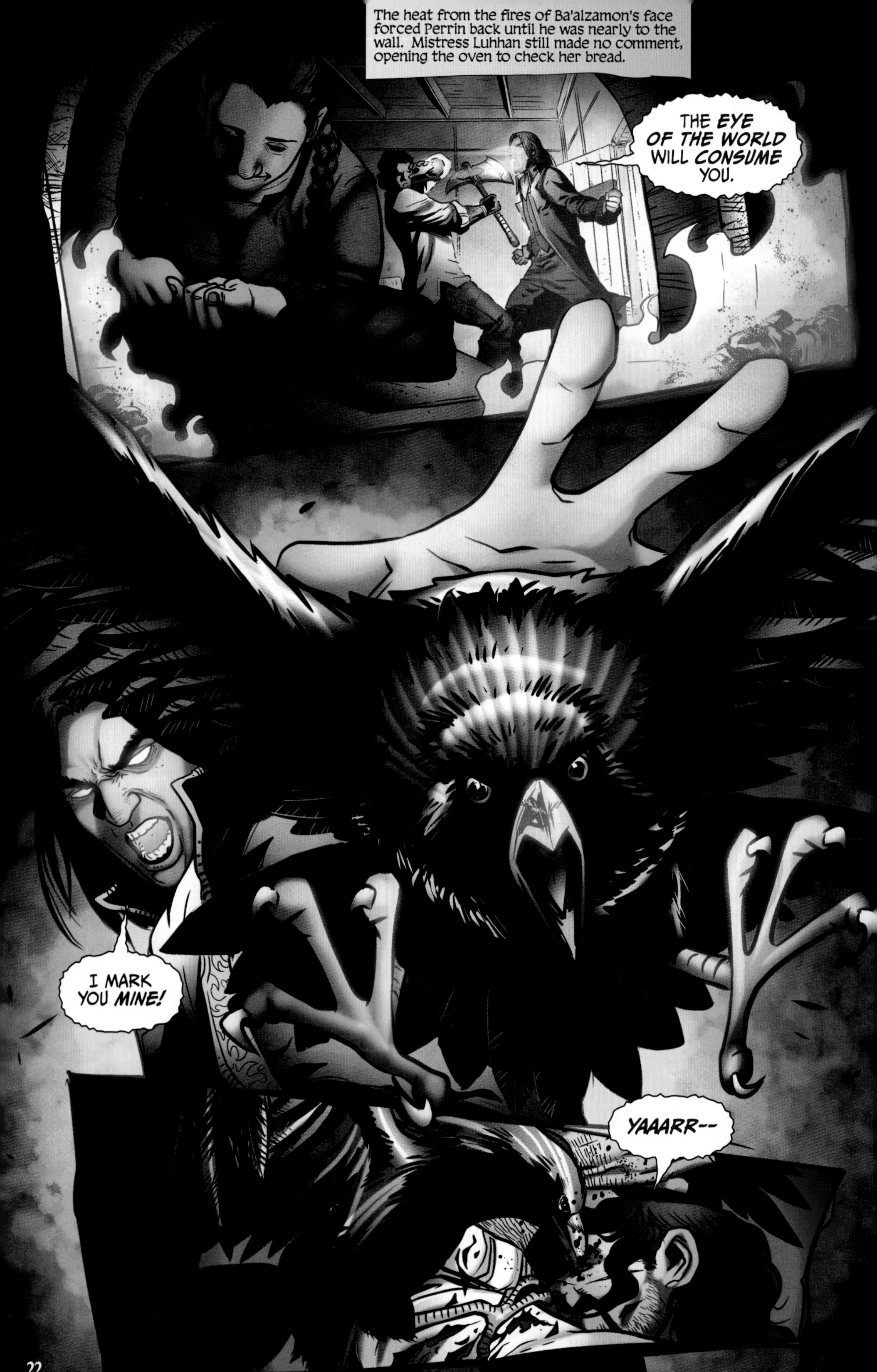
The heat from the fires of Ba'alzamon's face forced Perrin back until he was nearly to the wall. Mistress Luhhan still made no comment, opening the oven to check her bread.
THE EYE OF THE WORLD WILL CONSUME YOU.
I MARK YOU MINE!
YAAARR--

--NNNGH!

≡HH≡

≡HH≡

≡HH≡

There was no pain. No blood. It had been a dream. But Perrin could remember the pain, the stabbing agony.

Beyond the trees where the wagons lay, the wolves were howling, and he shared their sensations...

Fire. Pain. Fire. Hate. *Hate! Kill!*

GET UP, BOY... IT IS TIME FOR US TO *GO.*

While Perrin was still bundling his blanketroll, Raen came out of his wagon, rubbing the sleep from his eyes.

The Seeker glanced at the sky and froze halfway down the steps.

Only his eyes moved as he studied the sky intently, though Perrin could not understand what he was looking at.

A few clouds hung in the east, but there was nothing else to see.

Raen seemed to listen as well, and sme the air, but there was no sound excep wind in the trees and no smell but the smoky remnant of last night's campfi

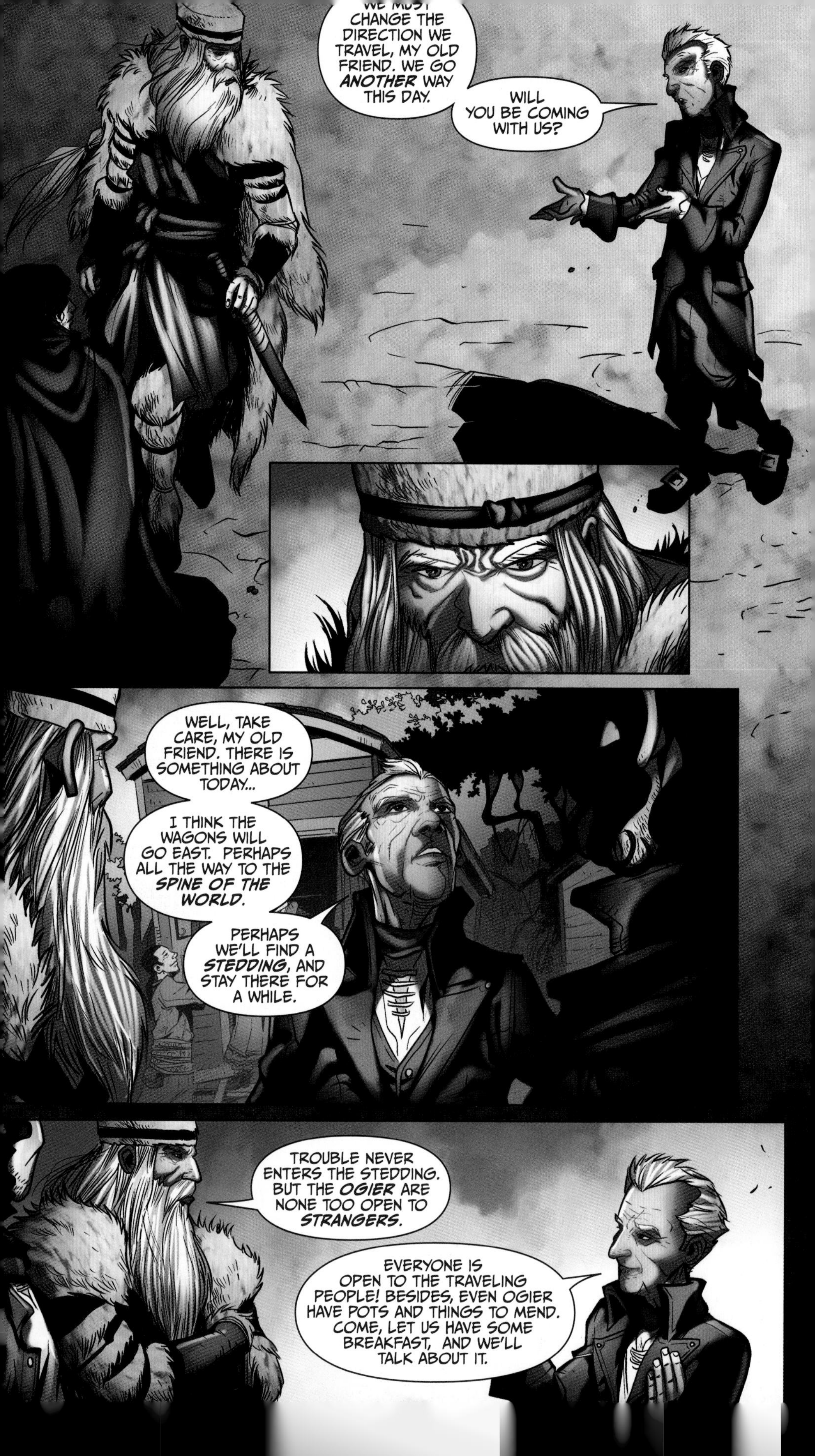
CHANGE THE DIRECTION WE TRAVEL, MY OLD FRIEND. WE GO ANOTHER WAY THIS DAY.
WILL YOU BE COMING WITH US?
WELL, TAKE CARE, MY OLD FRIEND. THERE IS SOMETHING ABOUT TODAY...
I THINK THE WAGONS WILL GO EAST. PERHAPS ALL THE WAY TO THE SPINE OF THE WORLD.
PERHAPS WE'LL FIND A STEDDING, AND STAY THERE FOR A WHILE.
TROUBLE NEVER ENTERS THE STEDDING. BUT THE OGIER ARE NONE TOO OPEN TO STRANGERS.
EVERYONE IS OPEN TO THE TRAVELING PEOPLE! BESIDES, EVEN OGIER HAVE POTS AND THINGS TO MEND. COME, LET US HAVE SOME BREAKFAST, AND WE'LL TALK ABOUT IT.

NO TIME. WE MOVE ON TODAY, TOO. AS SOON AS POSSIBLE.

IT'S A DAY FOR MOVING, IT SEEMS.

ARE YOU SURE? A LITTLE FOOD AND CONVERSATION NOW WILL MAKE LATER TRAVEL EASIER...

THERE IS NO TIME.

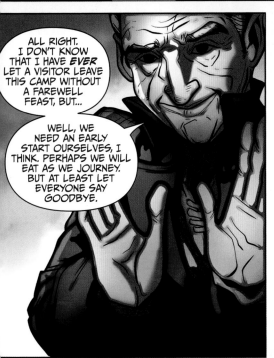

ALL RIGHT. I DON'T KNOW THAT I HAVE EVER LET A VISITOR LEAVE THIS CAMP WITHOUT A FAREWELL FEAST, BUT...

WELL, WE NEED AN EARLY START OURSELVES, I THINK. PERHAPS WE WILL EAT AS WE JOURNEY. BUT AT LEAST LET EVERYONE SAY GOODBYE.

≍YAWN≍

WHY IS THE SEEKER MAKING SUCH A RACKET SO EARLY?

HE'S ROUSING EVERYONE TO SAY GOODBYE.

GOODBYE?

WE PART WAYS WITH THE TRAVELING PEOPLE TODAY. IF YOU'RE COMING WITH US, COLLECT YOUR THINGS.

Perrin prepared himself, waiting for Egwene to say she wanted to stay with the Tuatha'an... instead, she simply nodded and hurried back into the wagon to get her things.

25

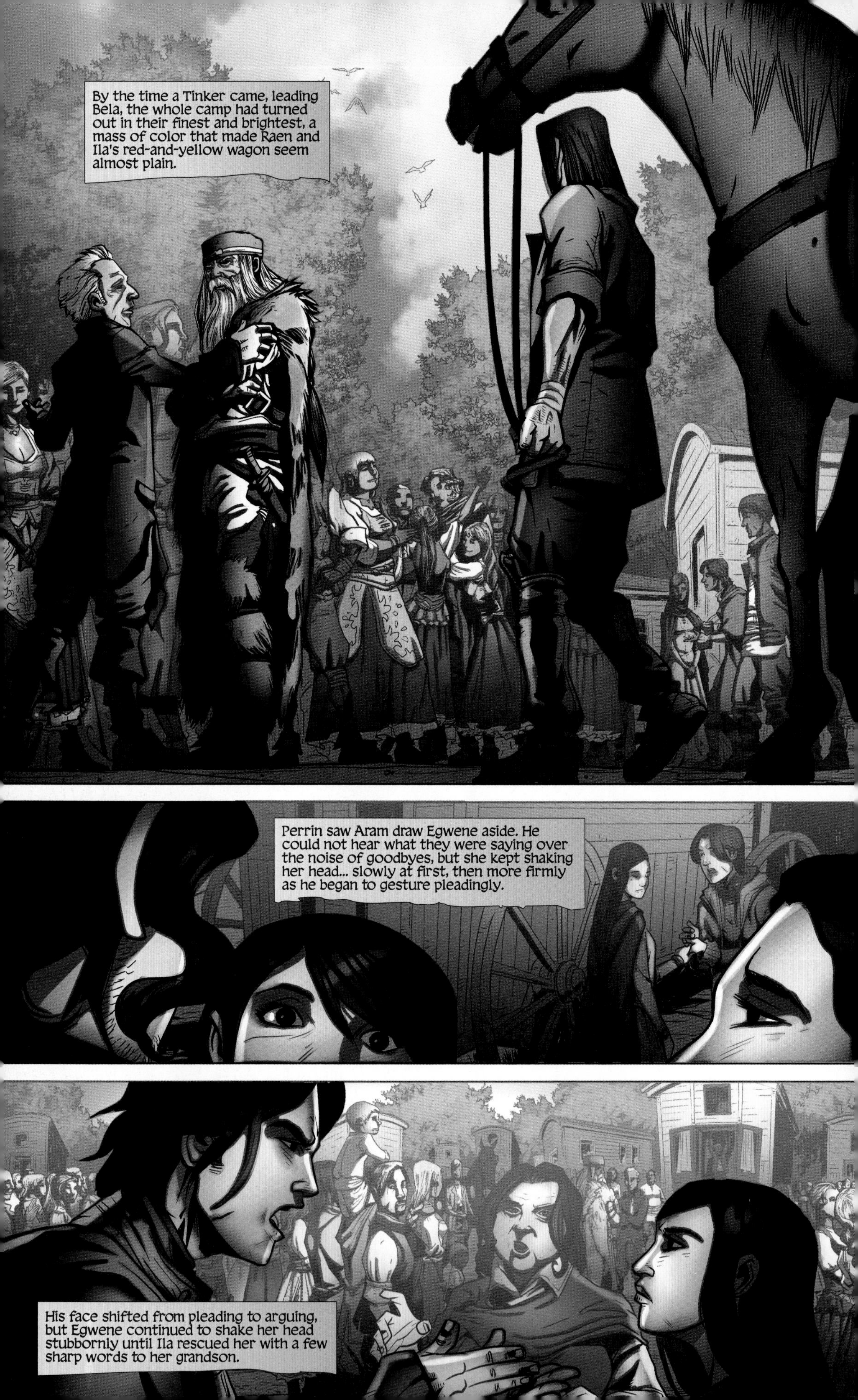
By the time a Tinker came, leading Bela, the whole camp had turned out in their finest and brightest, a mass of color that made Raen and Ila's red-and-yellow wagon seem almost plain.
Perrin saw Aram draw Egwene aside. He could not hear what they were saying over the noise of goodbyes, but she kept shaking her head... slowly at first, then more firmly as he began to gesture pleadingly.
His face shifted from pleading to arguing, but Egwene continued to shake her head stubbornly until Ila rescued her with a few sharp words to her grandson.

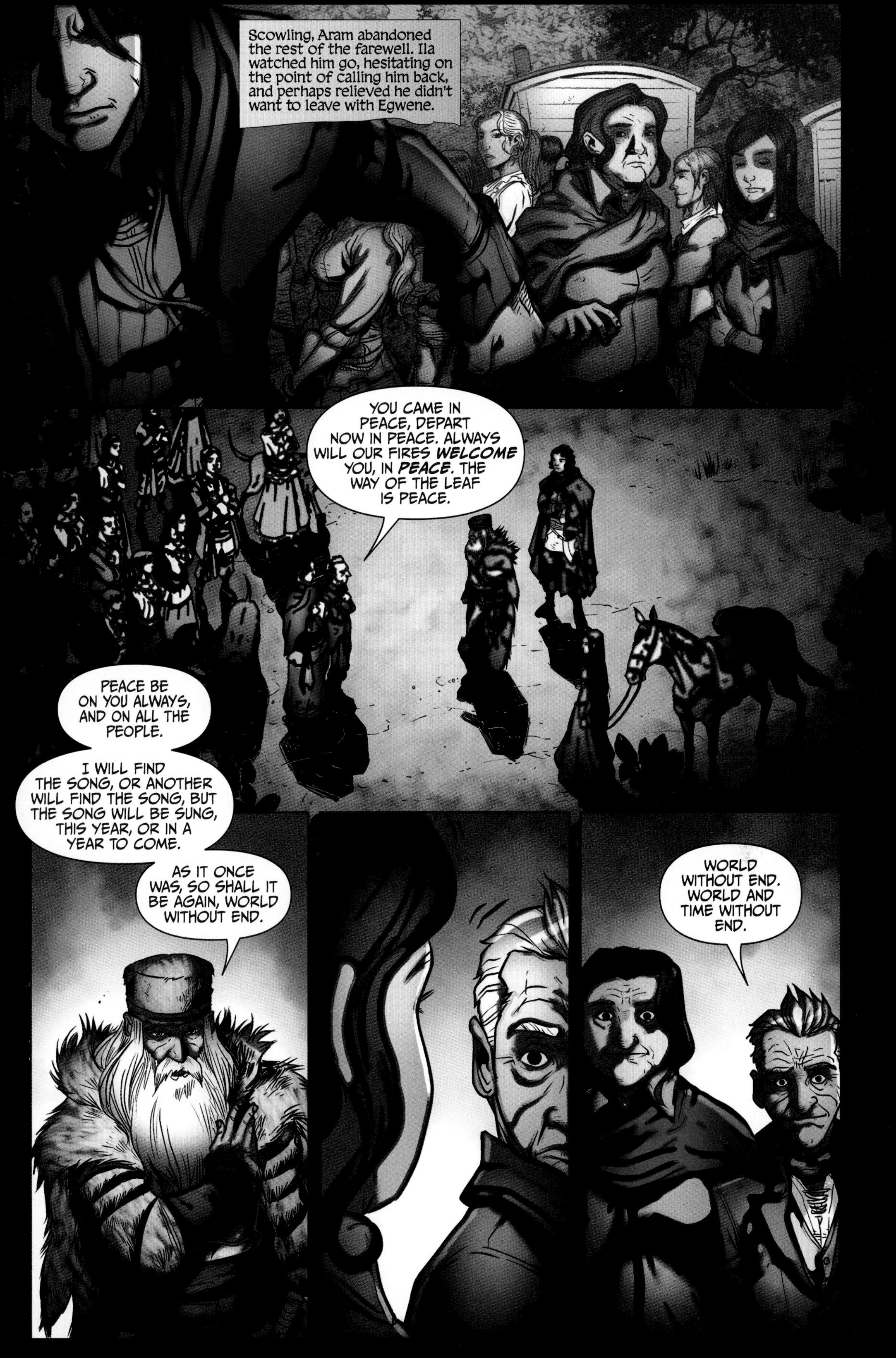
Scowling, Aram abandoned the rest of the farewell. Ila watched him go, hesitating on the point of calling him back, and perhaps relieved he didn't want to leave with Egwene.
YOU CAME IN PEACE, DEPART NOW IN PEACE. ALWAYS WILL OUR FIRES *WELCOME* YOU, IN *PEACE*. THE WAY OF THE LEAF IS PEACE.
PEACE BE ON YOU ALWAYS, AND ON ALL THE PEOPLE.
I WILL FIND THE SONG, OR ANOTHER WILL FIND THE SONG, BUT THE SONG WILL BE SUNG, THIS YEAR, OR IN A YEAR TO COME.
AS IT ONCE WAS, SO SHALL IT BE AGAIN, WORLD WITHOUT END.
WORLD WITHOUT END. WORLD AND TIME WITHOUT END.

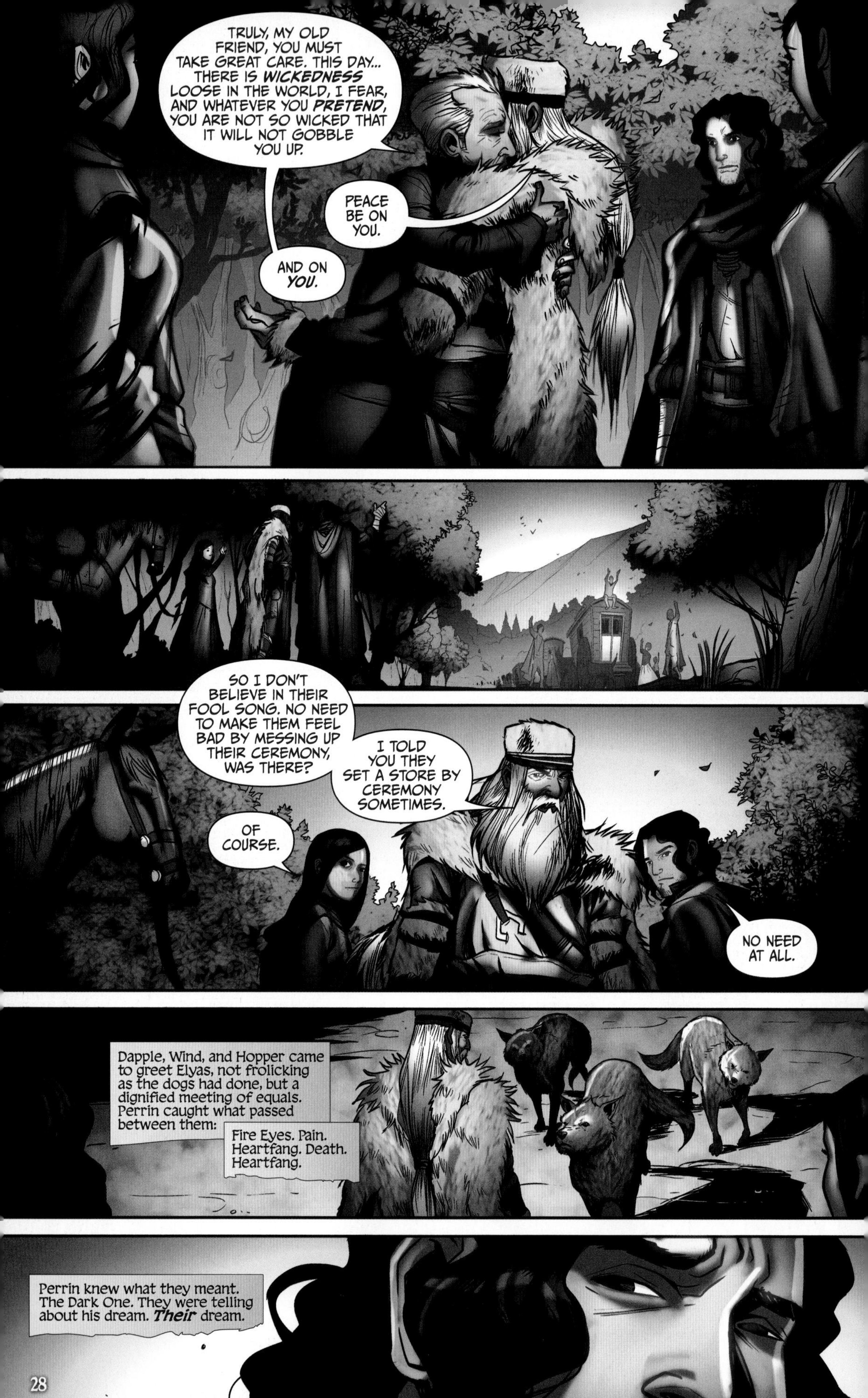

TRULY, MY OLD FRIEND, YOU MUST TAKE GREAT CARE. THIS DAY... THERE IS WICKEDNESS LOOSE IN THE WORLD, I FEAR, AND WHATEVER YOU PRETEND, YOU ARE NOT SO WICKED THAT IT WILL NOT GOBBLE YOU UP.
PEACE BE ON YOU.
AND ON YOU.
SO I DON'T BELIEVE IN THEIR FOOL SONG. NO NEED TO MAKE THEM FEEL BAD BY MESSING UP THEIR CEREMONY, WAS THERE?
I TOLD YOU THEY SET A STORE BY CEREMONY SOMETIMES.
OF COURSE.
NO NEED AT ALL.
Dapple, Wind, and Hopper came to greet Elyas, not frolicking as the dogs had done, but a dignified meeting of equals. Perrin caught what passed between them:
Fire Eyes. Pain. Heartfang. Death. Heartfang.
Perrin knew what they meant. The Dark One. They were telling about his dream. Their dream.

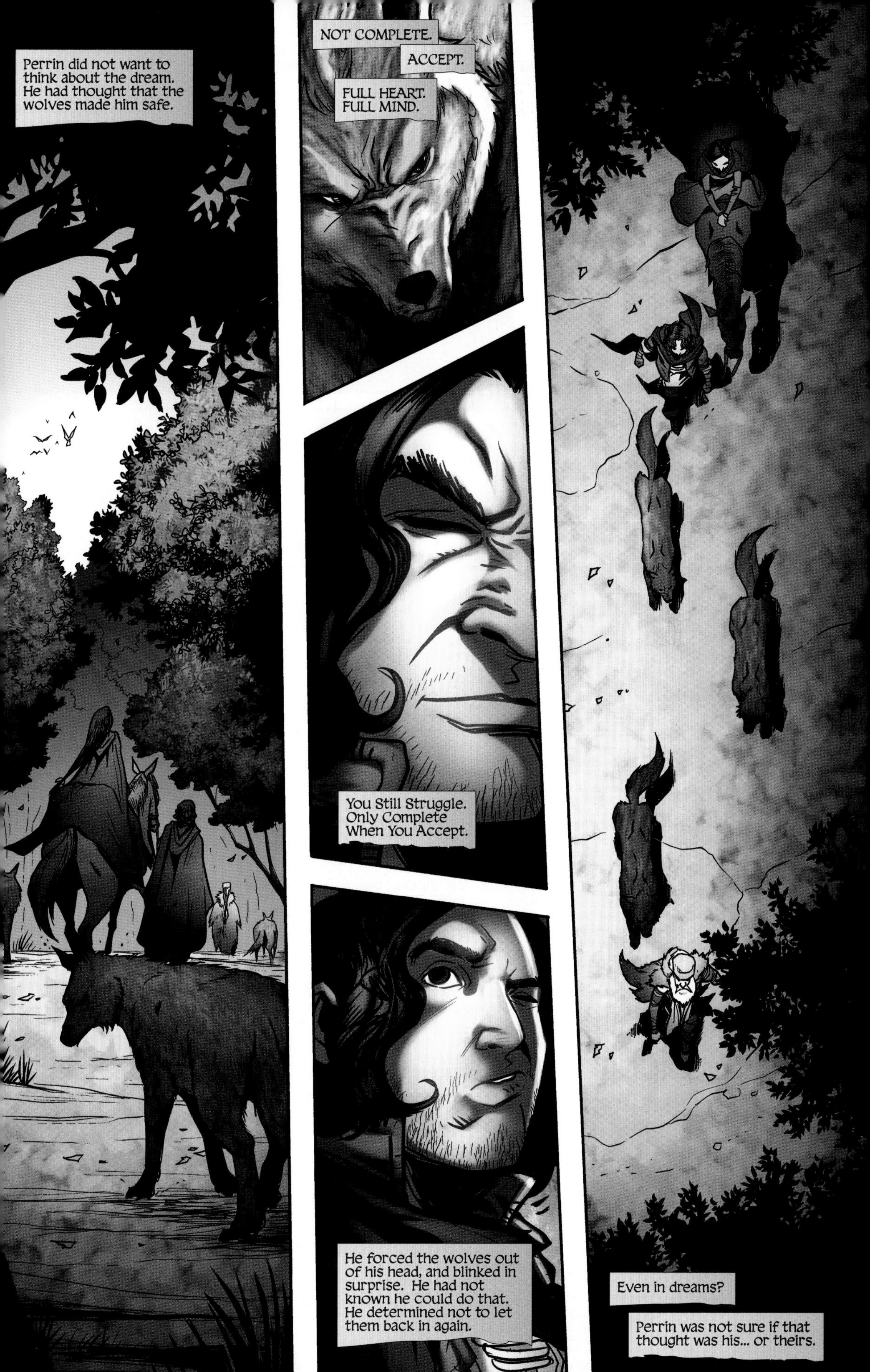

Perrin did not want to think about the dream. He had thought that the wolves made him safe.
NOT COMPLETE.
ACCEPT.
FULL HEART. FULL MIND.
You Still Struggle. Only Complete When You Accept.
He forced the wolves out of his head, and blinked in surprise. He had not known he could do that. He determined not to let them back in again.
Even in dreams?
Perrin was not sure if that thought was his... or theirs.

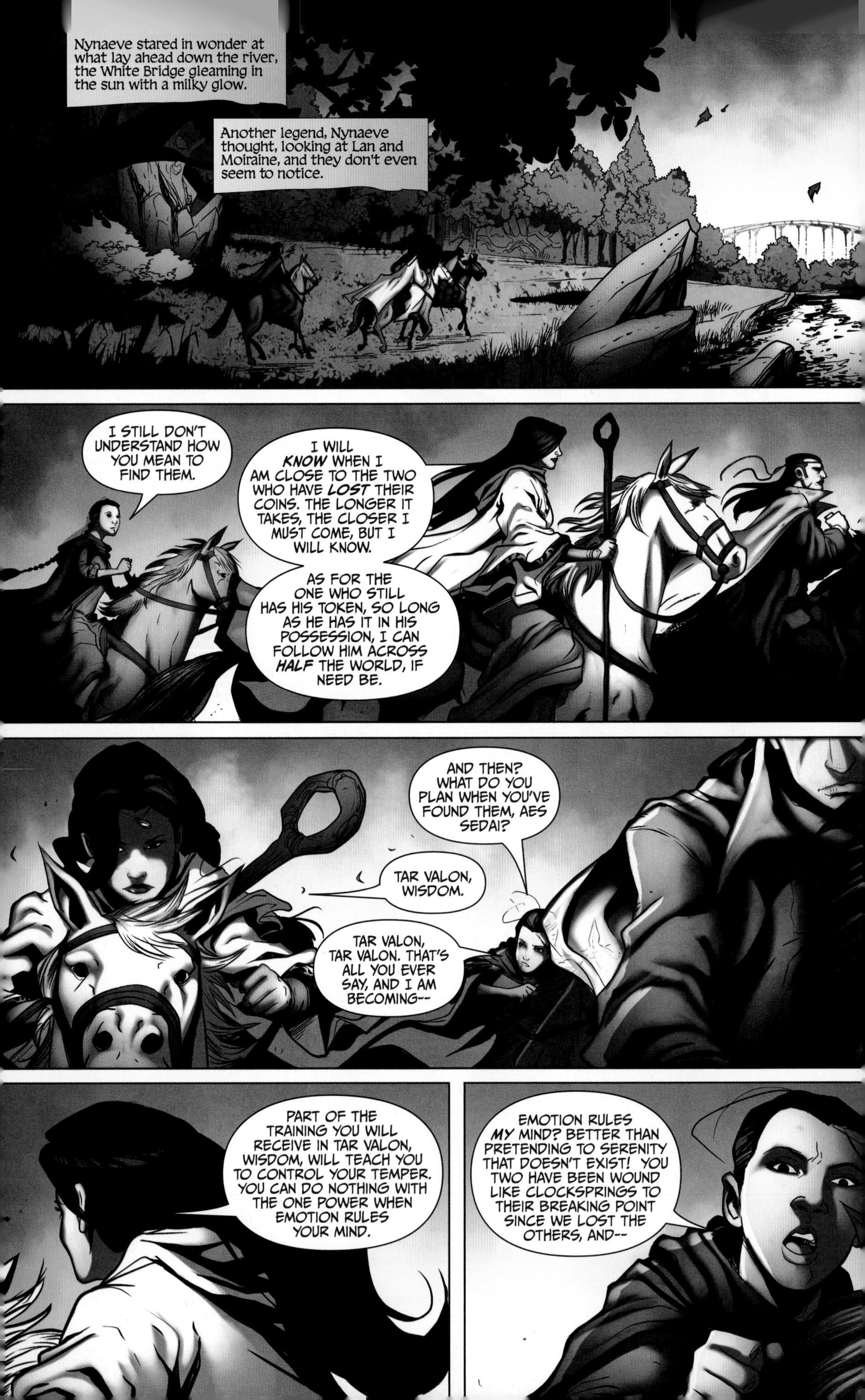
Nynaeve stared in wonder at what lay ahead down the river, the White Bridge gleaming in the sun with a milky glow.
Another legend, Nynaeve thought, looking at Lan and Moiraine, and they don't even seem to notice.
I STILL DON'T UNDERSTAND HOW YOU MEAN TO FIND THEM.
I WILL KNOW WHEN I AM CLOSE TO THE TWO WHO HAVE LOST THEIR COINS. THE LONGER IT TAKES, THE CLOSER I MUST COME, BUT I WILL KNOW.
AS FOR THE ONE WHO STILL HAS HIS TOKEN, SO LONG AS HE HAS IT IN HIS POSSESSION, I CAN FOLLOW HIM ACROSS HALF THE WORLD, IF NEED BE.
AND THEN? WHAT DO YOU PLAN WHEN YOU'VE FOUND THEM, AES SEDAI?
TAR VALON, WISDOM.
TAR VALON, TAR VALON. THAT'S ALL YOU EVER SAY, AND I AM BECOMING--
PART OF THE TRAINING YOU WILL RECEIVE IN TAR VALON, WISDOM, WILL TEACH YOU TO CONTROL YOUR TEMPER. YOU CAN DO NOTHING WITH THE ONE POWER WHEN EMOTION RULES YOUR MIND.
EMOTION RULES MY MIND? BETTER THAN PRETENDING TO SERENITY THAT DOESN'T EXIST! YOU TWO HAVE BEEN WOUND LIKE CLOCKSPRINGS TO THEIR BREAKING POINT SINCE WE LOST THE OTHERS, AND--

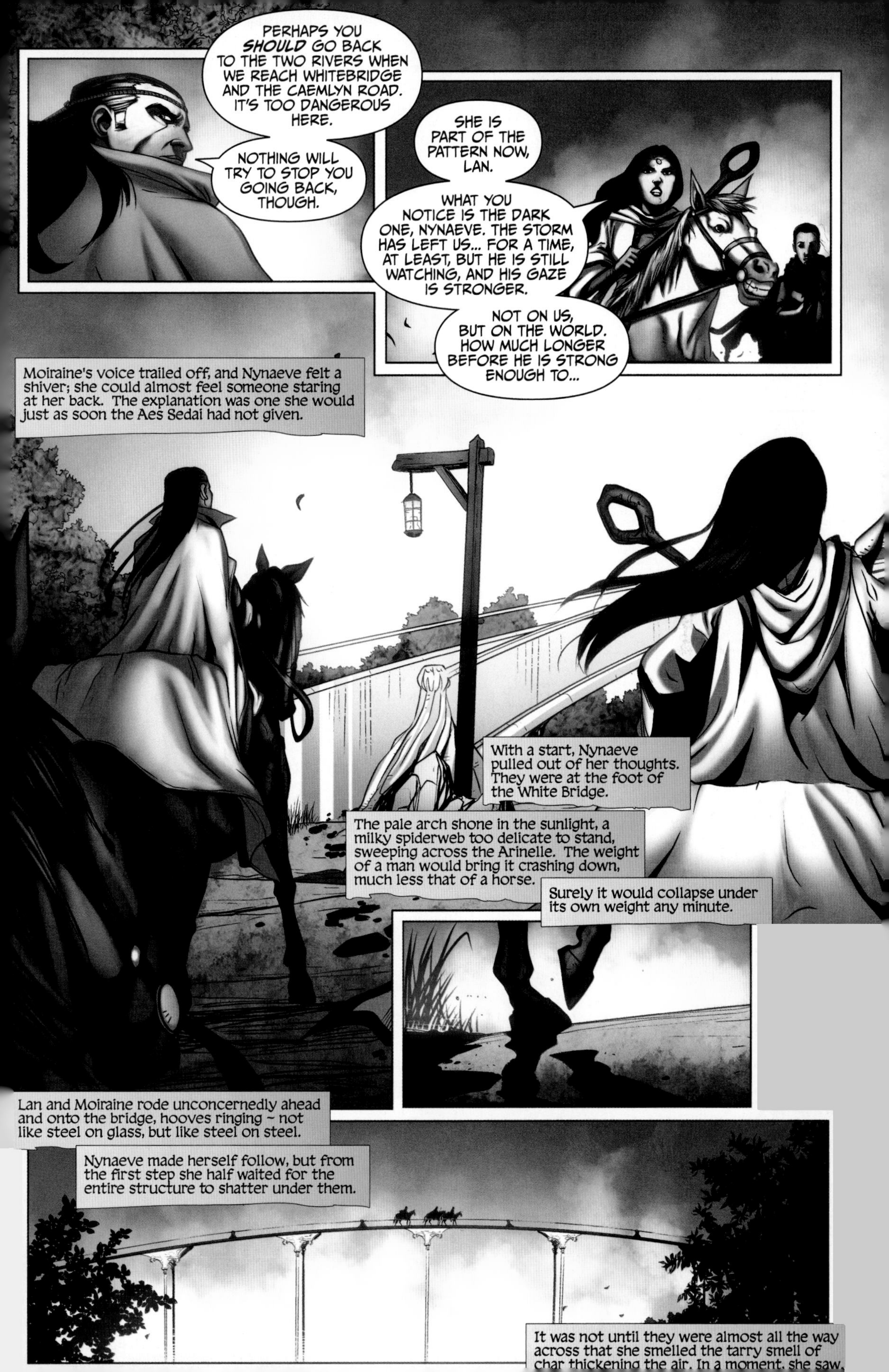
PERHAPS YOU SHOULD GO BACK TO THE TWO RIVERS WHEN WE REACH WHITEBRIDGE AND THE CAEMLYN ROAD. IT'S TOO DANGEROUS HERE.
NOTHING WILL TRY TO STOP YOU GOING BACK, THOUGH.
SHE IS PART OF THE PATTERN NOW, LAN.
WHAT YOU NOTICE IS THE DARK ONE, NYNAEVE. THE STORM HAS LEFT US... FOR A TIME, AT LEAST, BUT HE IS STILL WATCHING, AND HIS GAZE IS STRONGER.
NOT ON US, BUT ON THE WORLD. HOW MUCH LONGER BEFORE HE IS STRONG ENOUGH TO...
Moiraine's voice trailed off, and Nynaeve felt a shiver; she could almost feel someone staring at her back. The explanation was one she would just as soon the Aes Sedai had not given.
With a start, Nynaeve pulled out of her thoughts. They were at the foot of the White Bridge.
The pale arch shone in the sunlight, a milky spiderweb too delicate to stand, sweeping across the Arinelle. The weight of a man would bring it crashing down, much less that of a horse.
Surely it would collapse under its own weight any minute.
Lan and Moiraine rode unconcernedly ahead and onto the bridge, hooves ringing ~ not like steel on glass, but like steel on steel.
Nynaeve made herself follow, but from the first step she half waited for the entire structure to shatter under them.
It was not until they were almost all the way across that she smelled the tarry smell of char thickening the air. In a moment, she saw.

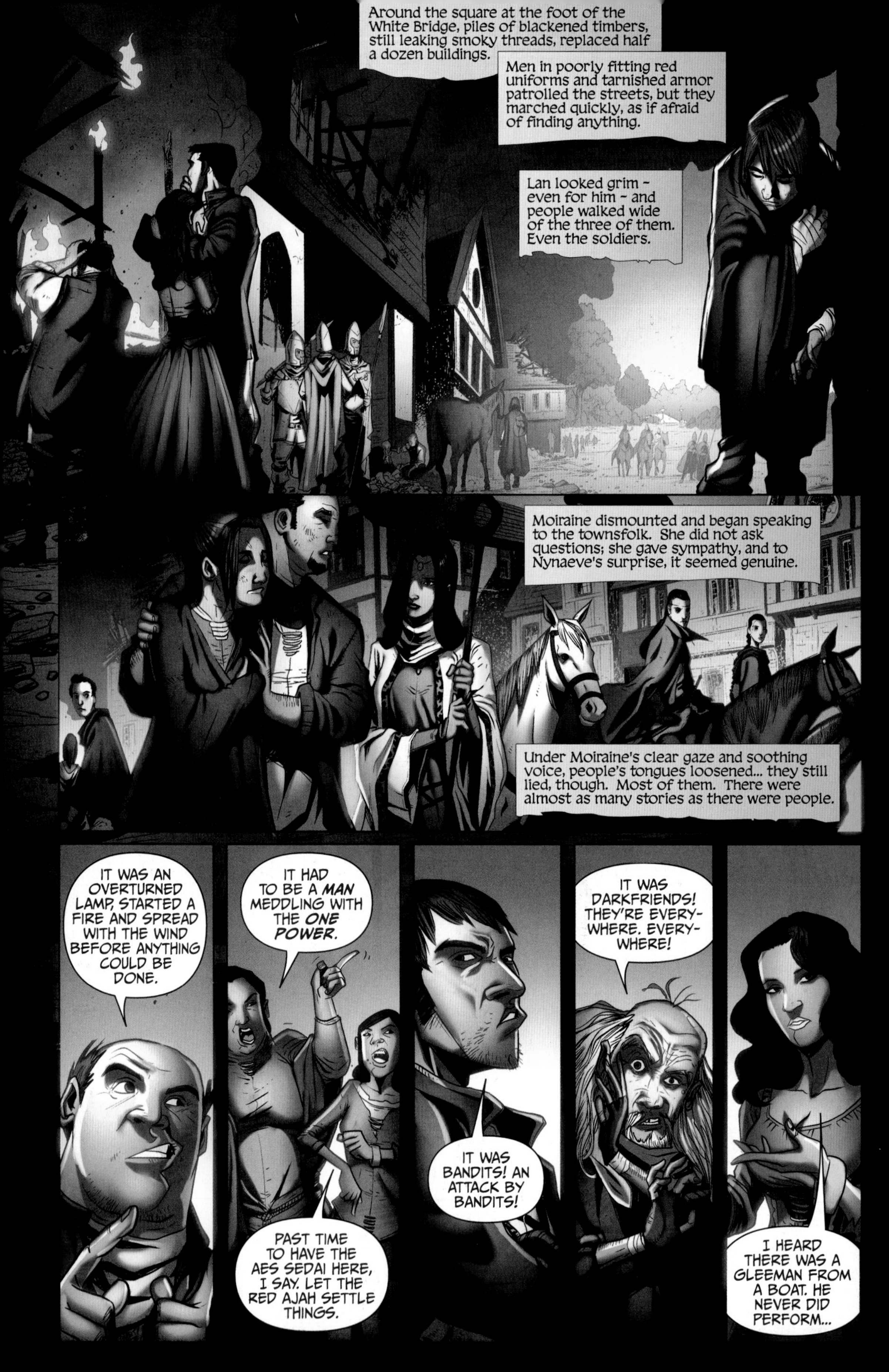
Around the square at the foot of the White Bridge, piles of blackened timbers, still leaking smoky threads, replaced half a dozen buildings.
Men in poorly fitting red uniforms and tarnished armor patrolled the streets, but they marched quickly, as if afraid of finding anything.
Lan looked grim - even for him - and people walked wide of the three of them. Even the soldiers.
Moiraine dismounted and began speaking to the townsfolk. She did not ask questions; she gave sympathy, and to Nynaeve's surprise, it seemed genuine.
Under Moiraine's clear gaze and soothing voice, people's tongues loosened... they still lied, though. Most of them. There were almost as many stories as there were people.
IT WAS AN OVERTURNED LAMP, STARTED A FIRE AND SPREAD WITH THE WIND BEFORE ANYTHING COULD BE DONE.
IT HAD TO BE A MAN MEDDLING WITH THE ONE POWER.
PAST TIME TO HAVE THE AES SEDAI HERE, I SAY. LET THE RED AJAH SETTLE THINGS.
IT WAS BANDITS! AN ATTACK BY BANDITS!
IT WAS DARKFRIENDS! THEY'RE EVERY-WHERE. EVERY-WHERE!
I HEARD THERE WAS A GLEEMAN FROM A BOAT. HE NEVER DID PERFORM...

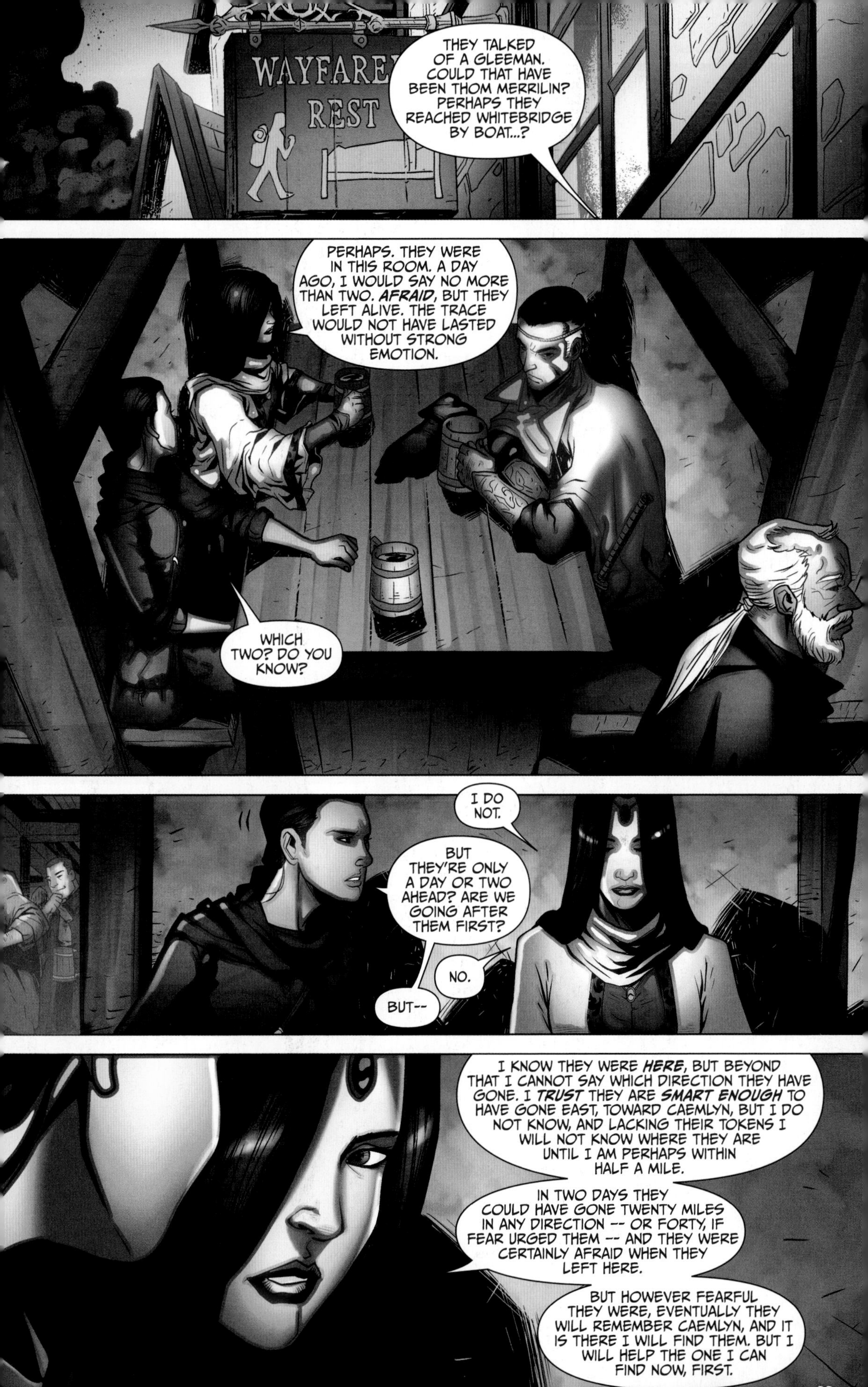
WAYFARER'S REST
THEY TALKED OF A GLEEMAN. COULD THAT HAVE BEEN THOM MERRILIN? PERHAPS THEY REACHED WHITEBRIDGE BY BOAT...?
PERHAPS. THEY WERE IN THIS ROOM. A DAY AGO, I WOULD SAY NO MORE THAN TWO. AFRAID, BUT THEY LEFT ALIVE. THE TRACE WOULD NOT HAVE LASTED WITHOUT STRONG EMOTION.
WHICH TWO? DO YOU KNOW?
I DO NOT.
BUT THEY'RE ONLY A DAY OR TWO AHEAD? ARE WE GOING AFTER THEM FIRST?
NO.
BUT--
I KNOW THEY WERE HERE, BUT BEYOND THAT I CANNOT SAY WHICH DIRECTION THEY HAVE GONE. I TRUST THEY ARE SMART ENOUGH TO HAVE GONE EAST, TOWARD CAEMLYN, BUT I DO NOT KNOW, AND LACKING THEIR TOKENS I WILL NOT KNOW WHERE THEY ARE UNTIL I AM PERHAPS WITHIN HALF A MILE.
IN TWO DAYS THEY COULD HAVE GONE TWENTY MILES IN ANY DIRECTION -- OR FORTY, IF FEAR URGED THEM -- AND THEY WERE CERTAINLY AFRAID WHEN THEY LEFT HERE.
BUT HOWEVER FEARFUL THEY WERE, EVENTUALLY THEY WILL REMEMBER CAEMLYN, AND IT IS THERE I WILL FIND THEM. BUT I WILL HELP THE ONE I CAN FIND NOW, FIRST.

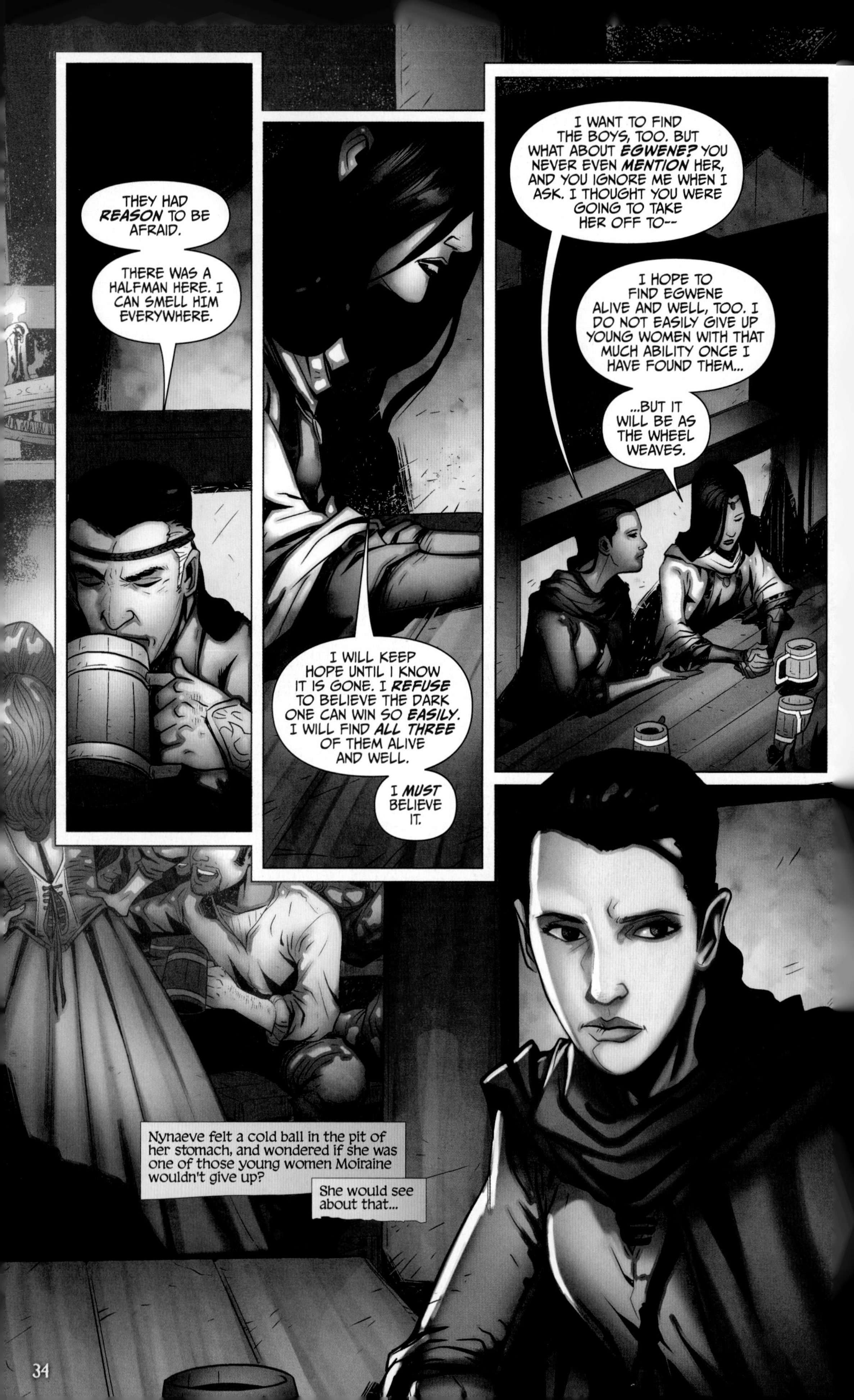
THEY HAD REASON TO BE AFRAID.
THERE WAS A HALFMAN HERE. I CAN SMELL HIM EVERYWHERE.
I WILL KEEP HOPE UNTIL I KNOW IT IS GONE. I REFUSE TO BELIEVE THE DARK ONE CAN WIN SO EASILY. I WILL FIND ALL THREE OF THEM ALIVE AND WELL.
I MUST BELIEVE IT.
I WANT TO FIND THE BOYS, TOO. BUT WHAT ABOUT EGWENE? YOU NEVER EVEN MENTION HER, AND YOU IGNORE ME WHEN I ASK. I THOUGHT YOU WERE GOING TO TAKE HER OFF TO--
I HOPE TO FIND EGWENE ALIVE AND WELL, TOO. I DO NOT EASILY GIVE UP YOUNG WOMEN WITH THAT MUCH ABILITY ONCE I HAVE FOUND THEM...
...BUT IT WILL BE AS THE WHEEL WEAVES.
Nynaeve felt a cold ball in the pit of her stomach, and wondered if she was one of those young women Moiraine wouldn't give up?
She would see about that...

chapter two

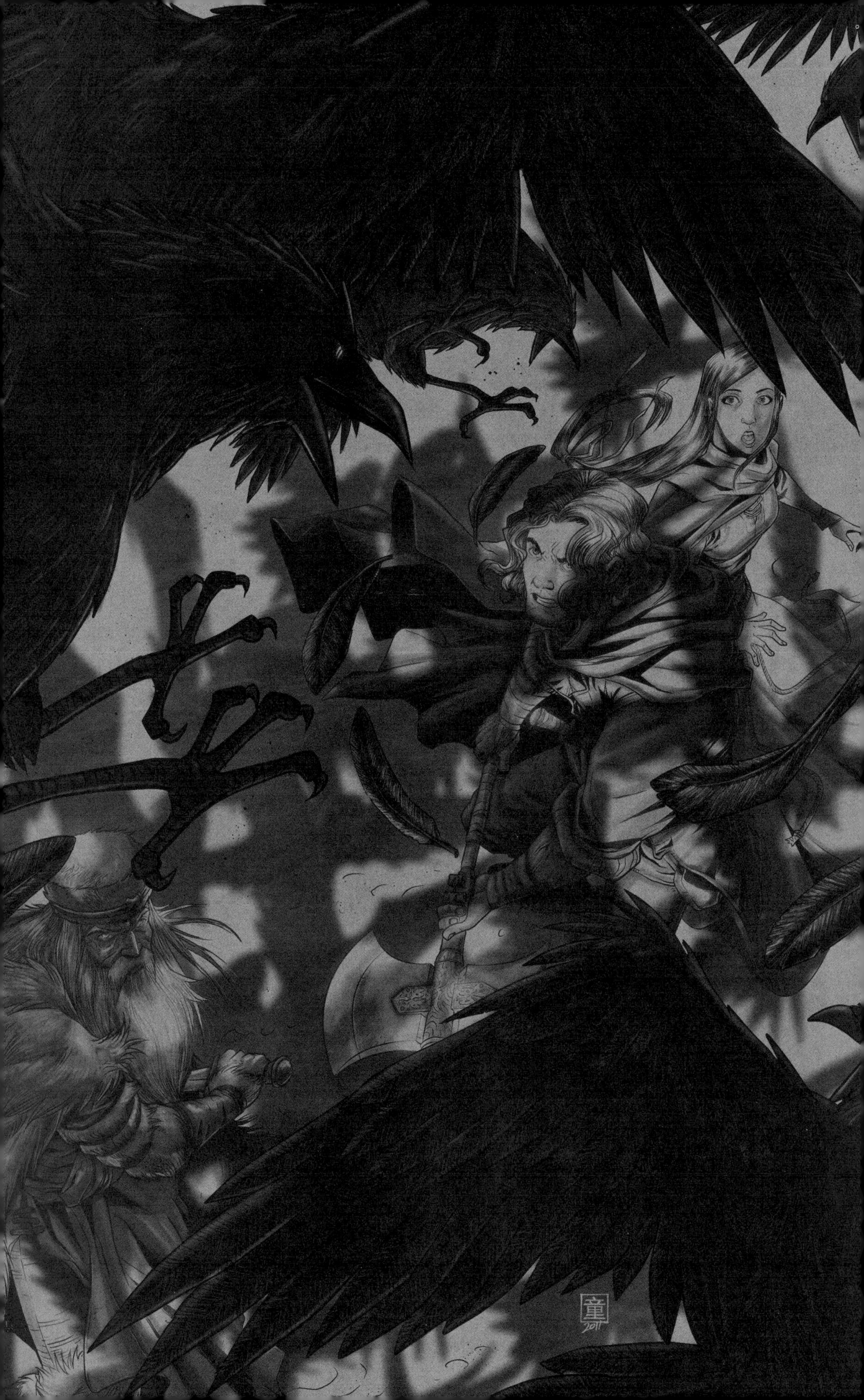

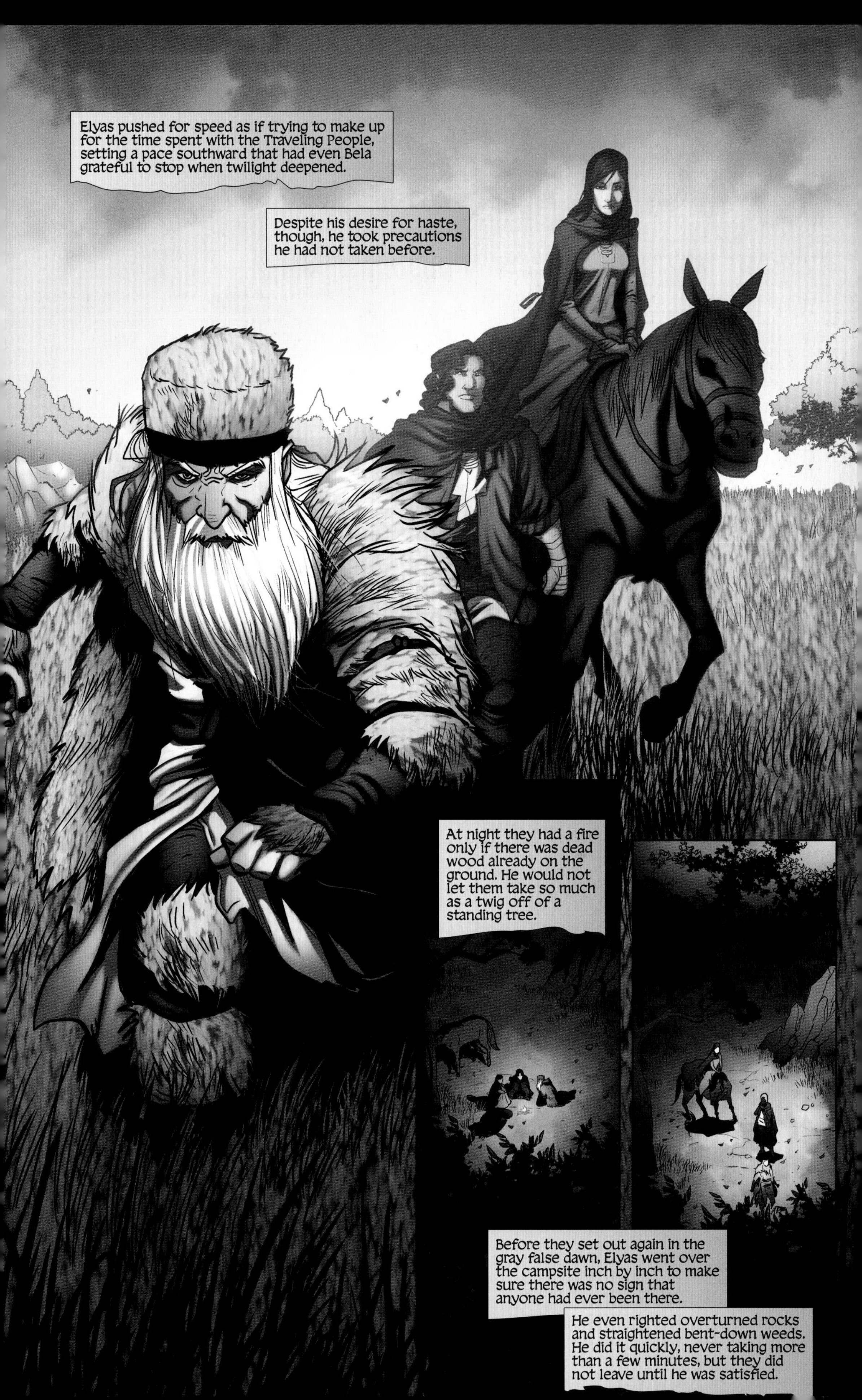
Elyas pushed for speed as if trying to make up for the time spent with the Traveling People, setting a pace southward that had even Bela grateful to stop when twilight deepened.
Despite his desire for haste, though, he took precautions he had not taken before.
At night they had a fire only if there was dead wood already on the ground. He would not let them take so much as a twig off of a standing tree.
Before they set out again in the gray false dawn, Elyas went over the campsite inch by inch to make sure there was no sign that anyone had ever been there.
He even righted overturned rocks and straightened bent-down weeds. He did it quickly, never taking more than a few minutes, but they did not leave until he was satisfied.

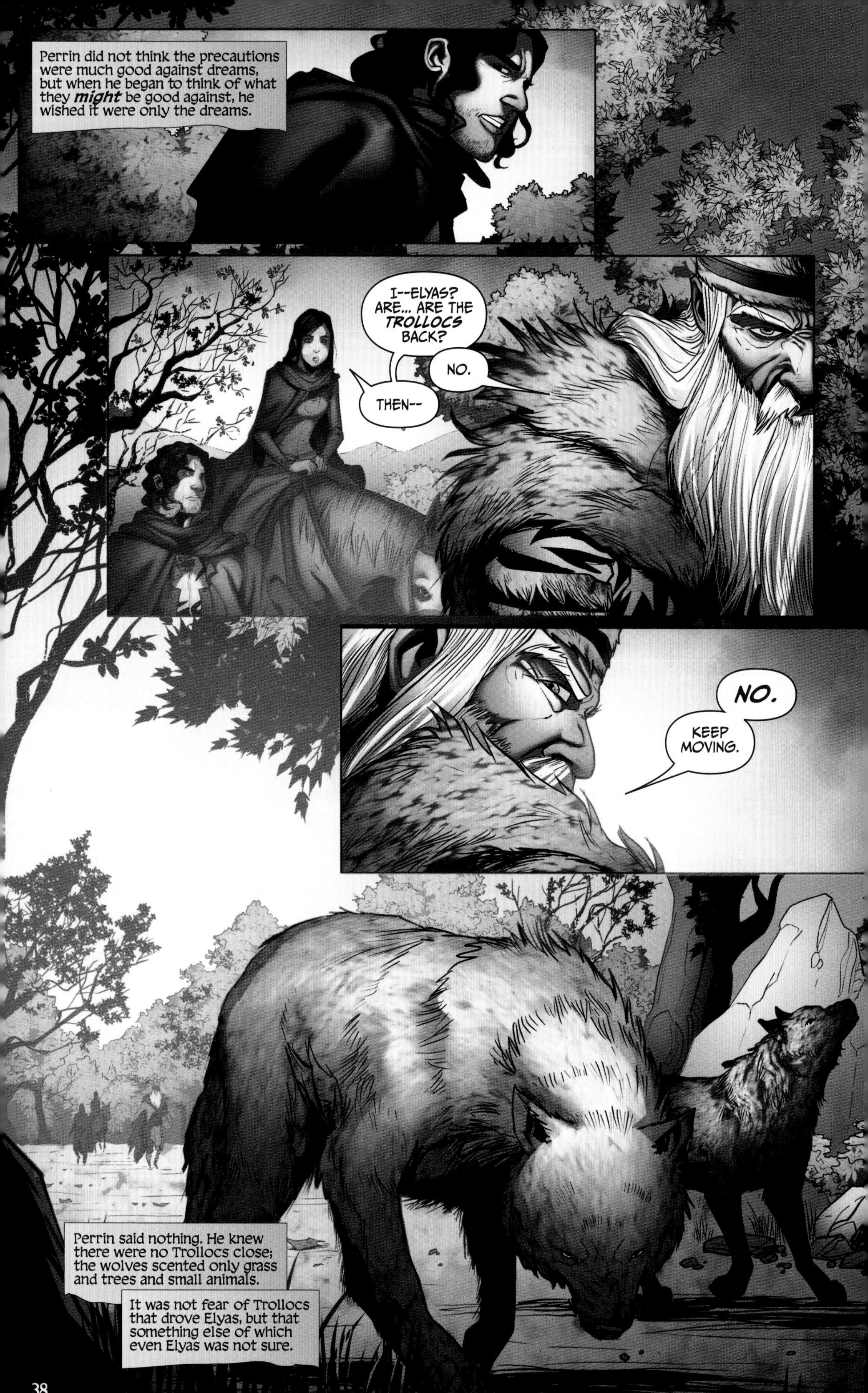
Perrin did not think the precautions were much good against dreams, but when he began to think of what they *might* be good against, he wished it were only the dreams.
I--ELYAS? ARE... ARE THE *TROLLOCS* BACK?
NO.
THEN--
NO.
KEEP MOVING.
Perrin said nothing. He knew there were no Trollocs close; the wolves scented only grass and trees and small animals.
It was not fear of Trollocs that drove Elyas, but that something else of which even Elyas was not sure.

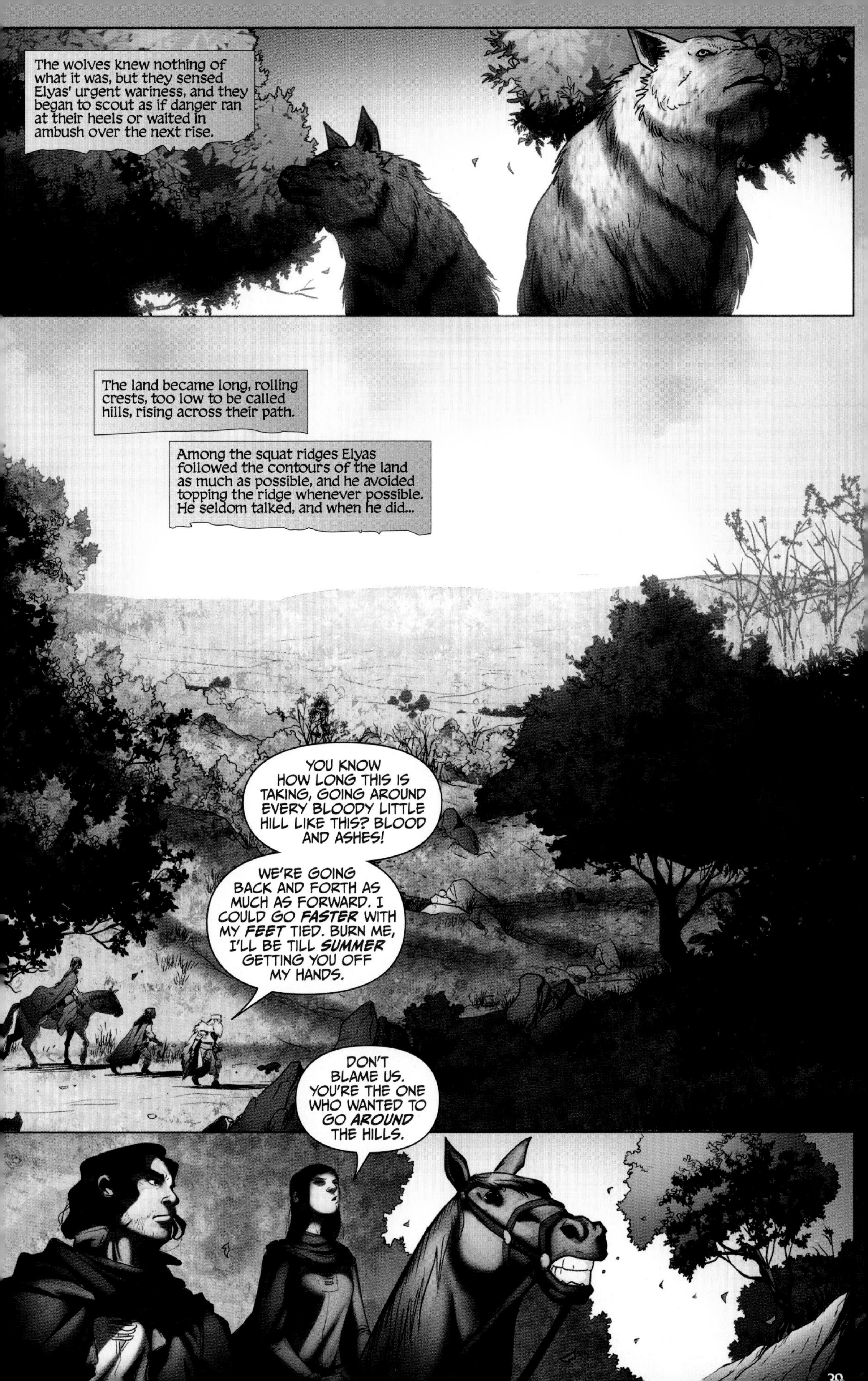

The wolves knew nothing of what it was, but they sensed Elyas' urgent wariness, and they began to scout as if danger ran at their heels or waited in ambush over the next rise.
The land became long, rolling crests, too low to be called hills, rising across their path.
Among the squat ridges Elyas followed the contours of the land as much as possible, and he avoided topping the ridge whenever possible. He seldom talked, and when he did...
YOU KNOW HOW LONG THIS IS TAKING, GOING AROUND EVERY BLOODY LITTLE HILL LIKE THIS? BLOOD AND ASHES!
WE'RE GOING BACK AND FORTH AS MUCH AS FORWARD. I COULD GO **FASTER** WITH MY **FEET** TIED. BURN ME, I'LL BE TILL **SUMMER** GETTING YOU OFF MY HANDS.
DON'T BLAME US. YOU'RE THE ONE WHO WANTED TO GO **AROUND** THE HILLS.

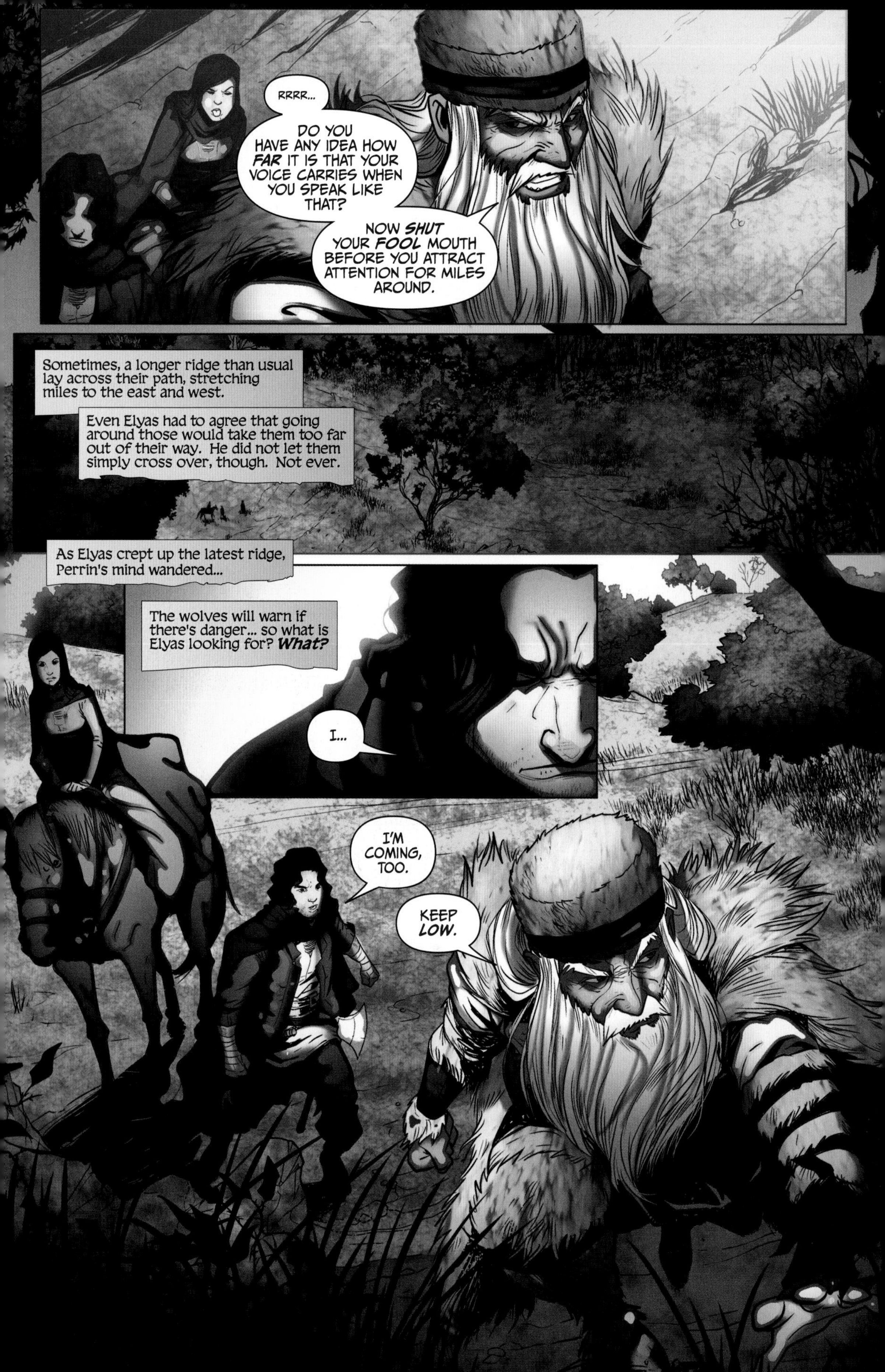
RRRR...
DO YOU HAVE ANY IDEA HOW FAR IT IS THAT YOUR VOICE CARRIES WHEN YOU SPEAK LIKE THAT?
NOW SHUT YOUR FOOL MOUTH BEFORE YOU ATTRACT ATTENTION FOR MILES AROUND.
Sometimes, a longer ridge than usual lay across their path, stretching miles to the east and west.
Even Elyas had to agree that going around those would take them too far out of their way. He did not let them simply cross over, though. Not ever.
As Elyas crept up the latest ridge, Perrin's mind wandered...
The wolves will warn if there's danger... so what is Elyas looking for? What?
I...
I'M COMING, TOO.
KEEP LOW.

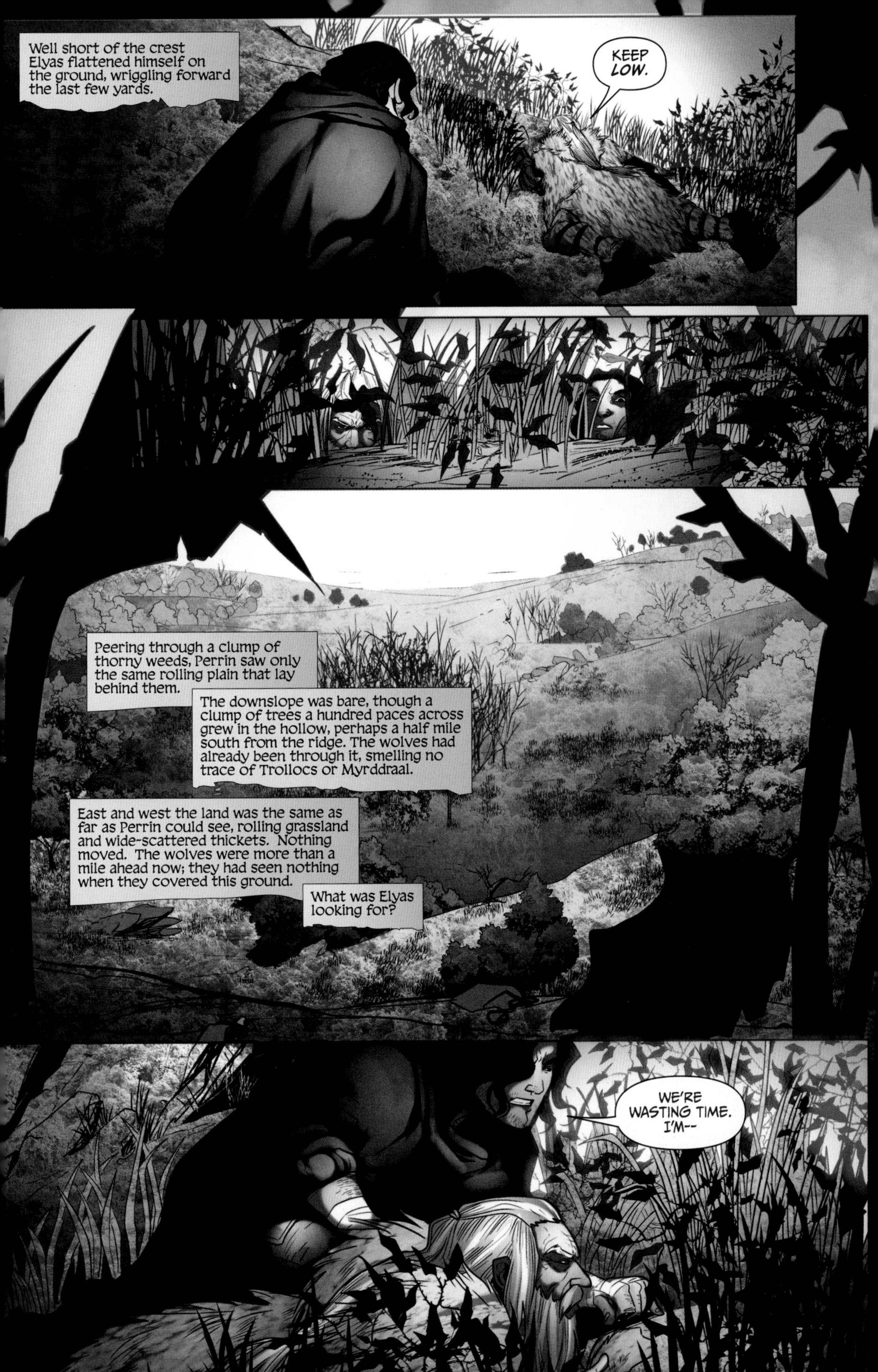
Well short of the crest Elyas flattened himself on the ground, wriggling forward the last few yards.
KEEP LOW.
Peering through a clump of thorny weeds, Perrin saw only the same rolling plain that lay behind them.
The downslope was bare, though a clump of trees a hundred paces across grew in the hollow, perhaps a half mile south from the ridge. The wolves had already been through it, smelling no trace of Trollocs or Myrddraal.
East and west the land was the same as far as Perrin could see, rolling grassland and wide-scattered thickets. Nothing moved. The wolves were more than a mile ahead now; they had seen nothing when they covered this ground.
What was Elyas looking for?
WE'RE WASTING TIME. I'M--

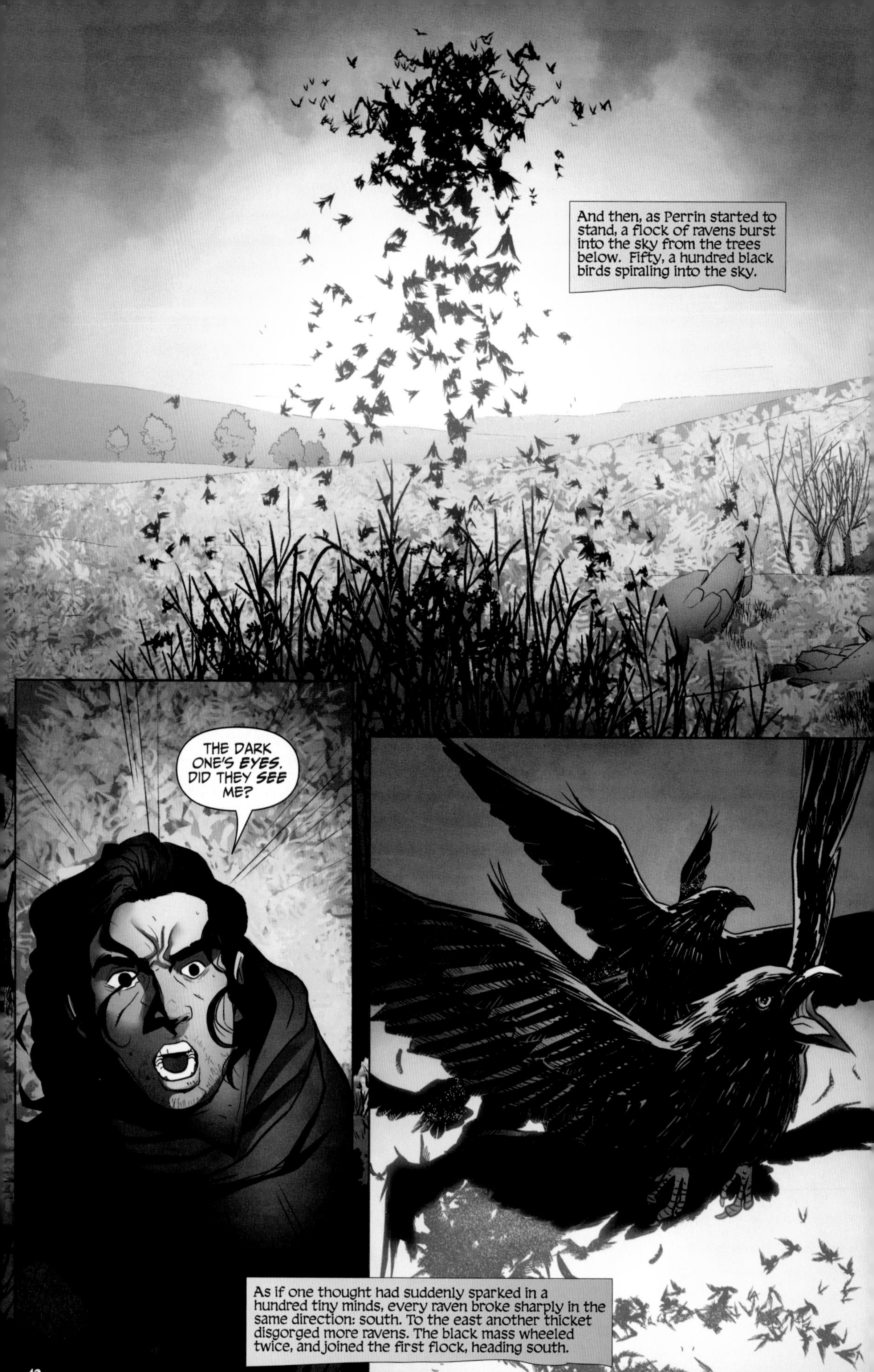
And then, as Perrin started to stand, a flock of ravens burst into the sky from the trees below. Fifty, a hundred black birds spiraling into the sky.
THE DARK ONE'S *EYES*. DID THEY *SEE* ME?
As if one thought had suddenly sparked in a hundred tiny minds, every raven broke sharply in the same direction: south. To the east another thicket disgorged more ravens. The black mass wheeled twice, and joined the first flock, heading south.

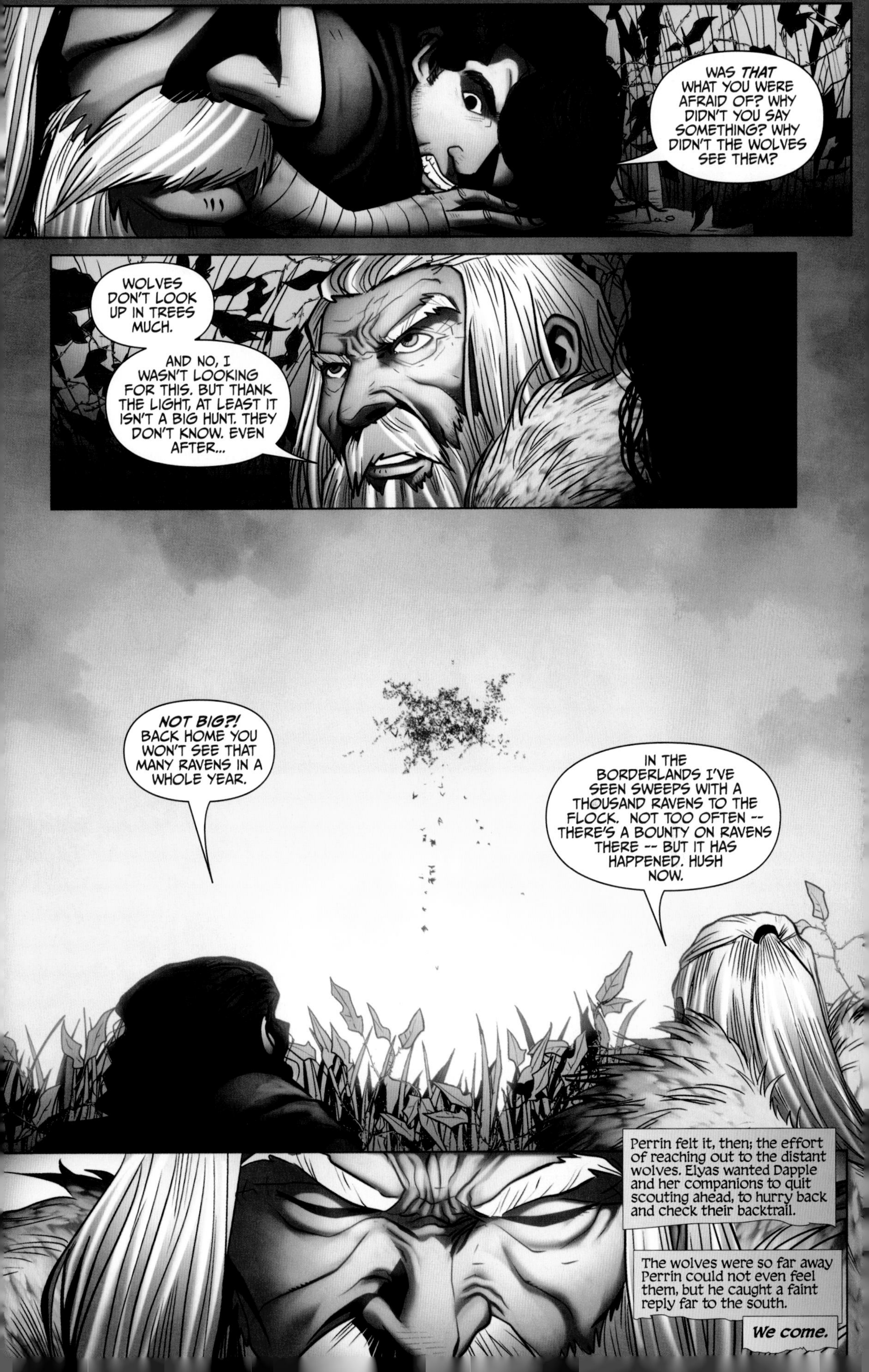
WAS *THAT* WHAT YOU WERE AFRAID OF? WHY DIDN'T YOU SAY SOMETHING? WHY DIDN'T THE WOLVES SEE THEM?
WOLVES DON'T LOOK UP IN TREES MUCH.
AND NO, I WASN'T LOOKING FOR THIS. BUT THANK THE LIGHT, AT LEAST IT ISN'T A BIG HUNT. THEY DON'T KNOW. EVEN AFTER...
NOT BIG?! BACK HOME YOU WON'T SEE THAT MANY RAVENS IN A WHOLE YEAR.
IN THE BORDERLANDS I'VE SEEN SWEEPS WITH A THOUSAND RAVENS TO THE FLOCK. NOT TOO OFTEN -- THERE'S A BOUNTY ON RAVENS THERE -- BUT IT HAS HAPPENED. HUSH NOW.
Perrin felt it, then; the effort of reaching out to the distant wolves. Elyas wanted Dapple and her companions to quit scouting ahead, to hurry back and check their backtrail.
The wolves were so far away Perrin could not even feel them, but he caught a faint reply far to the south.
We come.

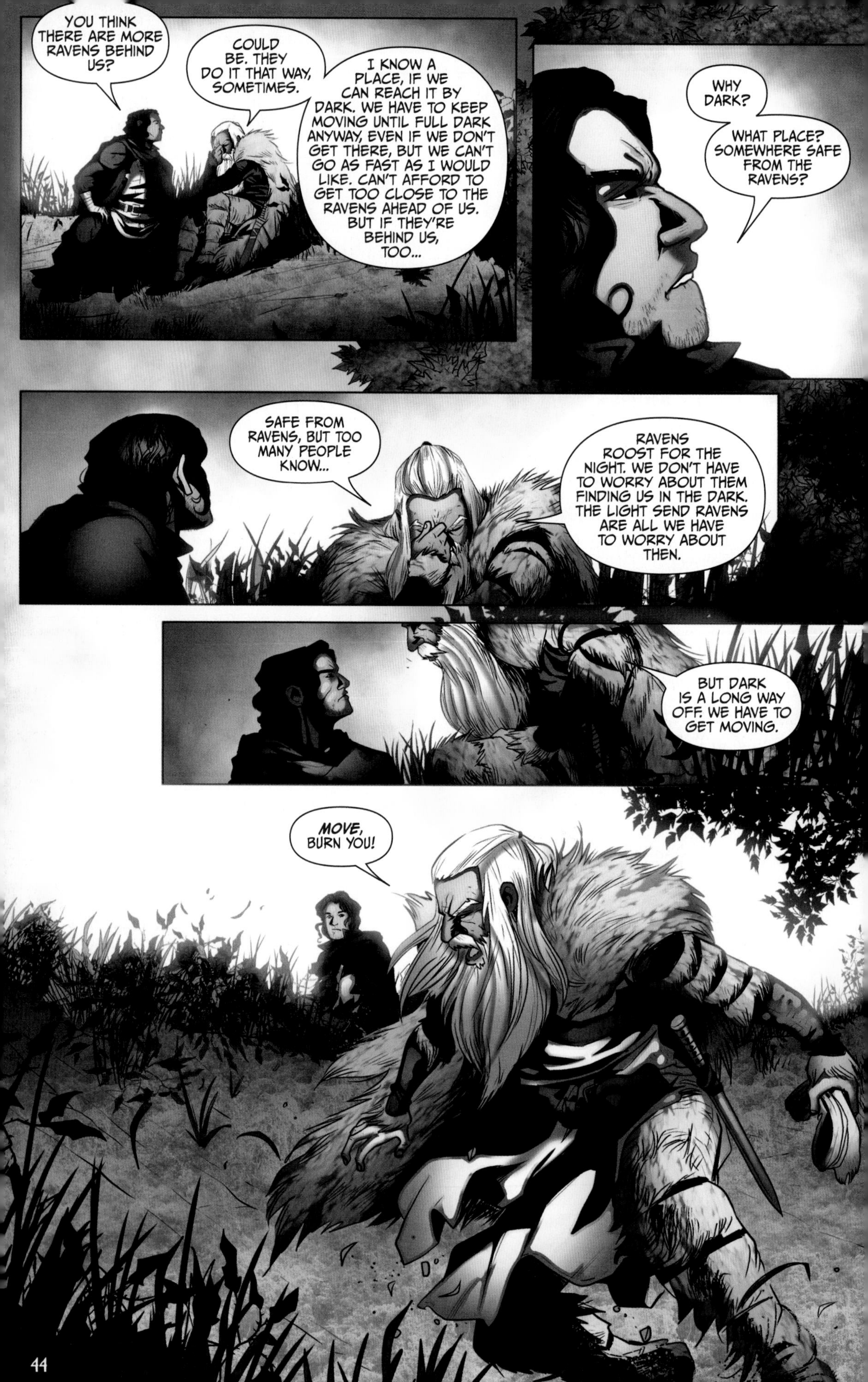
YOU THINK THERE ARE MORE RAVENS BEHIND US?
COULD BE. THEY DO IT THAT WAY, SOMETIMES.
I KNOW A PLACE, IF WE CAN REACH IT BY DARK. WE HAVE TO KEEP MOVING UNTIL FULL DARK ANYWAY, EVEN IF WE DON'T GET THERE, BUT WE CAN'T GO AS FAST AS I WOULD LIKE. CAN'T AFFORD TO GET TOO CLOSE TO THE RAVENS AHEAD OF US. BUT IF THEY'RE BEHIND US, TOO...
WHY DARK?
WHAT PLACE? SOMEWHERE SAFE FROM THE RAVENS?
SAFE FROM RAVENS, BUT TOO MANY PEOPLE KNOW...
RAVENS ROOST FOR THE NIGHT. WE DON'T HAVE TO WORRY ABOUT THEM FINDING US IN THE DARK. THE LIGHT SEND RAVENS ARE ALL WE HAVE TO WORRY ABOUT THEN.
BUT DARK IS A LONG WAY OFF. WE HAVE TO GET MOVING.
MOVE, BURN YOU!

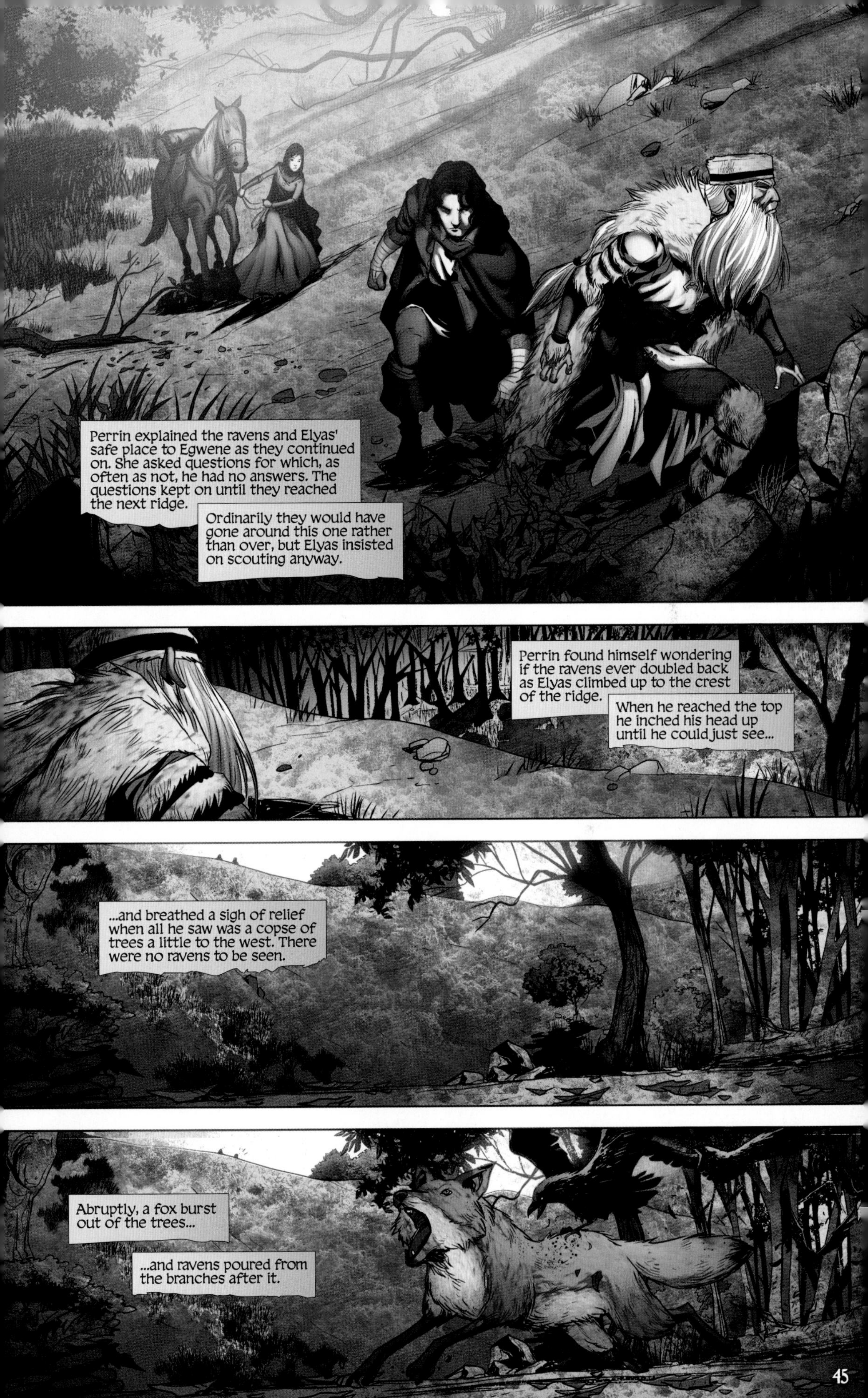

Perrin explained the ravens and Elyas' safe place to Egwene as they continued on. She asked questions for which, as often as not, he had no answers. The questions kept on until they reached the next ridge.
Ordinarily they would have gone around this one rather than over, but Elyas insisted on scouting anyway.
Perrin found himself wondering if the ravens ever doubled back as Elyas climbed up to the crest of the ridge.
When he reached the top he inched his head up until he could just see...
...and breathed a sigh of relief when all he saw was a copse of trees a little to the west. There were no ravens to be seen.
Abruptly, a fox burst out of the trees...
...and ravens poured from the branches after it.

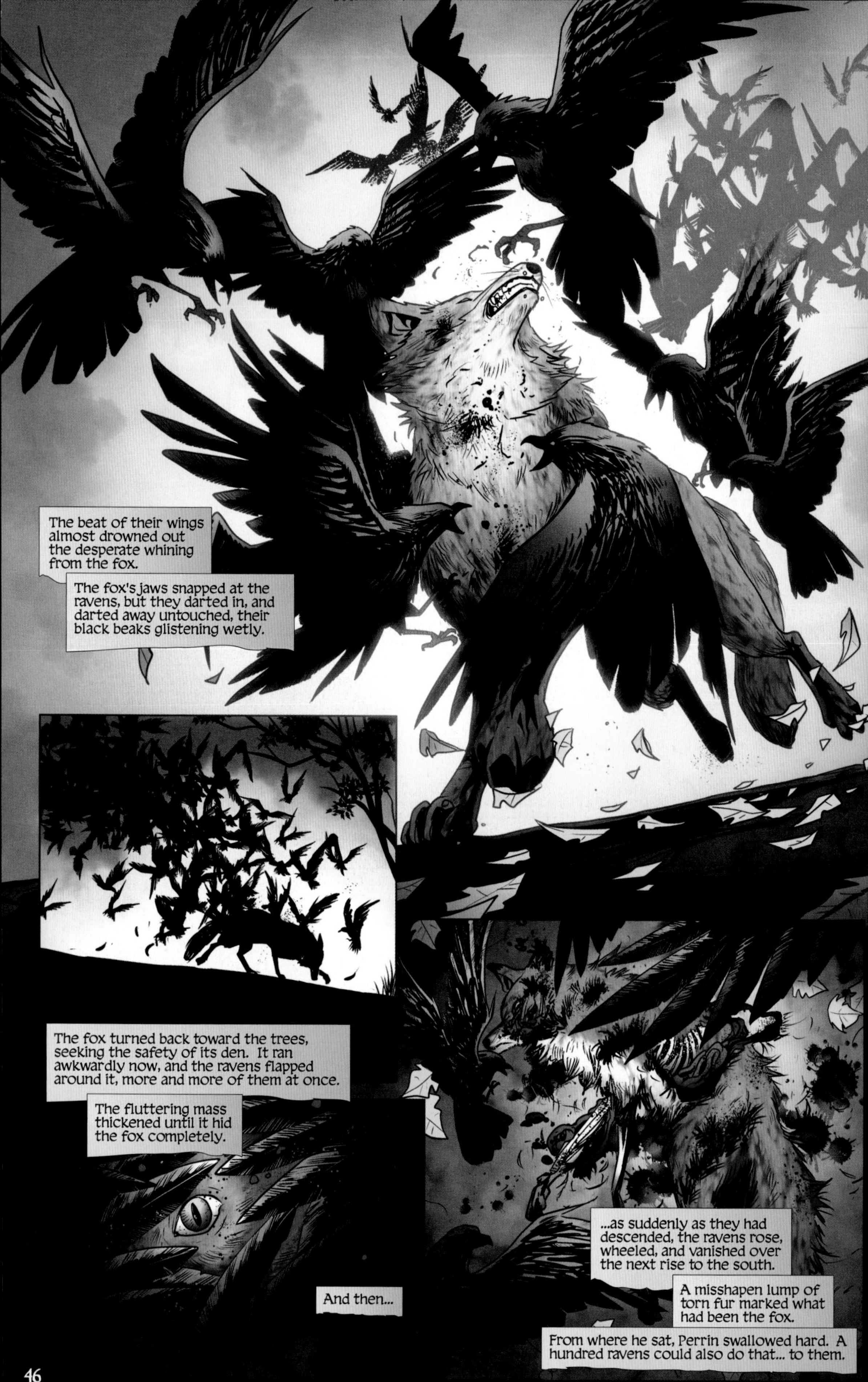
The beat of their wings almost drowned out the desperate whining from the fox.
The fox's jaws snapped at the ravens, but they darted in, and darted away untouched, their black beaks glistening wetly.
The fox turned back toward the trees, seeking the safety of its den. It ran awkwardly now, and the ravens flapped around it, more and more of them at once.
The fluttering mass thickened until it hid the fox completely.
And then...
...as suddenly as they had descended, the ravens rose, wheeled, and vanished over the next rise to the south.
A misshapen lump of torn fur marked what had been the fox.
From where he sat, Perrin swallowed hard. A hundred ravens could also do that... to them.

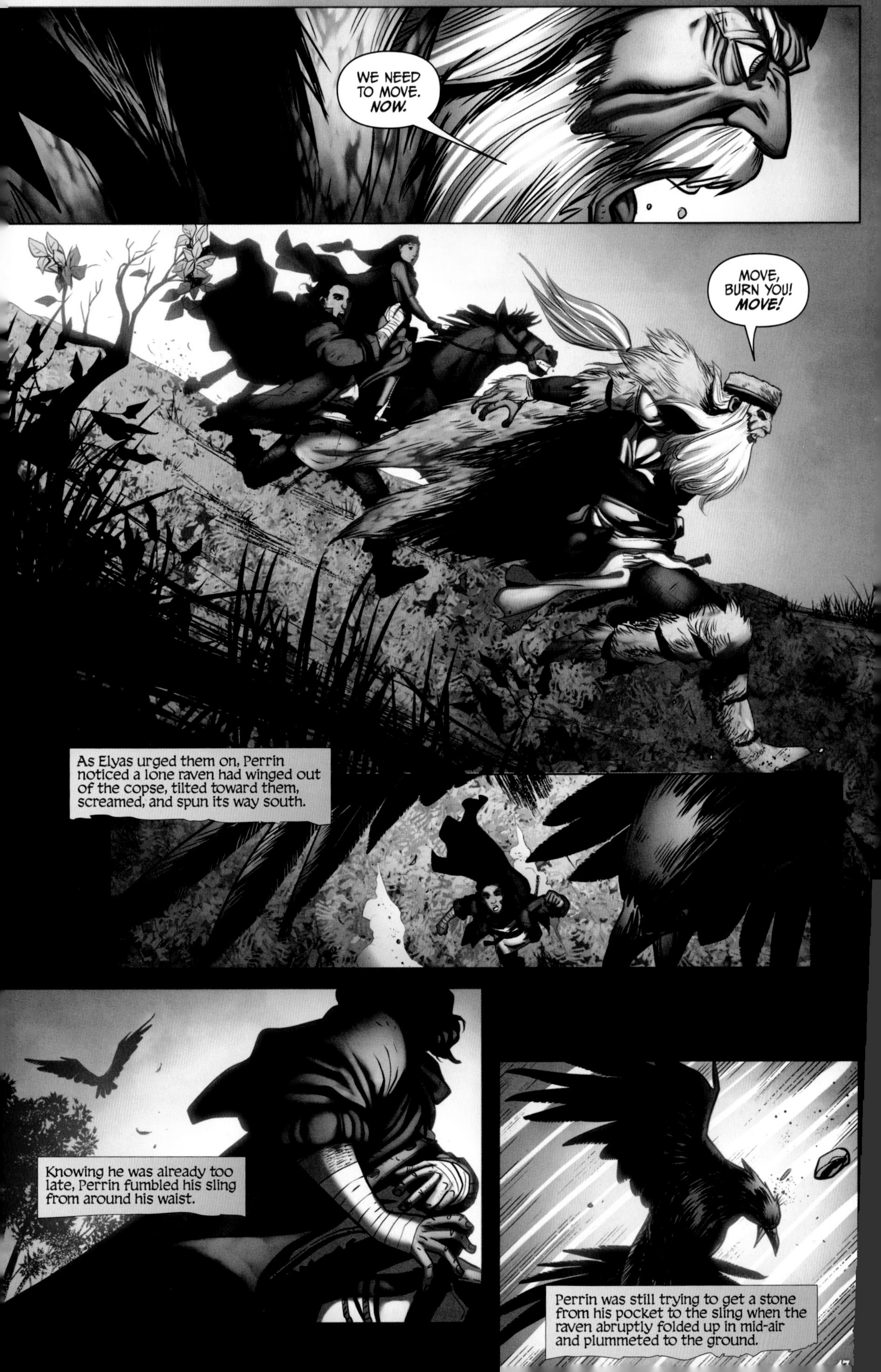
WE NEED TO MOVE. NOW.
MOVE, BURN YOU! MOVE!
As Elyas urged them on, Perrin noticed a lone raven had winged out of the copse, tilted toward them, screamed, and spun its way south.
Knowing he was already too late, Perrin fumbled his sling from around his waist.
Perrin was still trying to get a stone from his pocket to the sling when the raven abruptly folded up in mid-air and plummeted to the ground.

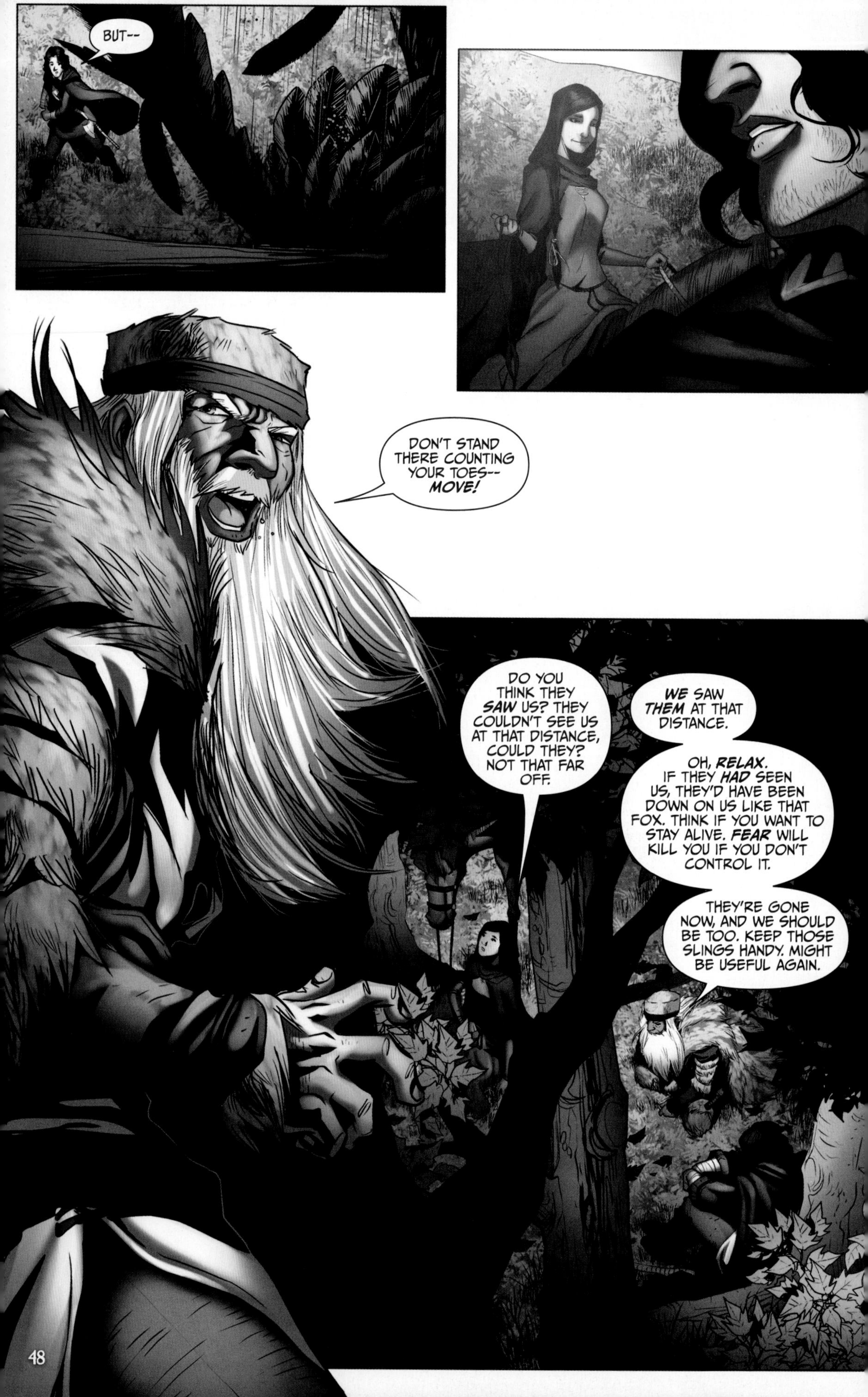
BUT--
DON'T STAND THERE COUNTING YOUR TOES-- MOVE!
DO YOU THINK THEY SAW US? THEY COULDN'T SEE US AT THAT DISTANCE, COULD THEY? NOT THAT FAR OFF.
WE SAW THEM AT THAT DISTANCE.
OH, RELAX. IF THEY HAD SEEN US, THEY'D HAVE BEEN DOWN ON US LIKE THAT FOX. THINK IF YOU WANT TO STAY ALIVE. FEAR WILL KILL YOU IF YOU DON'T CONTROL IT.
THEY'RE GONE NOW, AND WE SHOULD BE TOO. KEEP THOSE SLINGS HANDY. MIGHT BE USEFUL AGAIN.

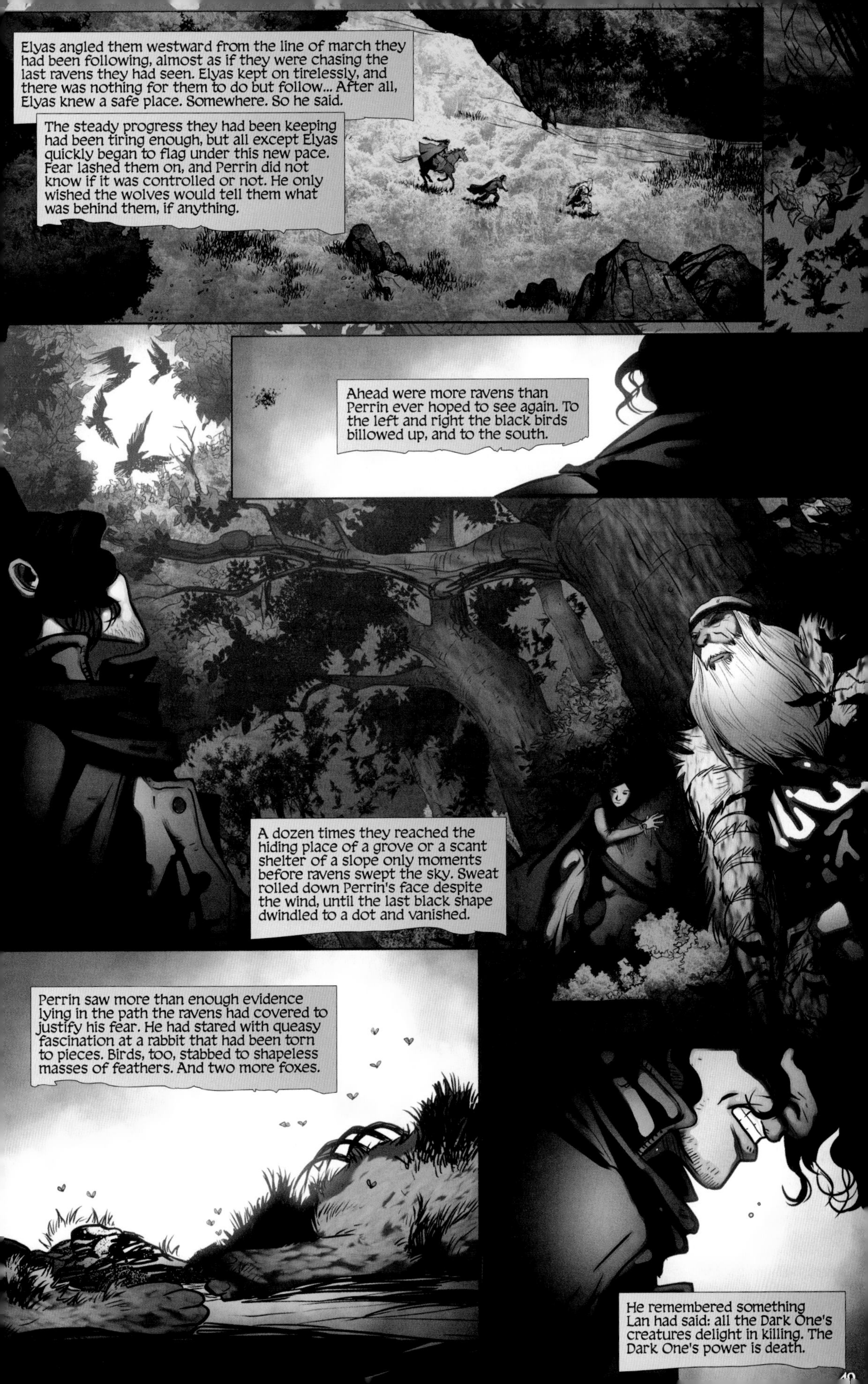
Elyas angled them westward from the line of march they had been following, almost as if they were chasing the last ravens they had seen. Elyas kept on tirelessly, and there was nothing for them to do but follow... After all, Elyas knew a safe place. Somewhere. So he said.
The steady progress they had been keeping had been tiring enough, but all except Elyas quickly began to flag under this new pace. Fear lashed them on, and Perrin did not know if it was controlled or not. He only wished the wolves would tell them what was behind them, if anything.
Ahead were more ravens than Perrin ever hoped to see again. To the left and right the black birds billowed up, and to the south.
A dozen times they reached the hiding place of a grove or a scant shelter of a slope only moments before ravens swept the sky. Sweat rolled down Perrin's face despite the wind, until the last black shape dwindled to a dot and vanished.
Perrin saw more than enough evidence lying in the path the ravens had covered to justify his fear. He had stared with queasy fascination at a rabbit that had been torn to pieces. Birds, too, stabbed to shapeless masses of feathers. And two more foxes.
He remembered something Lan had said: all the Dark One's creatures delight in killing. The Dark One's power is death.

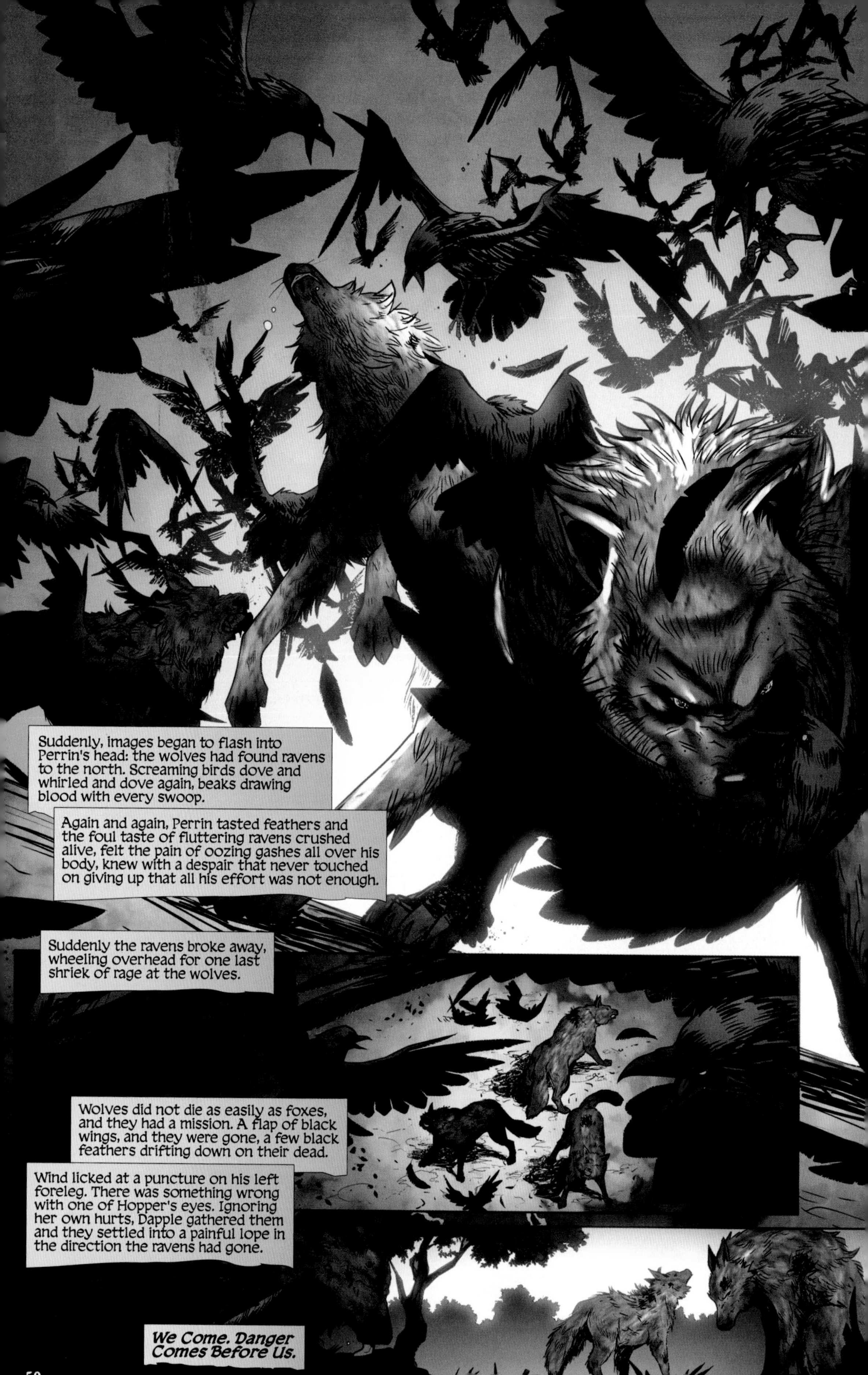

Suddenly, images began to flash into Perrin's head: the wolves had found ravens to the north. Screaming birds dove and whirled and dove again, beaks drawing blood with every swoop.
Again and again, Perrin tasted feathers and the foul taste of fluttering ravens crushed alive, felt the pain of oozing gashes all over his body, knew with a despair that never touched on giving up that all his effort was not enough.
Suddenly the ravens broke away, wheeling overhead for one last shriek of rage at the wolves.
Wolves did not die as easily as foxes, and they had a mission. A flap of black wings, and they were gone, a few black feathers drifting down on their dead.
Wind licked at a puncture on his left foreleg. There was something wrong with one of Hopper's eyes. Ignoring her own hurts, Dapple gathered them and they settled into a painful lope in the direction the ravens had gone.
We Come. Danger Comes Before Us.

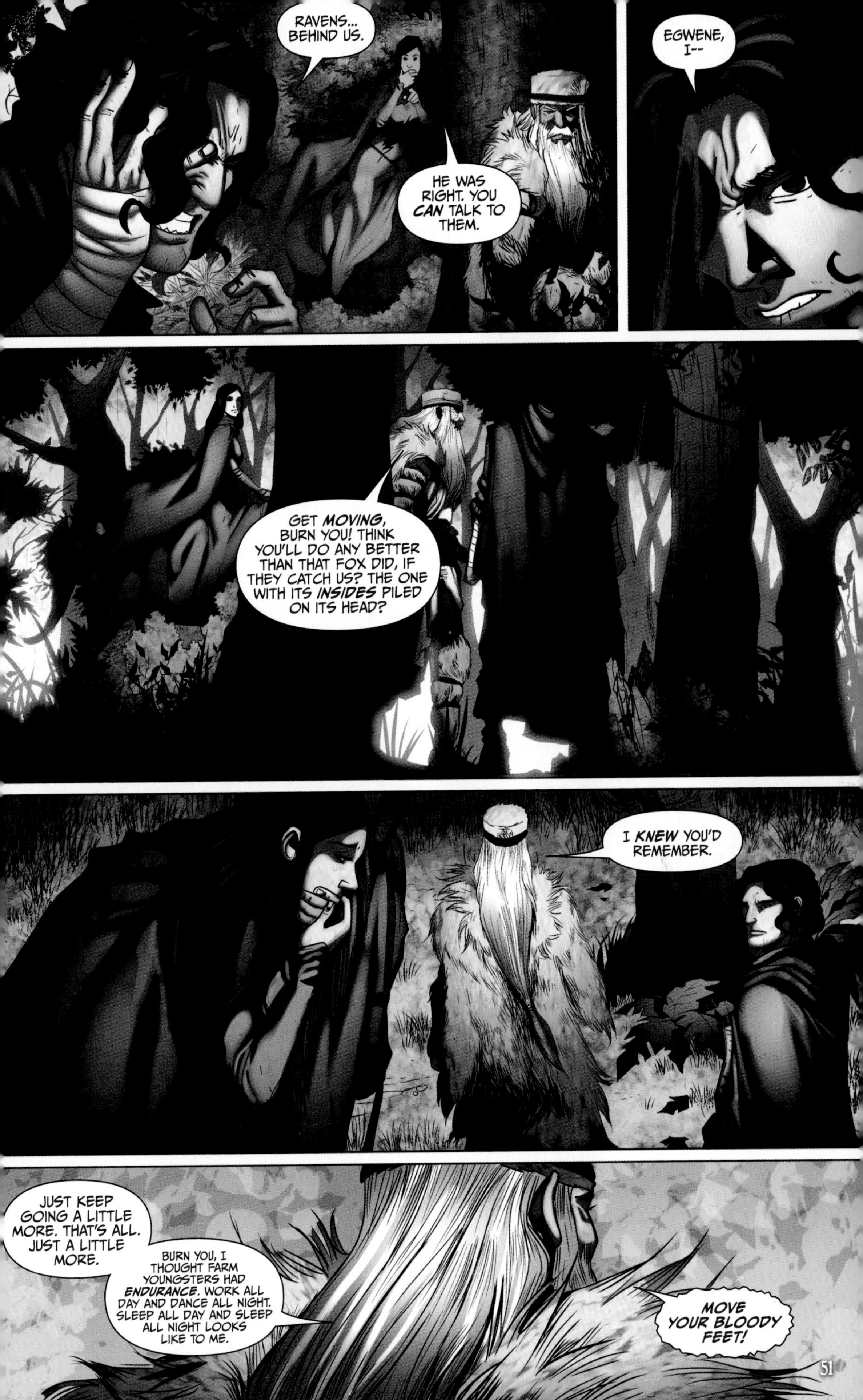
RAVENS... BEHIND US.
HE WAS RIGHT. YOU CAN TALK TO THEM.
EGWENE, I--
GET MOVING, BURN YOU! THINK YOU'LL DO ANY BETTER THAN THAT FOX DID, IF THEY CATCH US? THE ONE WITH ITS INSIDES PILED ON ITS HEAD?
I KNEW YOU'D REMEMBER.
JUST KEEP GOING A LITTLE MORE. THAT'S ALL. JUST A LITTLE MORE.
BURN YOU, I THOUGHT FARM YOUNGSTERS HAD ENDURANCE. WORK ALL DAY AND DANCE ALL NIGHT. SLEEP ALL DAY AND SLEEP ALL NIGHT LOOKS LIKE TO ME.
MOVE YOUR BLOODY FEET!

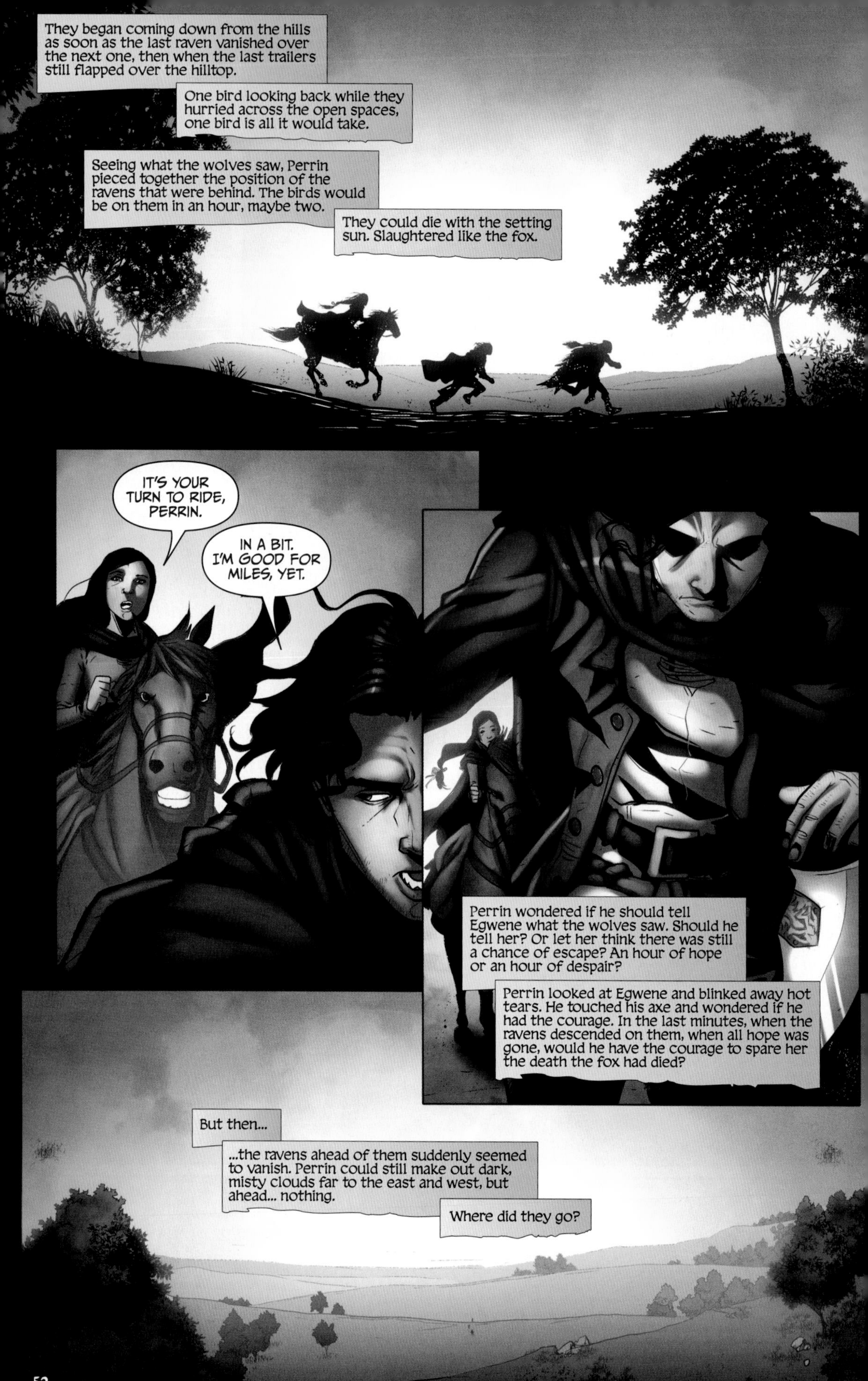
They began coming down from the hills as soon as the last raven vanished over the next one, then when the last trailers still flapped over the hilltop.
One bird looking back while they hurried across the open spaces, one bird is all it would take.
Seeing what the wolves saw, Perrin pieced together the position of the ravens that were behind. The birds would be on them in an hour, maybe two.
They could die with the setting sun. Slaughtered like the fox.
IT'S YOUR TURN TO RIDE, PERRIN.
IN A BIT. I'M GOOD FOR MILES, YET.
Perrin wondered if he should tell Egwene what the wolves saw. Should he tell her? Or let her think there was still a chance of escape? An hour of hope or an hour of despair?
Perrin looked at Egwene and blinked away hot tears. He touched his axe and wondered if he had the courage. In the last minutes, when the ravens descended on them, when all hope was gone, would he have the courage to spare her the death the fox had died?
But then...
...the ravens ahead of them suddenly seemed to vanish. Perrin could still make out dark, misty clouds far to the east and west, but ahead... nothing.
Where did they go?

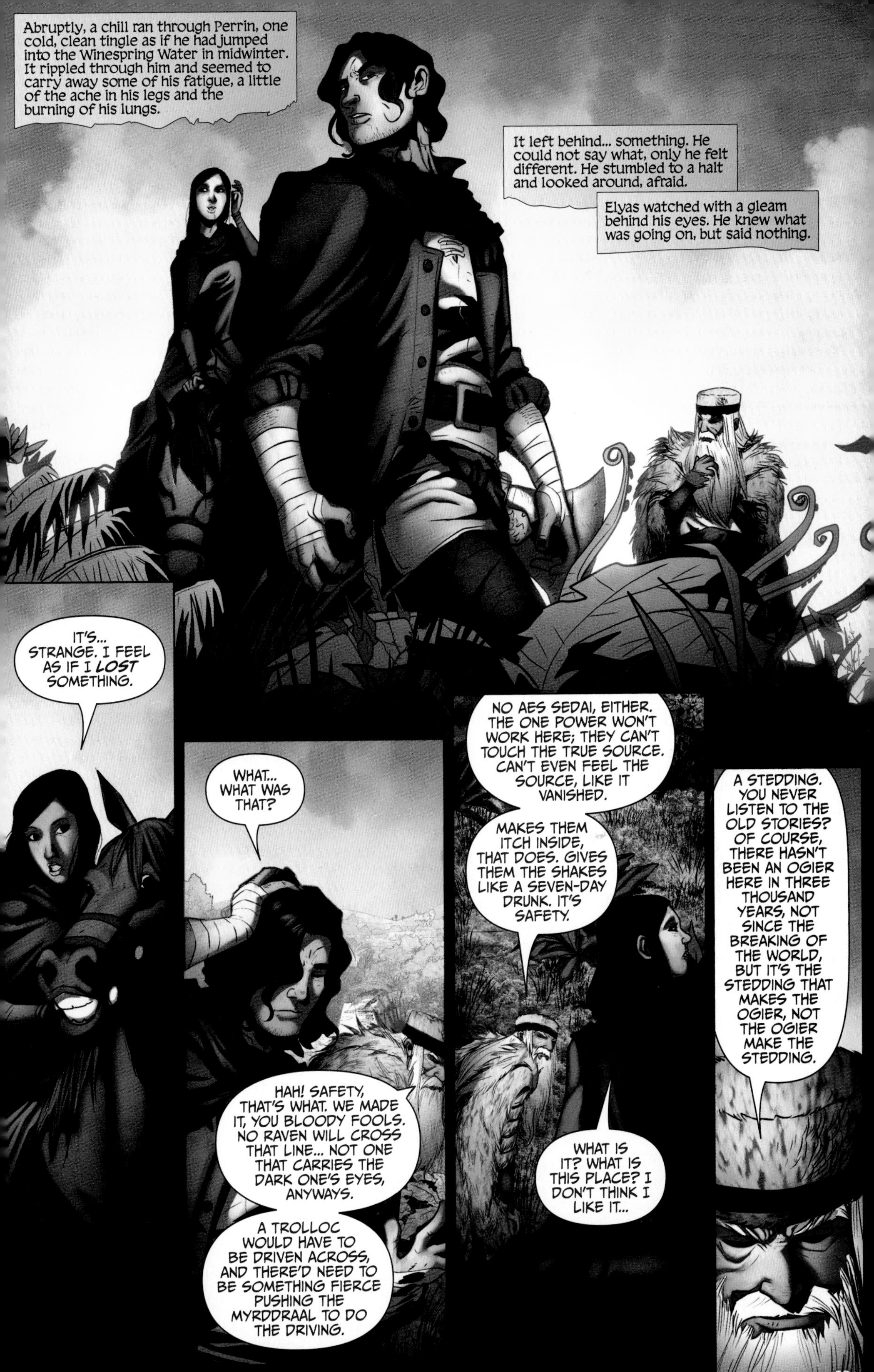
Abruptly, a chill ran through Perrin, one cold, clean tingle as if he had jumped into the Winespring Water in midwinter. It rippled through him and seemed to carry away some of his fatigue, a little of the ache in his legs and the burning of his lungs.
It left behind... something. He could not say what, only he felt different. He stumbled to a halt and looked around, afraid.
Elyas watched with a gleam behind his eyes. He knew what was going on, but said nothing.
IT'S... STRANGE. I FEEL AS IF I *LOST* SOMETHING.
WHAT... WHAT WAS THAT?
HAH! SAFETY, THAT'S WHAT. WE MADE IT, YOU BLOODY FOOLS. NO RAVEN WILL CROSS THAT LINE... NOT ONE THAT CARRIES THE DARK ONE'S EYES, ANYWAYS.
A TROLLOC WOULD HAVE TO BE DRIVEN ACROSS, AND THERE'D NEED TO BE SOMETHING FIERCE PUSHING THE MYRDDRAAL TO DO THE DRIVING.
NO AES SEDAI, EITHER. THE ONE POWER WON'T WORK HERE; THEY CAN'T TOUCH THE TRUE SOURCE. CAN'T EVEN FEEL THE SOURCE, LIKE IT VANISHED.
MAKES THEM ITCH INSIDE, THAT DOES. GIVES THEM THE SHAKES LIKE A SEVEN-DAY DRUNK. IT'S SAFETY.
WHAT IS IT? WHAT IS THIS PLACE? I DON'T THINK I LIKE IT...
A STEDDING. YOU NEVER LISTEN TO THE OLD STORIES? OF COURSE, THERE HASN'T BEEN AN OGIER HERE IN THREE THOUSAND YEARS, NOT SINCE THE BREAKING OF THE WORLD, BUT IT'S THE STEDDING THAT MAKES THE OGIER, NOT THE OGIER MAKE THE STEDDING.

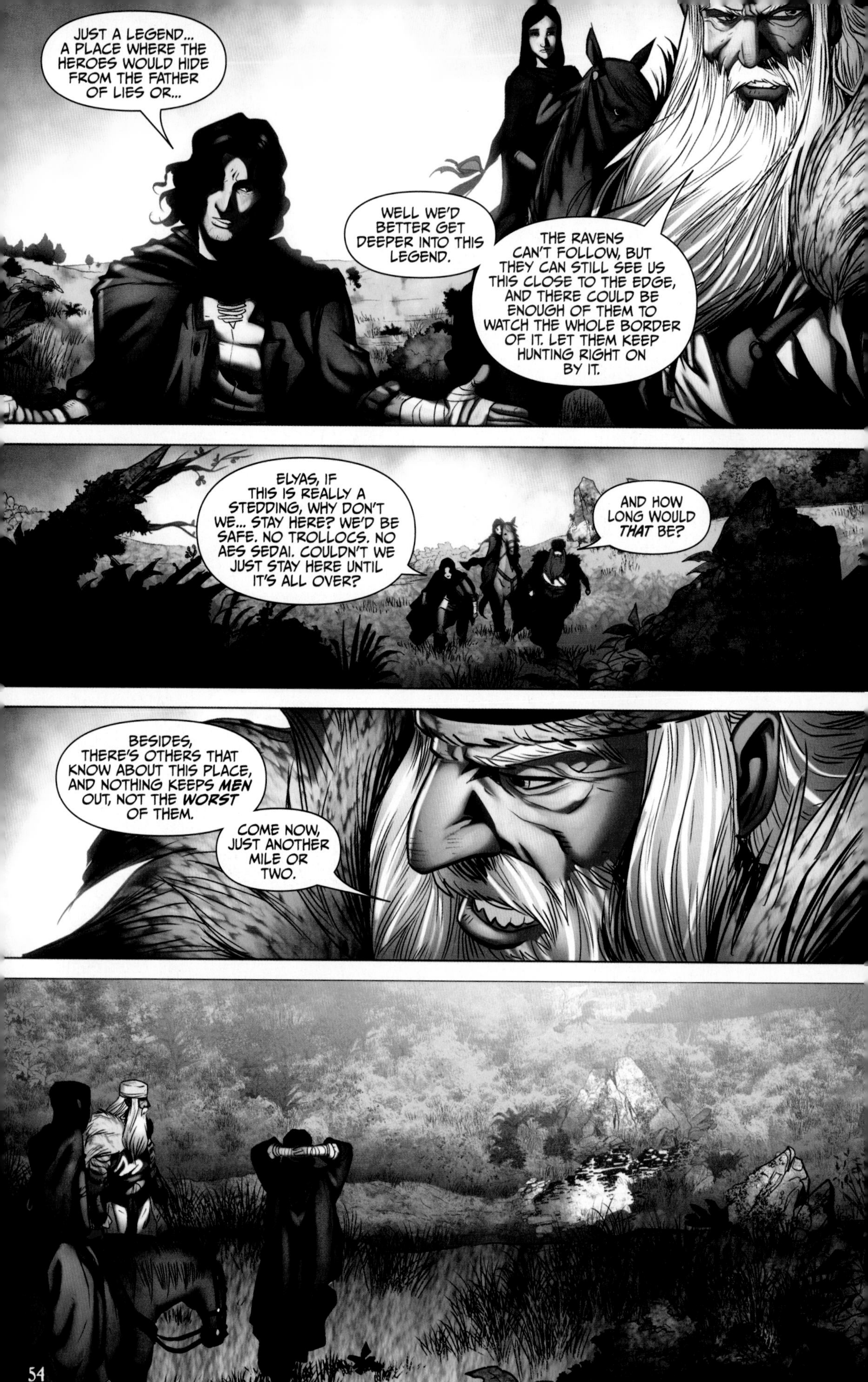
JUST A LEGEND... A PLACE WHERE THE HEROES WOULD HIDE FROM THE FATHER OF LIES OR...
WELL WE'D BETTER GET DEEPER INTO THIS LEGEND.
THE RAVENS CAN'T FOLLOW, BUT THEY CAN STILL SEE US THIS CLOSE TO THE EDGE, AND THERE COULD BE ENOUGH OF THEM TO WATCH THE WHOLE BORDER OF IT. LET THEM KEEP HUNTING RIGHT ON BY IT.
ELYAS, IF THIS IS REALLY A STEDDING, WHY DON'T WE... STAY HERE? WE'D BE SAFE. NO TROLLOCS. NO AES SEDAI. COULDN'T WE JUST STAY HERE UNTIL IT'S ALL OVER?
AND HOW LONG WOULD *THAT* BE?
BESIDES, THERE'S OTHERS THAT KNOW ABOUT THIS PLACE, AND NOTHING KEEPS *MEN* OUT, NOT THE *WORST* OF THEM.
COME NOW, JUST ANOTHER MILE OR TWO.

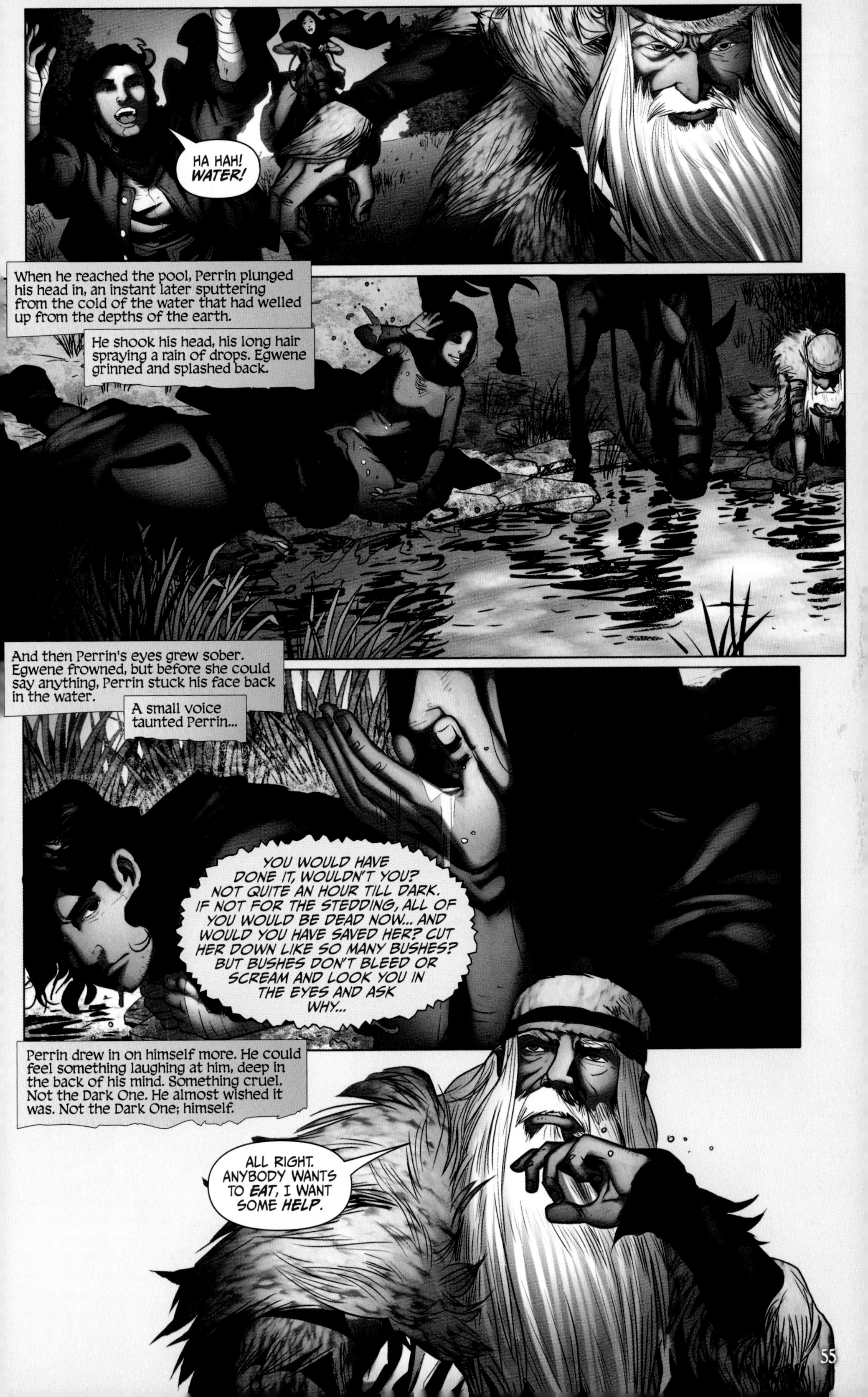
HA HAH! WATER!
When he reached the pool, Perrin plunged his head in, an instant later sputtering from the cold of the water that had welled up from the depths of the earth.
He shook his head, his long hair spraying a rain of drops. Egwene grinned and splashed back.
And then Perrin's eyes grew sober. Egwene frowned, but before she could say anything, Perrin stuck his face back in the water.
A small voice taunted Perrin...
YOU WOULD HAVE DONE IT, WOULDN'T YOU? NOT QUITE AN HOUR TILL DARK. IF NOT FOR THE STEDDING, ALL OF YOU WOULD BE DEAD NOW... AND WOULD YOU HAVE SAVED HER? CUT HER DOWN LIKE SO MANY BUSHES? BUT BUSHES DON'T BLEED OR SCREAM AND LOOK YOU IN THE EYES AND ASK WHY...
Perrin drew in on himself more. He could feel something laughing at him, deep in the back of his mind. Something cruel. Not the Dark One. He almost wished it was. Not the Dark One; himself.
ALL RIGHT. ANYBODY WANTS TO EAT, I WANT SOME HELP.

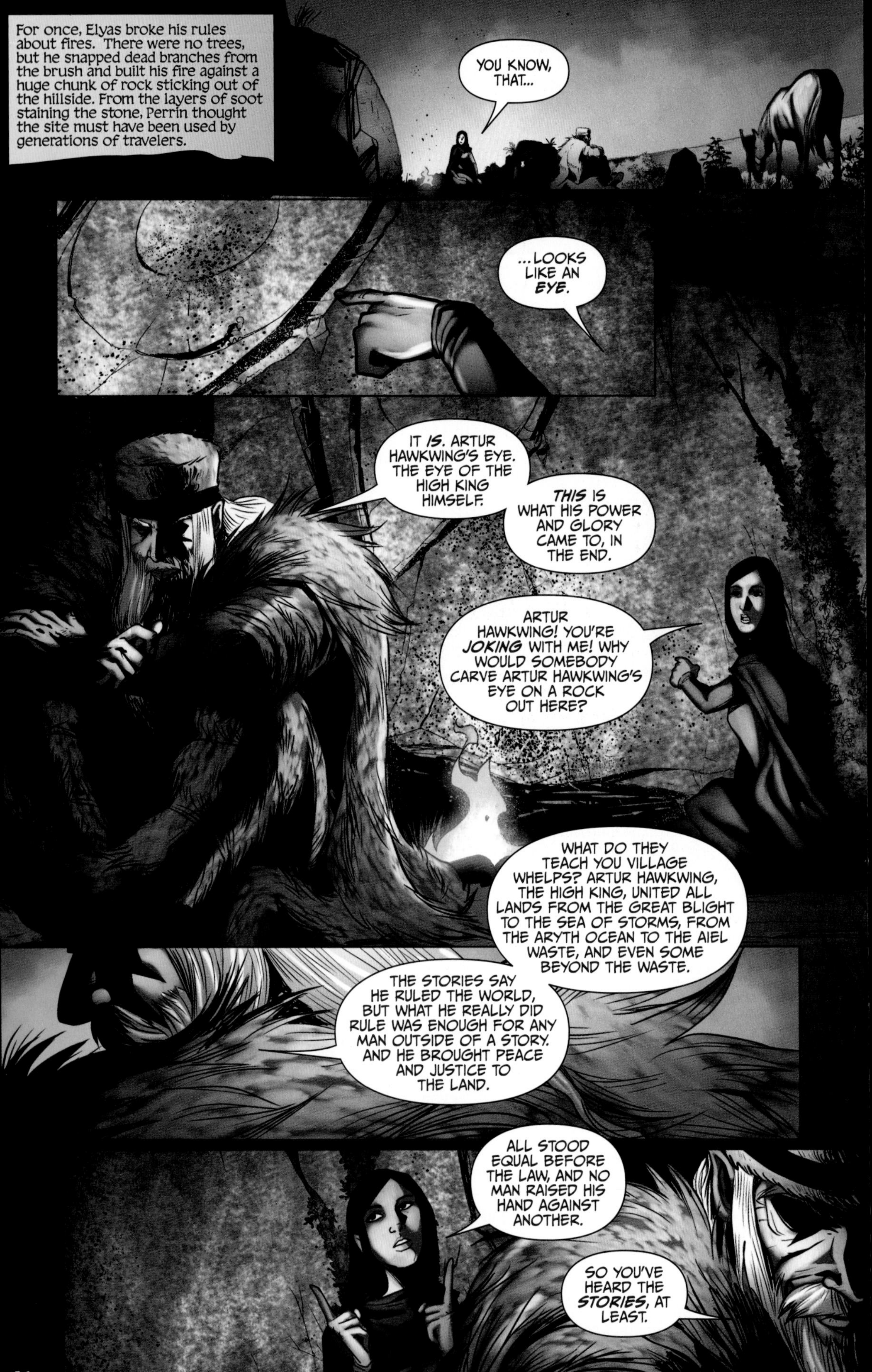
For once, Elyas broke his rules about fires. There were no trees, but he snapped dead branches from the brush and built his fire against a huge chunk of rock sticking out of the hillside. From the layers of soot staining the stone, Perrin thought the site must have been used by generations of travelers.
YOU KNOW, THAT...
...LOOKS LIKE AN *EYE.*
IT *IS.* ARTUR HAWKWING'S EYE. THE EYE OF THE HIGH KING HIMSELF.
THIS IS WHAT HIS POWER AND GLORY CAME TO, IN THE END.
ARTUR HAWKWING! YOU'RE *JOKING* WITH ME! WHY WOULD SOMEBODY CARVE ARTUR HAWKWING'S EYE ON A ROCK OUT HERE?
WHAT DO THEY TEACH YOU VILLAGE WHELPS? ARTUR HAWKWING, THE HIGH KING, UNITED ALL LANDS FROM THE GREAT BLIGHT TO THE SEA OF STORMS, FROM THE ARYTH OCEAN TO THE AIEL WASTE, AND EVEN SOME BEYOND THE WASTE.
THE STORIES SAY HE RULED THE WORLD, BUT WHAT HE REALLY DID RULE WAS ENOUGH FOR ANY MAN OUTSIDE OF A STORY. AND HE BROUGHT PEACE AND JUSTICE TO THE LAND.
ALL STOOD EQUAL BEFORE THE LAW, AND NO MAN RAISED HIS HAND AGAINST ANOTHER.
SO YOU'VE HEARD THE *STORIES,* AT LEAST.

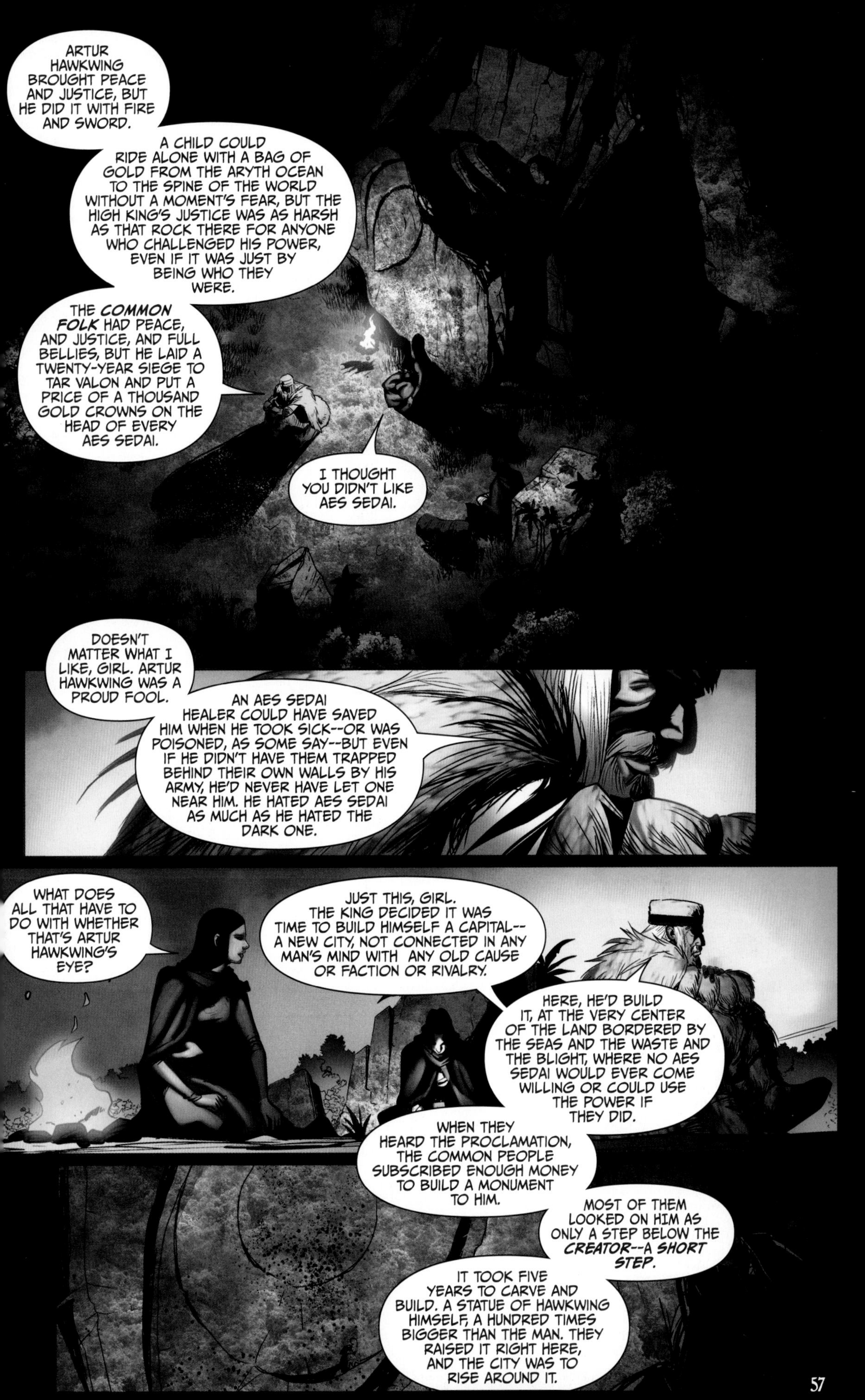
ARTUR HAWKWING BROUGHT PEACE AND JUSTICE, BUT HE DID IT WITH FIRE AND SWORD.
A CHILD COULD RIDE ALONE WITH A BAG OF GOLD FROM THE ARYTH OCEAN TO THE SPINE OF THE WORLD WITHOUT A MOMENT'S FEAR, BUT THE HIGH KING'S JUSTICE WAS AS HARSH AS THAT ROCK THERE FOR ANYONE WHO CHALLENGED HIS POWER, EVEN IF IT WAS JUST BY BEING WHO THEY WERE.
THE *COMMON FOLK* HAD PEACE, AND JUSTICE, AND FULL BELLIES, BUT HE LAID A TWENTY-YEAR SIEGE TO TAR VALON AND PUT A PRICE OF A THOUSAND GOLD CROWNS ON THE HEAD OF EVERY AES SEDAI.
I THOUGHT YOU DIDN'T LIKE AES SEDAI.
DOESN'T MATTER WHAT I LIKE, GIRL. ARTUR HAWKWING WAS A PROUD FOOL.
AN AES SEDAI HEALER COULD HAVE SAVED HIM WHEN HE TOOK SICK--OR WAS POISONED, AS SOME SAY--BUT EVEN IF HE DIDN'T HAVE THEM TRAPPED BEHIND THEIR OWN WALLS BY HIS ARMY, HE'D NEVER HAVE LET ONE NEAR HIM. HE HATED AES SEDAI AS MUCH AS HE HATED THE DARK ONE.
WHAT DOES ALL THAT HAVE TO DO WITH WHETHER THAT'S ARTUR HAWKWING'S EYE?
JUST THIS, GIRL. THE KING DECIDED IT WAS TIME TO BUILD HIMSELF A CAPITAL-- A NEW CITY, NOT CONNECTED IN ANY MAN'S MIND WITH ANY OLD CAUSE OR FACTION OR RIVALRY.
HERE, HE'D BUILD IT, AT THE VERY CENTER OF THE LAND BORDERED BY THE SEAS AND THE WASTE AND THE BLIGHT, WHERE NO AES SEDAI WOULD EVER COME WILLING OR COULD USE THE POWER IF THEY DID.
WHEN THEY HEARD THE PROCLAMATION, THE COMMON PEOPLE SUBSCRIBED ENOUGH MONEY TO BUILD A MONUMENT TO HIM.
MOST OF THEM LOOKED ON HIM AS ONLY A STEP BELOW THE *CREATOR*--A *SHORT STEP*.
IT TOOK FIVE YEARS TO CARVE AND BUILD. A STATUE OF HAWKWING HIMSELF, A HUNDRED TIMES BIGGER THAN THE MAN. THEY RAISED IT RIGHT HERE, AND THE CITY WAS TO RISE AROUND IT.

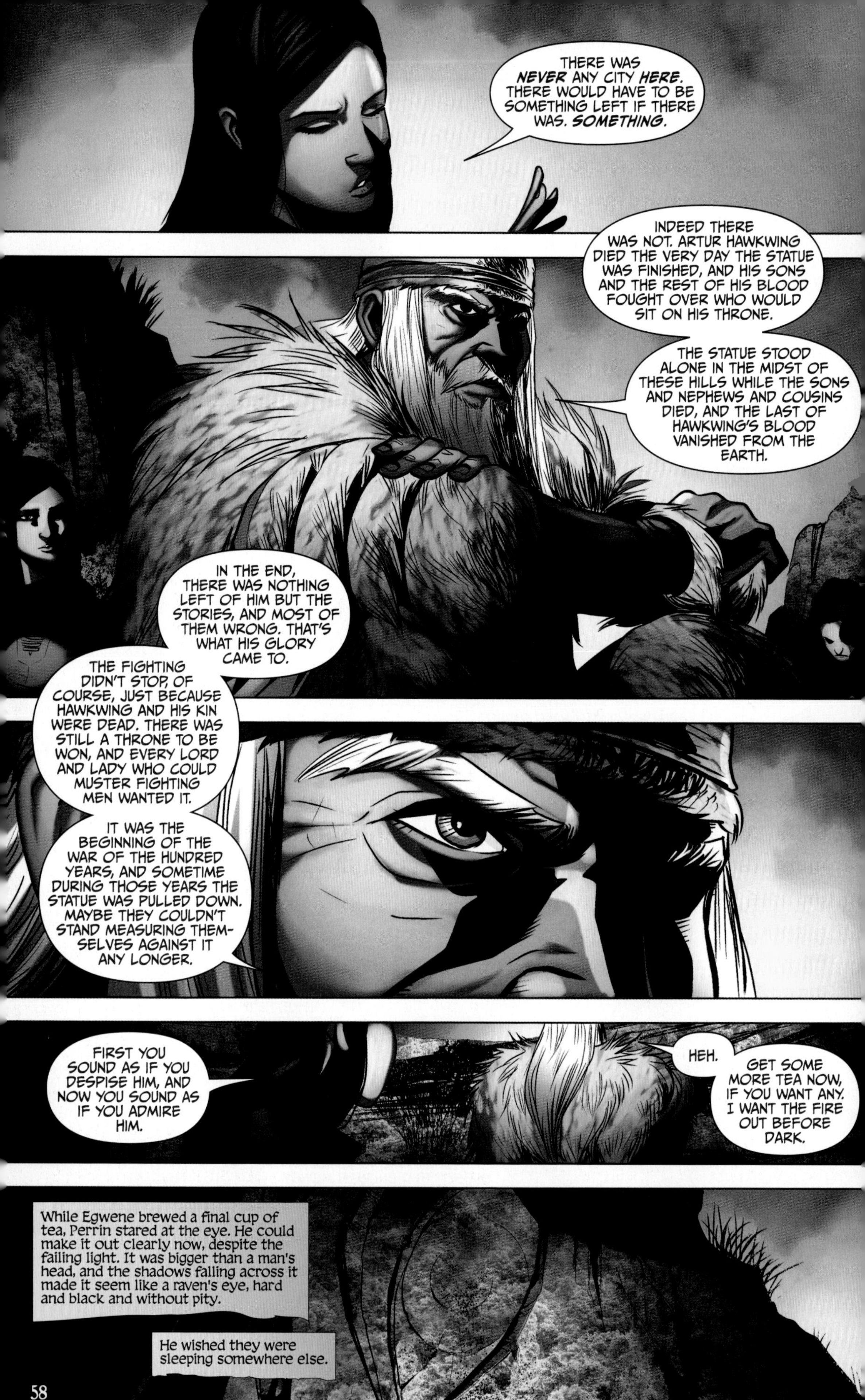
THERE WAS NEVER ANY CITY HERE. THERE WOULD HAVE TO BE SOMETHING LEFT IF THERE WAS. SOMETHING.
INDEED THERE WAS NOT. ARTUR HAWKWING DIED THE VERY DAY THE STATUE WAS FINISHED, AND HIS SONS AND THE REST OF HIS BLOOD FOUGHT OVER WHO WOULD SIT ON HIS THRONE.
THE STATUE STOOD ALONE IN THE MIDST OF THESE HILLS WHILE THE SONS AND NEPHEWS AND COUSINS DIED, AND THE LAST OF HAWKWING'S BLOOD VANISHED FROM THE EARTH.
IN THE END, THERE WAS NOTHING LEFT OF HIM BUT THE STORIES, AND MOST OF THEM WRONG. THAT'S WHAT HIS GLORY CAME TO.
THE FIGHTING DIDN'T STOP, OF COURSE, JUST BECAUSE HAWKWING AND HIS KIN WERE DEAD. THERE WAS STILL A THRONE TO BE WON, AND EVERY LORD AND LADY WHO COULD MUSTER FIGHTING MEN WANTED IT.
IT WAS THE BEGINNING OF THE WAR OF THE HUNDRED YEARS, AND SOMETIME DURING THOSE YEARS THE STATUE WAS PULLED DOWN. MAYBE THEY COULDN'T STAND MEASURING THEM-SELVES AGAINST IT ANY LONGER.
FIRST YOU SOUND AS IF YOU DESPISE HIM, AND NOW YOU SOUND AS IF YOU ADMIRE HIM.
HEH.
GET SOME MORE TEA NOW, IF YOU WANT ANY. I WANT THE FIRE OUT BEFORE DARK.
While Egwene brewed a final cup of tea, Perrin stared at the eye. He could make it out clearly now, despite the failing light. It was bigger than a man's head, and the shadows falling across it made it seem like a raven's eye, hard and black and without pity.
He wished they were sleeping somewhere else.

chapter three

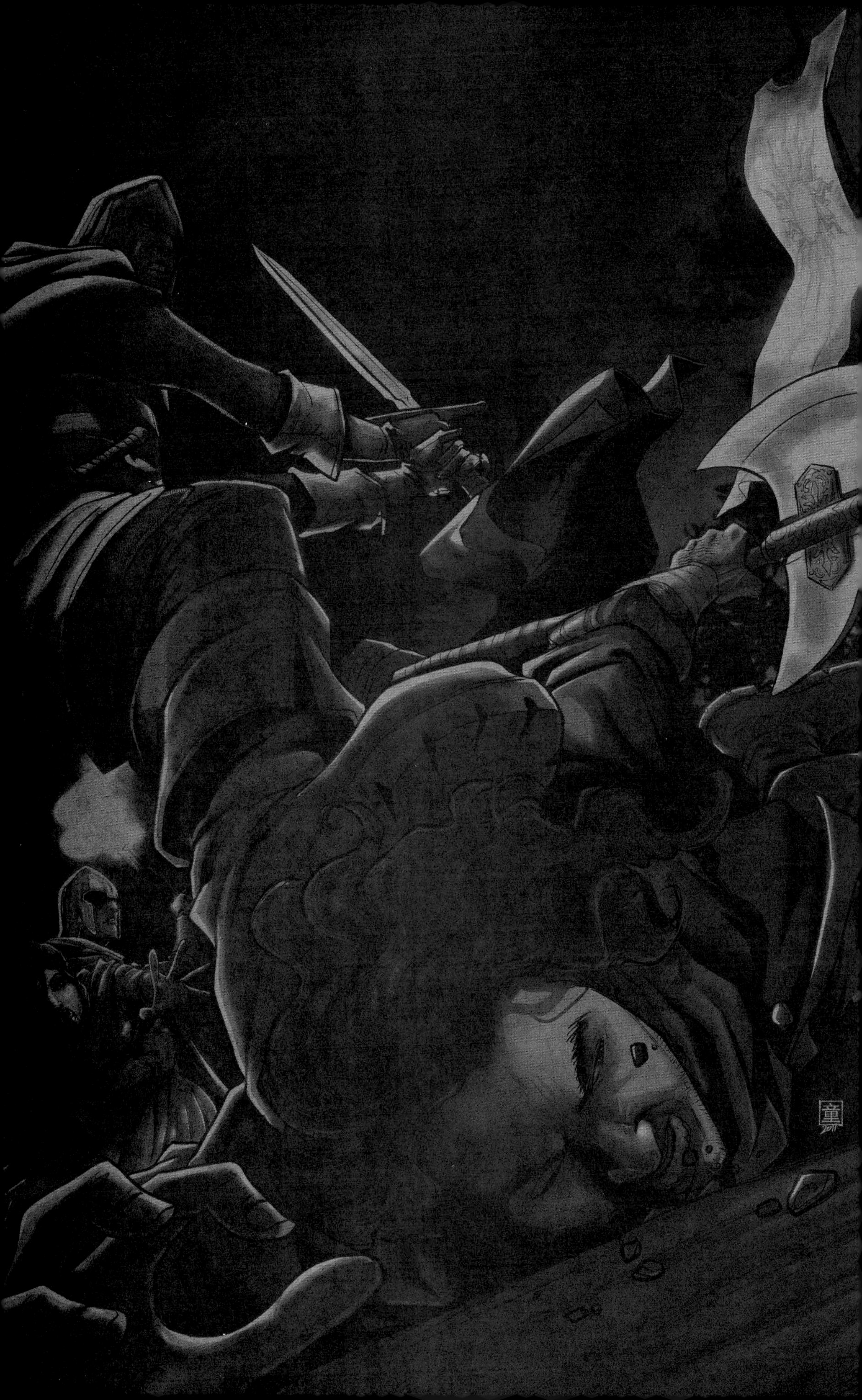

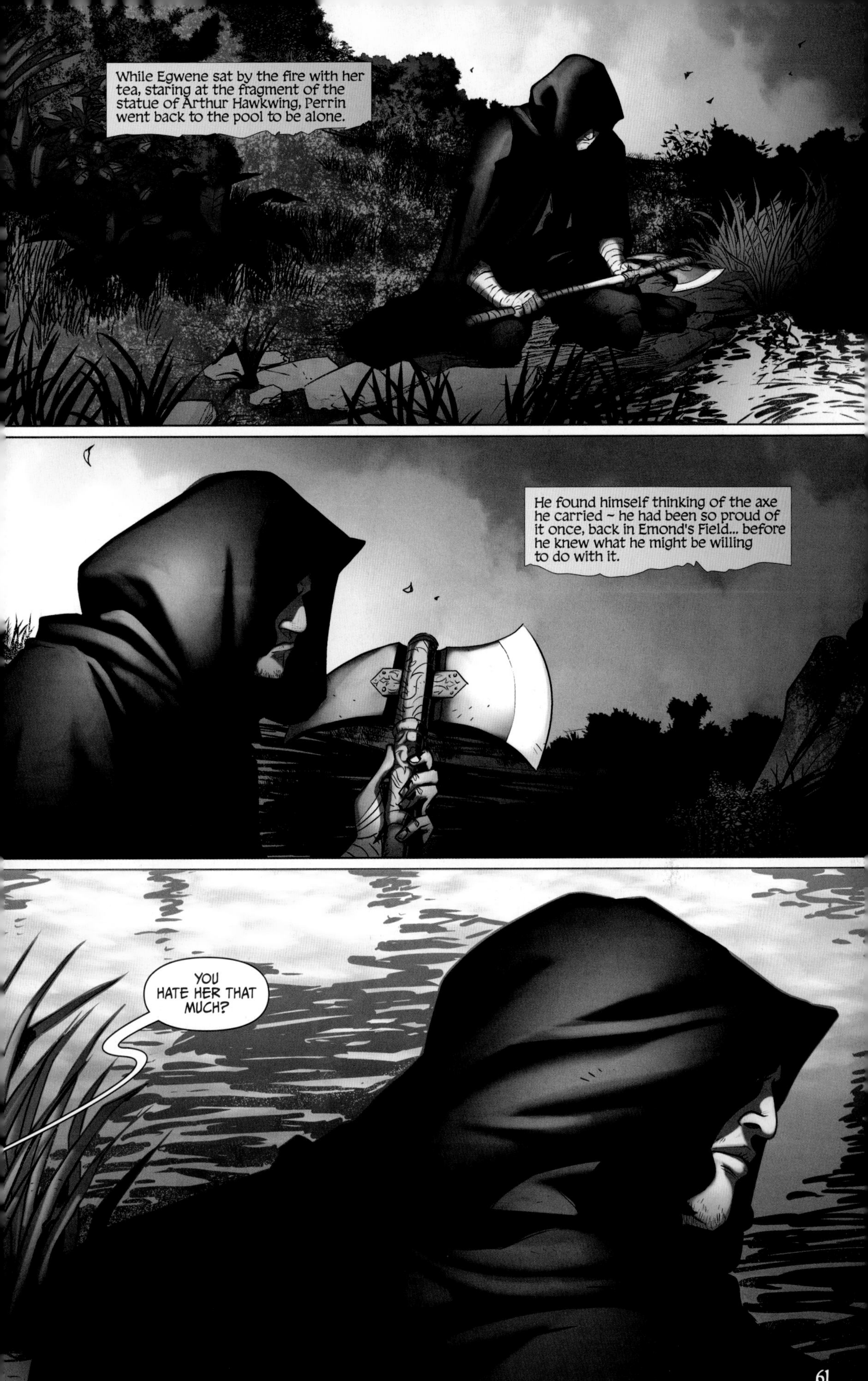
While Egwene sat by the fire with her tea, staring at the fragment of the statue of Arthur Hawkwing, Perrin went back to the pool to be alone.
He found himself thinking of the axe he carried ~ he had been so proud of it once, back in Emond's Field... before he knew what he might be willing to do with it.
YOU HATE HER THAT MUCH?

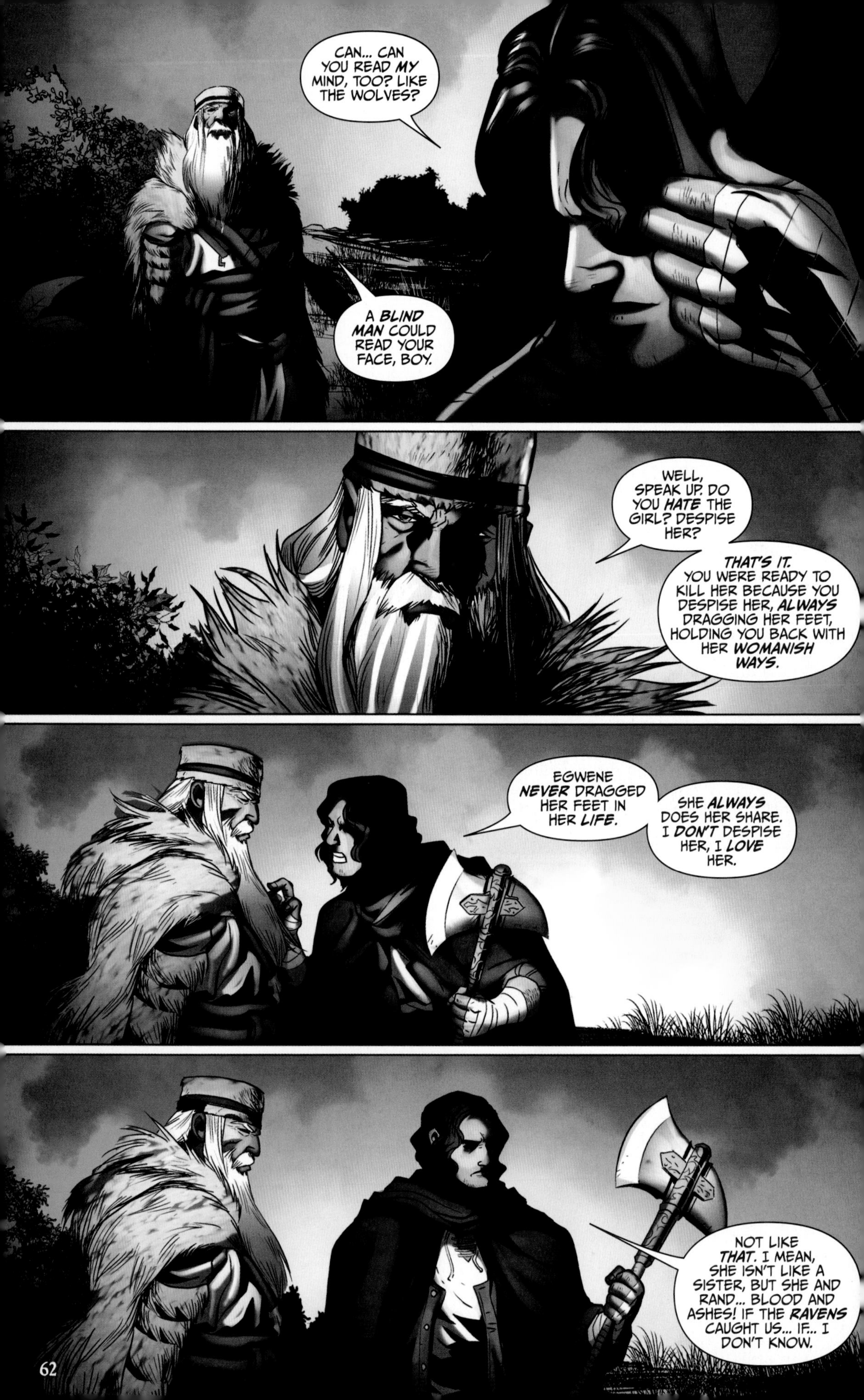
CAN... CAN YOU READ MY MIND, TOO? LIKE THE WOLVES?
A BLIND MAN COULD READ YOUR FACE, BOY.
WELL, SPEAK UP. DO YOU HATE THE GIRL? DESPISE HER?
THAT'S IT. YOU WERE READY TO KILL HER BECAUSE YOU DESPISE HER, ALWAYS DRAGGING HER FEET, HOLDING YOU BACK WITH HER WOMANISH WAYS.
EGWENE NEVER DRAGGED HER FEET IN HER LIFE.
SHE ALWAYS DOES HER SHARE. I DON'T DESPISE HER, I LOVE HER.
NOT LIKE THAT. I MEAN, SHE ISN'T LIKE A SISTER, BUT SHE AND RAND... BLOOD AND ASHES! IF THE RAVENS CAUGHT US... IF... I DON'T KNOW.

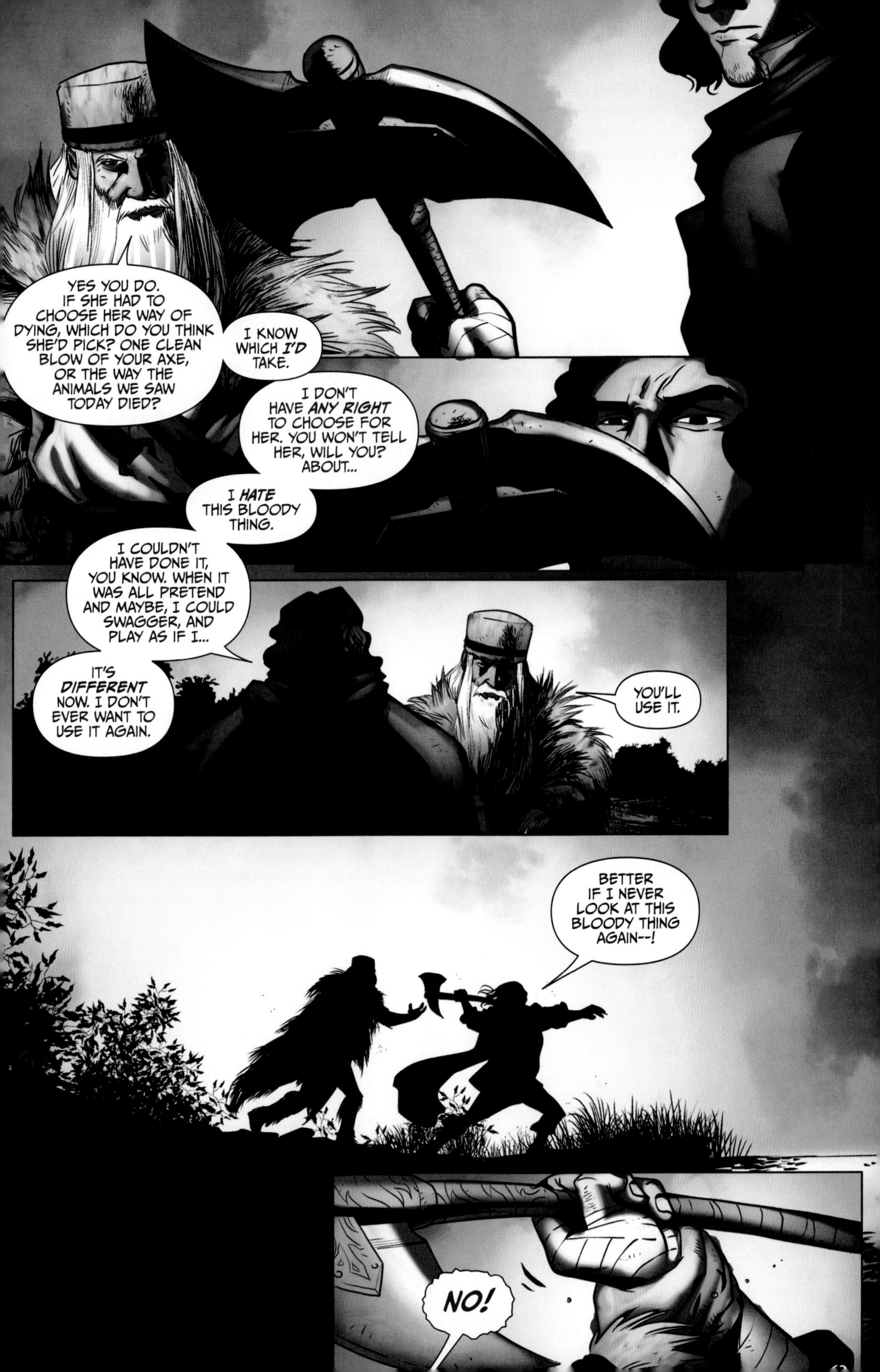
YES YOU DO. IF SHE HAD TO CHOOSE HER WAY OF DYING, WHICH DO YOU THINK SHE'D PICK? ONE CLEAN BLOW OF YOUR AXE, OR THE WAY THE ANIMALS WE SAW TODAY DIED?
I KNOW WHICH *I'D* TAKE.
I DON'T HAVE **ANY RIGHT** TO CHOOSE FOR HER. YOU WON'T TELL HER, WILL YOU? ABOUT...
I **HATE** THIS BLOODY THING.
I COULDN'T HAVE DONE IT, YOU KNOW. WHEN IT WAS ALL PRETEND AND MAYBE, I COULD SWAGGER, AND PLAY AS IF I...
IT'S **DIFFERENT** NOW. I DON'T EVER WANT TO USE IT AGAIN.
YOU'LL USE IT.
BETTER IF I NEVER LOOK AT THIS BLOODY THING AGAIN--!
NO!

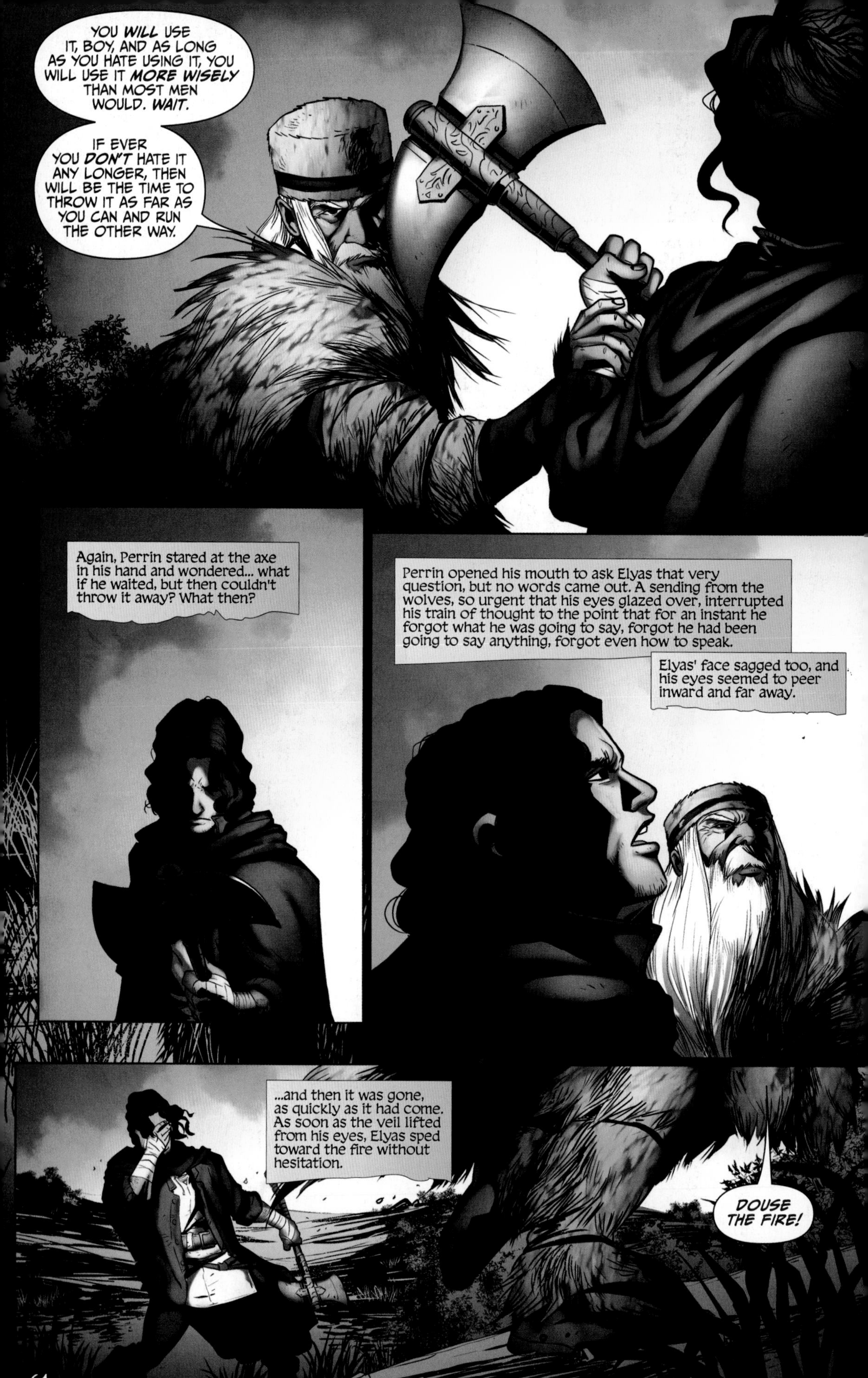

YOU WILL USE IT, BOY, AND AS LONG AS YOU HATE USING IT, YOU WILL USE IT MORE WISELY THAN MOST MEN WOULD. WAIT.
IF EVER YOU DON'T HATE IT ANY LONGER, THEN WILL BE THE TIME TO THROW IT AS FAR AS YOU CAN AND RUN THE OTHER WAY.
Again, Perrin stared at the axe in his hand and wondered... what if he waited, but then couldn't throw it away? What then?
Perrin opened his mouth to ask Elyas that very question, but no words came out. A sending from the wolves, so urgent that his eyes glazed over, interrupted his train of thought to the point that for an instant he forgot what he was going to say, forgot he had been going to say anything, forgot even how to speak.
Elyas' face sagged too, and his eyes seemed to peer inward and far away.
...and then it was gone, as quickly as it had come. As soon as the veil lifted from his eyes, Elyas sped toward the fire without hesitation.
DOUSE THE FIRE!

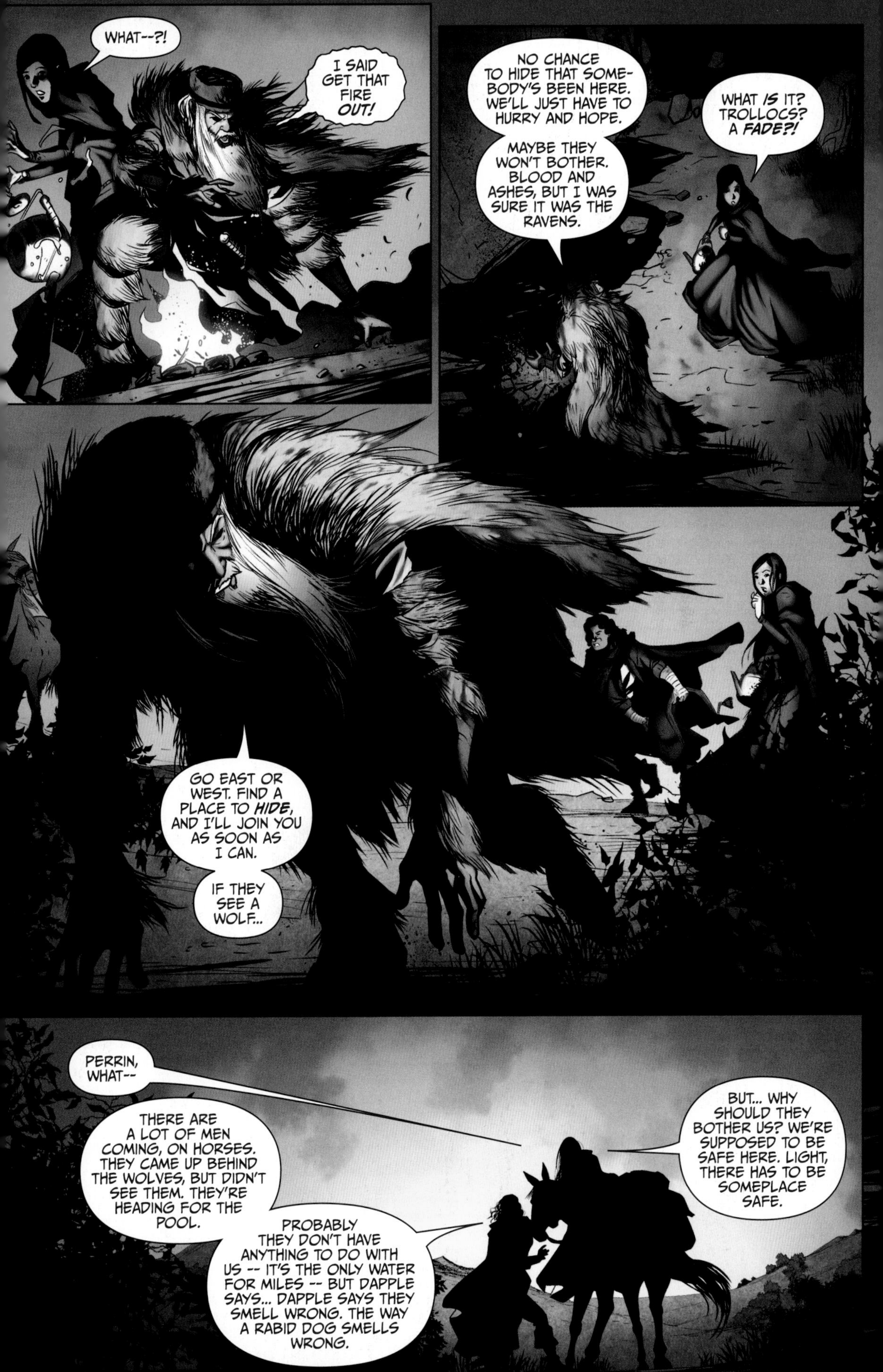
WHAT--?!
I SAID GET THAT FIRE OUT!
NO CHANCE TO HIDE THAT SOMEBODY'S BEEN HERE. WE'LL JUST HAVE TO HURRY AND HOPE.
MAYBE THEY WON'T BOTHER. BLOOD AND ASHES, BUT I WAS SURE IT WAS THE RAVENS.
WHAT IS IT? TROLLOCS? A FADE?!
GO EAST OR WEST. FIND A PLACE TO HIDE, AND I'LL JOIN YOU AS SOON AS I CAN.
IF THEY SEE A WOLF...
PERRIN, WHAT--
THERE ARE A LOT OF MEN COMING, ON HORSES. THEY CAME UP BEHIND THE WOLVES, BUT DIDN'T SEE THEM. THEY'RE HEADING FOR THE POOL.
BUT... WHY SHOULD THEY BOTHER US? WE'RE SUPPOSED TO BE SAFE HERE. LIGHT, THERE HAS TO BE SOMEPLACE SAFE.
PROBABLY THEY DON'T HAVE ANYTHING TO DO WITH US -- IT'S THE ONLY WATER FOR MILES -- BUT DAPPLE SAYS... DAPPLE SAYS THEY SMELL WRONG. THE WAY A RABID DOG SMELLS WRONG.

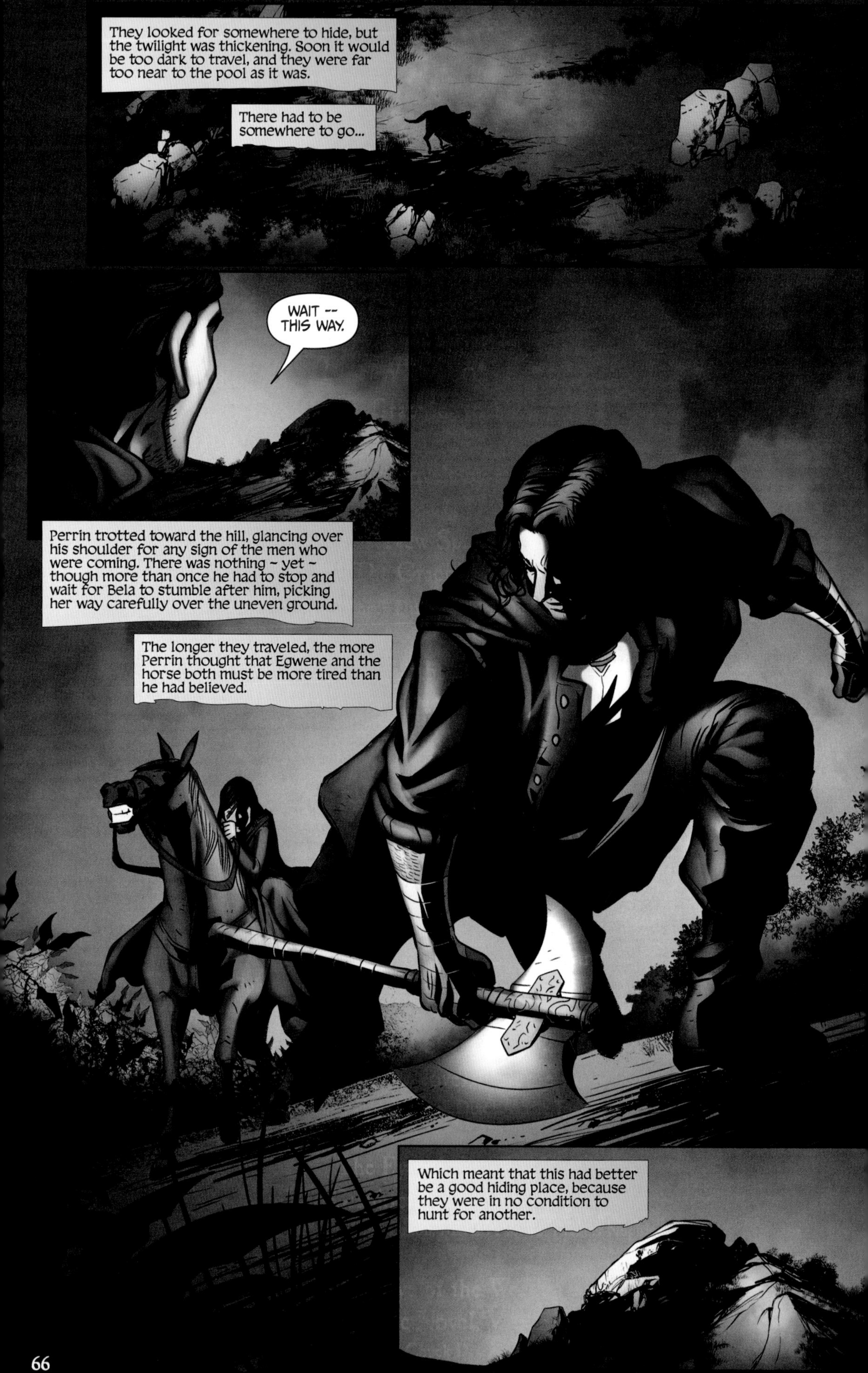
They looked for somewhere to hide, but the twilight was thickening. Soon it would be too dark to travel, and they were far too near to the pool as it was.
There had to be somewhere to go...
WAIT -- THIS WAY.
Perrin trotted toward the hill, glancing over his shoulder for any sign of the men who were coming. There was nothing ~ yet ~ though more than once he had to stop and wait for Bela to stumble after him, picking her way carefully over the uneven ground.
The longer they traveled, the more Perrin thought that Egwene and the horse both must be more tired than he had believed.
Which meant that this had better be a good hiding place, because they were in no condition to hunt for another.

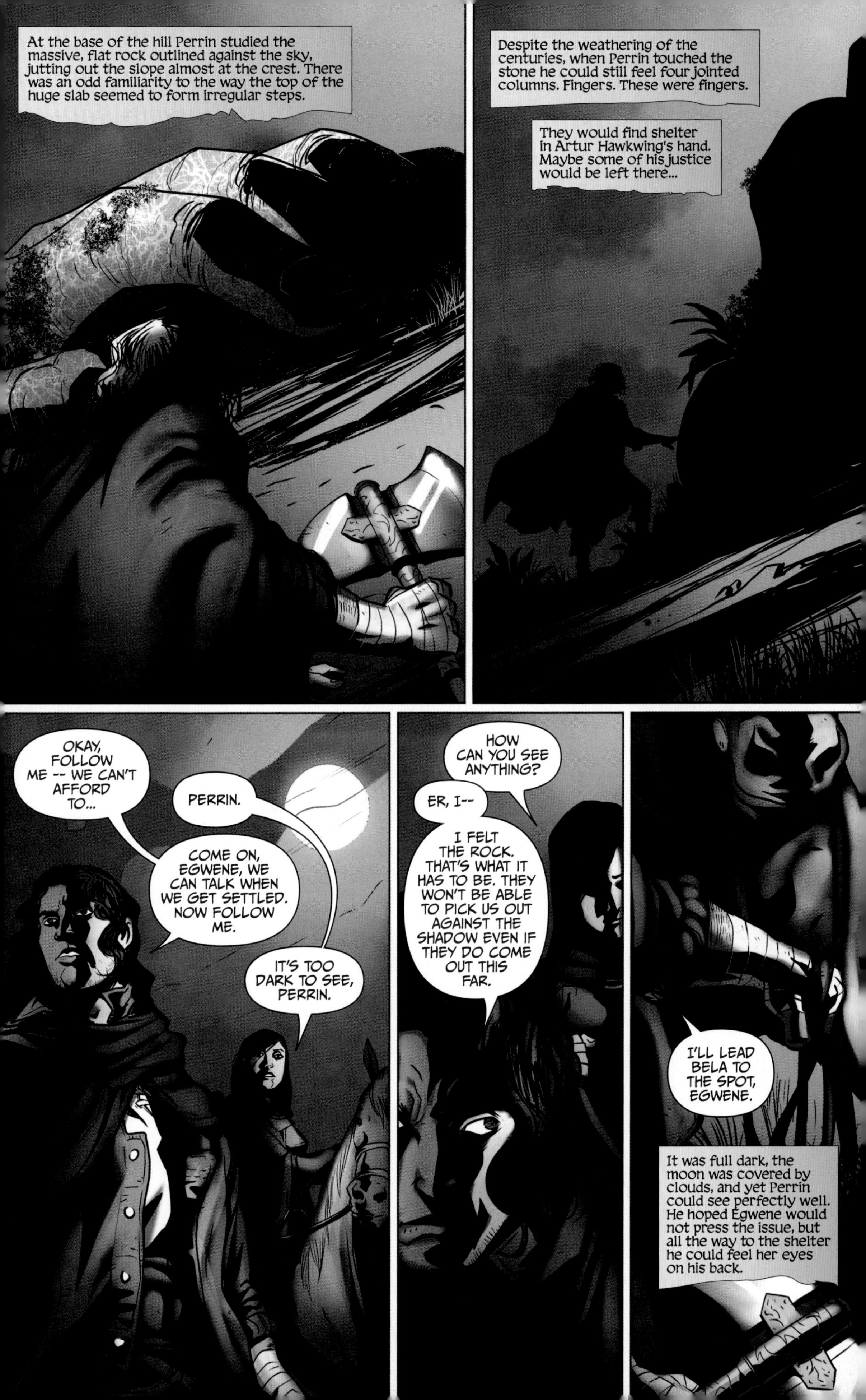
At the base of the hill Perrin studied the massive, flat rock outlined against the sky, jutting out the slope almost at the crest. There was an odd familiarity to the way the top of the huge slab seemed to form irregular steps.
Despite the weathering of the centuries, when Perrin touched the stone he could still feel four jointed columns. Fingers. These were fingers.
They would find shelter in Artur Hawkwing's hand. Maybe some of his justice would be left there...
OKAY, FOLLOW ME -- WE CAN'T AFFORD TO...
PERRIN.
COME ON, EGWENE, WE CAN TALK WHEN WE GET SETTLED. NOW FOLLOW ME.
IT'S TOO DARK TO SEE, PERRIN.
HOW CAN YOU SEE ANYTHING?
ER, I--
I FELT THE ROCK. THAT'S WHAT IT HAS TO BE. THEY WON'T BE ABLE TO PICK US OUT AGAINST THE SHADOW EVEN IF THEY DO COME OUT THIS FAR.
I'LL LEAD BELA TO THE SPOT, EGWENE.
It was full dark, the moon was covered by clouds, and yet Perrin could see perfectly well. He hoped Egwene would not press the issue, but all the way to the shelter he could feel her eyes on his back.

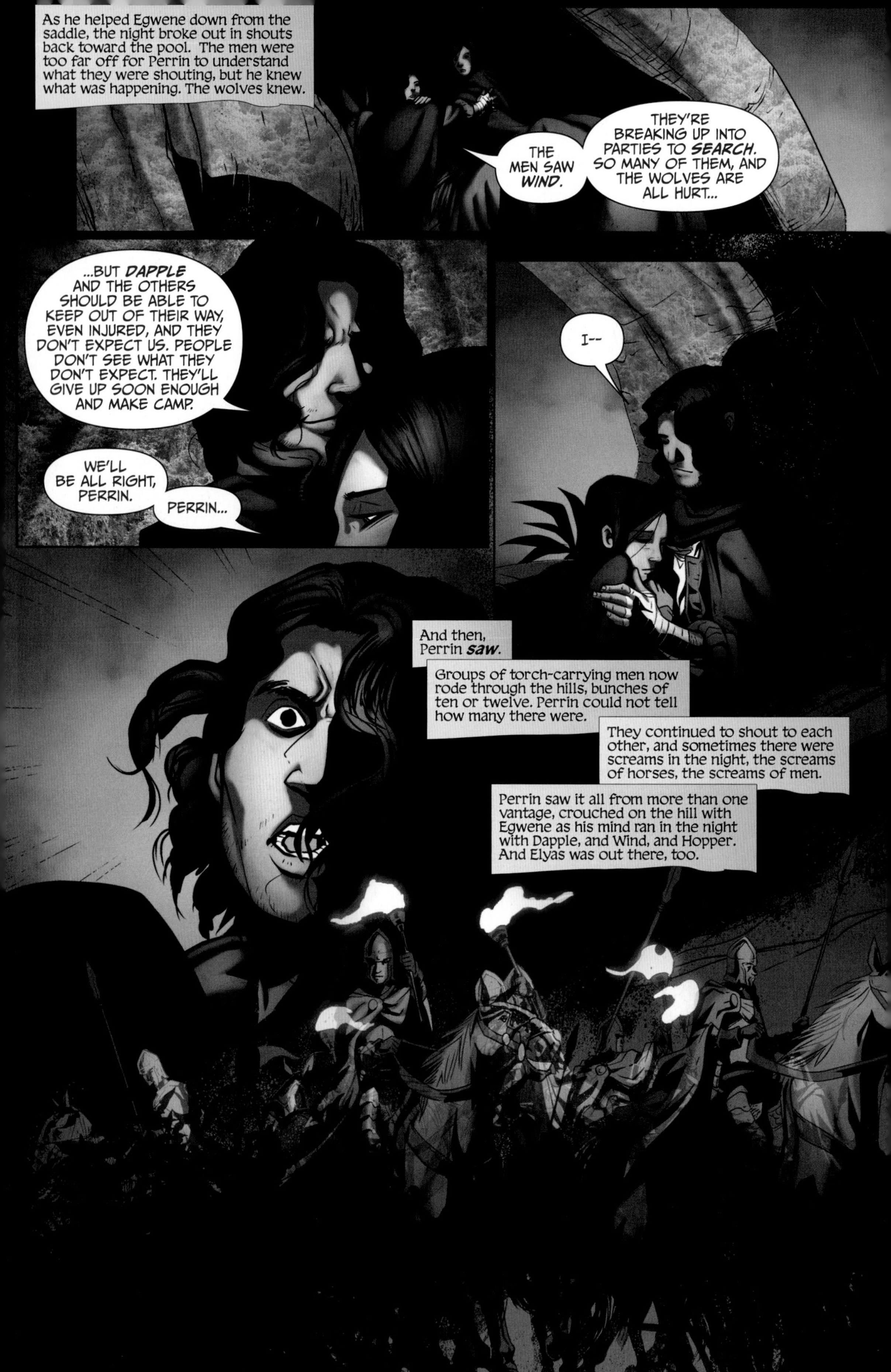

As he helped Egwene down from the saddle, the night broke out in shouts back toward the pool. The men were too far off for Perrin to understand what they were shouting, but he knew what was happening. The wolves knew.
THE MEN SAW *WIND*.
THEY'RE BREAKING UP INTO PARTIES TO *SEARCH*. SO MANY OF THEM, AND THE WOLVES ARE ALL HURT...
...BUT *DAPPLE* AND THE OTHERS SHOULD BE ABLE TO KEEP OUT OF THEIR WAY, EVEN INJURED, AND THEY DON'T EXPECT US. PEOPLE DON'T SEE WHAT THEY DON'T EXPECT. THEY'LL GIVE UP SOON ENOUGH AND MAKE CAMP.
WE'LL BE ALL RIGHT, PERRIN.
PERRIN...
I--
And then, Perrin *saw*.
Groups of torch-carrying men now rode through the hills, bunches of ten or twelve. Perrin could not tell how many there were.
They continued to shout to each other, and sometimes there were screams in the night, the screams of horses, the screams of men.
Perrin saw it all from more than one vantage, crouched on the hill with Egwene as his mind ran in the night with Dapple, and Wind, and Hopper. And Elyas was out there, too.

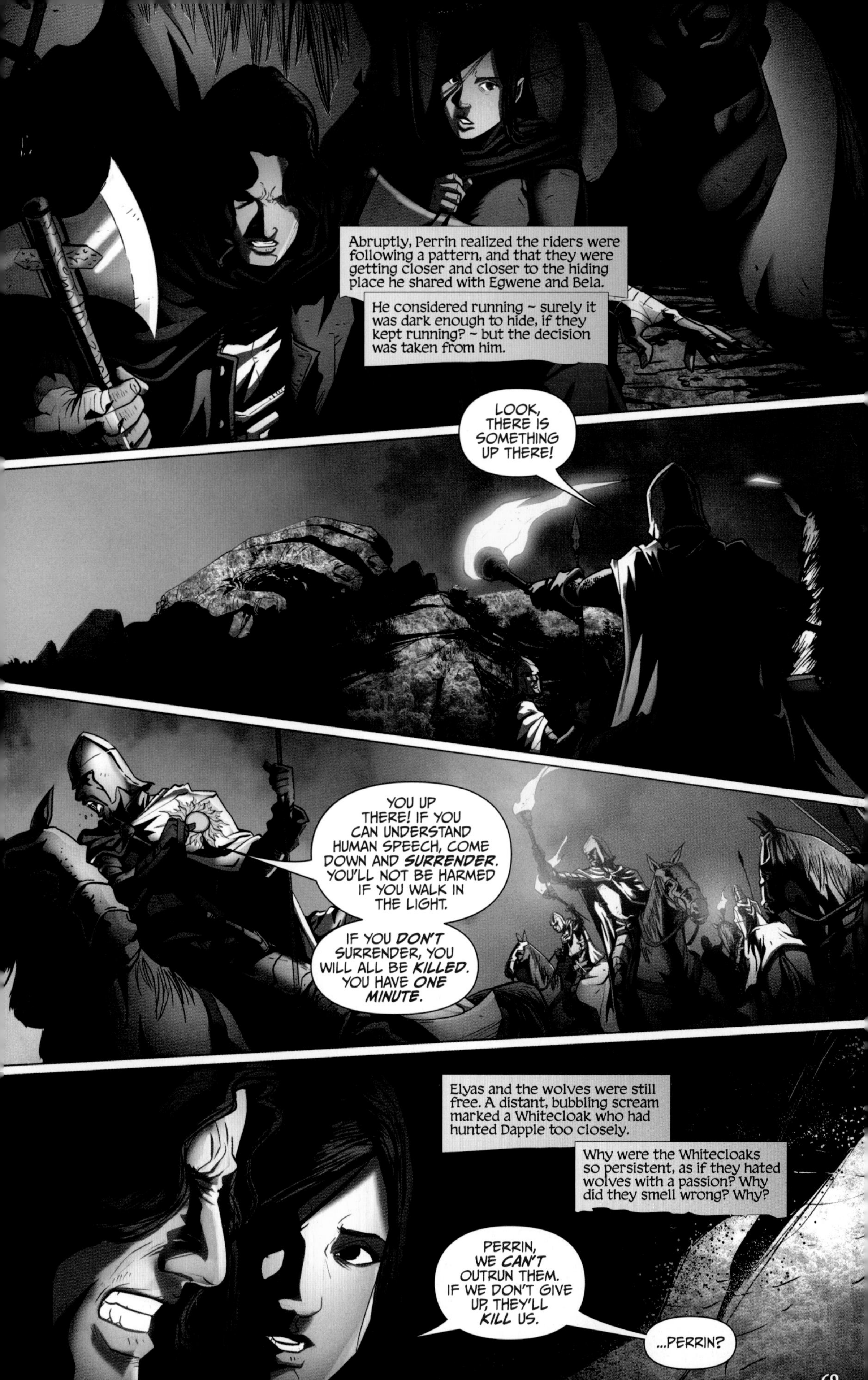
Abruptly, Perrin realized the riders were following a pattern, and that they were getting closer and closer to the hiding place he shared with Egwene and Bela.
He considered running ~ surely it was dark enough to hide, if they kept running? ~ but the decision was taken from him.
LOOK, THERE IS SOMETHING UP THERE!
YOU UP THERE! IF YOU CAN UNDERSTAND HUMAN SPEECH, COME DOWN AND SURRENDER. YOU'LL NOT BE HARMED IF YOU WALK IN THE LIGHT.
IF YOU DON'T SURRENDER, YOU WILL ALL BE KILLED. YOU HAVE ONE MINUTE.
Elyas and the wolves were still free. A distant, bubbling scream marked a Whitecloak who had hunted Dapple too closely.
Why were the Whitecloaks so persistent, as if they hated wolves with a passion? Why did they smell wrong? Why?
PERRIN, WE CAN'T OUTRUN THEM. IF WE DON'T GIVE UP, THEY'LL KILL US.
...PERRIN?

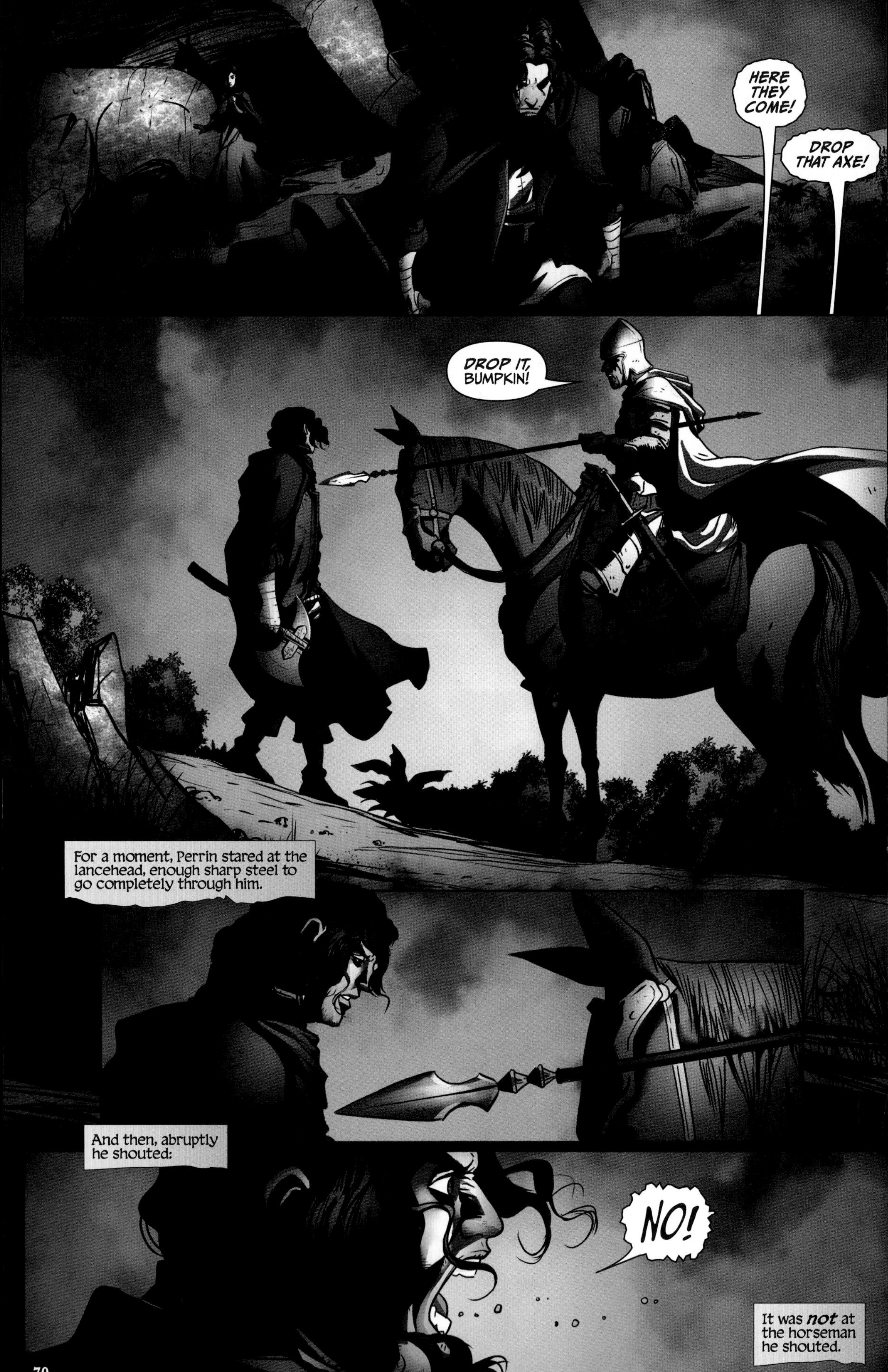
HERE THEY COME!
DROP THAT AXE!
DROP IT, BUMPKIN!
For a moment, Perrin stared at the lancehead, enough sharp steel to go completely through him.
And then, abruptly he shouted:
NO!
It was *not* at the horseman he shouted.

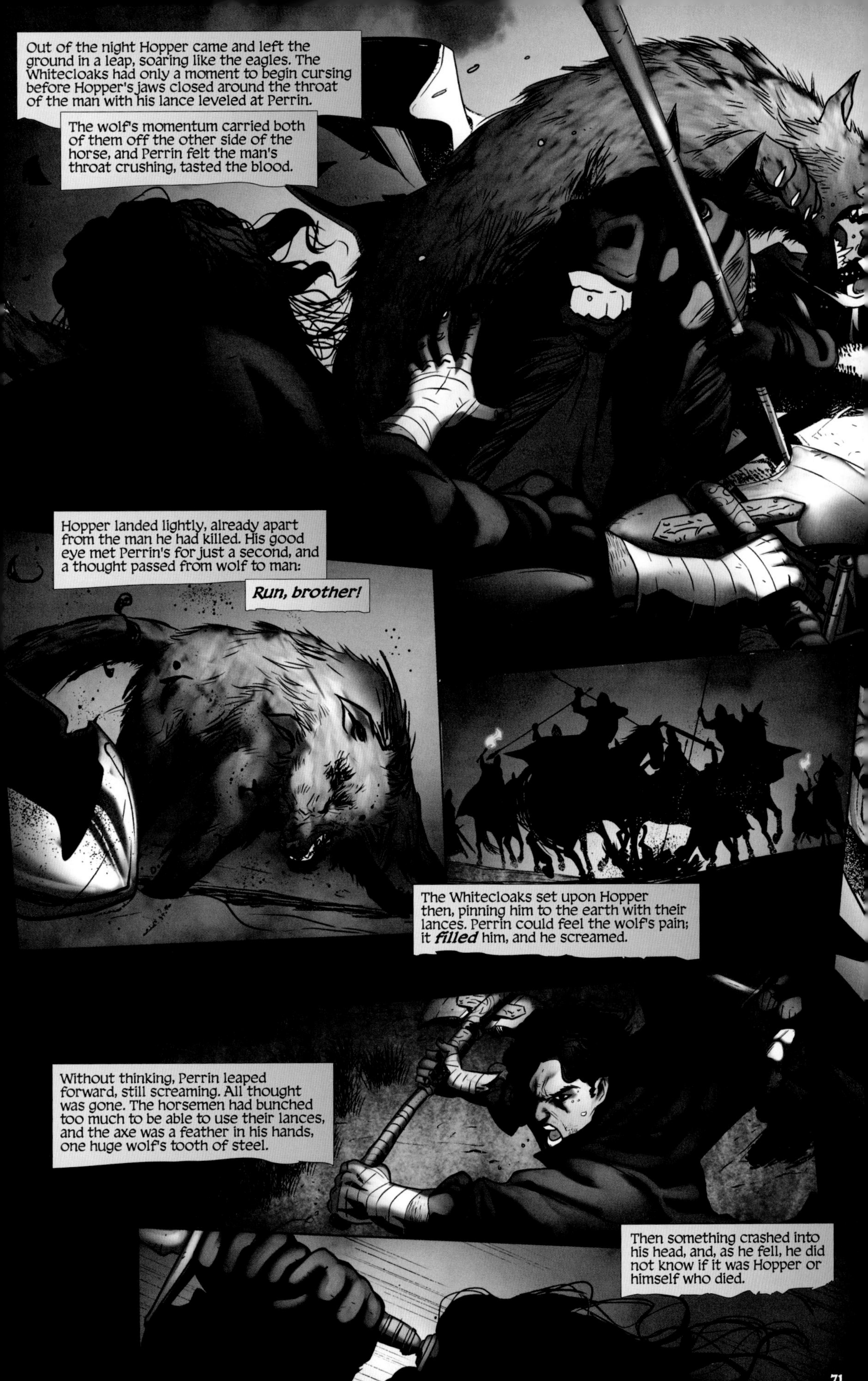

Out of the night Hopper came and left the ground in a leap, soaring like the eagles. The Whitecloaks had only a moment to begin cursing before Hopper's jaws closed around the throat of the man with his lance leveled at Perrin.
The wolf's momentum carried both of them off the other side of the horse, and Perrin felt the man's throat crushing, tasted the blood.
Hopper landed lightly, already apart from the man he had killed. His good eye met Perrin's for just a second, and a thought passed from wolf to man:
Run, brother!
The Whitecloaks set upon Hopper then, pinning him to the earth with their lances. Perrin could feel the wolf's pain; it filled him, and he screamed.
Without thinking, Perrin leaped forward, still screaming. All thought was gone. The horsemen had bunched too much to be able to use their lances, and the axe was a feather in his hands, one huge wolf's tooth of steel.
Then something crashed into his head, and, as he fell, he did not know if it was Hopper or himself who died.

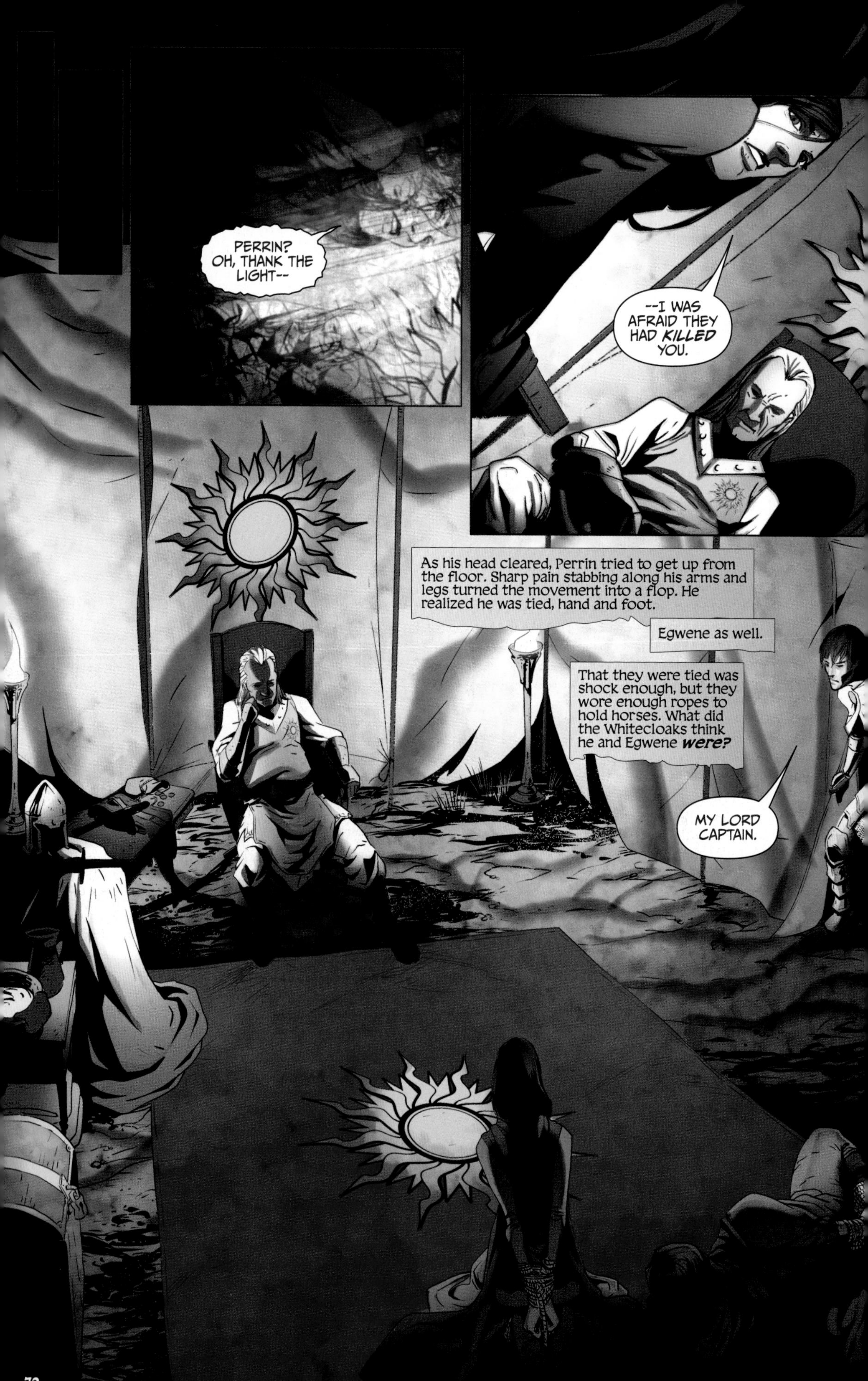
PERRIN? OH, THANK THE LIGHT--
--I WAS AFRAID THEY HAD *KILLED* YOU.
As his head cleared, Perrin tried to get up from the floor. Sharp pain stabbing along his arms and legs turned the movement into a flop. He realized he was tied, hand and foot.
Egwene as well.
That they were tied was shock enough, but they wore enough ropes to hold horses. What did the Whitecloaks think he and Egwene ***were?***
MY LORD CAPTAIN.

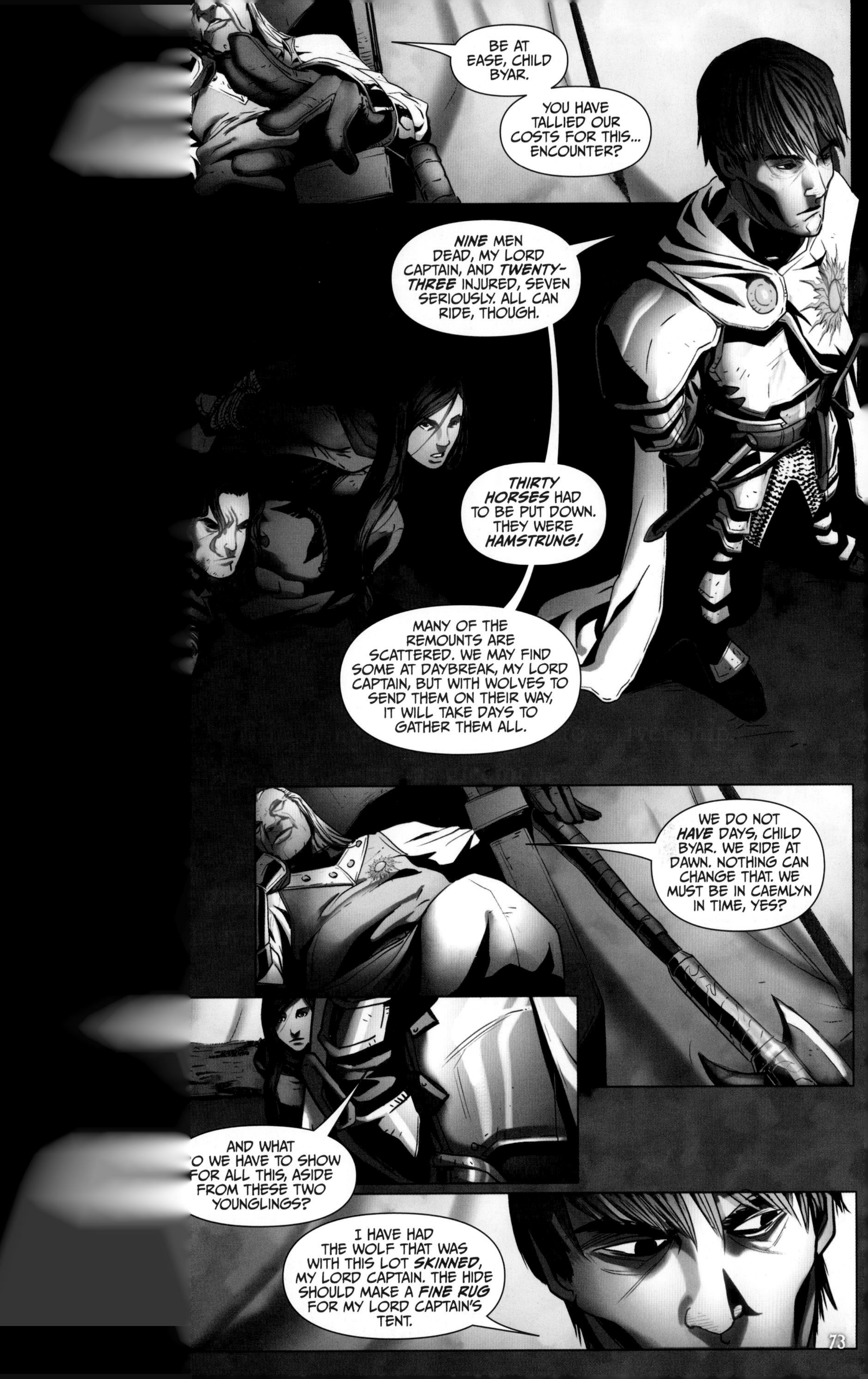

BE AT EASE, CHILD BYAR.
YOU HAVE TALLIED OUR COSTS FOR THIS... ENCOUNTER?
NINE MEN DEAD, MY LORD CAPTAIN, AND TWENTY-THREE INJURED, SEVEN SERIOUSLY. ALL CAN RIDE, THOUGH.
THIRTY HORSES HAD TO BE PUT DOWN. THEY WERE HAMSTRUNG!
MANY OF THE REMOUNTS ARE SCATTERED. WE MAY FIND SOME AT DAYBREAK, MY LORD CAPTAIN, BUT WITH WOLVES TO SEND THEM ON THEIR WAY, IT WILL TAKE DAYS TO GATHER THEM ALL.
WE DO NOT HAVE DAYS, CHILD BYAR. WE RIDE AT DAWN. NOTHING CAN CHANGE THAT. WE MUST BE IN CAEMLYN IN TIME, YES?
AND WHAT O WE HAVE TO SHOW FOR ALL THIS, ASIDE FROM THESE TWO YOUNGLINGS?
I HAVE HAD THE WOLF THAT WAS WITH THIS LOT SKINNED, MY LORD CAPTAIN. THE HIDE SHOULD MAKE A FINE RUG FOR MY LORD CAPTAIN'S TENT.

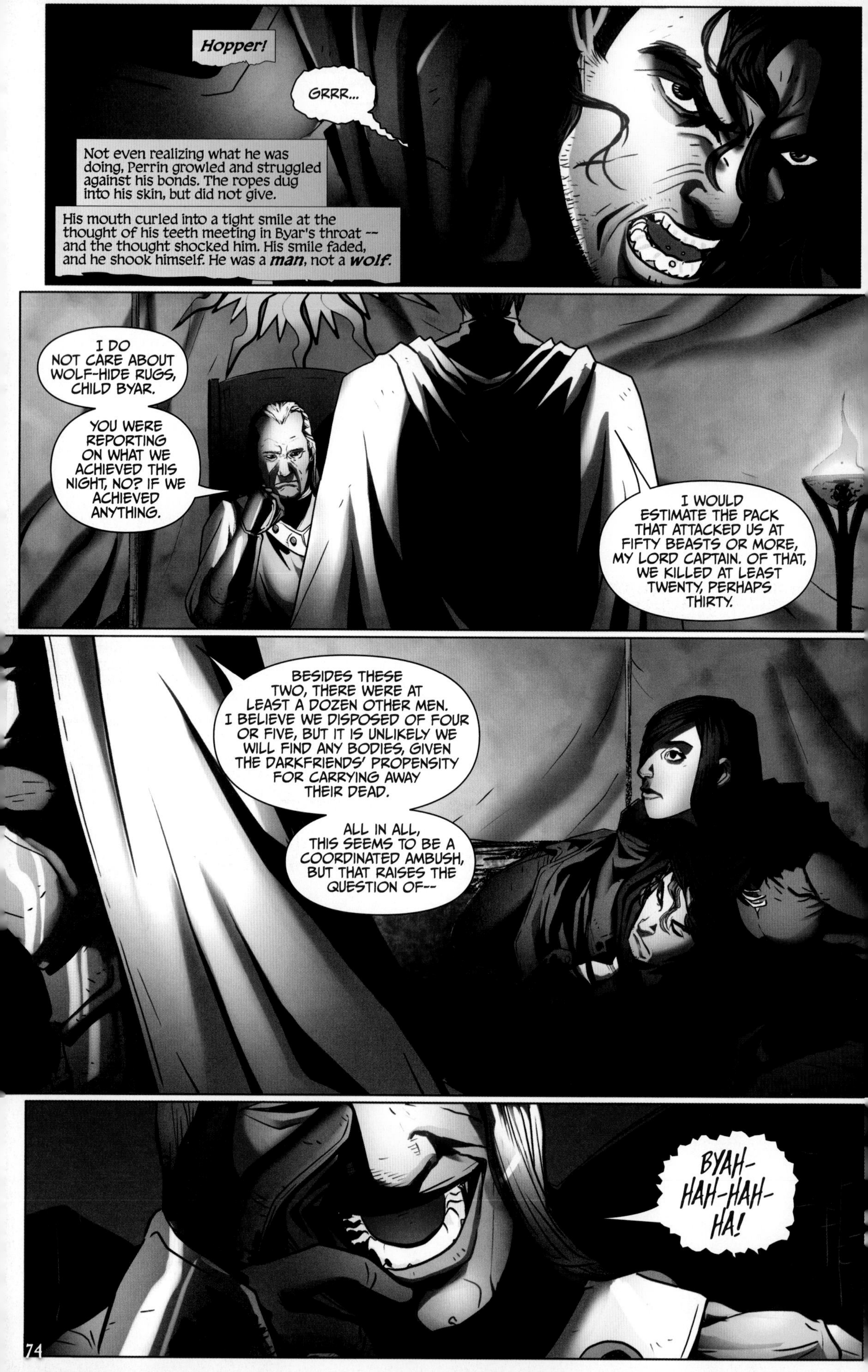
Hopper!
GRRR...
Not even realizing what he was doing, Perrin growled and struggled against his bonds. The ropes dug into his skin, but did not give.
His mouth curled into a tight smile at the thought of his teeth meeting in Byar's throat -- and the thought shocked him. His smile faded, and he shook himself. He was a *man*, not a *wolf*.
I DO NOT CARE ABOUT WOLF-HIDE RUGS, CHILD BYAR.
YOU WERE REPORTING ON WHAT WE ACHIEVED THIS NIGHT, NO? IF WE ACHIEVED ANYTHING.
I WOULD ESTIMATE THE PACK THAT ATTACKED US AT FIFTY BEASTS OR MORE, MY LORD CAPTAIN. OF THAT, WE KILLED AT LEAST TWENTY, PERHAPS THIRTY.
BESIDES THESE TWO, THERE WERE AT LEAST A DOZEN OTHER MEN. I BELIEVE WE DISPOSED OF FOUR OR FIVE, BUT IT IS UNLIKELY WE WILL FIND ANY BODIES, GIVEN THE DARKFRIENDS' PROPENSITY FOR CARRYING AWAY THEIR DEAD.
ALL IN ALL, THIS SEEMS TO BE A COORDINATED AMBUSH, BUT THAT RAISES THE QUESTION OF--
BYAH-HAH-HAH-HA!

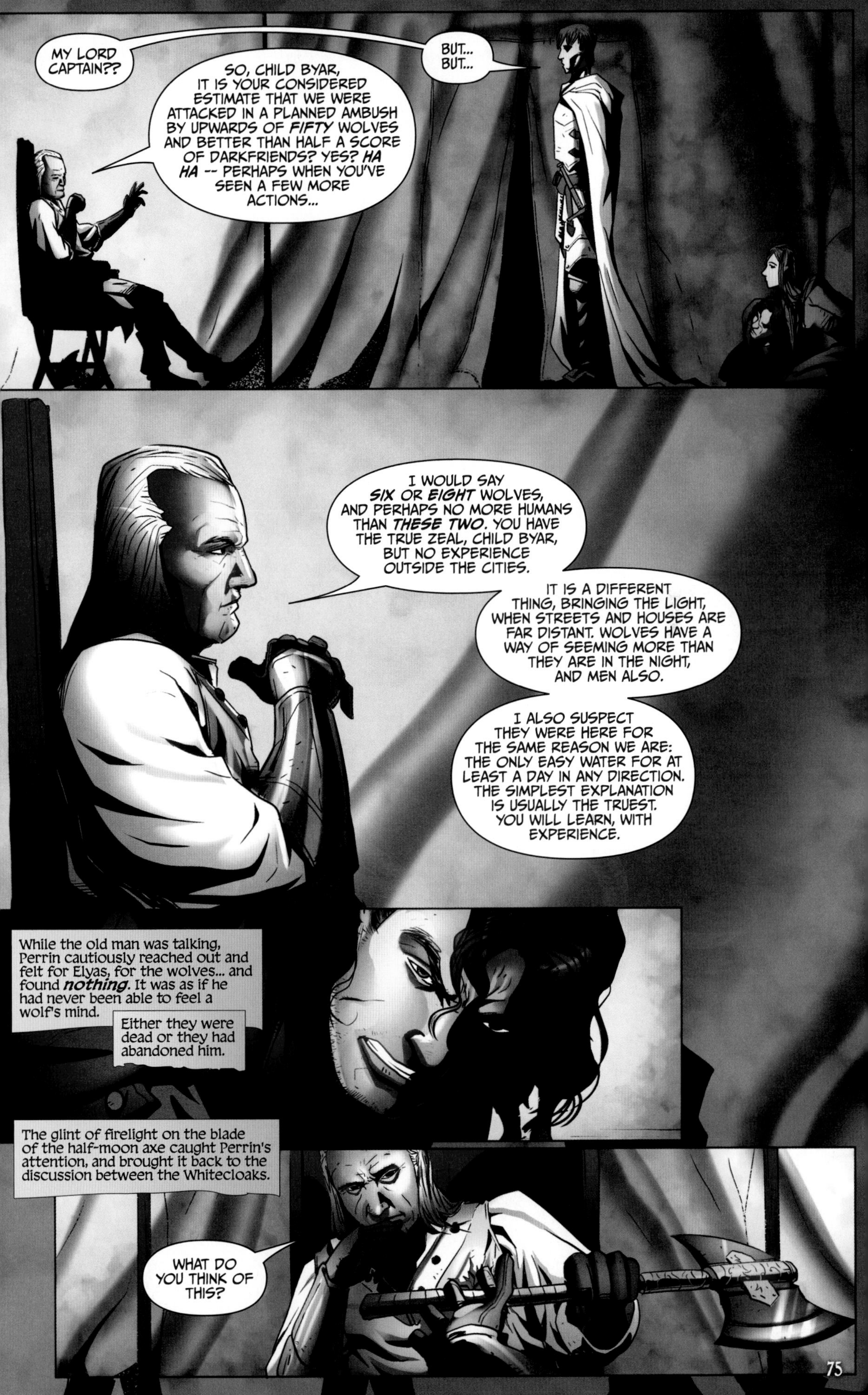
MY LORD CAPTAIN??
SO, CHILD BYAR, IT IS YOUR CONSIDERED ESTIMATE THAT WE WERE ATTACKED IN A PLANNED AMBUSH BY UPWARDS OF *FIFTY* WOLVES AND BETTER THAN HALF A SCORE OF DARKFRIENDS? YES? ***HA HA*** -- PERHAPS WHEN YOU'VE SEEN A FEW MORE ACTIONS...
BUT... BUT...
I WOULD SAY ***SIX*** OR ***EIGHT*** WOLVES, AND PERHAPS NO MORE HUMANS THAN ***THESE TWO***. YOU HAVE THE TRUE ZEAL, CHILD BYAR, BUT NO EXPERIENCE OUTSIDE THE CITIES.
IT IS A DIFFERENT THING, BRINGING THE LIGHT, WHEN STREETS AND HOUSES ARE FAR DISTANT. WOLVES HAVE A WAY OF SEEMING MORE THAN THEY ARE IN THE NIGHT, AND MEN ALSO.
I ALSO SUSPECT THEY WERE HERE FOR THE SAME REASON WE ARE: THE ONLY EASY WATER FOR AT LEAST A DAY IN ANY DIRECTION. THE SIMPLEST EXPLANATION IS USUALLY THE TRUEST. YOU WILL LEARN, WITH EXPERIENCE.
While the old man was talking, Perrin cautiously reached out and felt for Elyas, for the wolves... and found ***nothing***. It was as if he had never been able to feel a wolf's mind.
Either they were dead or they had abandoned him.
The glint of firelight on the blade of the half-moon axe caught Perrin's attention, and brought it back to the discussion between the Whitecloaks.
WHAT DO YOU THINK OF THIS?

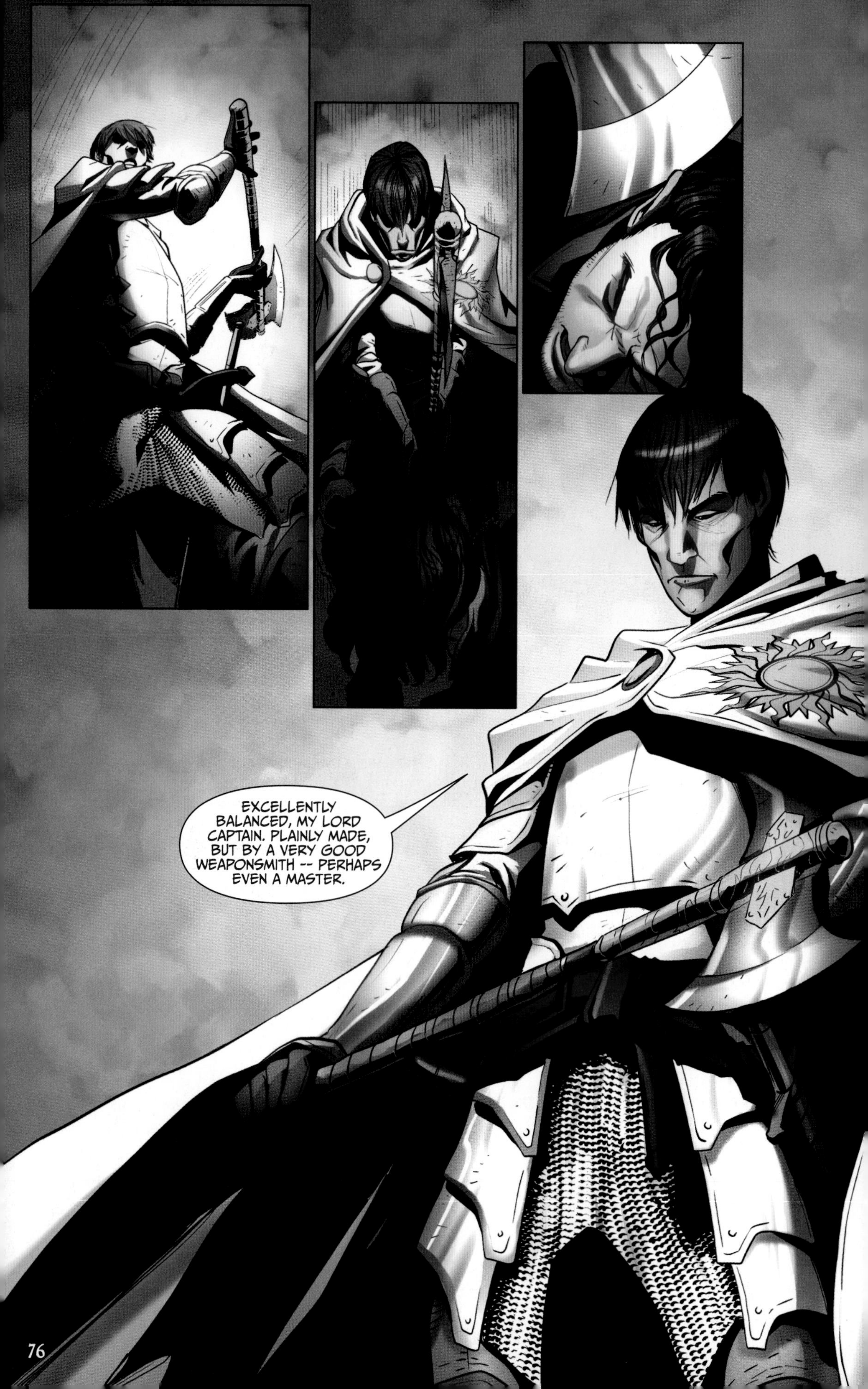
EXCELLENTLY BALANCED, MY LORD CAPTAIN. PLAINLY MADE, BUT BY A VERY GOOD WEAPONSMITH -- PERHAPS EVEN A MASTER.

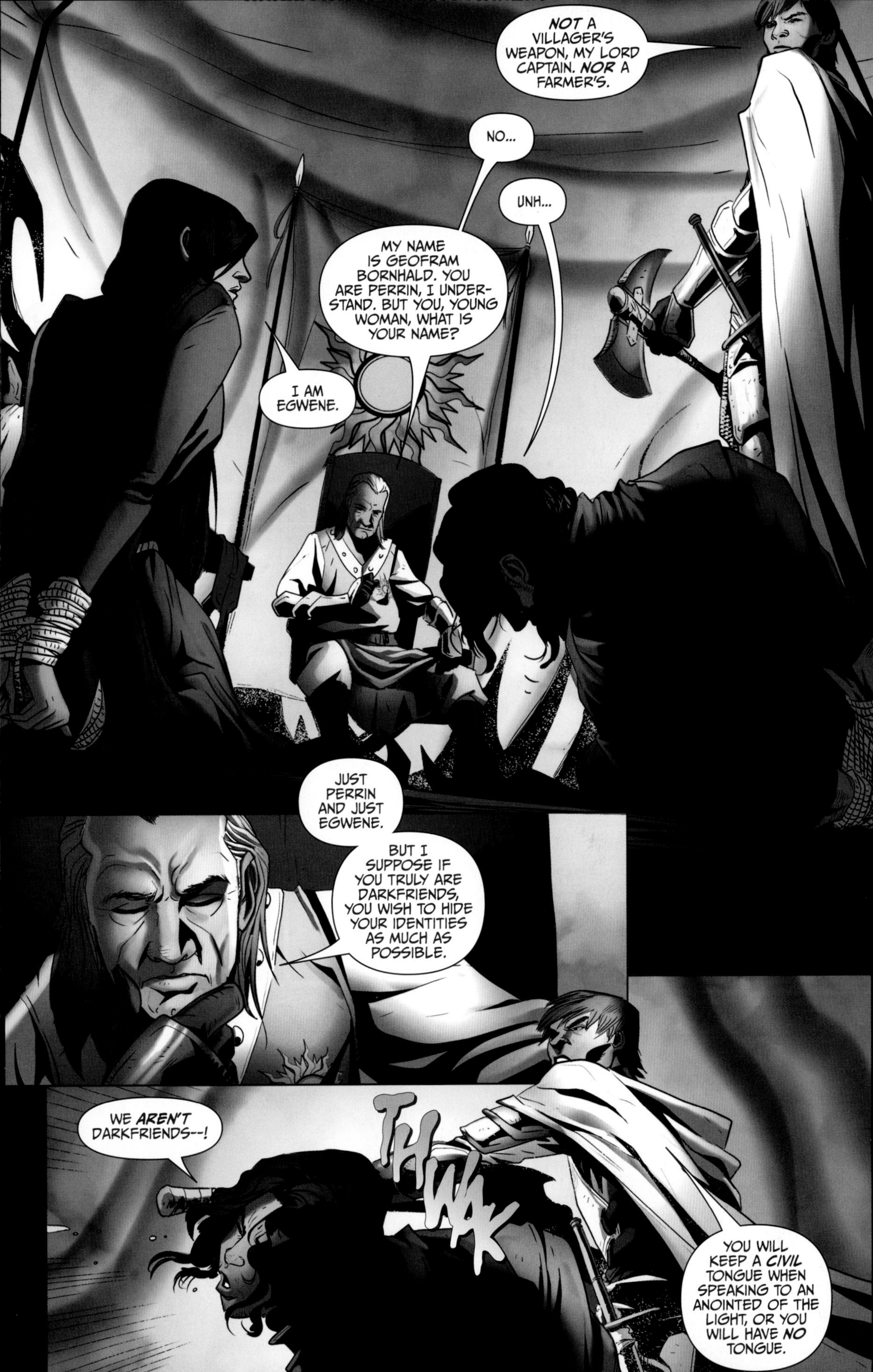
NOT A VILLAGER'S WEAPON, MY LORD CAPTAIN. NOR A FARMER'S.
NO...
UNH...
MY NAME IS GEOFRAM BORNHALD. YOU ARE PERRIN, I UNDERSTAND. BUT YOU, YOUNG WOMAN, WHAT IS YOUR NAME?
I AM EGWENE.
JUST PERRIN AND JUST EGWENE.
BUT I SUPPOSE IF YOU TRULY ARE DARKFRIENDS, YOU WISH TO HIDE YOUR IDENTITIES AS MUCH AS POSSIBLE.
WE AREN'T DARKFRIENDS--!
THWAK
YOU WILL KEEP A CIVIL TONGUE WHEN SPEAKING TO AN ANOINTED OF THE LIGHT, OR YOU WILL HAVE NO TONGUE.

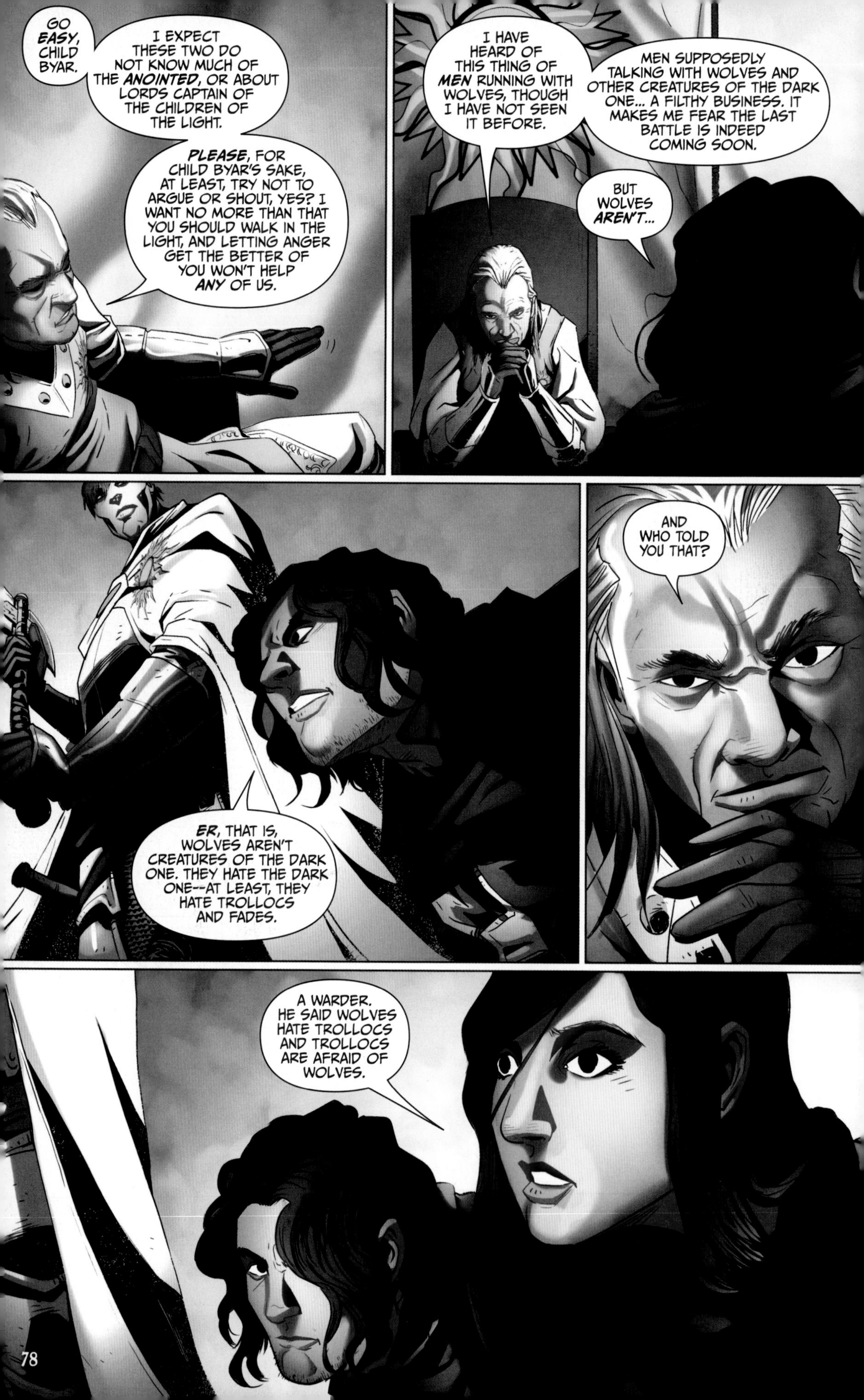
GO EASY, CHILD BYAR.
I EXPECT THESE TWO DO NOT KNOW MUCH OF THE ANOINTED, OR ABOUT LORDS CAPTAIN OF THE CHILDREN OF THE LIGHT.
PLEASE, FOR CHILD BYAR'S SAKE, AT LEAST, TRY NOT TO ARGUE OR SHOUT, YES? I WANT NO MORE THAN THAT YOU SHOULD WALK IN THE LIGHT, AND LETTING ANGER GET THE BETTER OF YOU WON'T HELP ANY OF US.
I HAVE HEARD OF THIS THING OF MEN RUNNING WITH WOLVES, THOUGH I HAVE NOT SEEN IT BEFORE.
MEN SUPPOSEDLY TALKING WITH WOLVES AND OTHER CREATURES OF THE DARK ONE... A FILTHY BUSINESS. IT MAKES ME FEAR THE LAST BATTLE IS INDEED COMING SOON.
BUT WOLVES AREN'T...
ER, THAT IS, WOLVES AREN'T CREATURES OF THE DARK ONE. THEY HATE THE DARK ONE--AT LEAST, THEY HATE TROLLOCS AND FADES.
AND WHO TOLD YOU THAT?
A WARDER. HE SAID WOLVES HATE TROLLOCS AND TROLLOCS ARE AFRAID OF WOLVES.

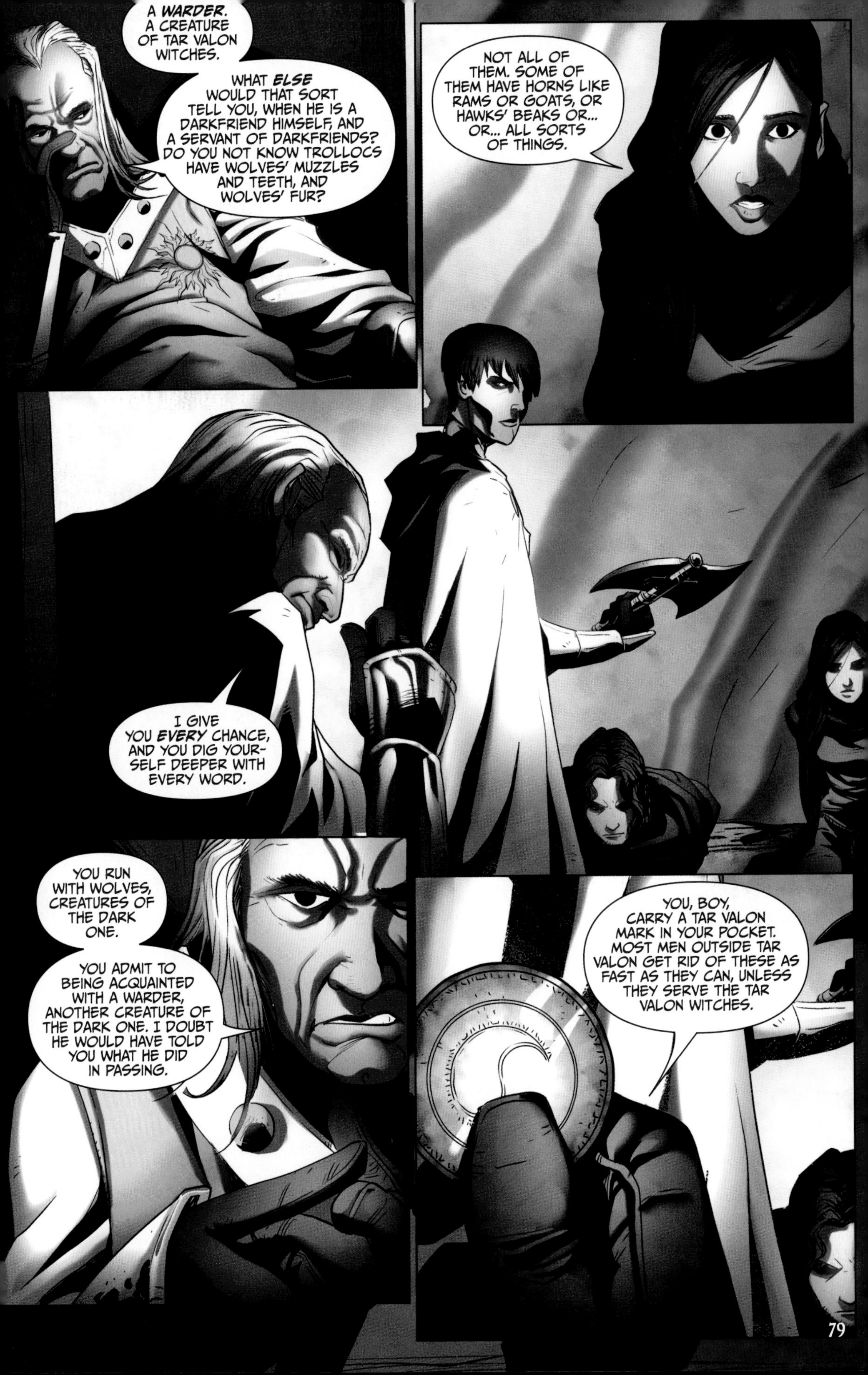
A WARDER. A CREATURE OF TAR VALON WITCHES.
WHAT ELSE WOULD THAT SORT TELL YOU, WHEN HE IS A DARKFRIEND HIMSELF, AND A SERVANT OF DARKFRIENDS? DO YOU NOT KNOW TROLLOCS HAVE WOLVES' MUZZLES AND TEETH, AND WOLVES' FUR?
NOT ALL OF THEM. SOME OF THEM HAVE HORNS LIKE RAMS OR GOATS, OR HAWKS' BEAKS OR... OR... ALL SORTS OF THINGS.
I GIVE YOU EVERY CHANCE, AND YOU DIG YOURSELF DEEPER WITH EVERY WORD.
YOU RUN WITH WOLVES, CREATURES OF THE DARK ONE.
YOU ADMIT TO BEING ACQUAINTED WITH A WARDER, ANOTHER CREATURE OF THE DARK ONE. I DOUBT HE WOULD HAVE TOLD YOU WHAT HE DID IN PASSING.
YOU, BOY, CARRY A TAR VALON MARK IN YOUR POCKET. MOST MEN OUTSIDE TAR VALON GET RID OF THESE AS FAST AS THEY CAN, UNLESS THEY SERVE THE TAR VALON WITCHES.

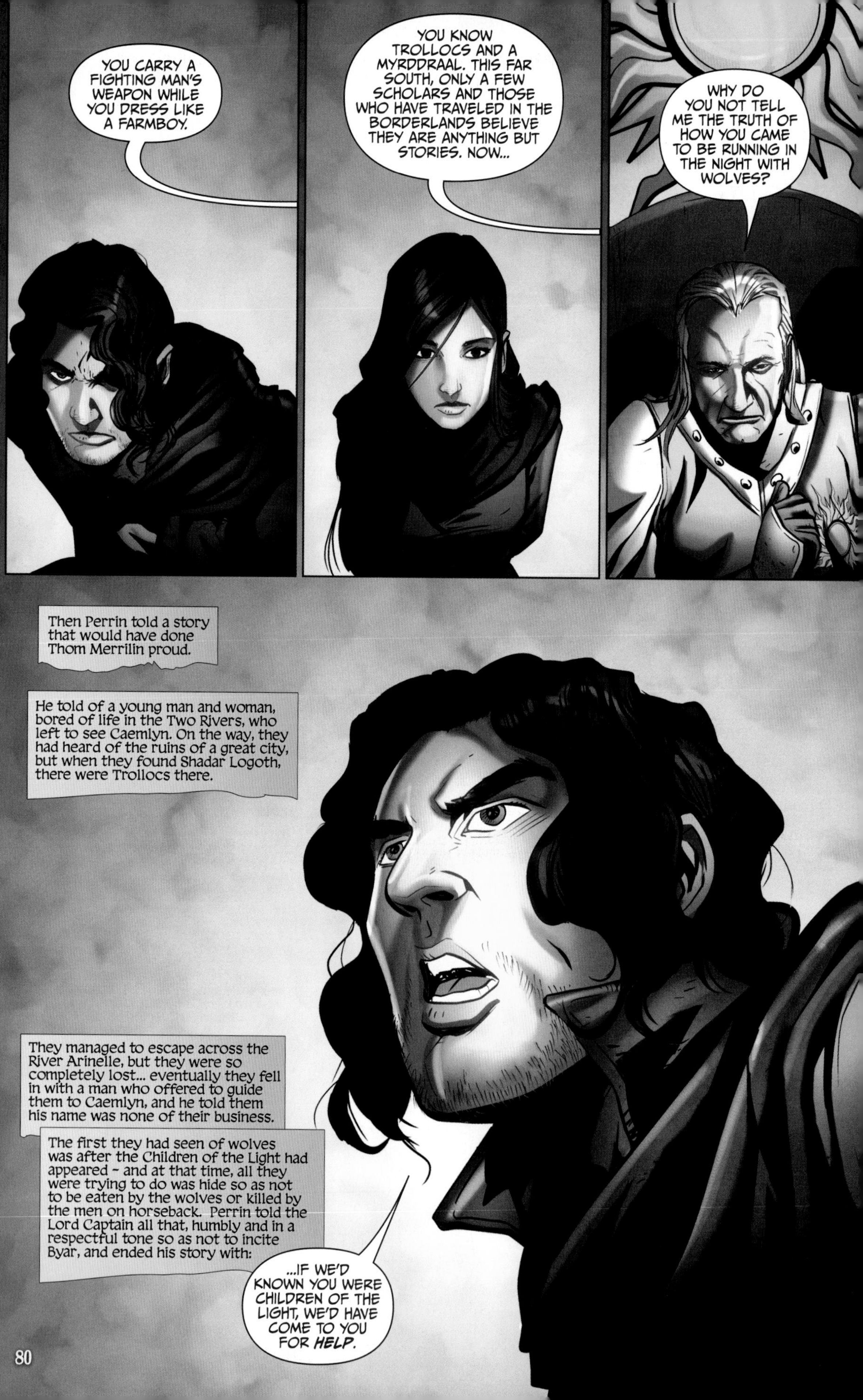
YOU CARRY A FIGHTING MAN'S WEAPON WHILE YOU DRESS LIKE A FARMBOY.
YOU KNOW TROLLOCS AND A MYRDDRAAL. THIS FAR SOUTH, ONLY A FEW SCHOLARS AND THOSE WHO HAVE TRAVELED IN THE BORDERLANDS BELIEVE THEY ARE ANYTHING BUT STORIES. NOW...
WHY DO YOU NOT TELL ME THE TRUTH OF HOW YOU CAME TO BE RUNNING IN THE NIGHT WITH WOLVES?
Then Perrin told a story that would have done Thom Merrilin proud.
He told of a young man and woman, bored of life in the Two Rivers, who left to see Caemlyn. On the way, they had heard of the ruins of a great city, but when they found Shadar Logoth, there were Trollocs there.
They managed to escape across the River Arinelle, but they were so completely lost... eventually they fell in with a man who offered to guide them to Caemlyn, and he told them his name was none of their business.
The first they had seen of wolves was after the Children of the Light had appeared – and at that time, all they were trying to do was hide so as not to be eaten by the wolves or killed by the men on horseback. Perrin told the Lord Captain all that, humbly and in a respectful tone so as not to incite Byar, and ended his story with:
...IF WE'D KNOWN YOU WERE CHILDREN OF THE LIGHT, WE'D HAVE COME TO YOU FOR *HELP*.

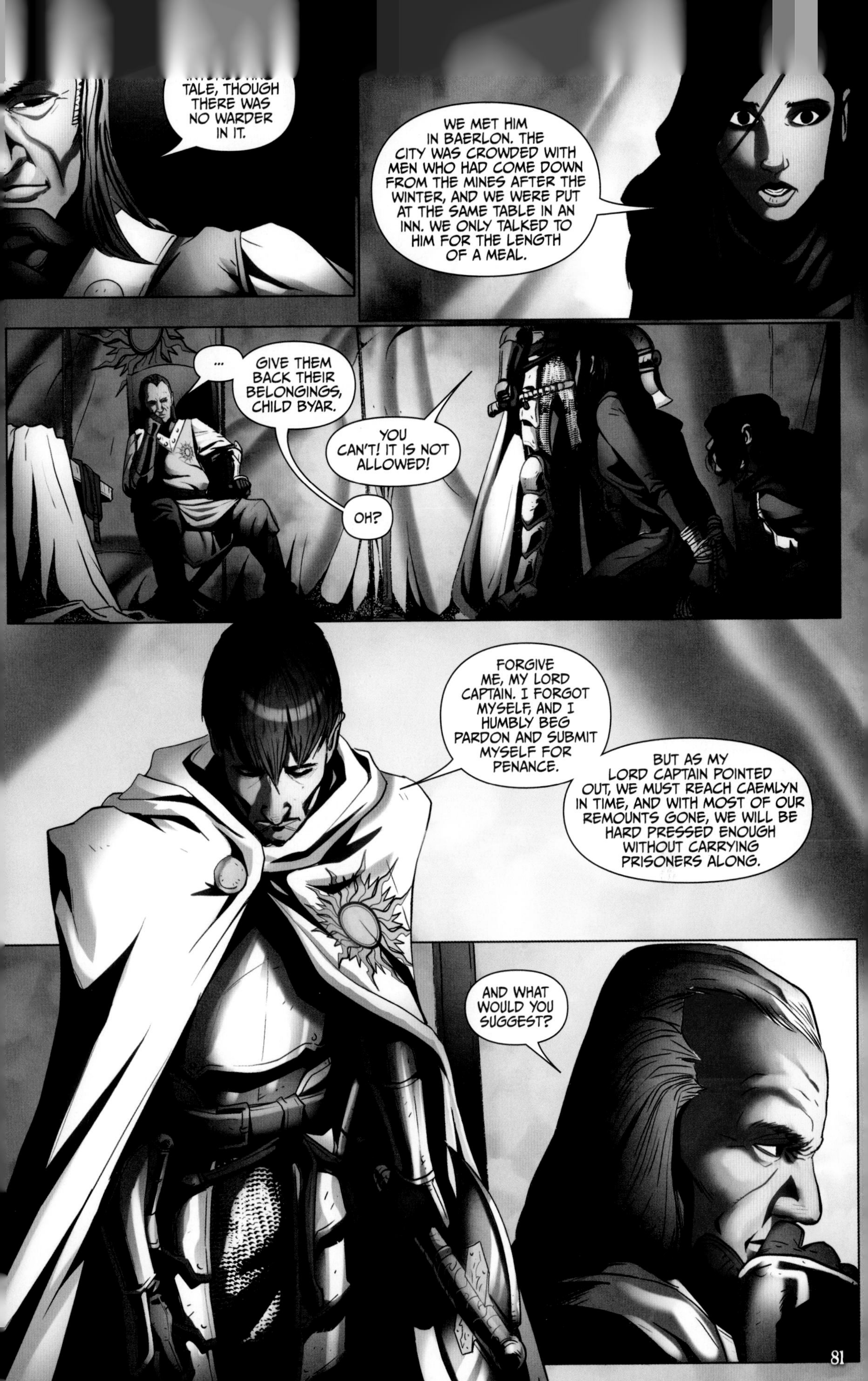
TALE, THOUGH THERE WAS NO WARDER IN IT.
WE MET HIM IN BAERLON. THE CITY WAS CROWDED WITH MEN WHO HAD COME DOWN FROM THE MINES AFTER THE WINTER, AND WE WERE PUT AT THE SAME TABLE IN AN INN. WE ONLY TALKED TO HIM FOR THE LENGTH OF A MEAL.
...
GIVE THEM BACK THEIR BELONGINGS, CHILD BYAR.
YOU CAN'T! IT IS NOT ALLOWED!
OH?
FORGIVE ME, MY LORD CAPTAIN. I FORGOT MYSELF, AND I HUMBLY BEG PARDON AND SUBMIT MYSELF FOR PENANCE.
BUT AS MY LORD CAPTAIN POINTED OUT, WE MUST REACH CAEMLYN IN TIME, AND WITH MOST OF OUR REMOUNTS GONE, WE WILL BE HARD PRESSED ENOUGH WITHOUT CARRYING PRISONERS ALONG.
AND WHAT WOULD YOU SUGGEST?

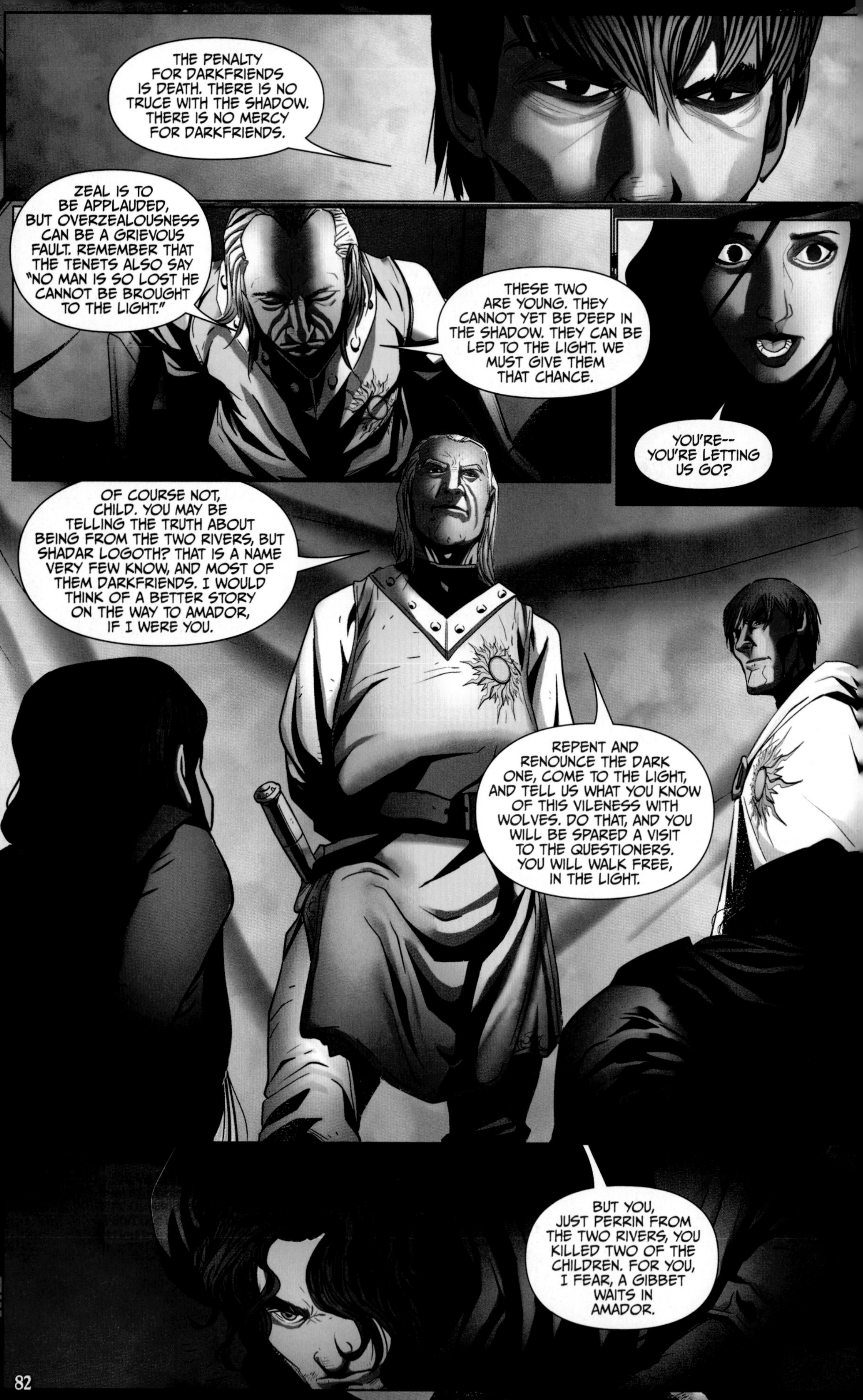
THE PENALTY FOR DARKFRIENDS IS DEATH. THERE IS NO TRUCE WITH THE SHADOW. THERE IS NO MERCY FOR DARKFRIENDS.
ZEAL IS TO BE APPLAUDED, BUT OVERZEALOUSNESS CAN BE A GRIEVOUS FAULT. REMEMBER THAT THE TENETS ALSO SAY "NO MAN IS SO LOST HE CANNOT BE BROUGHT TO THE LIGHT."
THESE TWO ARE YOUNG. THEY CANNOT YET BE DEEP IN THE SHADOW. THEY CAN BE LED TO THE LIGHT. WE MUST GIVE THEM THAT CHANCE.
YOU'RE-- YOU'RE LETTING US GO?
OF COURSE NOT, CHILD. YOU MAY BE TELLING THE TRUTH ABOUT BEING FROM THE TWO RIVERS, BUT SHADAR LOGOTH? THAT IS A NAME VERY FEW KNOW, AND MOST OF THEM DARKFRIENDS. I WOULD THINK OF A BETTER STORY ON THE WAY TO AMADOR, IF I WERE YOU.
REPENT AND RENOUNCE THE DARK ONE, COME TO THE LIGHT, AND TELL US WHAT YOU KNOW OF THIS VILENESS WITH WOLVES. DO THAT, AND YOU WILL BE SPARED A VISIT TO THE QUESTIONERS. YOU WILL WALK FREE, IN THE LIGHT.
BUT YOU, JUST PERRIN FROM THE TWO RIVERS, YOU KILLED TWO OF THE CHILDREN. FOR YOU, I FEAR, A GIBBET WAITS IN AMADOR.

chapter four

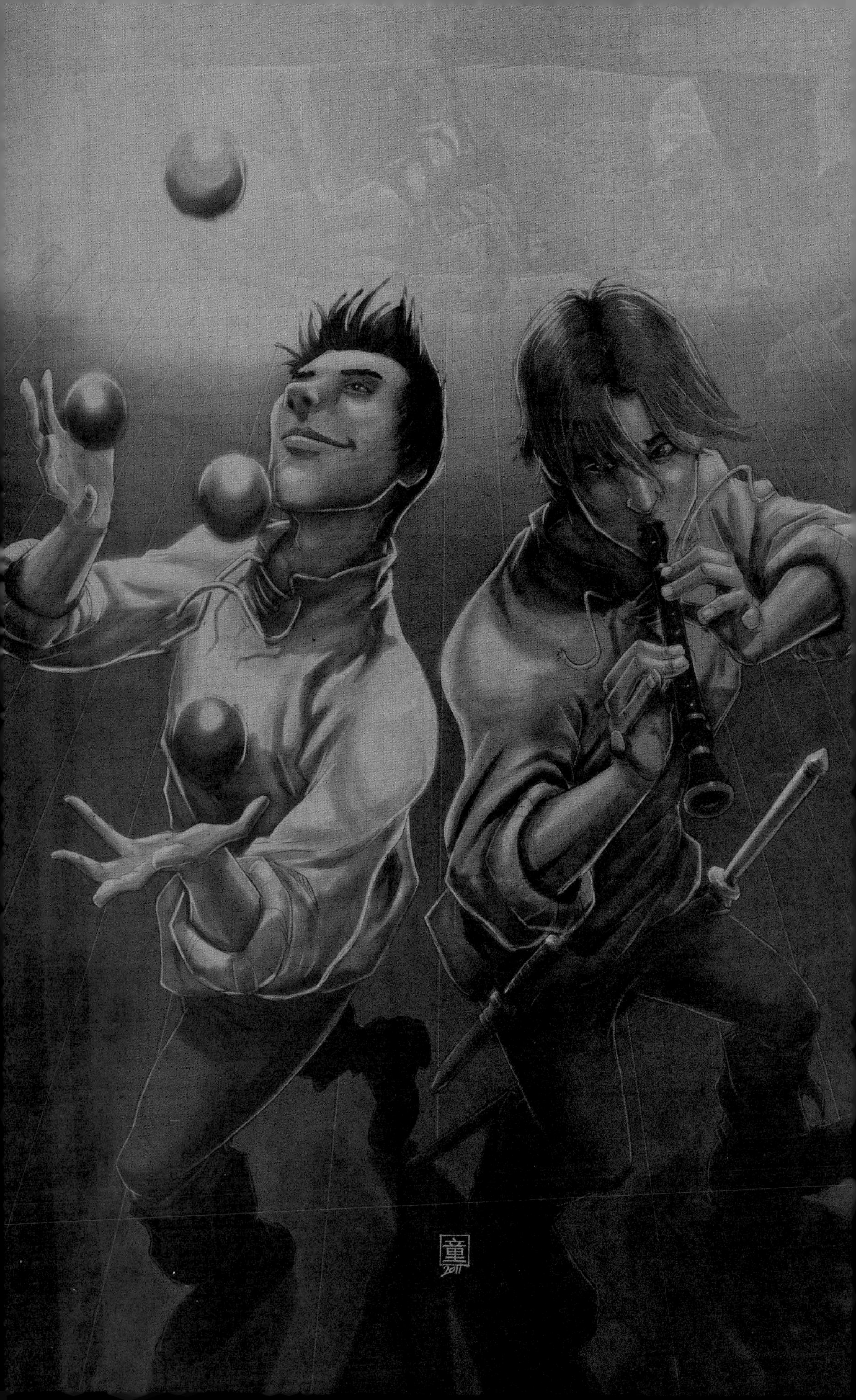

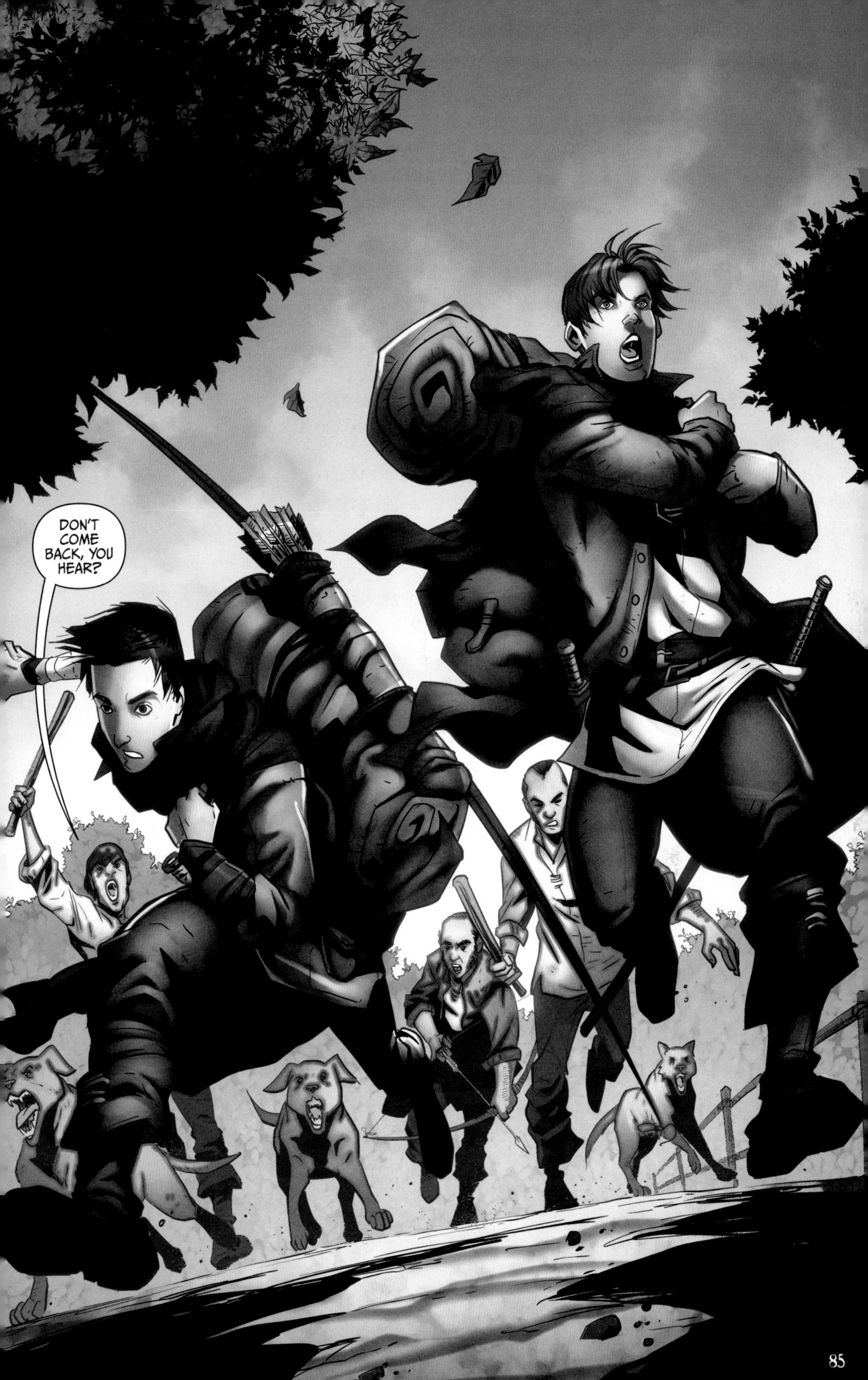
DON'T COME BACK, YOU HEAR?

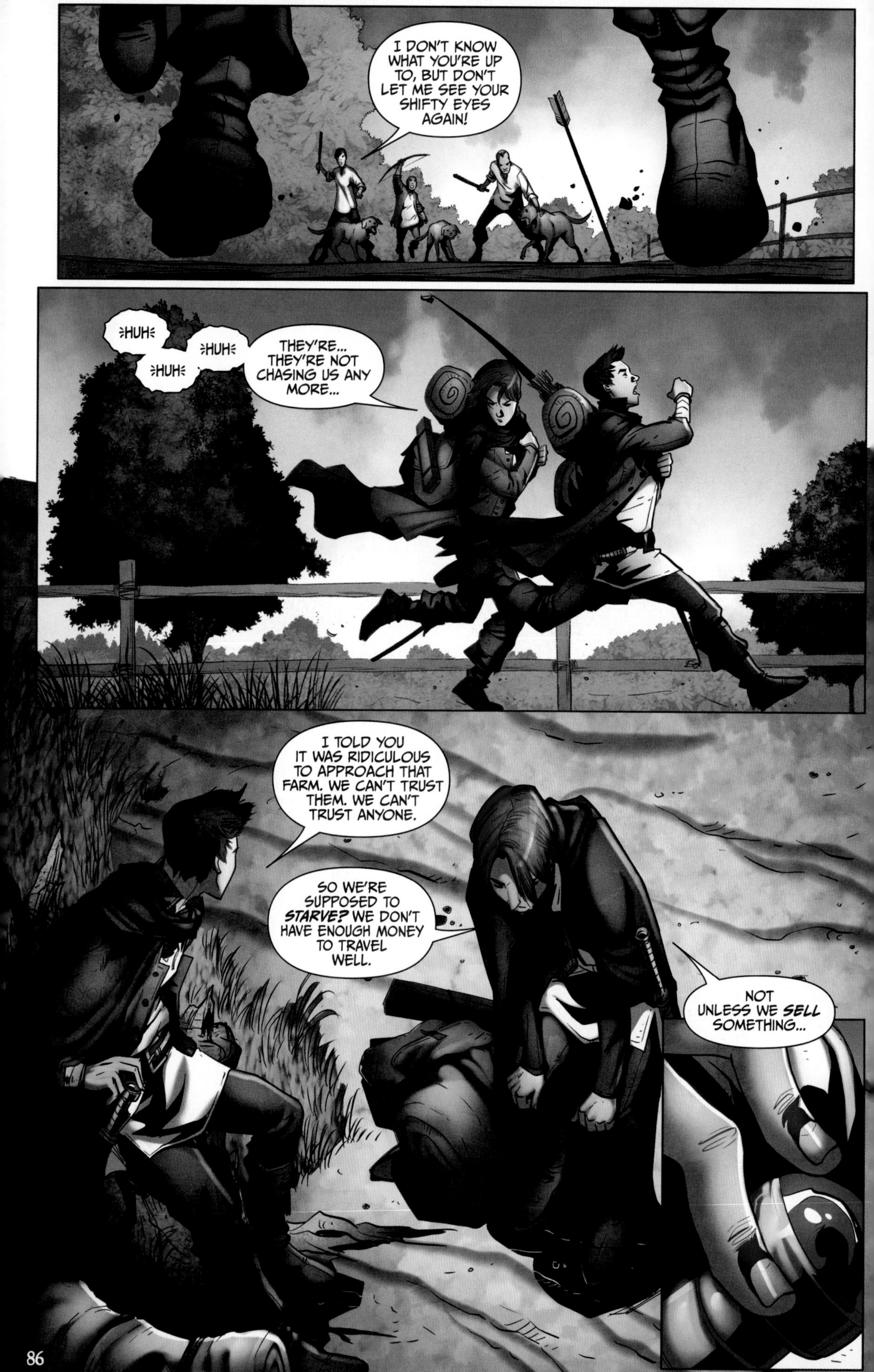
I DON'T KNOW WHAT YOU'RE UP TO, BUT DON'T LET ME SEE YOUR SHIFTY EYES AGAIN!
HUH
HUH
HUH
THEY'RE... THEY'RE NOT CHASING US ANY MORE...
I TOLD YOU IT WAS RIDICULOUS TO APPROACH THAT FARM. WE CAN'T TRUST THEM. WE CAN'T TRUST ANYONE.
SO WE'RE SUPPOSED TO STARVE? WE DON'T HAVE ENOUGH MONEY TO TRAVEL WELL.
NOT UNLESS WE SELL SOMETHING...

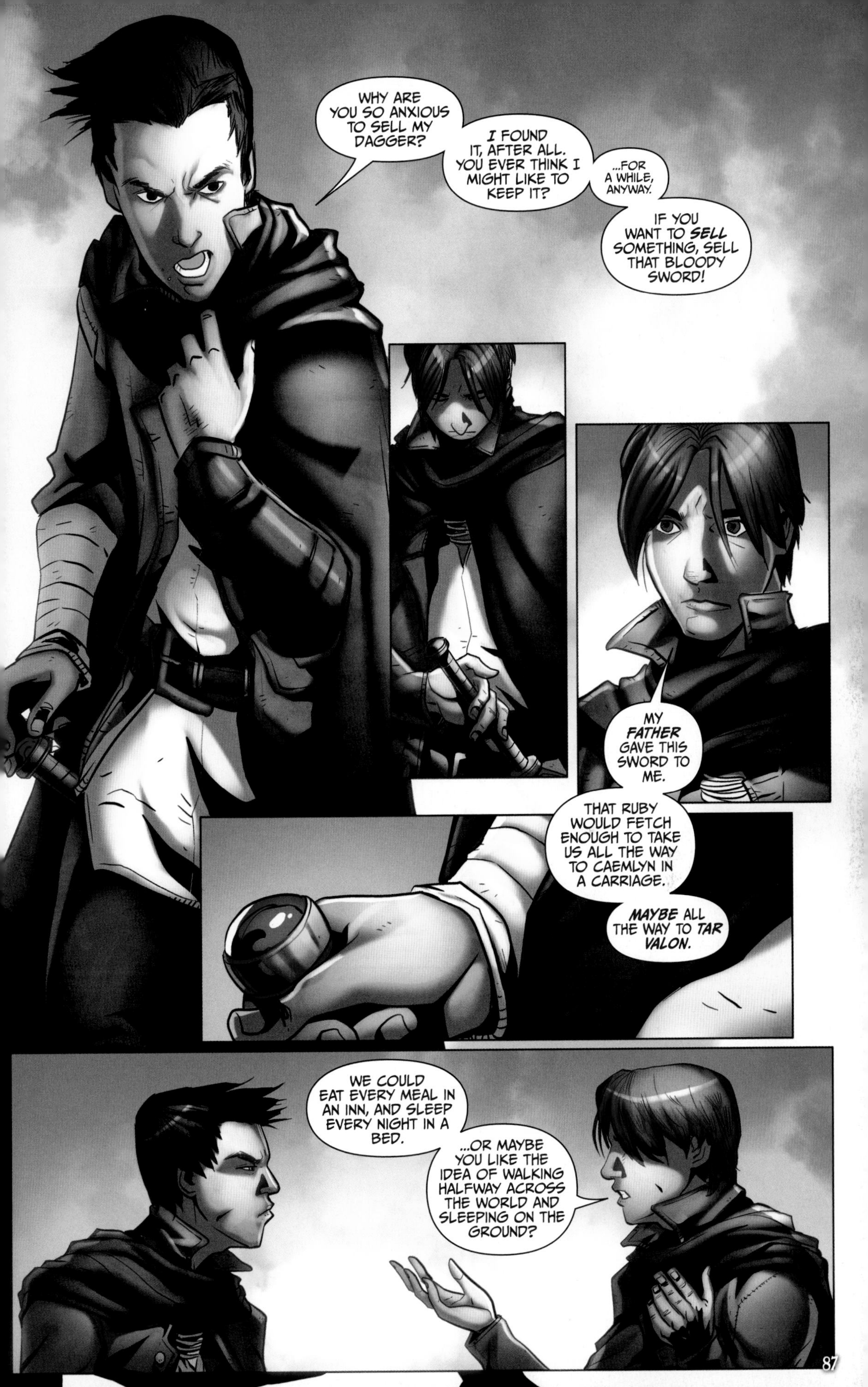
WHY ARE YOU SO ANXIOUS TO SELL MY DAGGER?
I FOUND IT, AFTER ALL. YOU EVER THINK I MIGHT LIKE TO KEEP IT?
...FOR A WHILE, ANYWAY.
IF YOU WANT TO SELL SOMETHING, SELL THAT BLOODY SWORD!
MY FATHER GAVE THIS SWORD TO ME.
THAT RUBY WOULD FETCH ENOUGH TO TAKE US ALL THE WAY TO CAEMLYN IN A CARRIAGE.
MAYBE ALL THE WAY TO TAR VALON.
WE COULD EAT EVERY MEAL IN AN INN, AND SLEEP EVERY NIGHT IN A BED.
...OR MAYBE YOU LIKE THE IDEA OF WALKING HALFWAY ACROSS THE WORLD AND SLEEPING ON THE GROUND?

≈SIGH≈ WHO WOULD I EVEN SELL IT TO, RAND? A *FARMER?* HE WOULD HAVE TO PAY IN *CHICKENS;* WE COULDN'T BUY A CARRIAGE WITH CHICKENS.

AND IF I EVEN SHOWED IT IN ANY VILLAGE WE'VE BEEN THROUGH, THEY'D PROBABLY THINK WE STOLE IT. LIGHT KNOWS WHAT WOULD HAPPEN THEN.

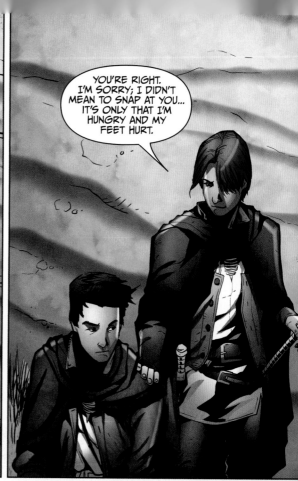

YOU'RE RIGHT. I'M SORRY; I DIDN'T MEAN TO SNAP AT YOU... IT'S ONLY THAT I'M HUNGRY AND MY FEET HURT.

MINE, TOO.

Rand sometimes wondered if it was worthwhile stopping at farms, as they had been. The further they went, the more suspicious of strangers Mat became, and the less he was able to hide it.

The meals got skimpier for the same work, and sometimes not even a barn was offered as a place to sleep. But then a solution to all their problems came to Rand, or so it seemed.

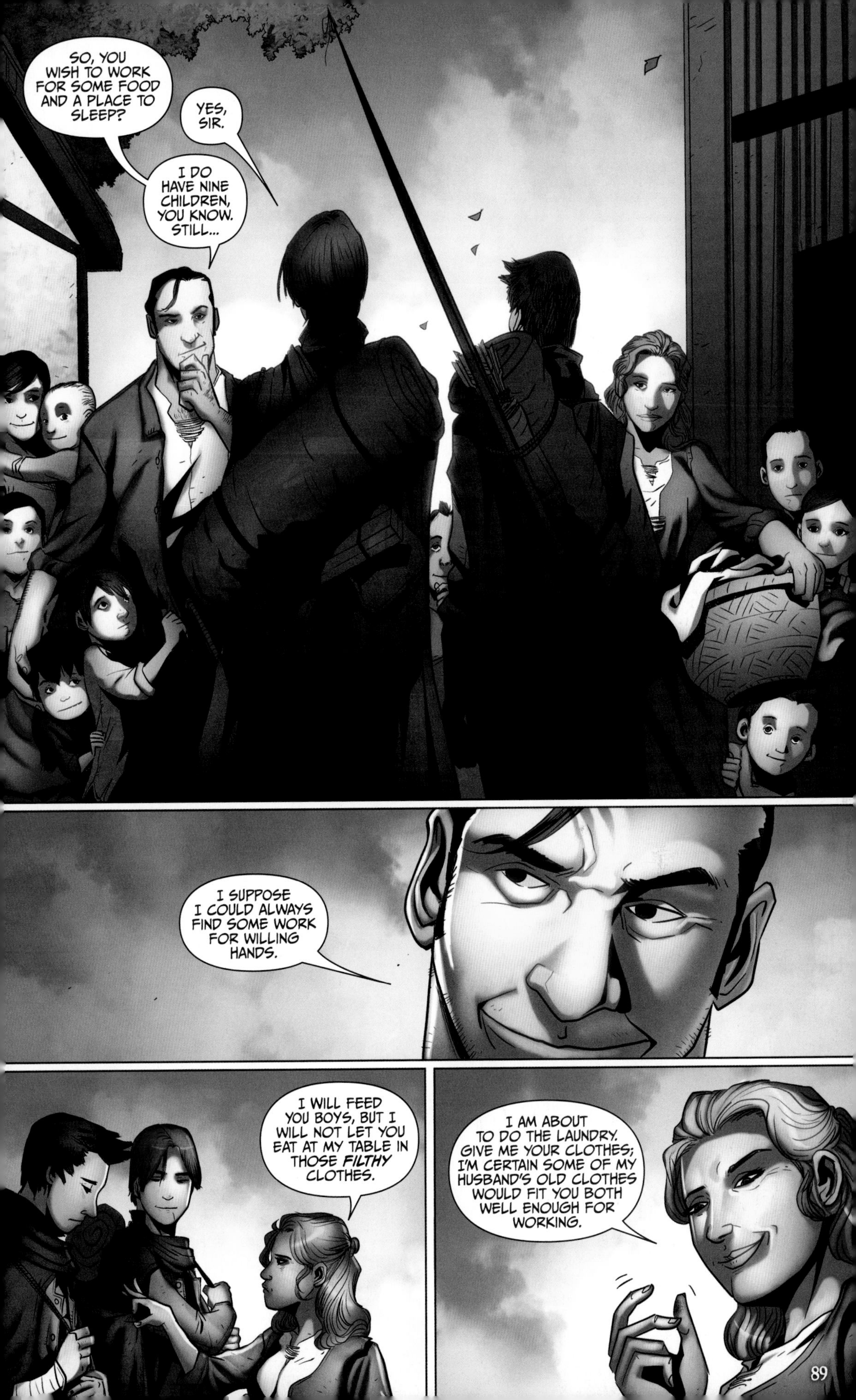
SO, YOU WISH TO WORK FOR SOME FOOD AND A PLACE TO SLEEP?
YES, SIR.
I DO HAVE NINE CHILDREN, YOU KNOW. STILL...
I SUPPOSE I COULD ALWAYS FIND SOME WORK FOR WILLING HANDS.
I WILL FEED YOU BOYS, BUT I WILL NOT LET YOU EAT AT MY TABLE IN THOSE *FILTHY* CLOTHES.
I AM ABOUT TO DO THE LAUNDRY. GIVE ME YOUR CLOTHES; I'M CERTAIN SOME OF MY HUSBAND'S OLD CLOTHES WOULD FIT YOU BOTH WELL ENOUGH FOR WORKING.

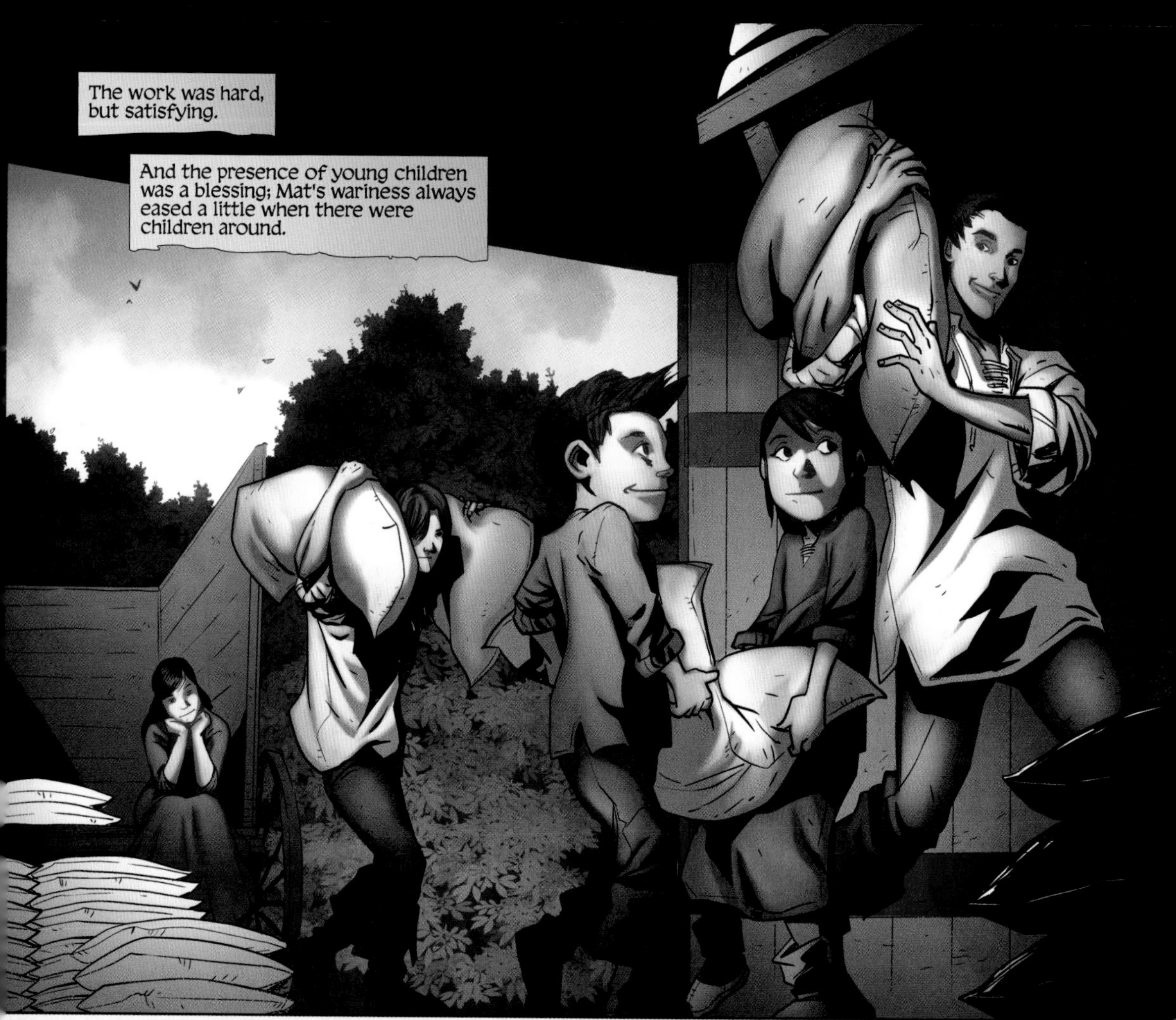
The work was hard, but satisfying.
And the presence of young children was a blessing; Mat's wariness always eased a little when there were children around.

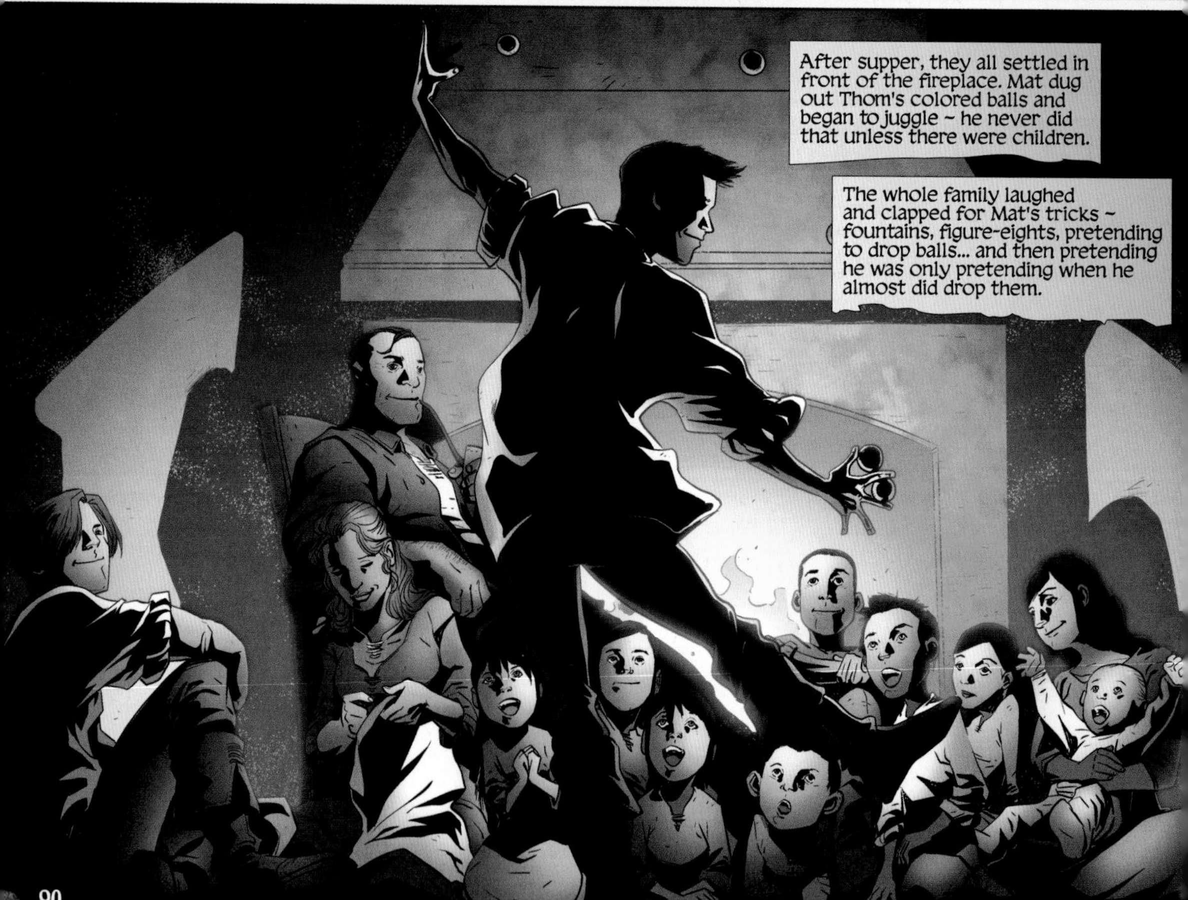
After supper, they all settled in front of the fireplace. Mat dug out Thom's colored balls and began to juggle ~ he never did that unless there were children.
The whole family laughed and clapped for Mat's tricks ~ fountains, figure-eights, pretending to drop balls... and then pretending he was only pretending when he almost did drop them.

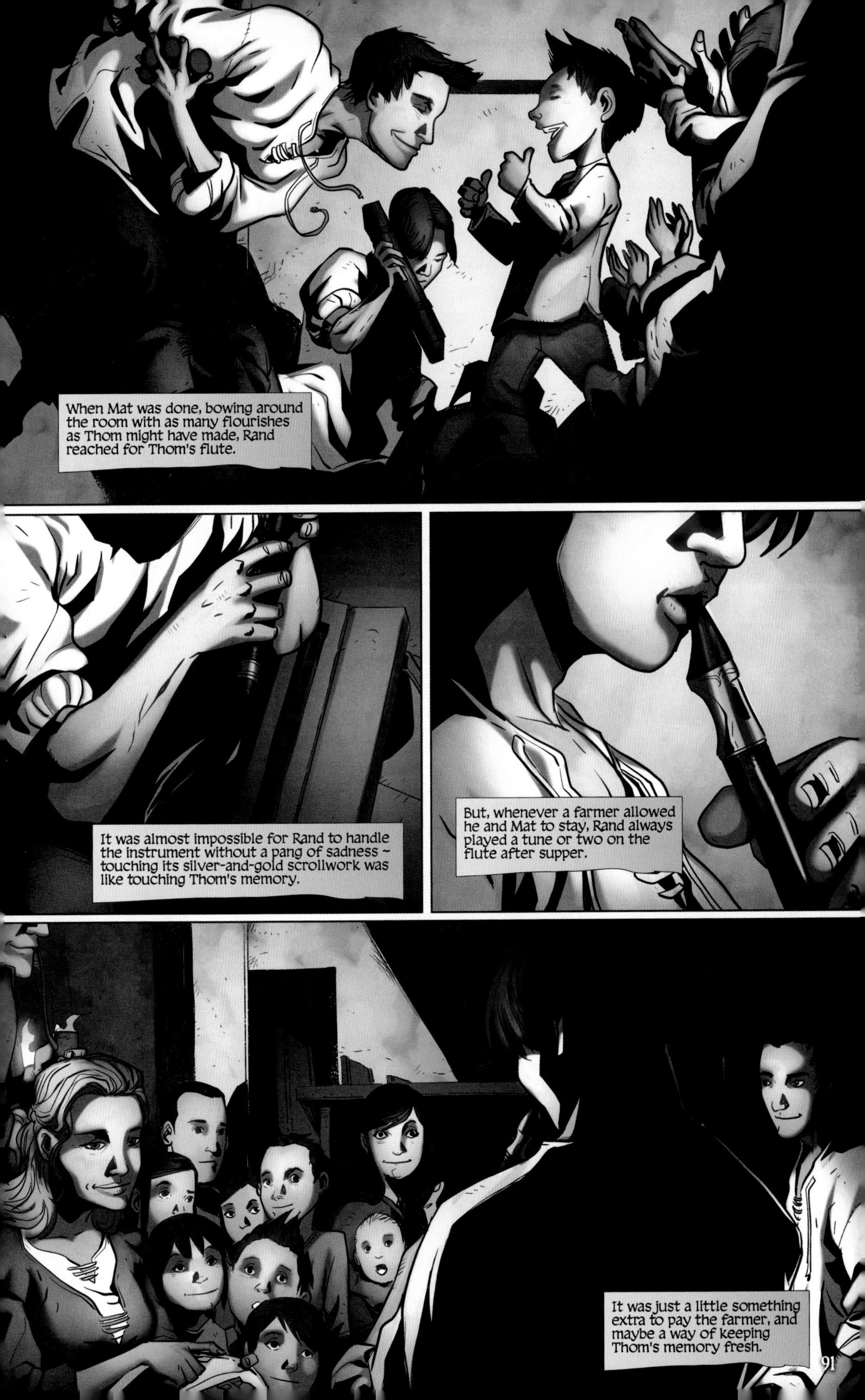
When Mat was done, bowing around the room with as many flourishes as Thom might have made, Rand reached for Thom's flute.
It was almost impossible for Rand to handle the instrument without a pang of sadness - touching its silver-and-gold scrollwork was like touching Thom's memory.
But, whenever a farmer allowed he and Mat to stay, Rand always played a tune or two on the flute after supper.
It was just a little something extra to pay the farmer, and maybe a way of keeping Thom's memory fresh.

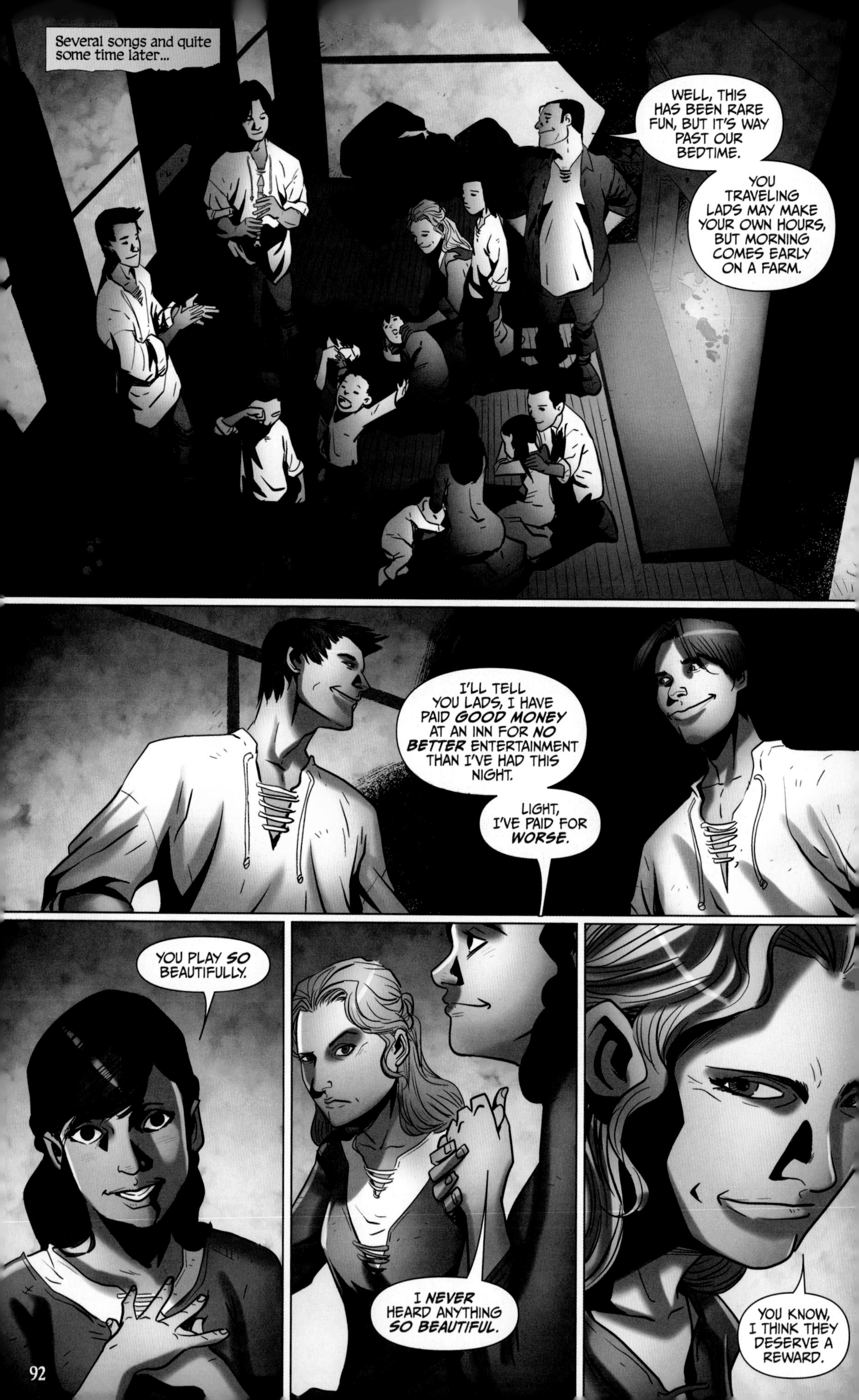

Several songs and quite some time later...
WELL, THIS HAS BEEN RARE FUN, BUT IT'S WAY PAST OUR BEDTIME.
YOU TRAVELING LADS MAY MAKE YOUR OWN HOURS, BUT MORNING COMES EARLY ON A FARM.
I'LL TELL YOU LADS, I HAVE PAID GOOD MONEY AT AN INN FOR NO BETTER ENTERTAINMENT THAN I'VE HAD THIS NIGHT.
LIGHT, I'VE PAID FOR WORSE.
YOU PLAY SO BEAUTIFULLY.
I NEVER HEARD ANYTHING SO BEAUTIFUL.
YOU KNOW, I THINK THEY DESERVE A REWARD.

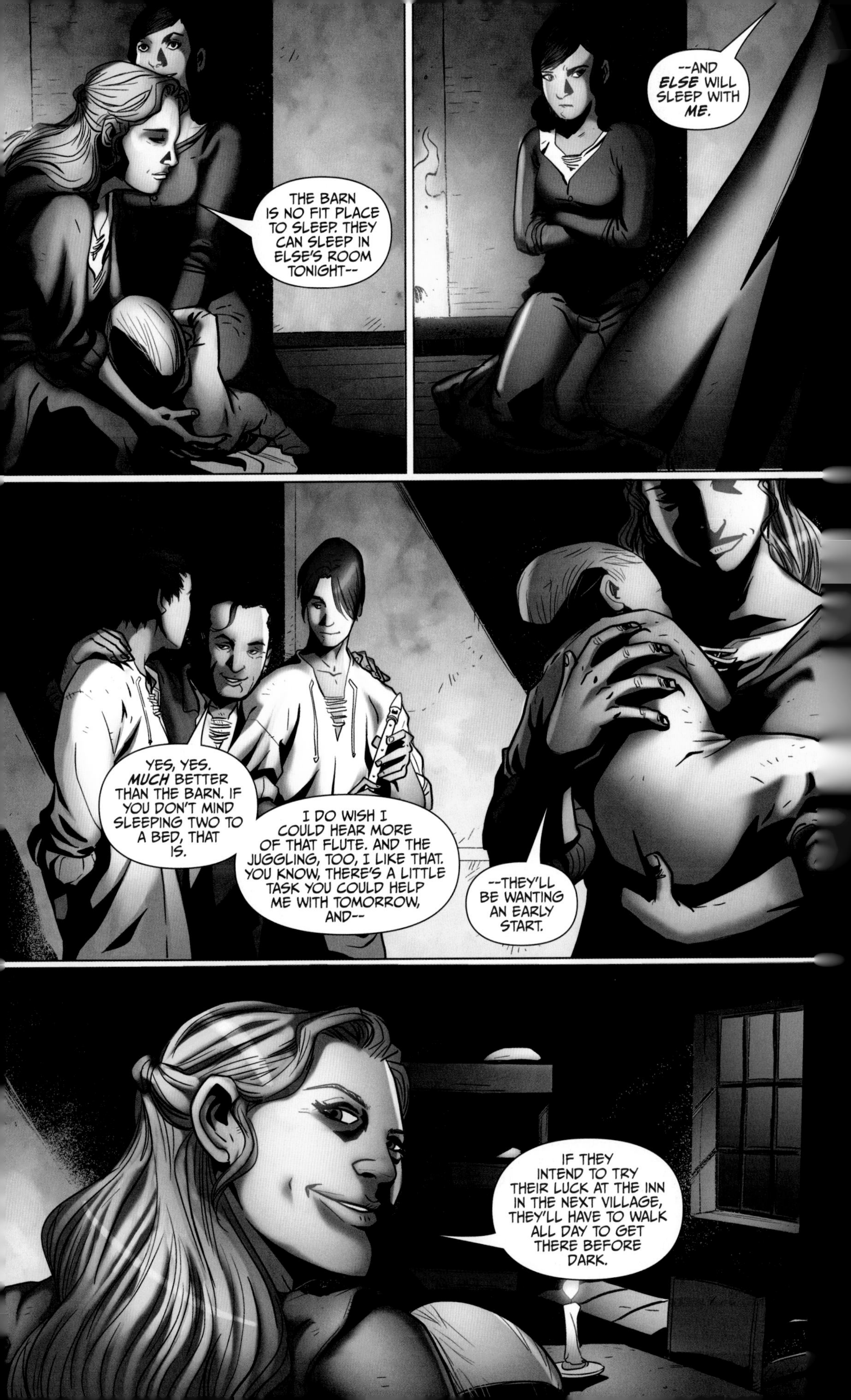
THE BARN IS NO FIT PLACE TO SLEEP. THEY CAN SLEEP IN ELSE'S ROOM TONIGHT--
--AND *ELSE* WILL SLEEP WITH *ME.*
YES, YES. *MUCH* BETTER THAN THE BARN. IF YOU DON'T MIND SLEEPING TWO TO A BED, THAT IS.
I DO WISH I COULD HEAR MORE OF THAT FLUTE. AND THE JUGGLING, TOO, I LIKE THAT. YOU KNOW, THERE'S A LITTLE TASK YOU COULD HELP ME WITH TOMORROW, AND--
--THEY'LL BE WANTING AN EARLY START.
IF THEY INTEND TO TRY THEIR LUCK AT THE INN IN THE NEXT VILLAGE, THEY'LL HAVE TO WALK ALL DAY TO GET THERE BEFORE DARK.

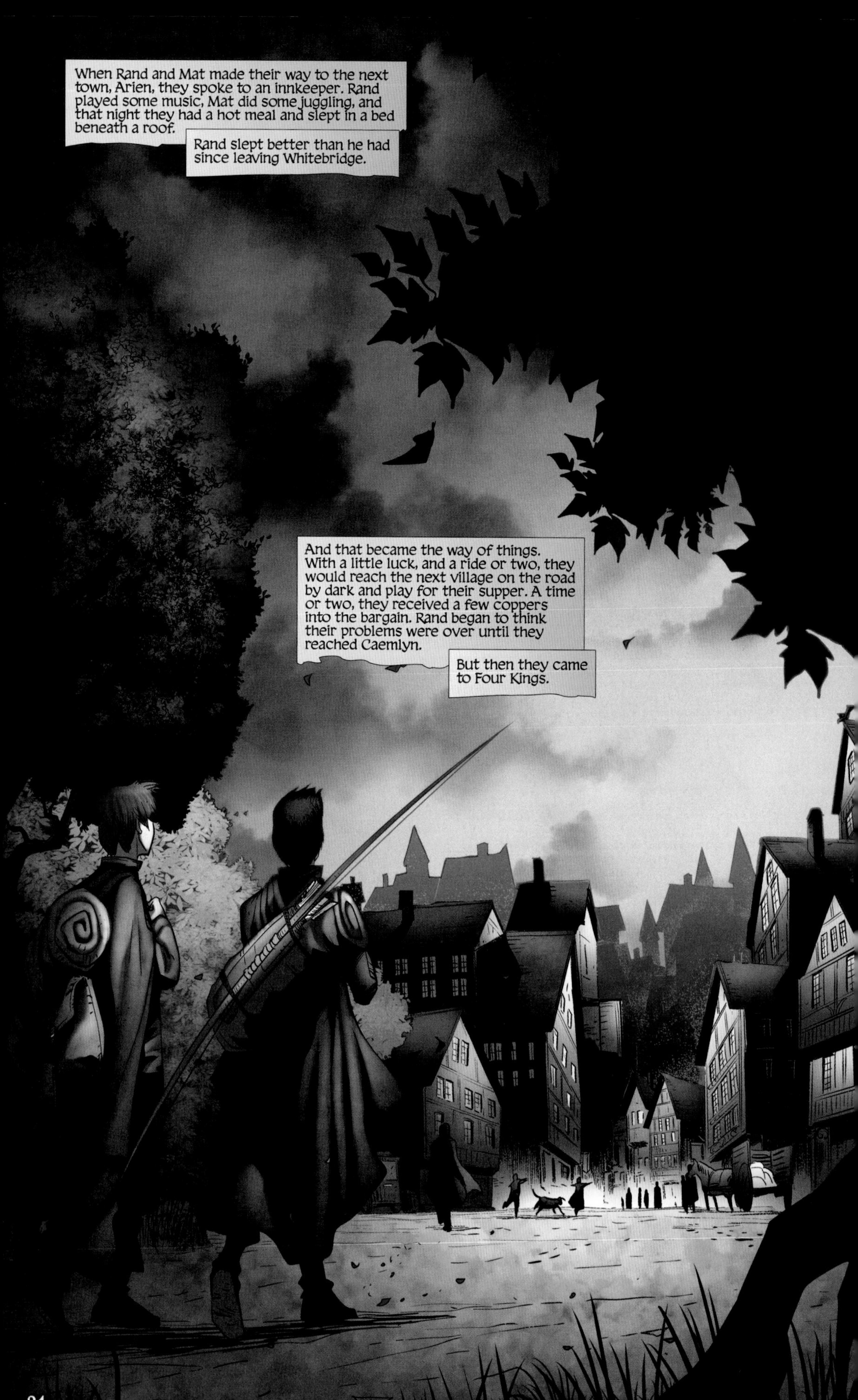
When Rand and Mat made their way to the next town, Arien, they spoke to an innkeeper. Rand played some music, Mat did some juggling, and that night they had a hot meal and slept in a bed beneath a roof.
Rand slept better than he had since leaving Whitebridge.
And that became the way of things. With a little luck, and a ride or two, they would reach the next village on the road by dark and play for their supper. A time or two, they received a few coppers into the bargain. Rand began to think their problems were over until they reached Caemlyn.
But then they came to Four Kings.

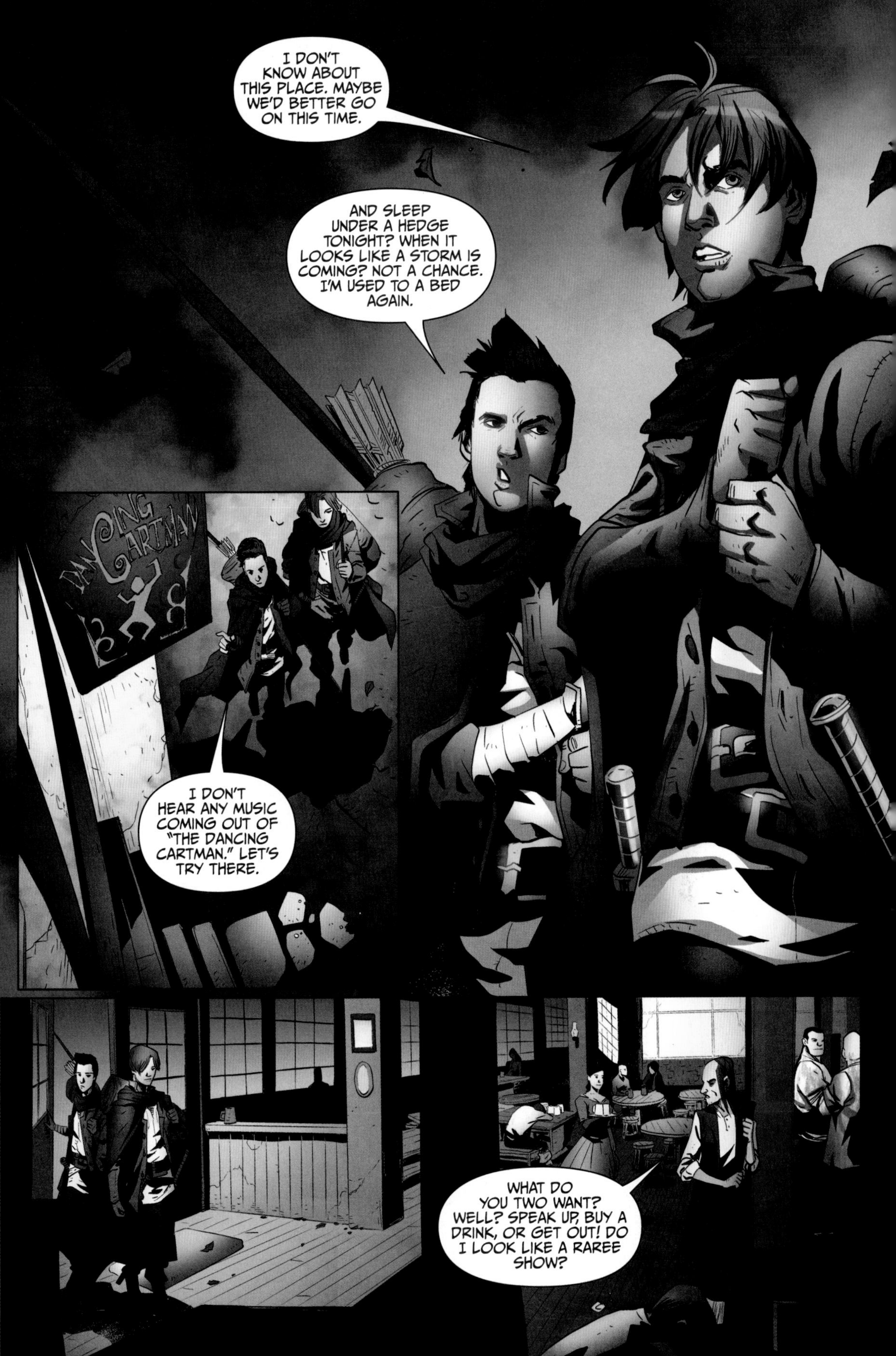
I DON'T KNOW ABOUT THIS PLACE. MAYBE WE'D BETTER GO ON THIS TIME.
AND SLEEP UNDER A HEDGE TONIGHT? WHEN IT LOOKS LIKE A STORM IS COMING? NOT A CHANCE. I'M USED TO A BED AGAIN.
DANCING CARTMAN
I DON'T HEAR ANY MUSIC COMING OUT OF "THE DANCING CARTMAN." LET'S TRY THERE.
WHAT DO YOU TWO WANT? WELL? SPEAK UP, BUY A DRINK, OR GET OUT! DO I LOOK LIKE A RAREE SHOW?

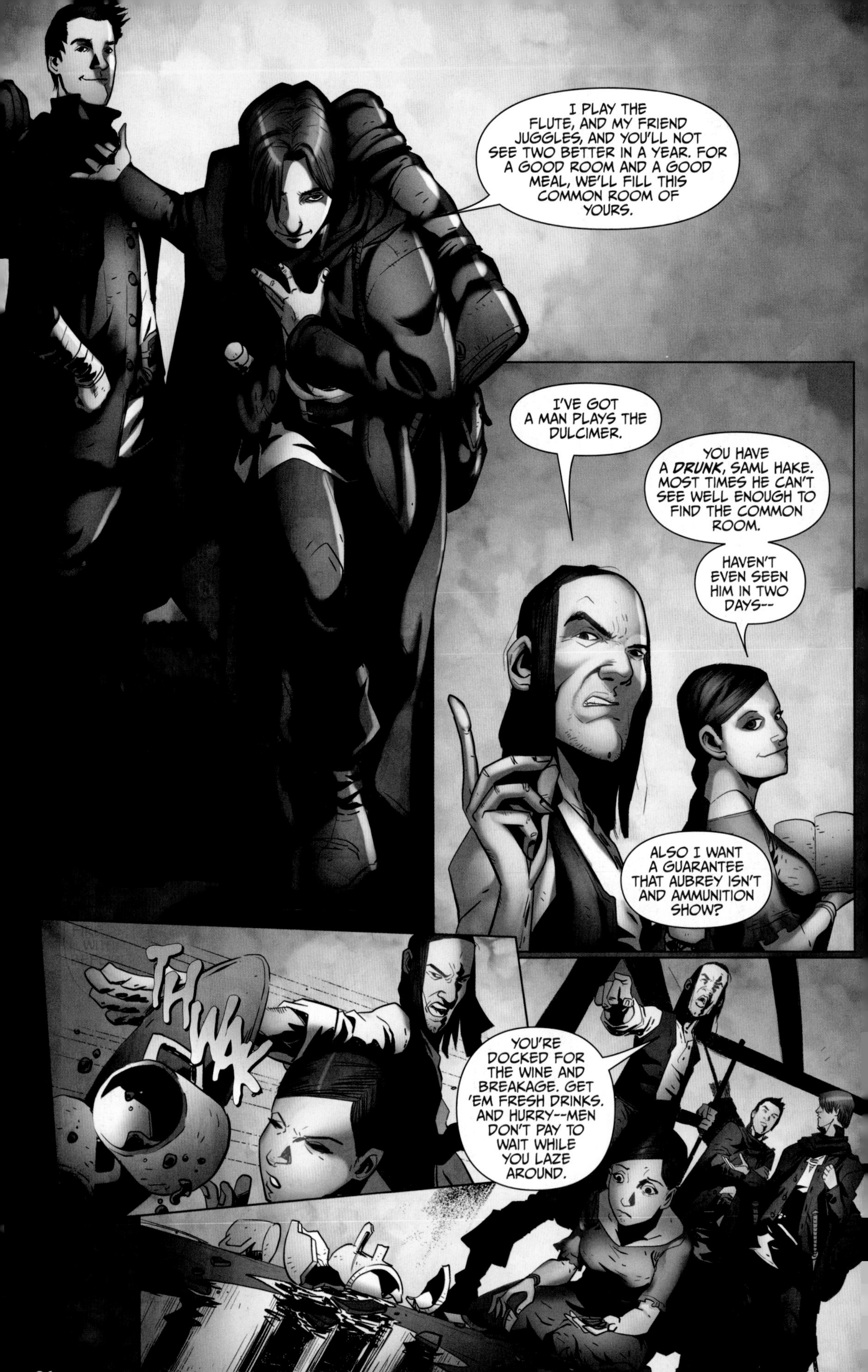
I PLAY THE FLUTE, AND MY FRIEND JUGGLES, AND YOU'LL NOT SEE TWO BETTER IN A YEAR. FOR A GOOD ROOM AND A GOOD MEAL, WE'LL FILL THIS COMMON ROOM OF YOURS.
I'VE GOT A MAN PLAYS THE DULCIMER.
YOU HAVE A *DRUNK*, SAML HAKE. MOST TIMES HE CAN'T SEE WELL ENOUGH TO FIND THE COMMON ROOM.
HAVEN'T EVEN SEEN HIM IN TWO DAYS--
ALSO I WANT A GUARANTEE THAT AUBREY ISN'T AND AMMUNITION SHOW?
THWAK
YOU'RE DOCKED FOR THE WINE AND BREAKAGE. GET 'EM FRESH DRINKS. AND HURRY--MEN DON'T PAY TO WAIT WHILE YOU LAZE AROUND.

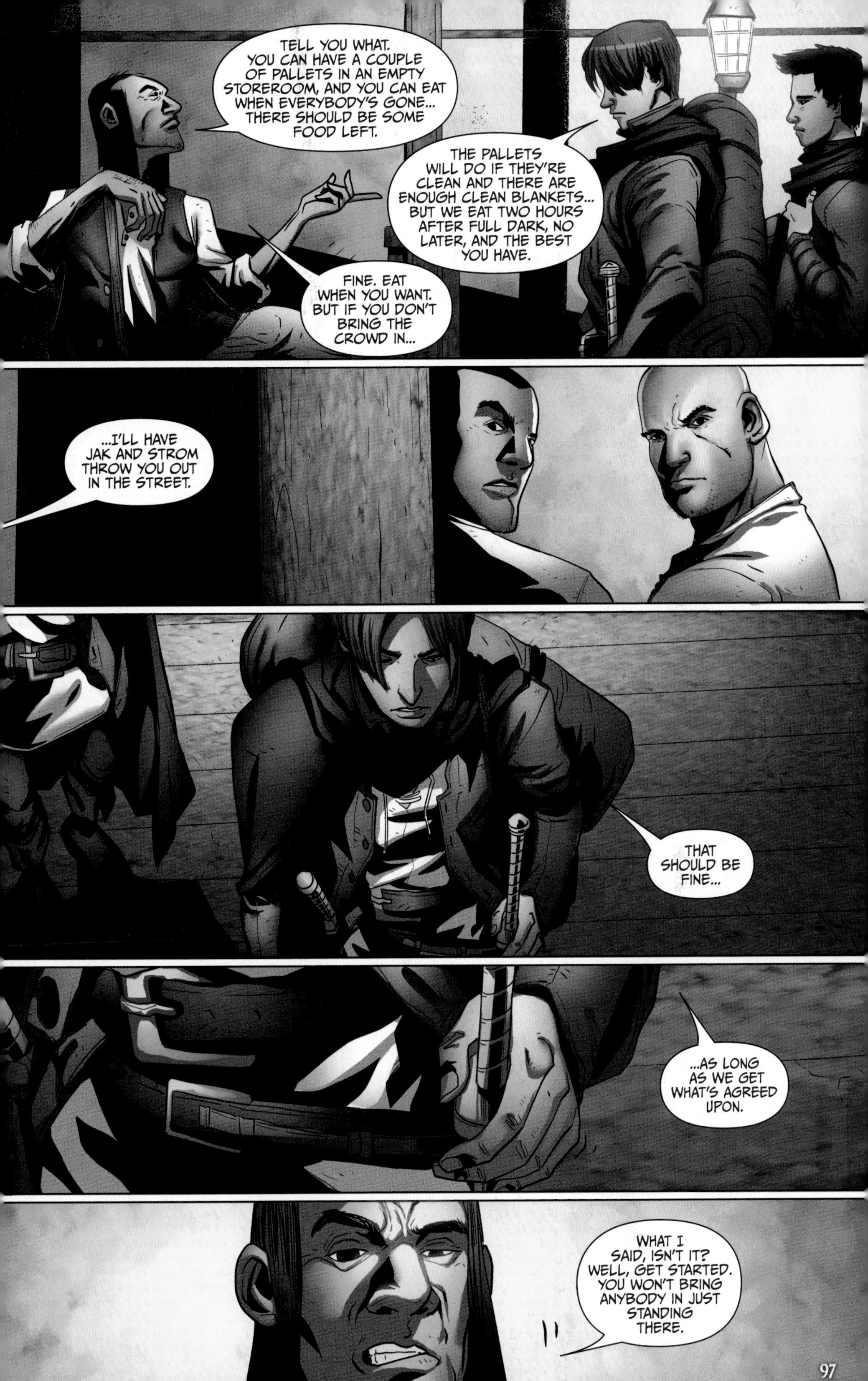
TELL YOU WHAT. YOU CAN HAVE A COUPLE OF PALLETS IN AN EMPTY STOREROOM, AND YOU CAN EAT WHEN EVERYBODY'S GONE... THERE SHOULD BE SOME FOOD LEFT.
THE PALLETS WILL DO IF THEY'RE CLEAN AND THERE ARE ENOUGH CLEAN BLANKETS... BUT WE EAT TWO HOURS AFTER FULL DARK, NO LATER, AND THE BEST YOU HAVE.
FINE. EAT WHEN YOU WANT. BUT IF YOU DON'T BRING THE CROWD IN...
...I'LL HAVE JAK AND STROM THROW YOU OUT IN THE STREET.
THAT SHOULD BE FINE...
...AS LONG AS WE GET WHAT'S AGREED UPON.
WHAT I SAID, ISN'T IT? WELL, GET STARTED. YOU WON'T BRING ANYBODY IN JUST STANDING THERE.

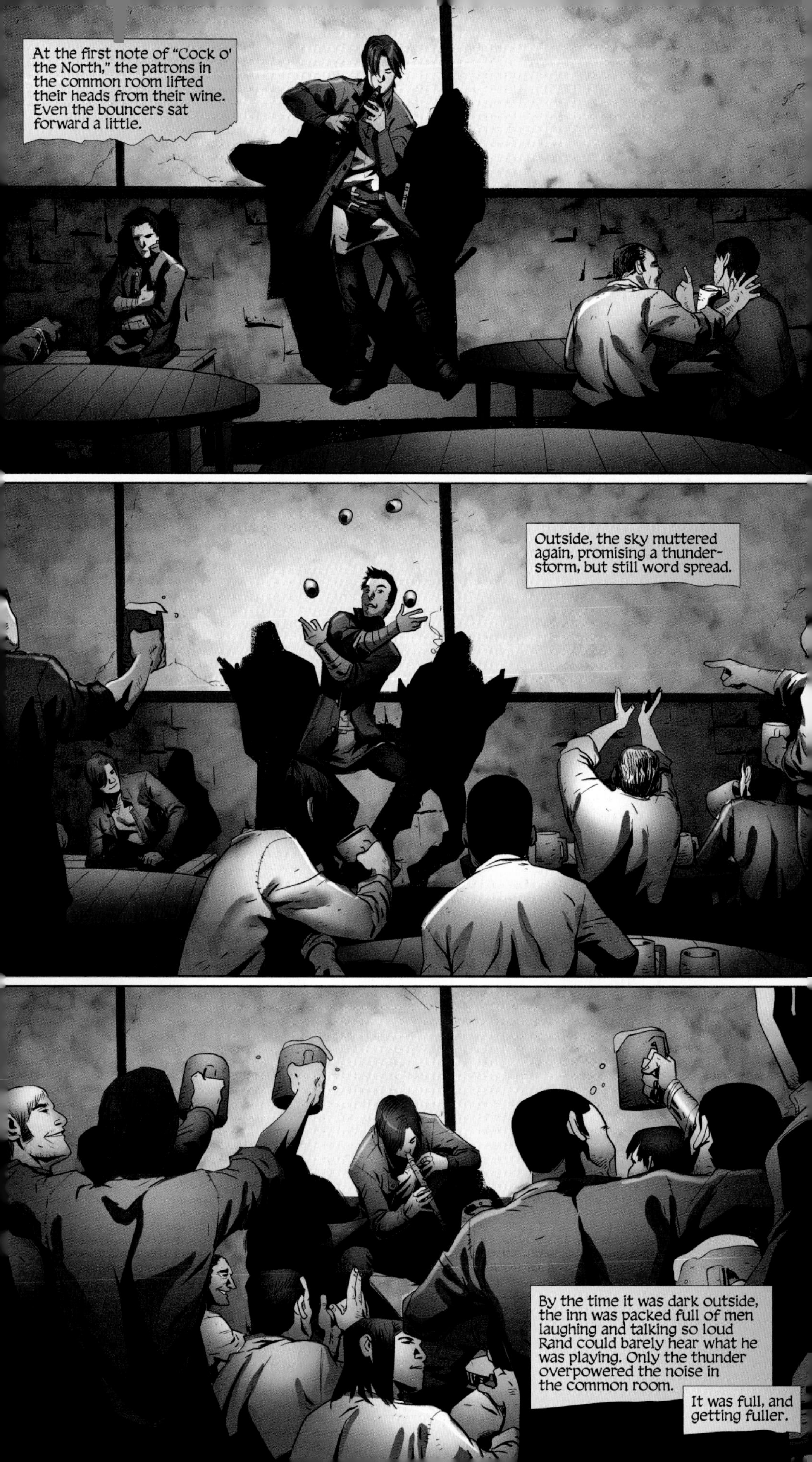
At the first note of "Cock o' the North," the patrons in the common room lifted their heads from their wine. Even the bouncers sat forward a little.
Outside, the sky muttered again, promising a thunder-storm, but still word spread.
By the time it was dark outside, the inn was packed full of men laughing and talking so loud Rand could barely hear what he was playing. Only the thunder overpowered the noise in the common room.
It was full, and getting fuller.

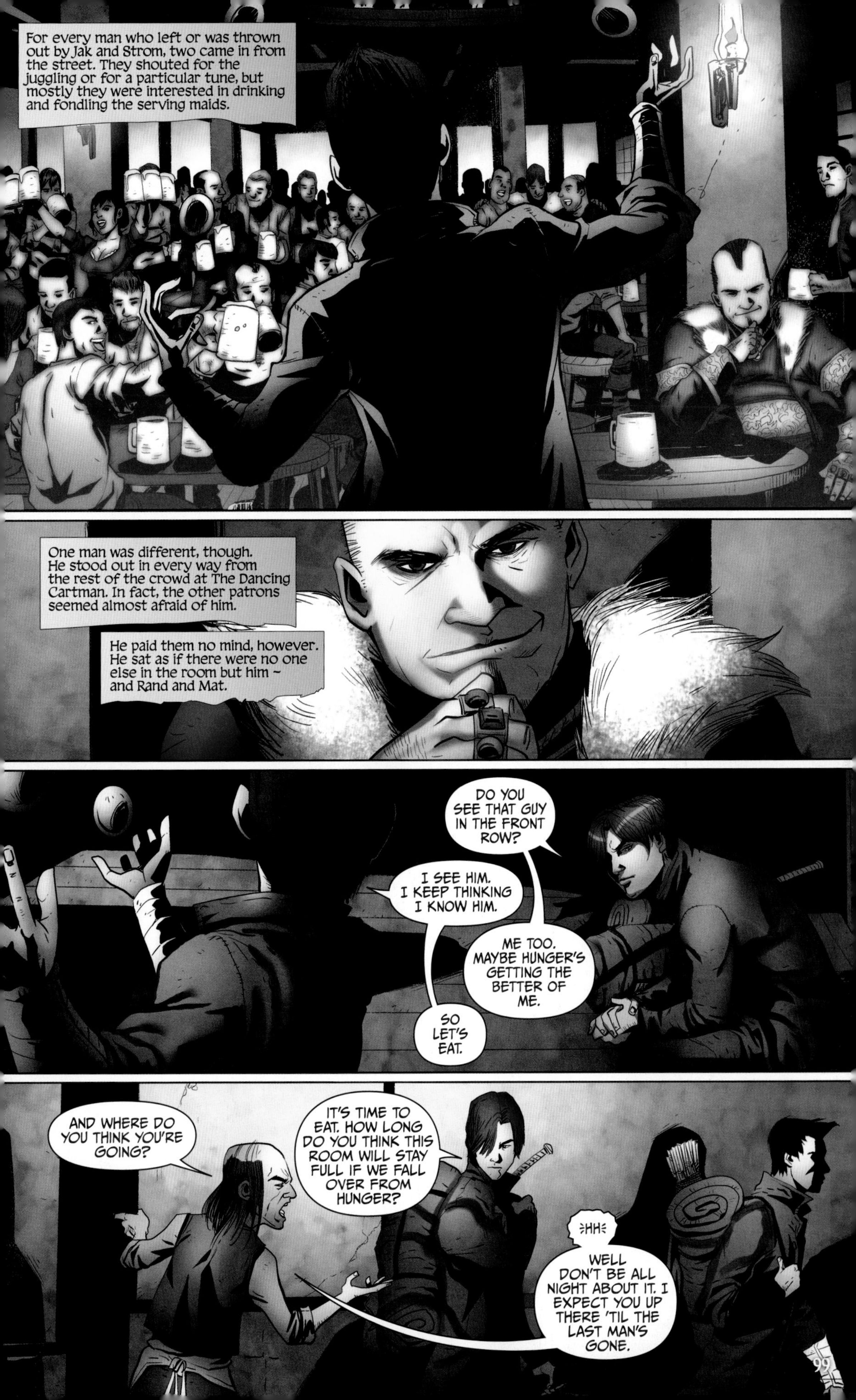
For every man who left or was thrown out by Jak and Strom, two came in from the street. They shouted for the juggling or for a particular tune, but mostly they were interested in drinking and fondling the serving maids.
One man was different, though. He stood out in every way from the rest of the crowd at The Dancing Cartman. In fact, the other patrons seemed almost afraid of him.
He paid them no mind, however. He sat as if there were no one else in the room but him ~ and Rand and Mat.
DO YOU SEE THAT GUY IN THE FRONT ROW?
I SEE HIM. I KEEP THINKING I KNOW HIM.
ME TOO. MAYBE HUNGER'S GETTING THE BETTER OF ME.
SO LET'S EAT.
AND WHERE DO YOU THINK YOU'RE GOING?
IT'S TIME TO EAT. HOW LONG DO YOU THINK THIS ROOM WILL STAY FULL IF WE FALL OVER FROM HUNGER?
HH
WELL DON'T BE ALL NIGHT ABOUT IT. I EXPECT YOU UP THERE 'TIL THE LAST MAN'S GONE.

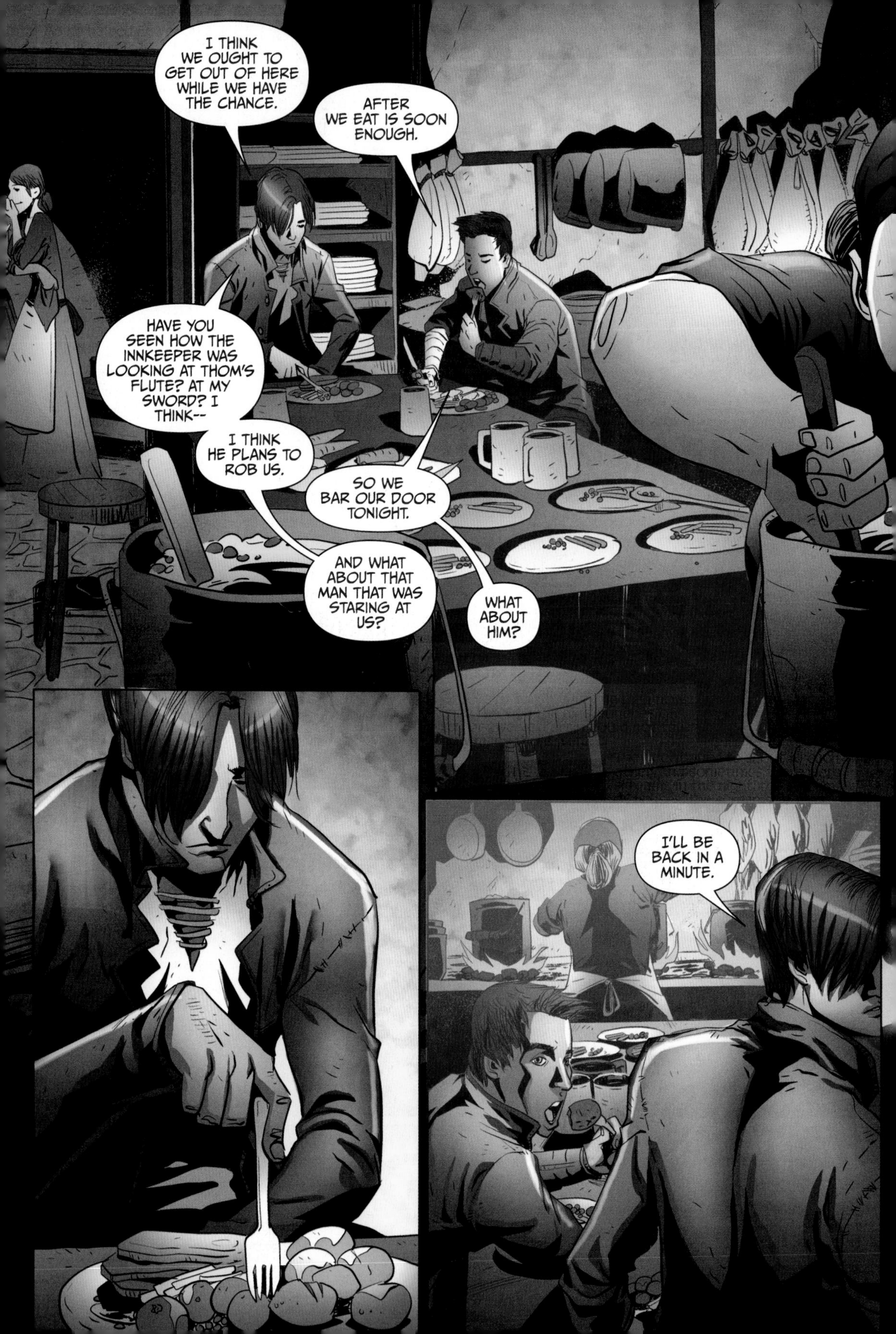
I THINK WE OUGHT TO GET OUT OF HERE WHILE WE HAVE THE CHANCE.
AFTER WE EAT IS SOON ENOUGH.
HAVE YOU SEEN HOW THE INNKEEPER WAS LOOKING AT THOM'S FLUTE? AT MY SWORD? I THINK--
I THINK HE PLANS TO ROB US.
SO WE BAR OUR DOOR TONIGHT.
AND WHAT ABOUT THAT MAN THAT WAS STARING AT US?
WHAT ABOUT HIM?
I'LL BE BACK IN A MINUTE.

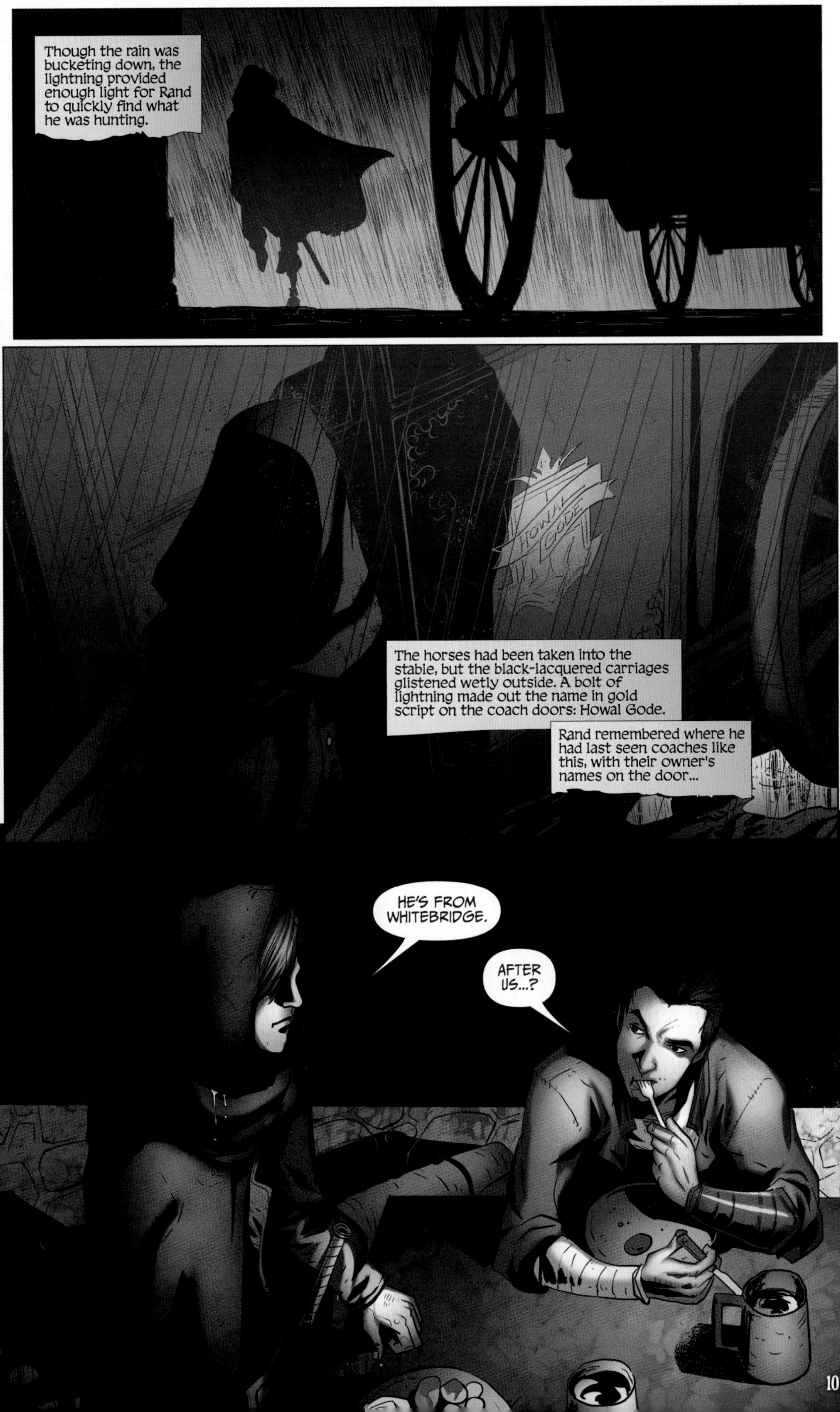
Though the rain was bucketing down, the lightning provided enough light for Rand to quickly find what he was hunting.
HOWAL GODE
The horses had been taken into the stable, but the black-lacquered carriages glistened wetly outside. A bolt of lightning made out the name in gold script on the coach doors: Howal Gode.
Rand remembered where he had last seen coaches like this, with their owner's names on the door...
HE'S FROM WHITEBRIDGE.
AFTER US...?

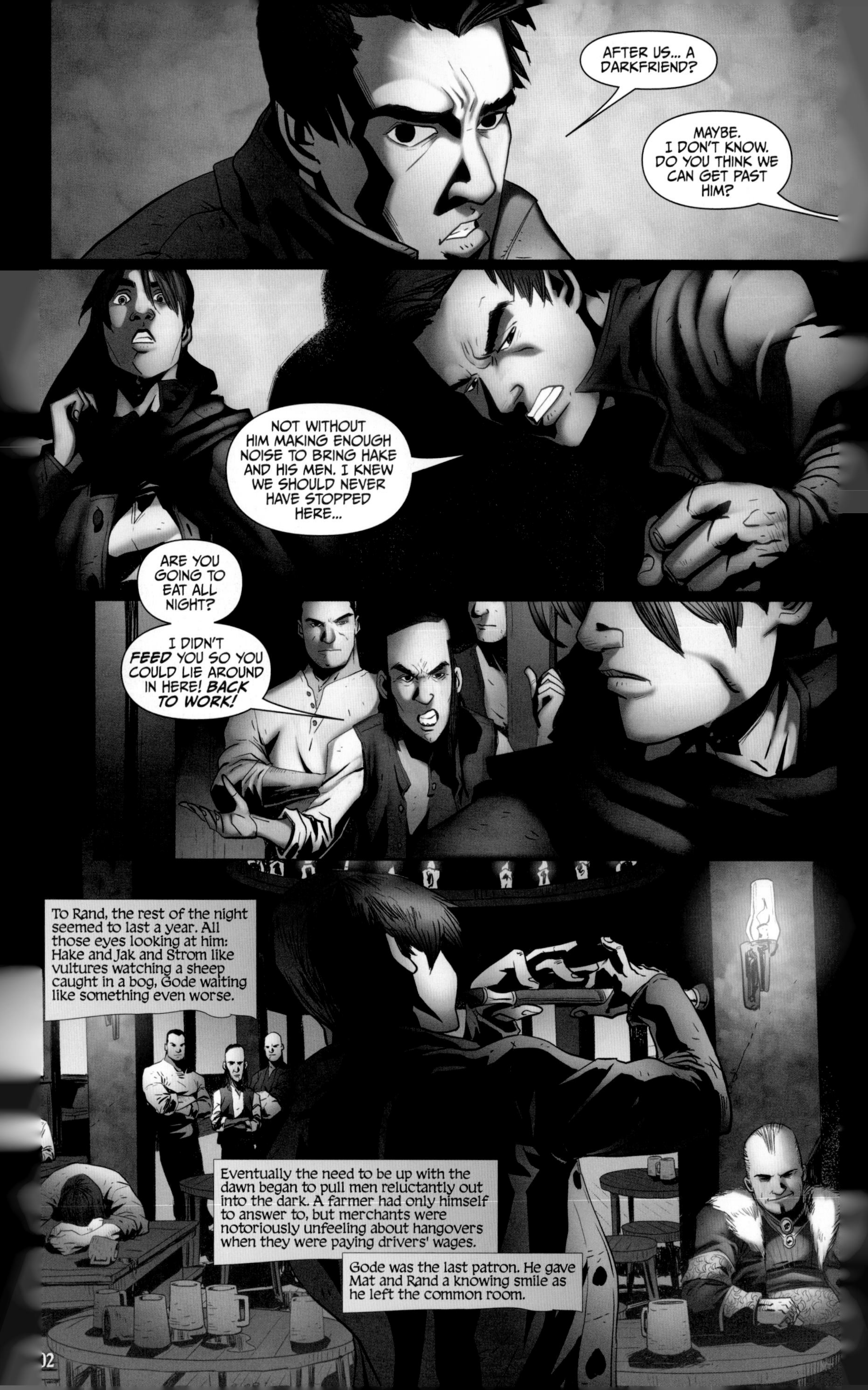
AFTER US... A DARKFRIEND?
MAYBE. I DON'T KNOW. DO YOU THINK WE CAN GET PAST HIM?
NOT WITHOUT HIM MAKING ENOUGH NOISE TO BRING HAKE AND HIS MEN. I KNEW WE SHOULD NEVER HAVE STOPPED HERE...
ARE YOU GOING TO EAT ALL NIGHT?
I DIDN'T *FEED* YOU SO YOU COULD LIE AROUND IN HERE! ***BACK TO WORK!***
To Rand, the rest of the night seemed to last a year. All those eyes looking at him: Hake and Jak and Strom like vultures watching a sheep caught in a bog, Gode waiting like something even worse.
Eventually the need to be up with the dawn began to pull men reluctantly out into the dark. A farmer had only himself to answer to, but merchants were notoriously unfeeling about hangovers when they were paying drivers' wages.
Gode was the last patron. He gave Mat and Rand a knowing smile as he left the common room.

YOU TWO. YOUR PALLETS ARE THIS WAY.

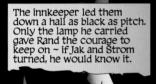

YOU NEED THOSE TWO TO SHOW US OUR BEDS?

I'M A MAN OF PROPERTY, AND MEN OF PROPERTY CAN'T BE TOO CAREFUL.

DO YOU WANT TO SEE YOUR BEDS OR NOT?

LEAD THE WAY. I DON'T LIKE HAVING ANYBODY BEHIND ME.

The innkeeper led them down a hall as black as pitch. Only the lamp he carried gave Rand the courage to keep on ~ if Jak and Strom turned, he would know it.

HERE IT IS.

THIS'LL DO. LEAVE THE LAMP.

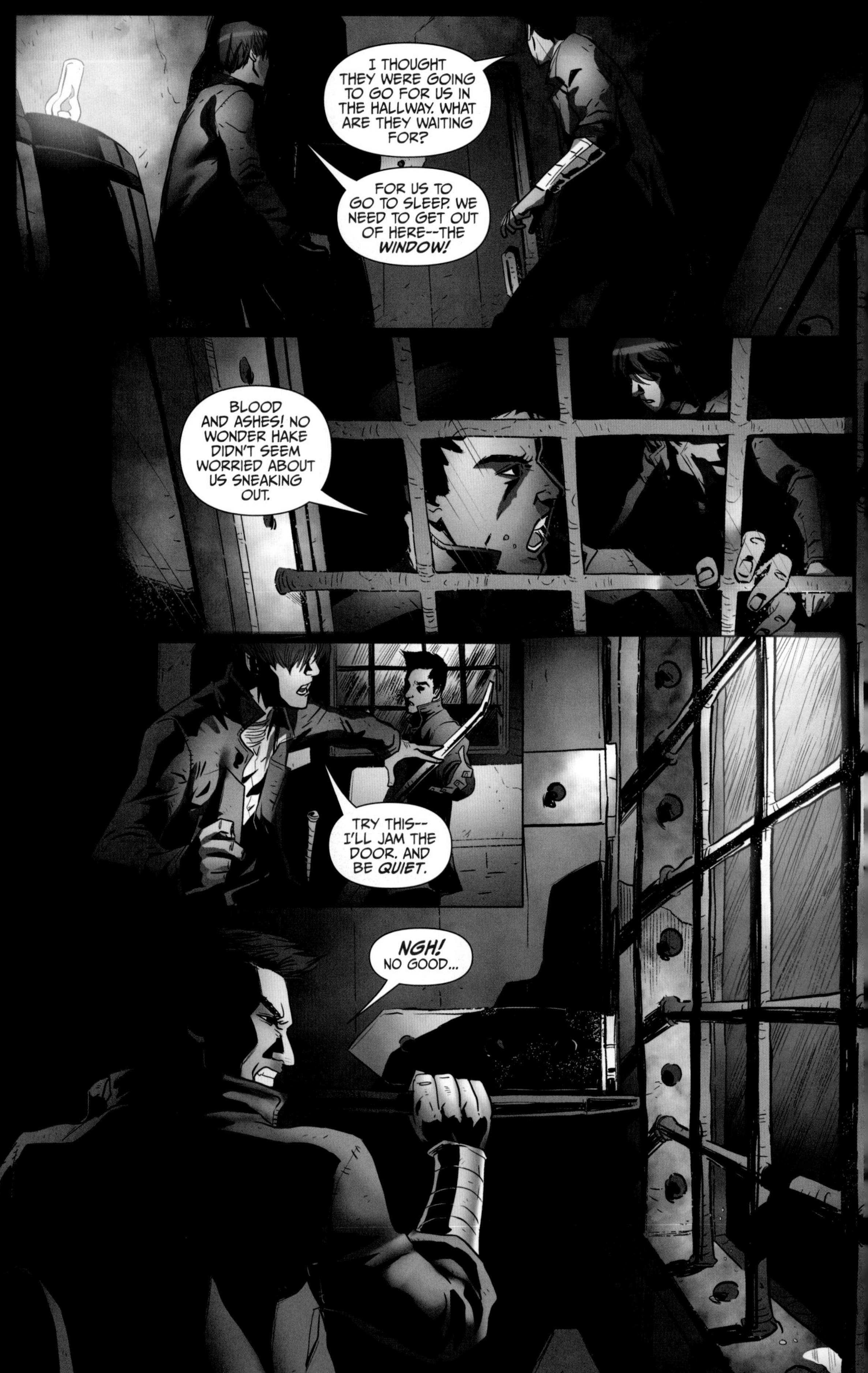

I THOUGHT THEY WERE GOING TO GO FOR US IN THE HALLWAY. WHAT ARE THEY WAITING FOR?
FOR US TO GO TO SLEEP. WE NEED TO GET OUT OF HERE--THE *WINDOW!*
BLOOD AND ASHES! NO WONDER HAKE DIDN'T SEEM WORRIED ABOUT US SNEAKING OUT.
TRY THIS-- I'LL JAM THE DOOR. AND BE *QUIET*.
NGH! NO GOOD...

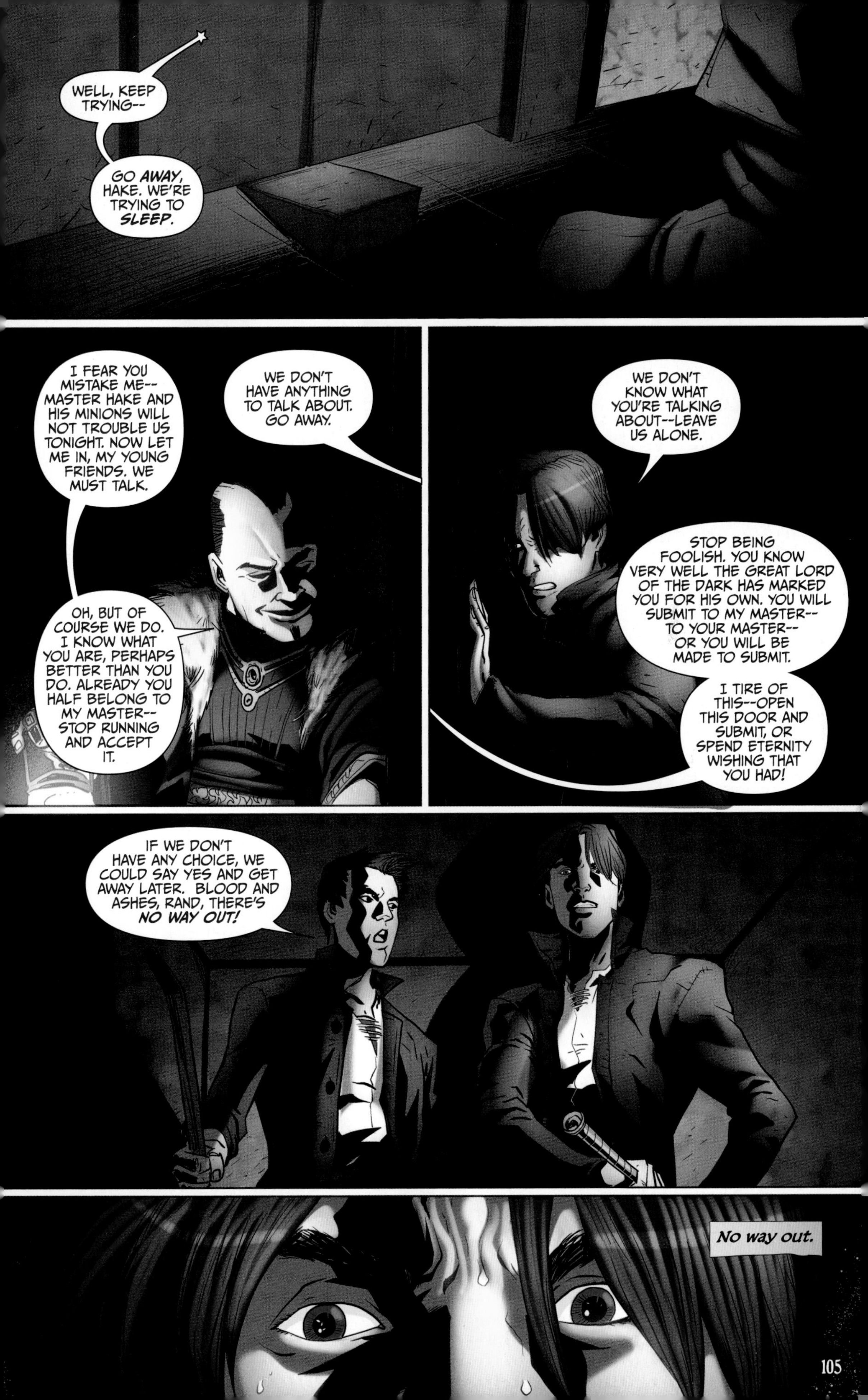
WELL, KEEP TRYING--
GO AWAY, HAKE. WE'RE TRYING TO SLEEP.
I FEAR YOU MISTAKE ME--MASTER HAKE AND HIS MINIONS WILL NOT TROUBLE US TONIGHT. NOW LET ME IN, MY YOUNG FRIENDS. WE MUST TALK.
WE DON'T HAVE ANYTHING TO TALK ABOUT. GO AWAY.
OH, BUT OF COURSE WE DO. I KNOW WHAT YOU ARE, PERHAPS BETTER THAN YOU DO. ALREADY YOU HALF BELONG TO MY MASTER--STOP RUNNING AND ACCEPT IT.
WE DON'T KNOW WHAT YOU'RE TALKING ABOUT--LEAVE US ALONE.
STOP BEING FOOLISH. YOU KNOW VERY WELL THE GREAT LORD OF THE DARK HAS MARKED YOU FOR HIS OWN. YOU WILL SUBMIT TO MY MASTER--TO YOUR MASTER--OR YOU WILL BE MADE TO SUBMIT.
I TIRE OF THIS--OPEN THIS DOOR AND SUBMIT, OR SPEND ETERNITY WISHING THAT YOU HAD!
IF WE DON'T HAVE ANY CHOICE, WE COULD SAY YES AND GET AWAY LATER. BLOOD AND ASHES, RAND, THERE'S NO WAY OUT!
No way out.

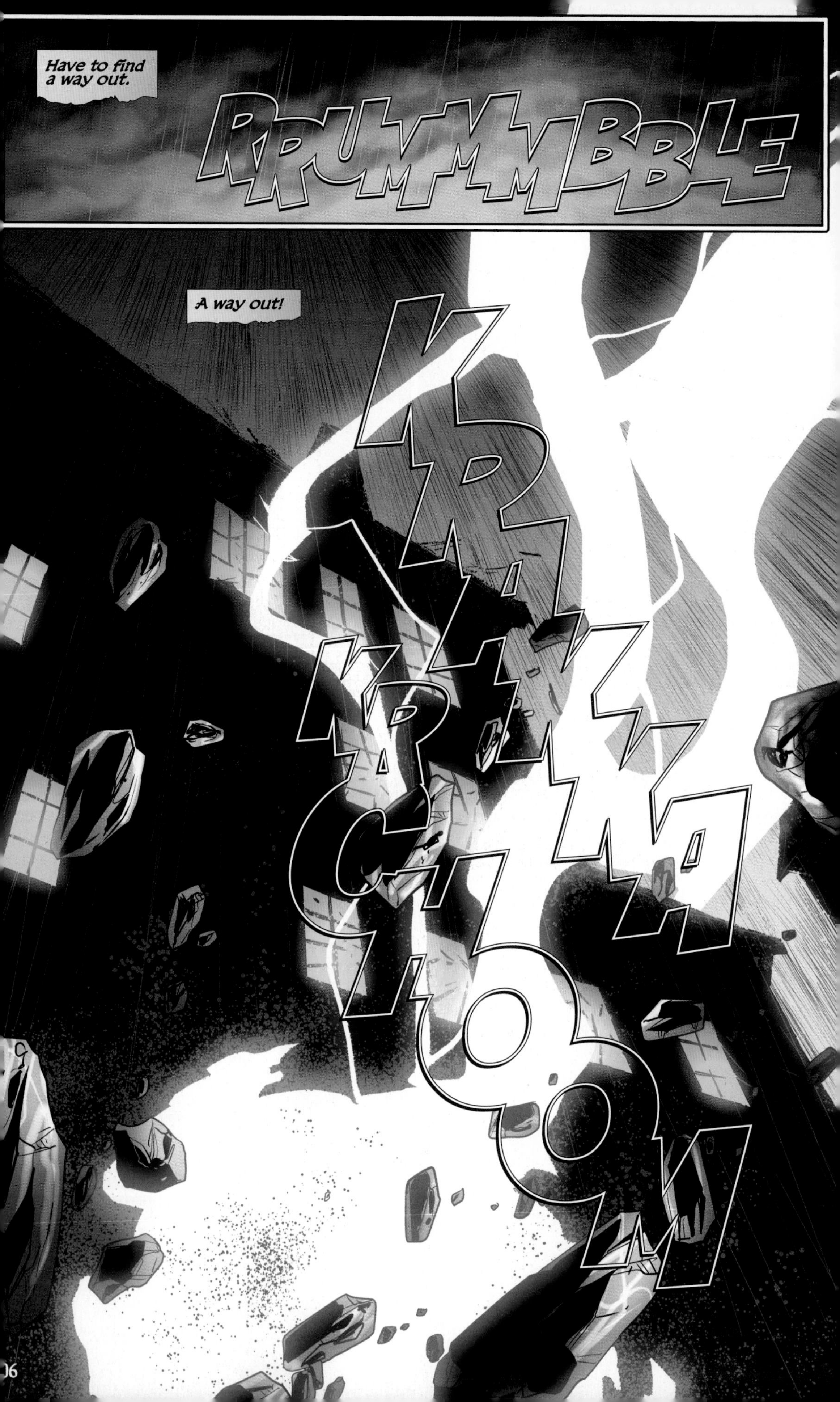
Have to find a way out.
RRUMMMBBLE
A way out!
KRAKKKAKKKA
KRACHOOM

chapter five

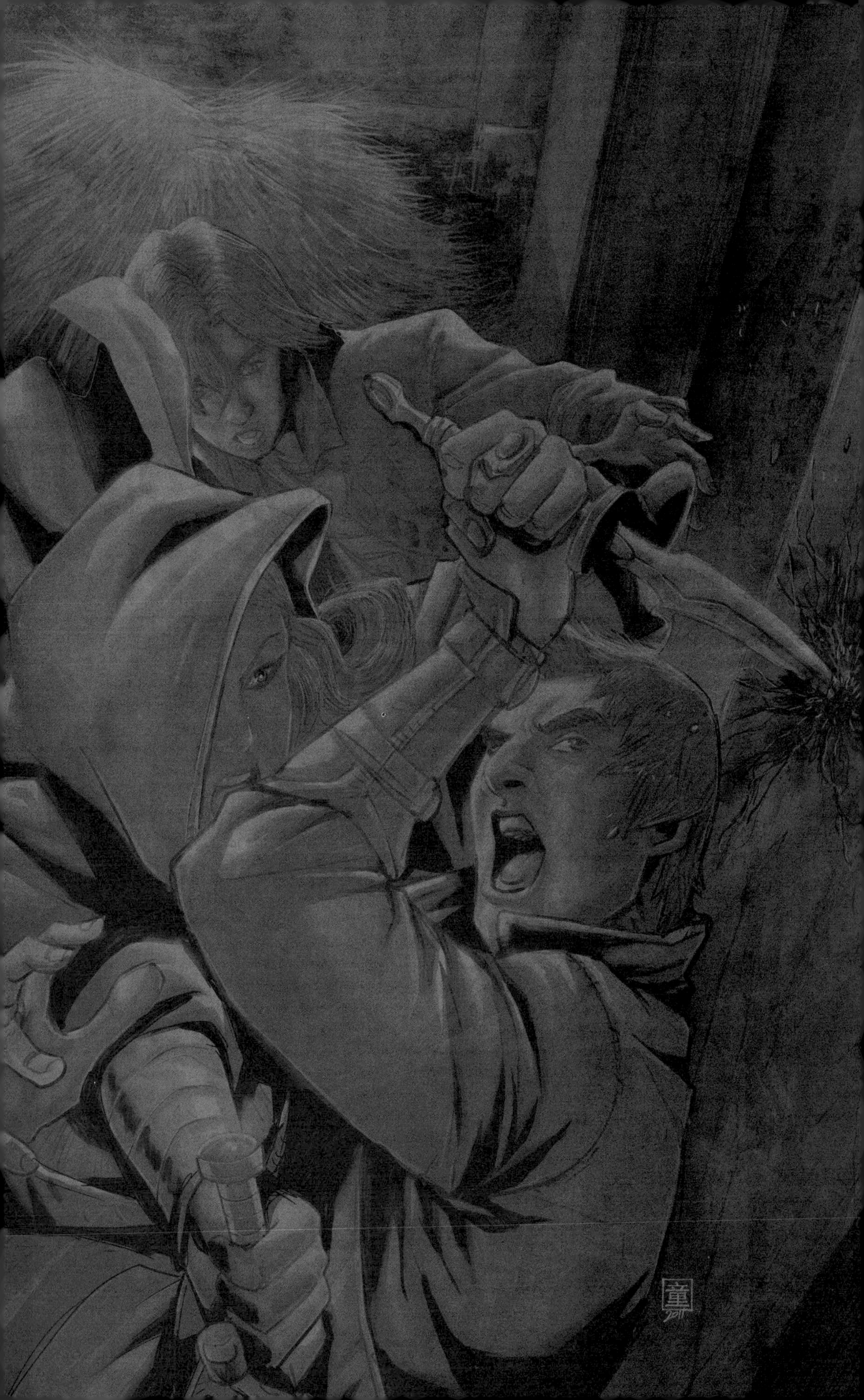

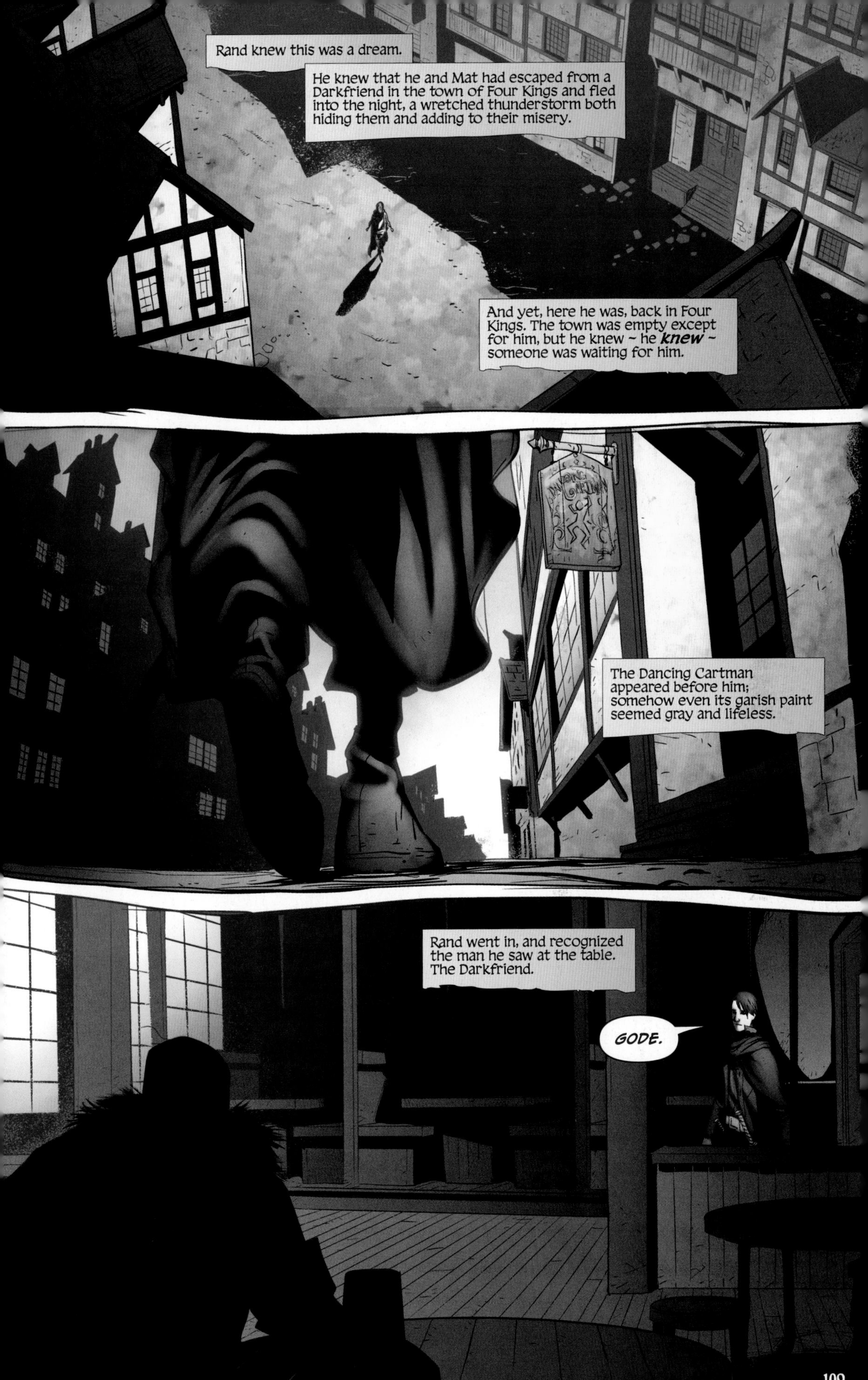

Rand knew this was a dream.
He knew that he and Mat had escaped from a Darkfriend in the town of Four Kings and fled into the night, a wretched thunderstorm both hiding them and adding to their misery.
And yet, here he was, back in Four Kings. The town was empty except for him, but he knew ~ he *knew* ~ someone was waiting for him.
The Dancing Cartman appeared before him; somehow even its garish paint seemed gray and lifeless.
Rand went in, and recognized the man he saw at the table. The Darkfriend.
GODE.

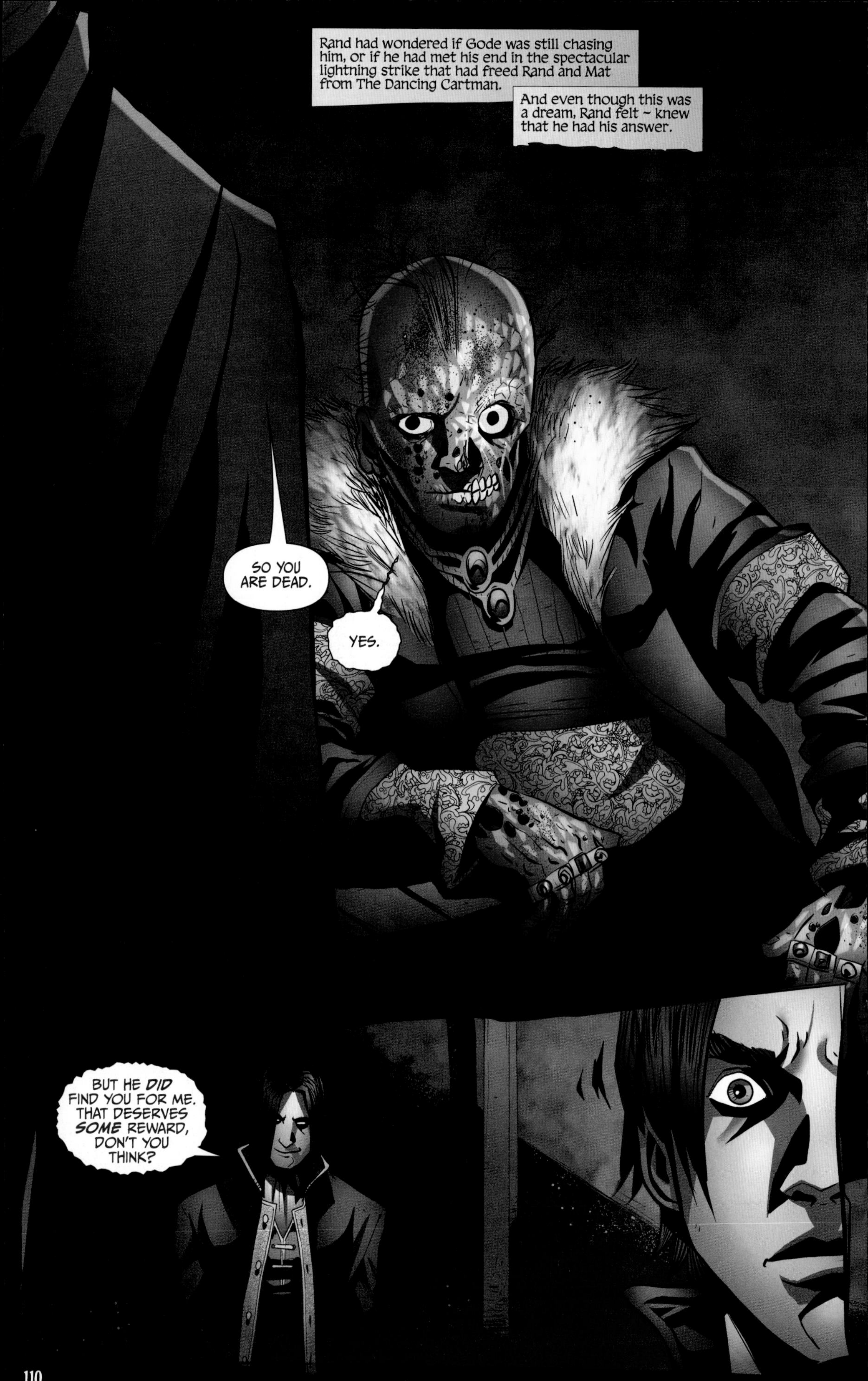
Rand had wondered if Gode was still chasing him, or if he had met his end in the spectacular lightning strike that had freed Rand and Mat from The Dancing Cartman.
And even though this was a dream, Rand felt ~ knew that he had his answer.
SO YOU ARE DEAD.
YES.
BUT HE *DID* FIND YOU FOR ME. THAT DESERVES *SOME* REWARD, DON'T YOU THINK?

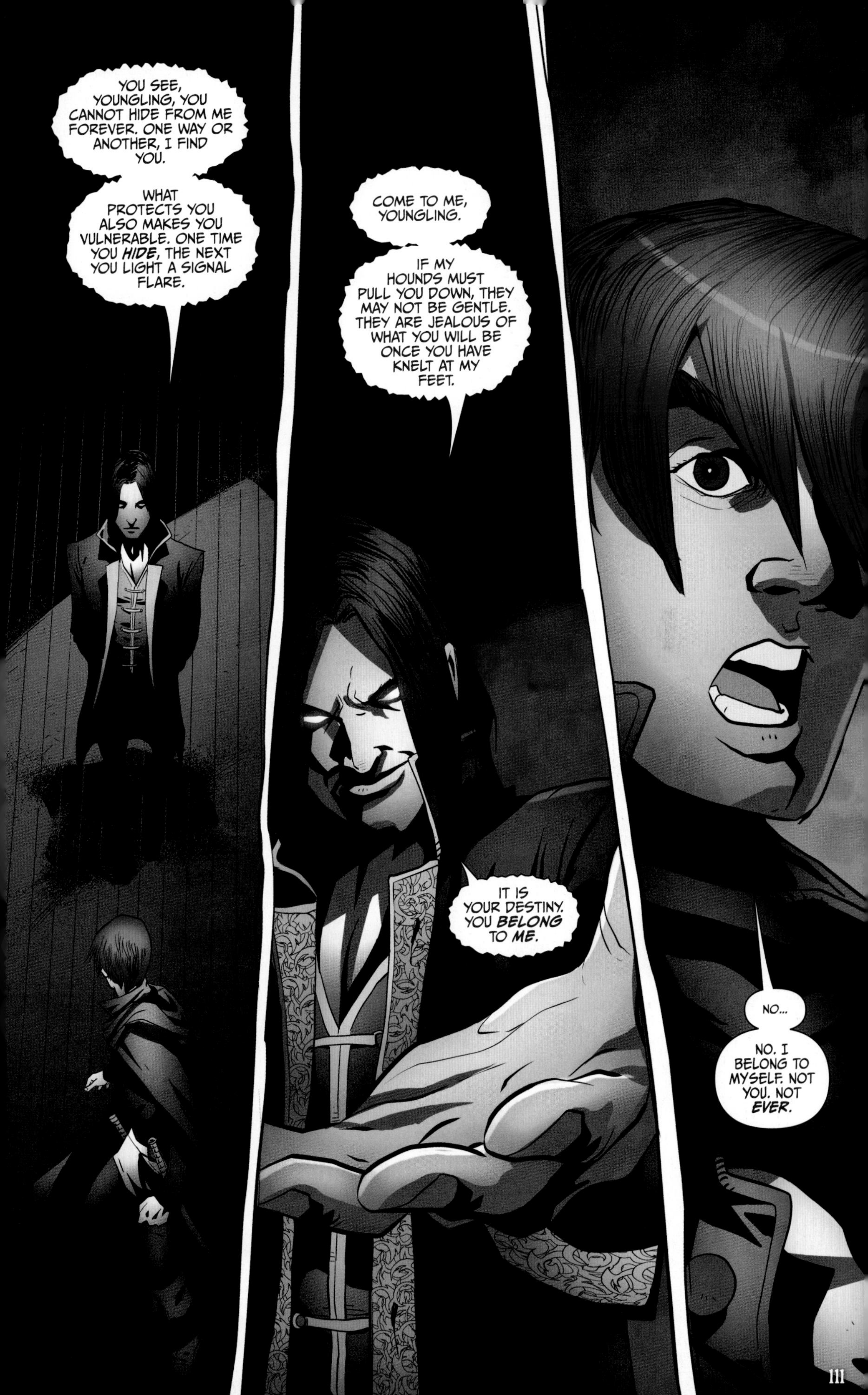
YOU SEE, YOUNGLING, YOU CANNOT HIDE FROM ME FOREVER. ONE WAY OR ANOTHER, I FIND YOU.
WHAT PROTECTS YOU ALSO MAKES YOU VULNERABLE. ONE TIME YOU *HIDE*, THE NEXT YOU LIGHT A SIGNAL FLARE.
COME TO ME, YOUNGLING.
IF MY HOUNDS MUST PULL YOU DOWN, THEY MAY NOT BE GENTLE. THEY ARE JEALOUS OF WHAT YOU WILL BE ONCE YOU HAVE KNELT AT MY FEET.
IT IS YOUR DESTINY. YOU *BELONG* TO *ME*.
NO...
NO. I BELONG TO MYSELF. NOT YOU. NOT *EVER*.

IF YOUR DARKFRIENDS KILL ME, YOU'LL NEVER HAVE ME.
ALIVE OR DEAD, YOUNGLING, YOU ARE MINE.
THE GRAVE BELONGS TO ME. EASIER DEAD, BUT BETTER ALIVE. BETTER FOR YOU, YOUNGLING...
...THE LIVING HAVE MORE POWER IN MOST THINGS.
WHIMPER
YES, MY GOOD HOUND.
HERE IS YOUR REWARD.

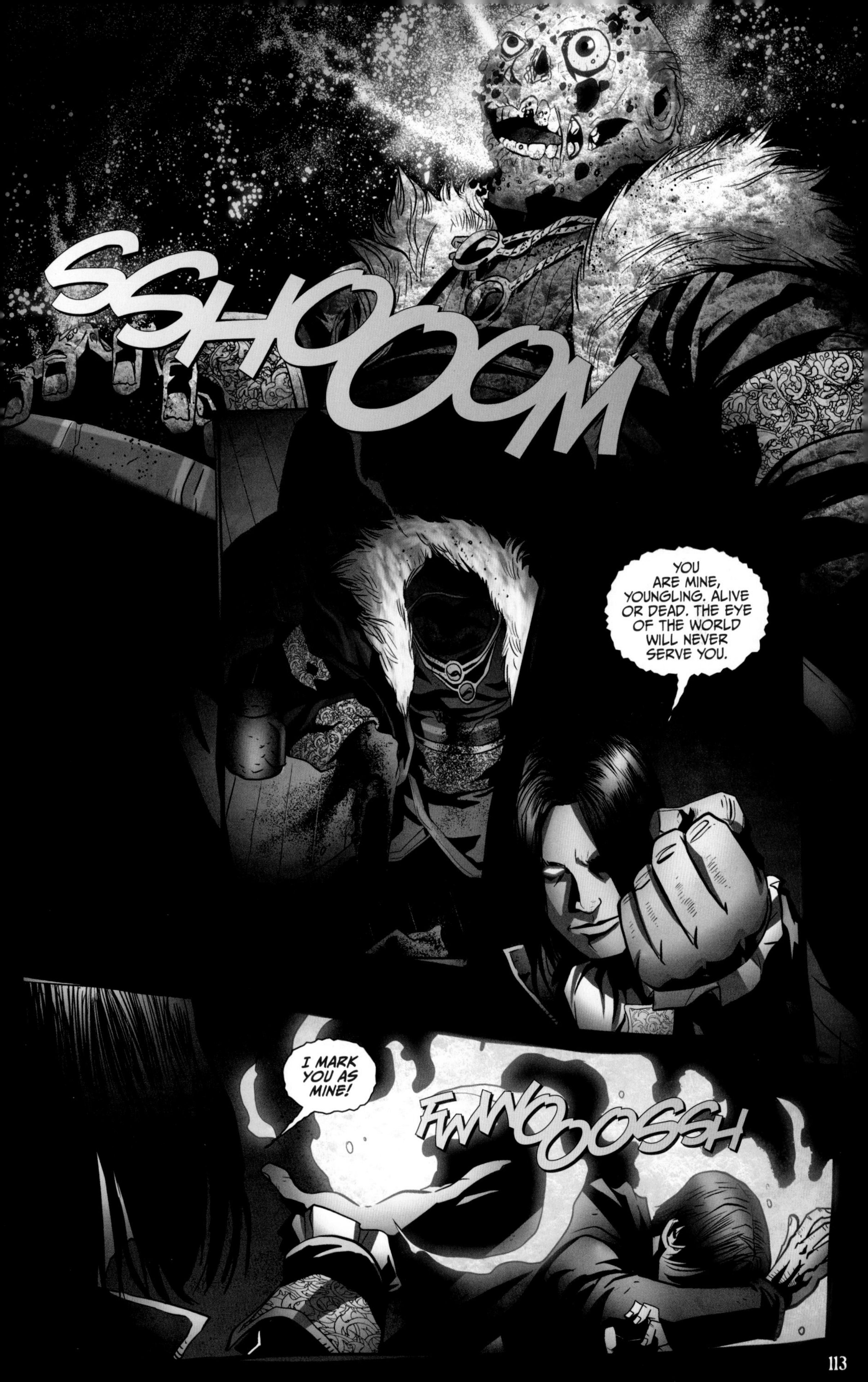
SSHOOOOM
YOU ARE MINE, YOUNGLING. ALIVE OR DEAD. THE EYE OF THE WORLD WILL NEVER SERVE YOU.
I MARK YOU AS MINE!
FWWOOOSSH

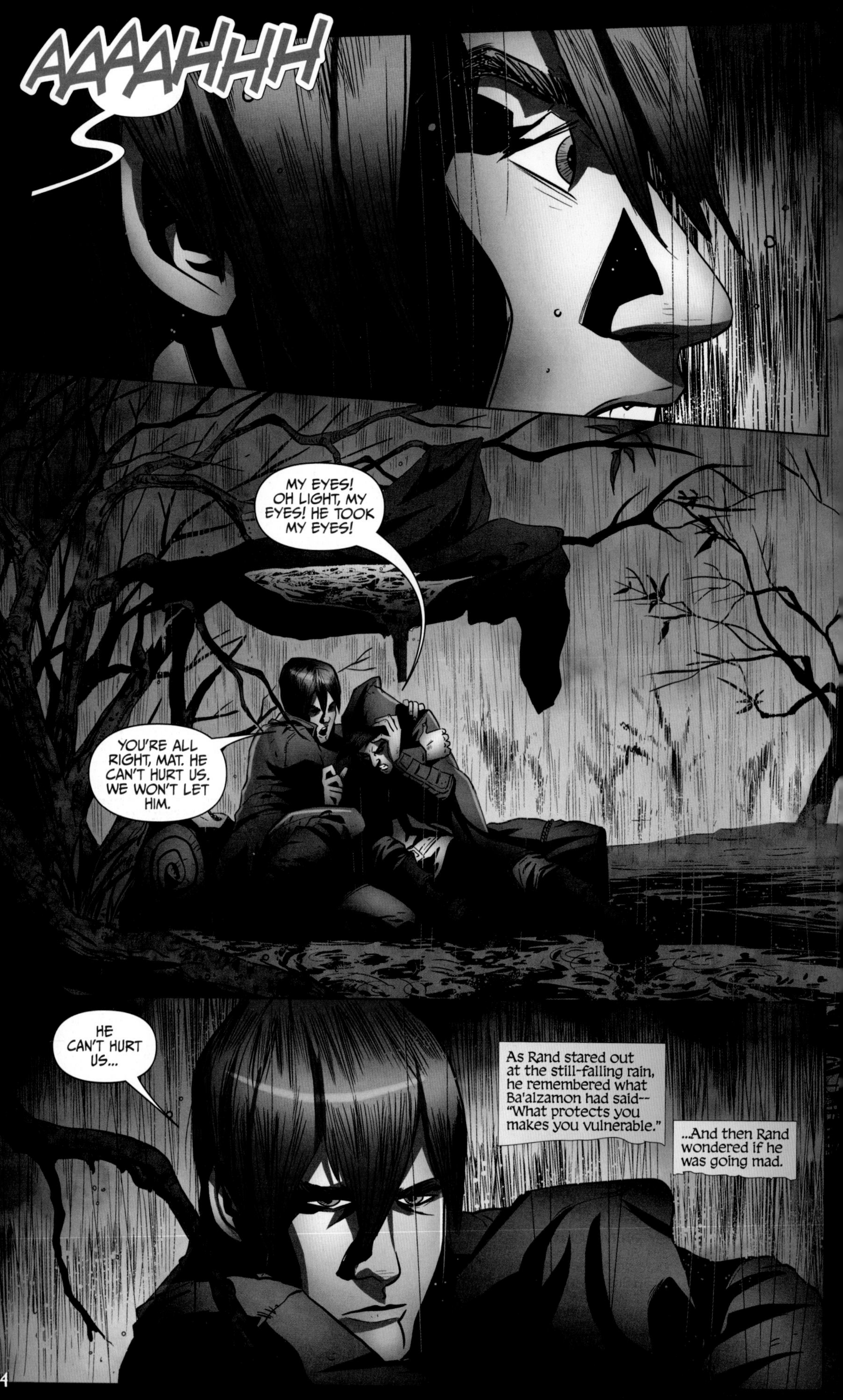
AAAAHHH
MY EYES! OH LIGHT, MY EYES! HE TOOK MY EYES!
YOU'RE ALL RIGHT, MAT. HE CAN'T HURT US. WE WON'T LET HIM.
HE CAN'T HURT US...
As Rand stared out at the still-falling rain, he remembered what Ba'alzamon had said--"What protects you makes you vulnerable."
...And then Rand wondered if he was going mad.

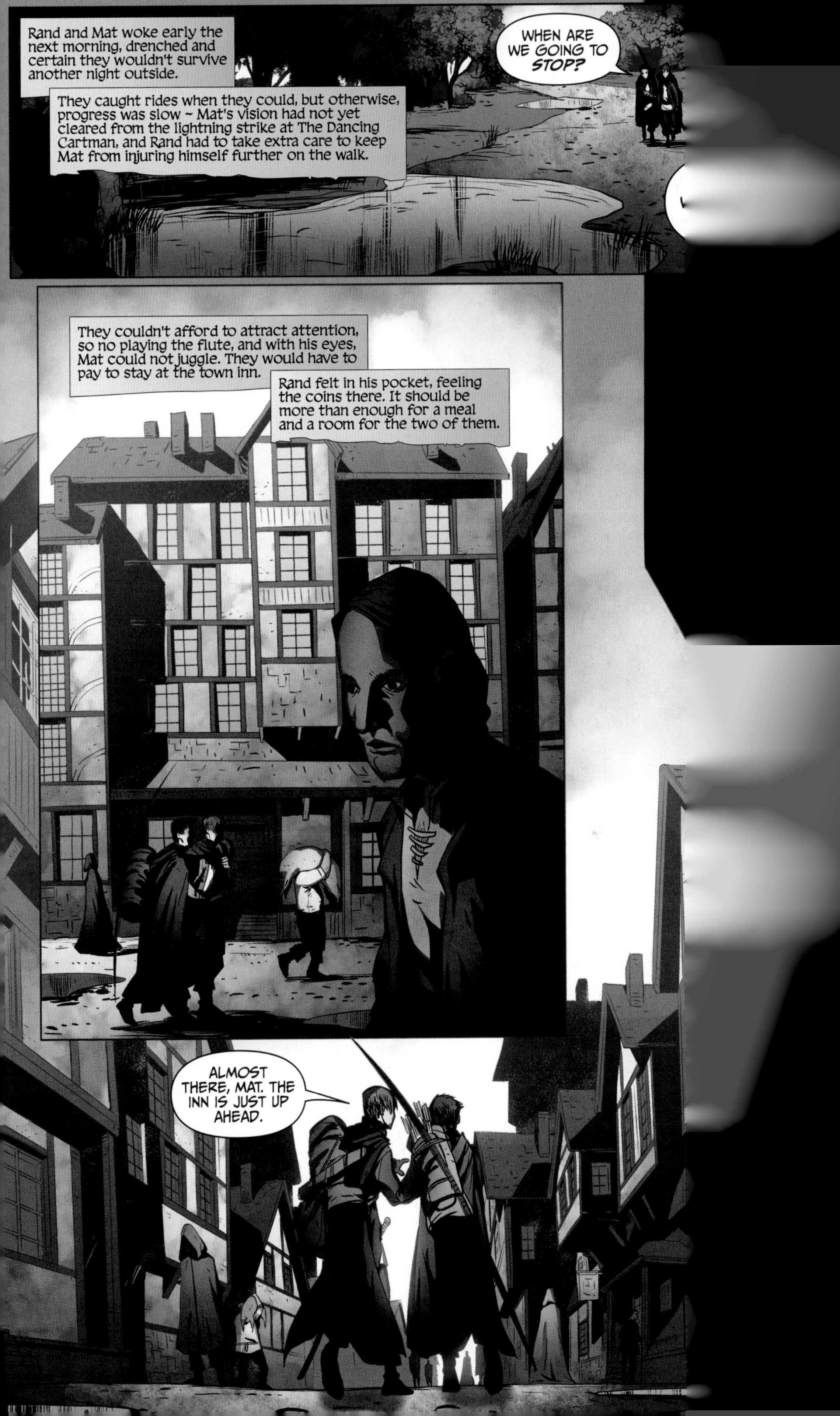
Rand and Mat woke early the next morning, drenched and certain they wouldn't survive another night outside.
WHEN ARE WE GOING TO STOP?
They caught rides when they could, but otherwise, progress was slow ~ Mat's vision had not yet cleared from the lightning strike at The Dancing Cartman, and Rand had to take extra care to keep Mat from injuring himself further on the walk.
They couldn't afford to attract attention, so no playing the flute, and with his eyes, Mat could not juggle. They would have to pay to stay at the town inn.
Rand felt in his pocket, feeling the coins there. It should be more than enough for a meal and a room for the two of them.
ALMOST THERE, MAT. THE INN IS JUST UP AHEAD.

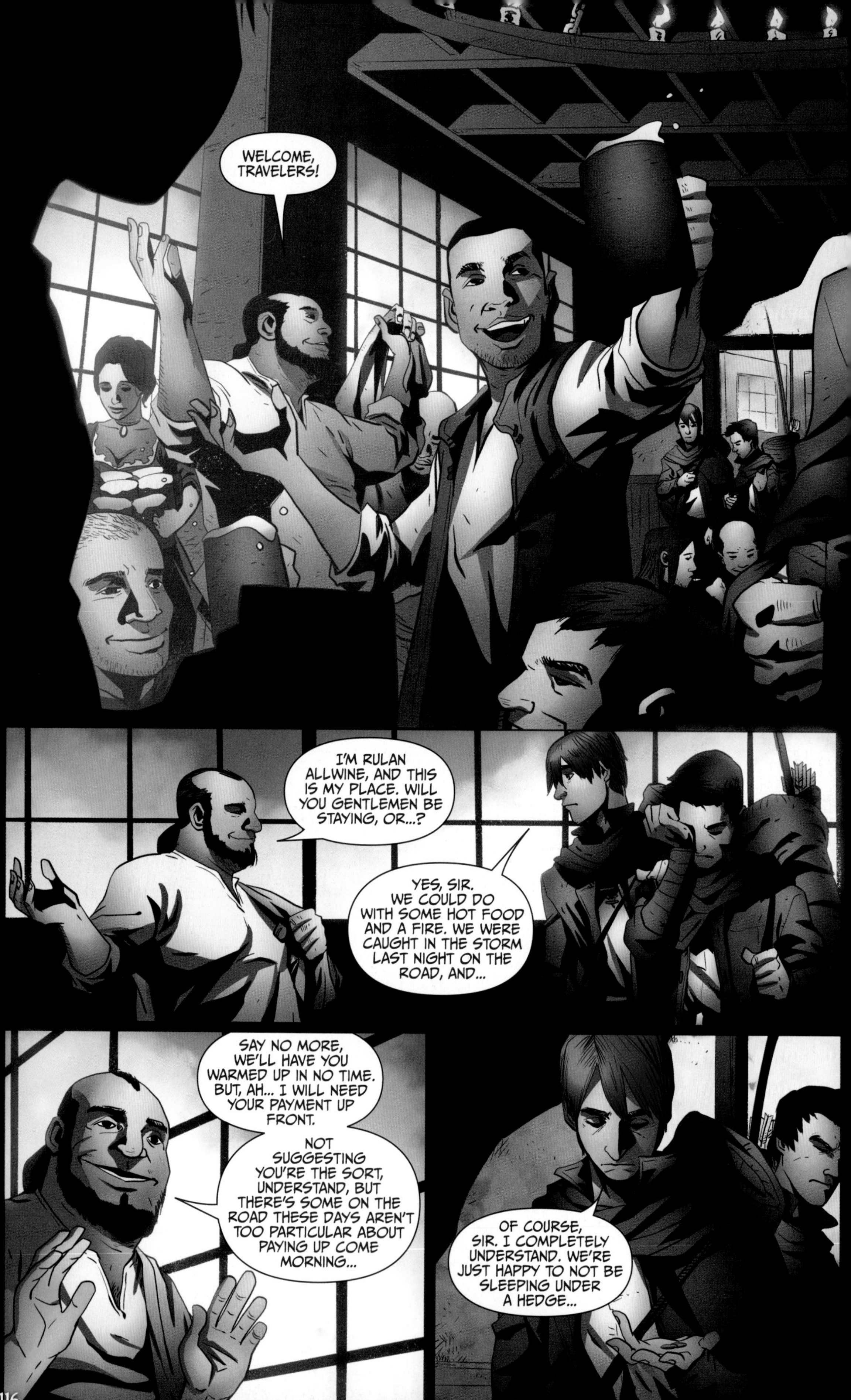
WELCOME, TRAVELERS!
I'M RULAN ALLWINE, AND THIS IS MY PLACE. WILL YOU GENTLEMEN BE STAYING, OR...?
YES, SIR. WE COULD DO WITH SOME HOT FOOD AND A FIRE. WE WERE CAUGHT IN THE STORM LAST NIGHT ON THE ROAD, AND...
SAY NO MORE, WE'LL HAVE YOU WARMED UP IN NO TIME. BUT, AH... I WILL NEED YOUR PAYMENT UP FRONT.
NOT SUGGESTING YOU'RE THE SORT, UNDERSTAND, BUT THERE'S SOME ON THE ROAD THESE DAYS AREN'T TOO PARTICULAR ABOUT PAYING UP COME MORNING...
OF COURSE, SIR. I COMPLETELY UNDERSTAND. WE'RE JUST HAPPY TO NOT BE SLEEPING UNDER A HEDGE...

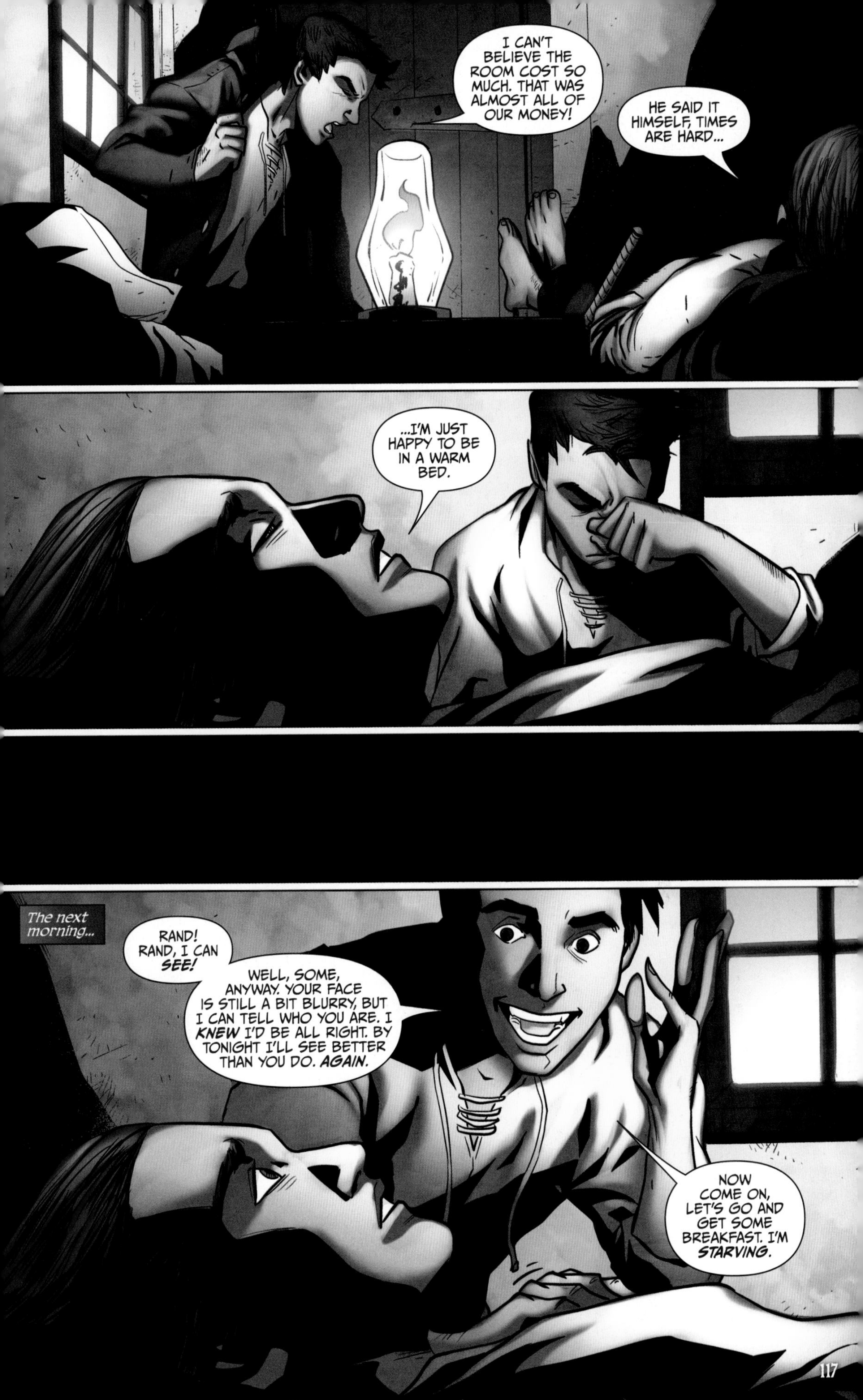
I CAN'T BELIEVE THE ROOM COST SO MUCH. THAT WAS ALMOST ALL OF OUR MONEY!
HE SAID IT HIMSELF, TIMES ARE HARD...
...I'M JUST HAPPY TO BE IN A WARM BED.
The next morning...
RAND! RAND, I CAN ***SEE!***
WELL, SOME, ANYWAY. YOUR FACE IS STILL A BIT BLURRY, BUT I CAN TELL WHO YOU ARE. I ***KNEW*** I'D BE ALL RIGHT. BY TONIGHT I'LL SEE BETTER THAN YOU DO. ***AGAIN.***
NOW COME ON, LET'S GO AND GET SOME BREAKFAST. I'M ***STARVING.***

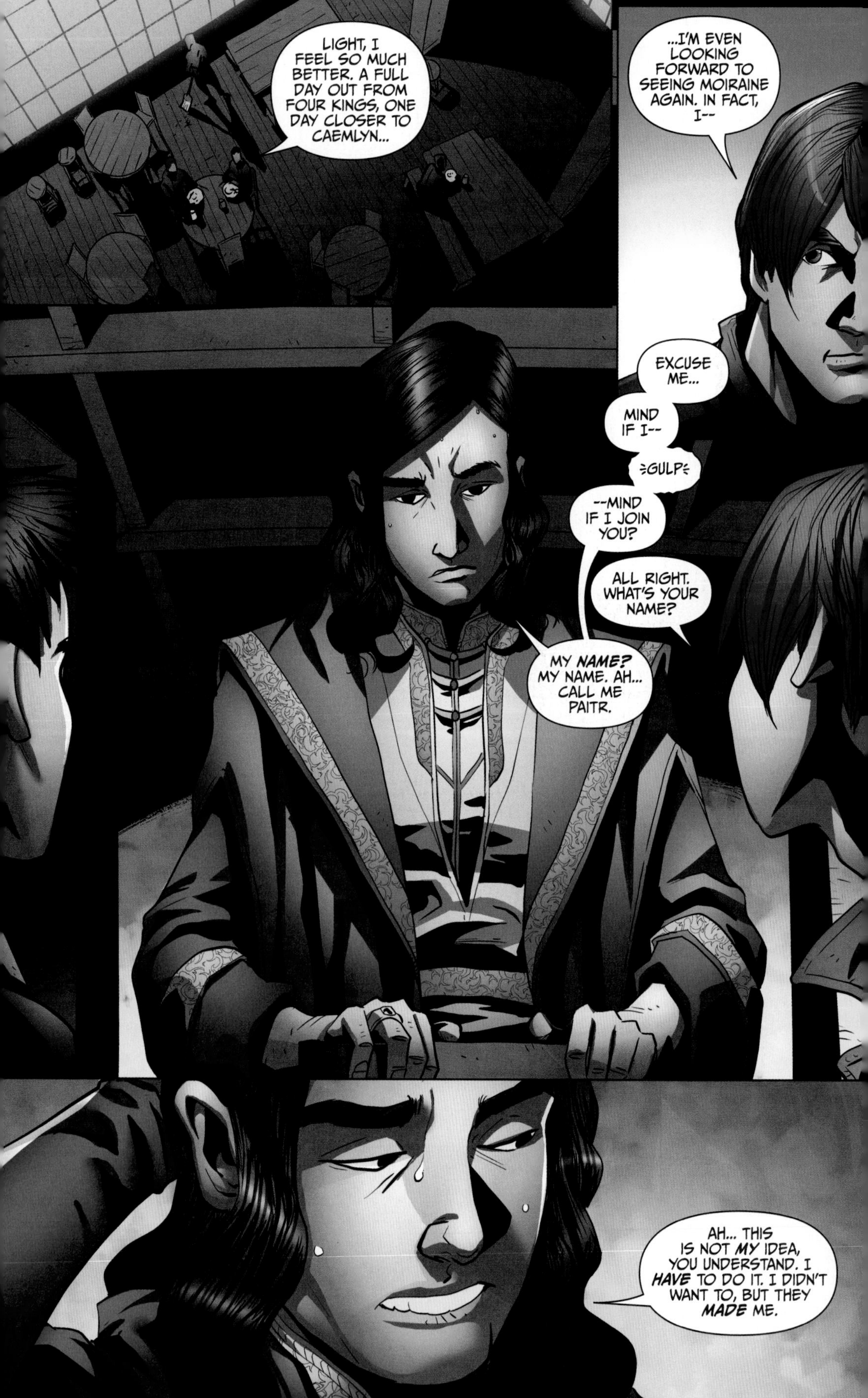
LIGHT, I FEEL SO MUCH BETTER. A FULL DAY OUT FROM FOUR KINGS, ONE DAY CLOSER TO CAEMLYN...
...I'M EVEN LOOKING FORWARD TO SEEING MOIRAINE AGAIN. IN FACT, I--
EXCUSE ME...
MIND IF I--
GULP
--MIND IF I JOIN YOU?
ALL RIGHT. WHAT'S YOUR NAME?
MY *NAME?* MY NAME. AH... CALL ME PAITR.
AH... THIS IS NOT *MY* IDEA, YOU UNDERSTAND. I *HAVE* TO DO IT. I DIDN'T WANT TO, BUT THEY *MADE* ME.

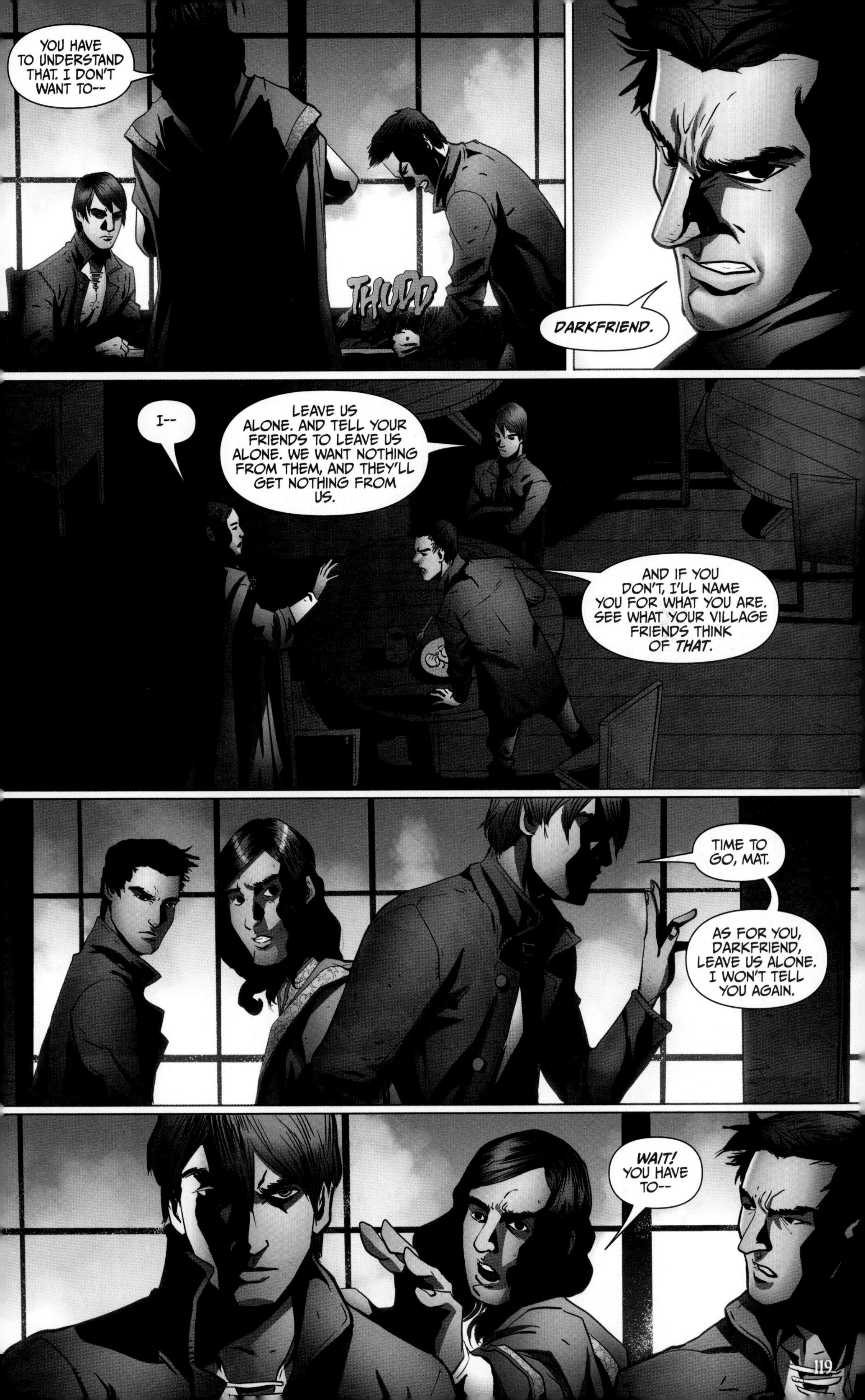

YOU HAVE TO UNDERSTAND THAT. I DON'T WANT TO--
THUDD
DARKFRIEND.
I--
LEAVE US ALONE. AND TELL YOUR FRIENDS TO LEAVE US ALONE. WE WANT NOTHING FROM THEM, AND THEY'LL GET NOTHING FROM US.
AND IF YOU DON'T, I'LL NAME YOU FOR WHAT YOU ARE. SEE WHAT YOUR VILLAGE FRIENDS THINK OF *THAT*.
TIME TO GO, MAT.
AS FOR YOU, DARKFRIEND, LEAVE US ALONE. I WON'T TELL YOU AGAIN.
WAIT! YOU HAVE TO--

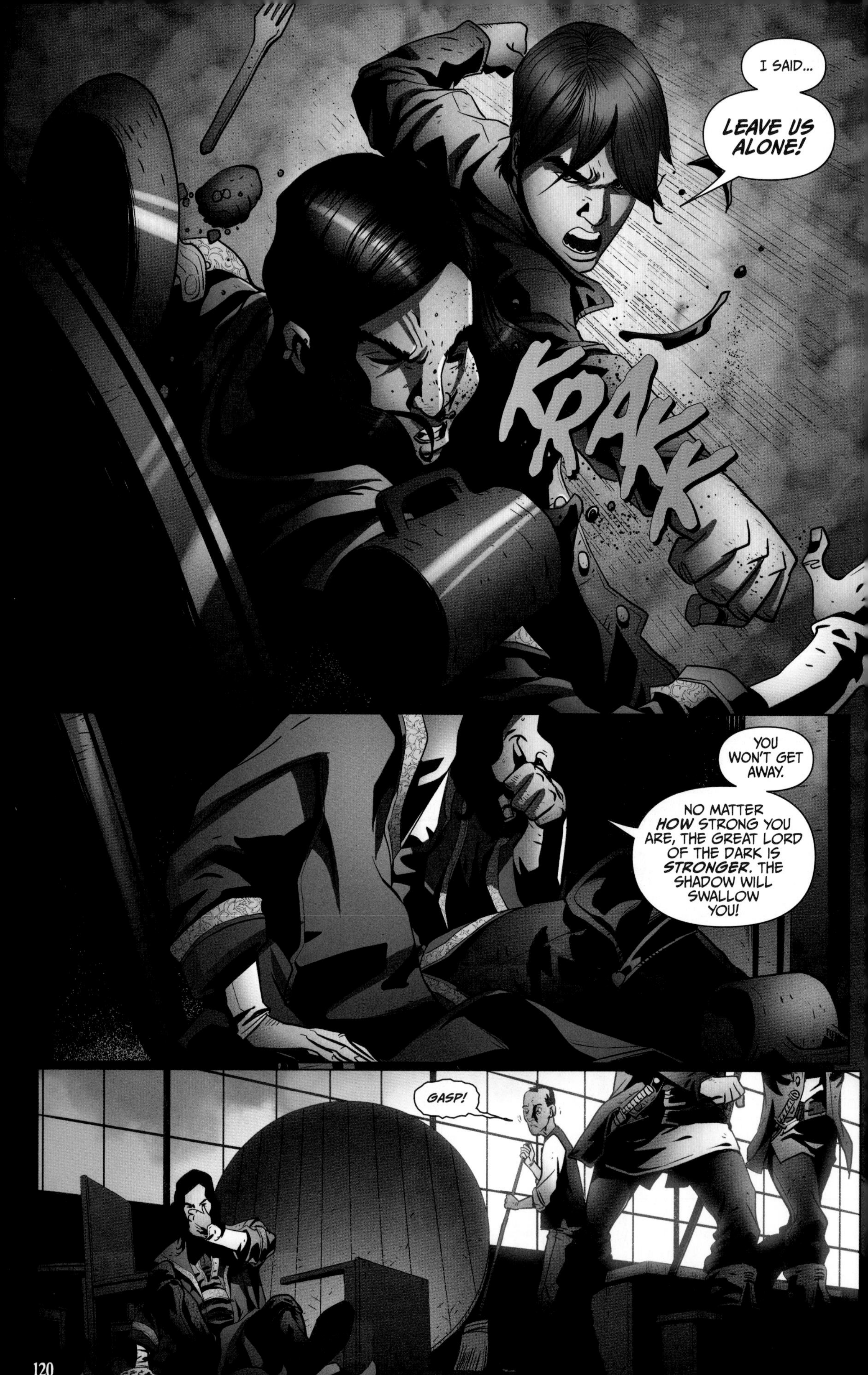
I SAID...
LEAVE US ALONE!
KRAKK
YOU WON'T GET AWAY.
NO MATTER HOW STRONG YOU ARE, THE GREAT LORD OF THE DARK IS STRONGER. THE SHADOW WILL SWALLOW YOU!
GASP!

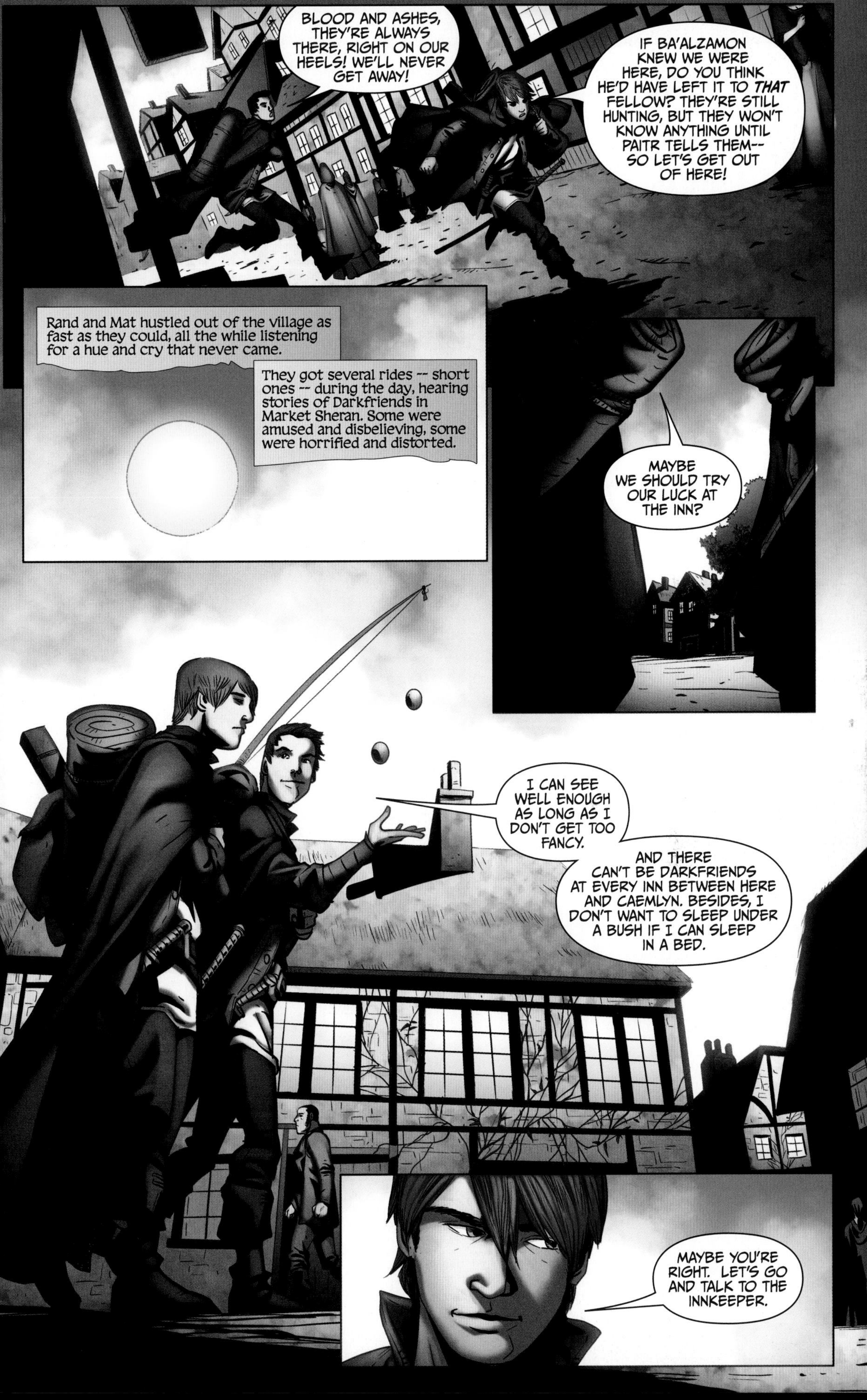
BLOOD AND ASHES, THEY'RE ALWAYS THERE, RIGHT ON OUR HEELS! WE'LL NEVER GET AWAY!
IF BA'ALZAMON KNEW WE WERE HERE, DO YOU THINK HE'D HAVE LEFT IT TO *THAT* FELLOW? THEY'RE STILL HUNTING, BUT THEY WON'T KNOW ANYTHING UNTIL PAITR TELLS THEM-- SO LET'S GET OUT OF HERE!
Rand and Mat hustled out of the village as fast as they could, all the while listening for a hue and cry that never came.
They got several rides -- short ones -- during the day, hearing stories of Darkfriends in Market Sheran. Some were amused and disbelieving, some were horrified and distorted.
MAYBE WE SHOULD TRY OUR LUCK AT THE INN?
I CAN SEE WELL ENOUGH AS LONG AS I DON'T GET TOO FANCY.
AND THERE CAN'T BE DARKFRIENDS AT EVERY INN BETWEEN HERE AND CAEMLYN. BESIDES, I DON'T WANT TO SLEEP UNDER A BUSH IF I CAN SLEEP IN A BED.
MAYBE YOU'RE RIGHT. LET'S GO AND TALK TO THE INNKEEPER.

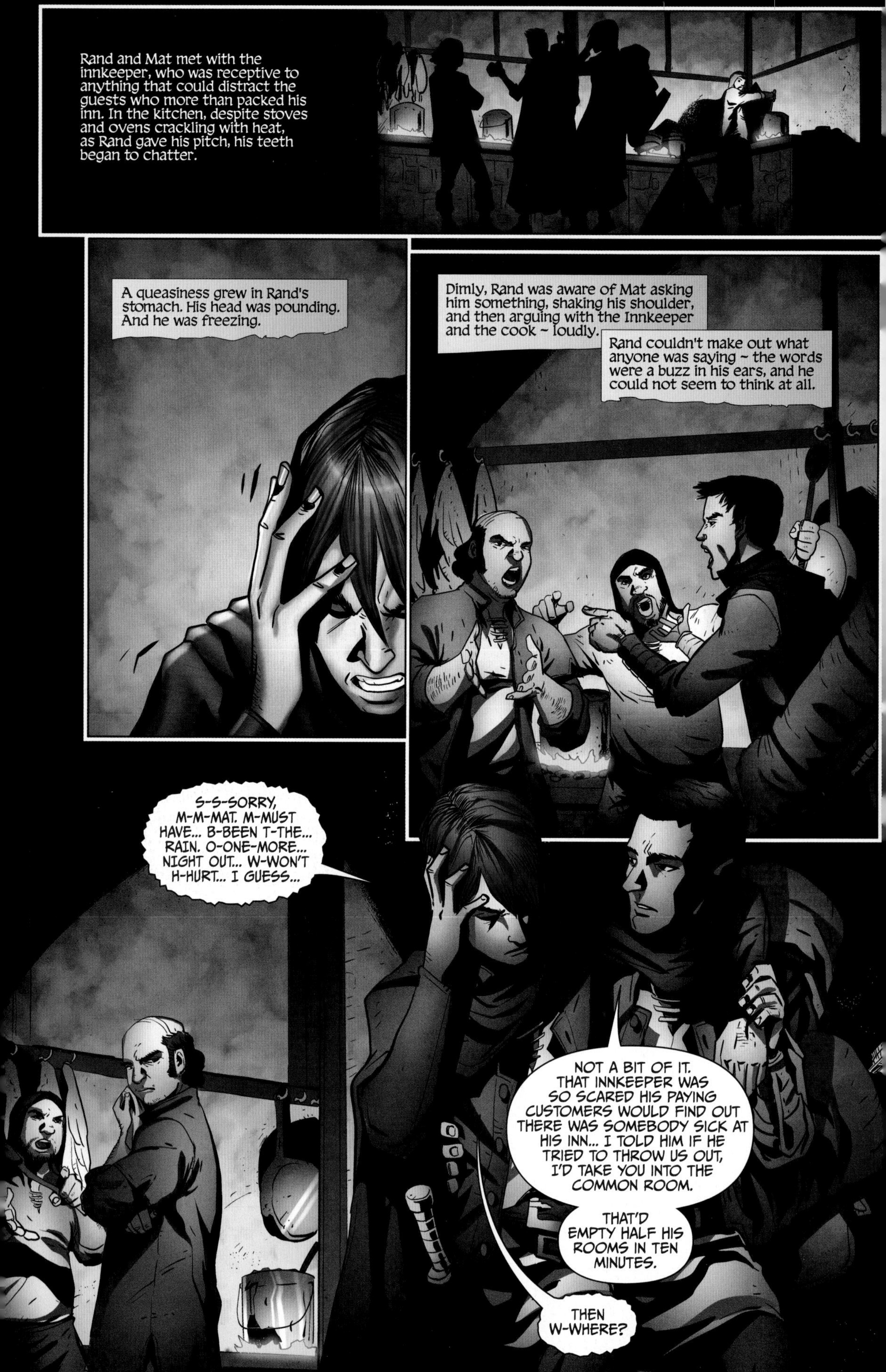

Rand and Mat met with the innkeeper, who was receptive to anything that could distract the guests who more than packed his inn. In the kitchen, despite stoves and ovens crackling with heat, as Rand gave his pitch, his teeth began to chatter.
A queasiness grew in Rand's stomach. His head was pounding. And he was freezing.
Dimly, Rand was aware of Mat asking him something, shaking his shoulder, and then arguing with the Innkeeper and the cook ~ loudly.
Rand couldn't make out what anyone was saying ~ the words were a buzz in his ears, and he could not seem to think at all.
S-S-SORRY, M-M-MAT. M-MUST HAVE... B-BEEN T-THE... RAIN. O-ONE-MORE... NIGHT OUT... W-WON'T H-HURT... I GUESS...
NOT A BIT OF IT. THAT INNKEEPER WAS SO SCARED HIS PAYING CUSTOMERS WOULD FIND OUT THERE WAS SOMEBODY SICK AT HIS INN... I TOLD HIM IF HE TRIED TO THROW US OUT, I'D TAKE YOU INTO THE COMMON ROOM.
THAT'D EMPTY HALF HIS ROOMS IN TEN MINUTES.
THEN W-WHERE?

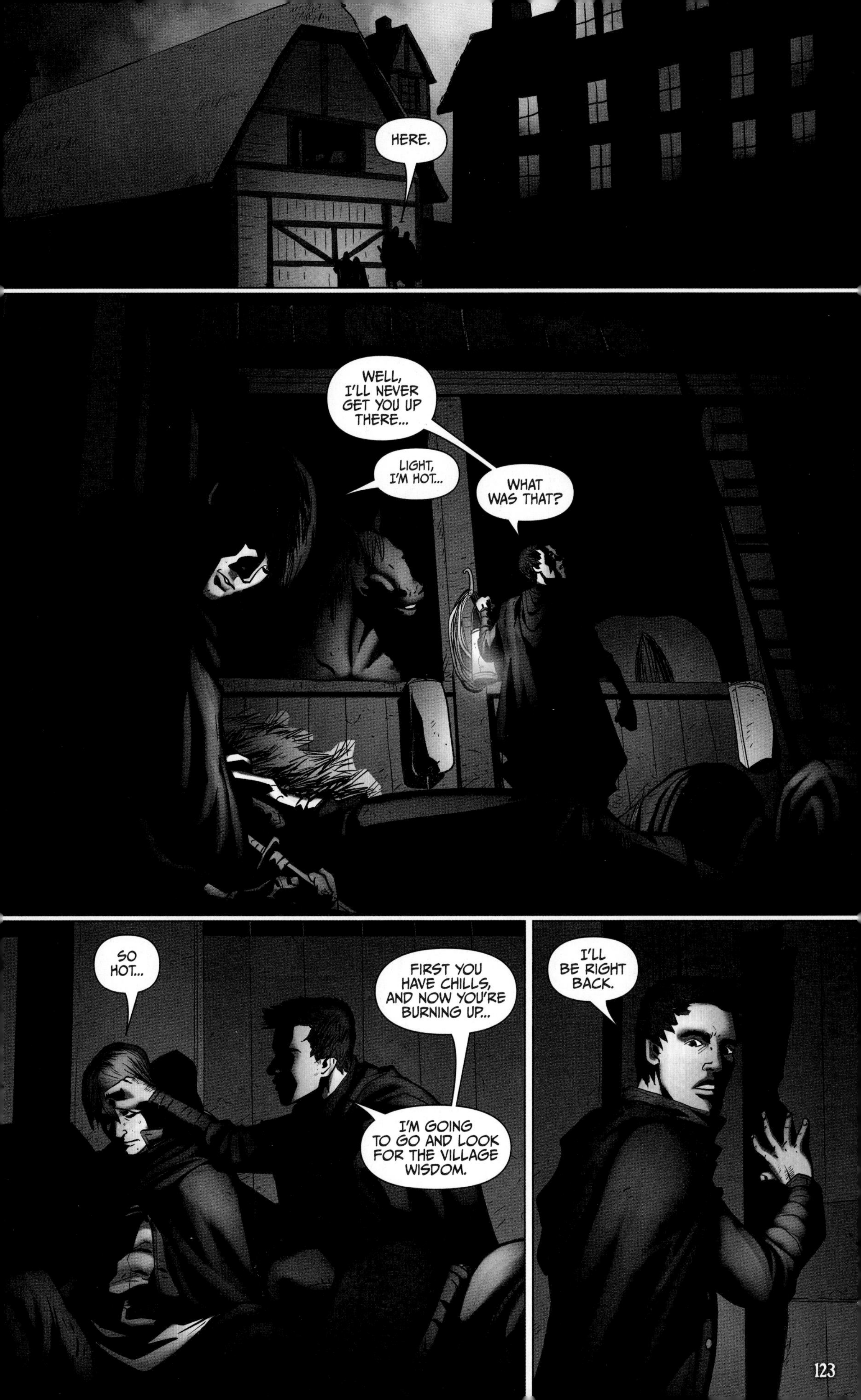
HERE.
WELL, I'LL NEVER GET YOU UP THERE...
LIGHT, I'M HOT...
WHAT WAS THAT?
SO HOT...
FIRST YOU HAVE CHILLS, AND NOW YOU'RE BURNING UP...
I'M GOING TO GO AND LOOK FOR THE VILLAGE WISDOM.
I'LL BE RIGHT BACK.

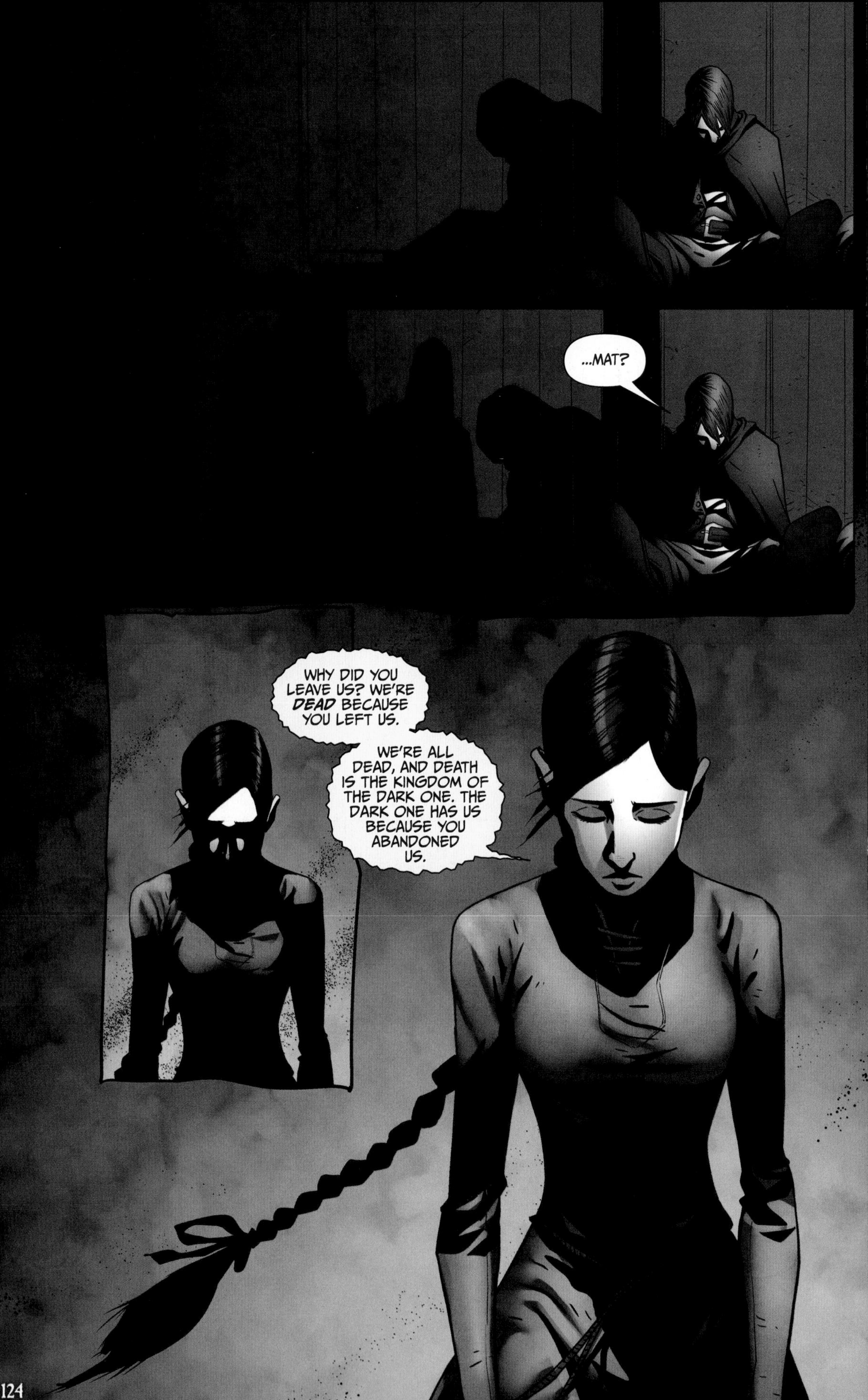
...MAT?
WHY DID YOU LEAVE US? WE'RE *DEAD* BECAUSE YOU LEFT US.
WE'RE ALL DEAD, AND DEATH IS THE KINGDOM OF THE DARK ONE. THE DARK ONE HAS US BECAUSE YOU ABANDONED US.

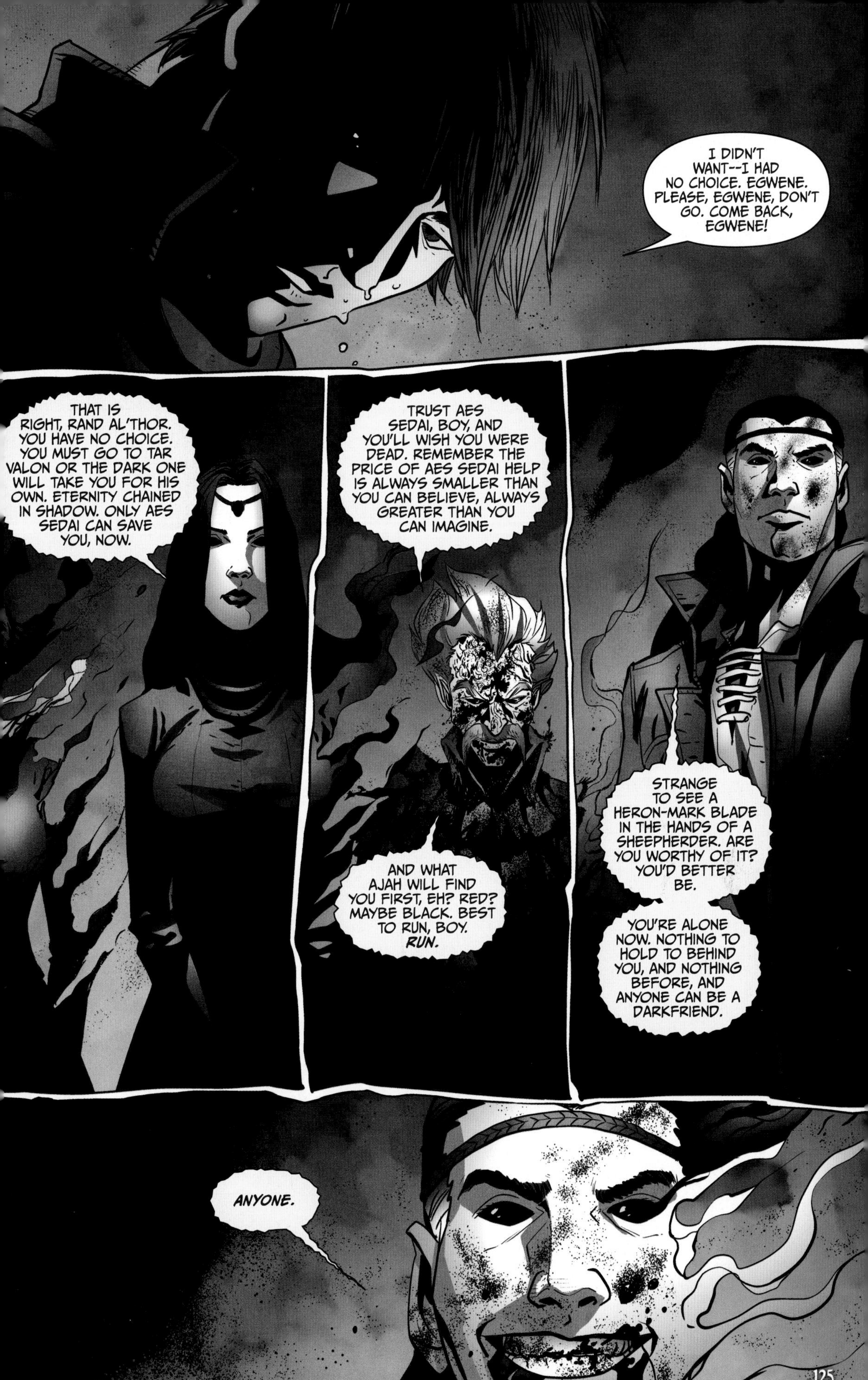
I DIDN'T WANT--I HAD NO CHOICE. EGWENE. PLEASE, EGWENE, DON'T GO. COME BACK, EGWENE!
THAT IS RIGHT, RAND AL'THOR. YOU HAVE NO CHOICE. YOU MUST GO TO TAR VALON OR THE DARK ONE WILL TAKE YOU FOR HIS OWN. ETERNITY CHAINED IN SHADOW. ONLY AES SEDAI CAN SAVE YOU, NOW.
TRUST AES SEDAI, BOY, AND YOU'LL WISH YOU WERE DEAD. REMEMBER THE PRICE OF AES SEDAI HELP IS ALWAYS SMALLER THAN YOU CAN BELIEVE, ALWAYS GREATER THAN YOU CAN IMAGINE.
AND WHAT AJAH WILL FIND YOU FIRST, EH? RED? MAYBE BLACK. BEST TO RUN, BOY. *RUN.*
STRANGE TO SEE A HERON-MARK BLADE IN THE HANDS OF A SHEEPHERDER. ARE YOU WORTHY OF IT? YOU'D BETTER BE.
YOU'RE ALONE NOW. NOTHING TO HOLD TO BEHIND YOU, AND NOTHING BEFORE, AND ANYONE CAN BE A DARKFRIEND.
ANYONE.

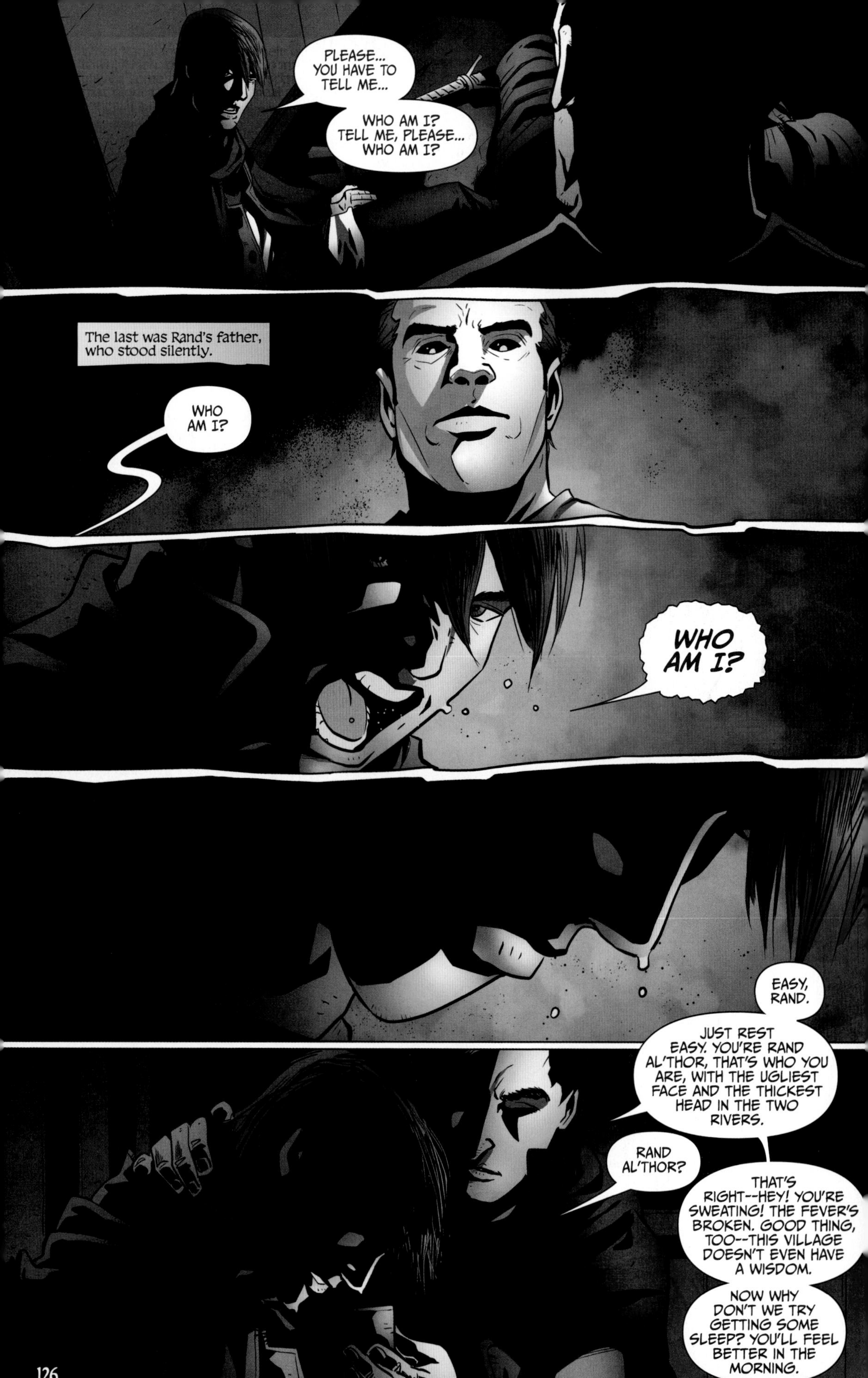
PLEASE... YOU HAVE TO TELL ME...
WHO AM I? TELL ME, PLEASE... WHO AM I?
The last was Rand's father, who stood silently.
WHO AM I?
WHO AM I?
EASY, RAND.
JUST REST EASY. YOU'RE RAND AL'THOR, THAT'S WHO YOU ARE, WITH THE UGLIEST FACE AND THE THICKEST HEAD IN THE TWO RIVERS.
RAND AL'THOR?
THAT'S RIGHT--HEY! YOU'RE SWEATING! THE FEVER'S BROKEN. GOOD THING, TOO--THIS VILLAGE DOESN'T EVEN HAVE A WISDOM.
NOW WHY DON'T WE TRY GETTING SOME SLEEP? YOU'LL FEEL BETTER IN THE MORNING.

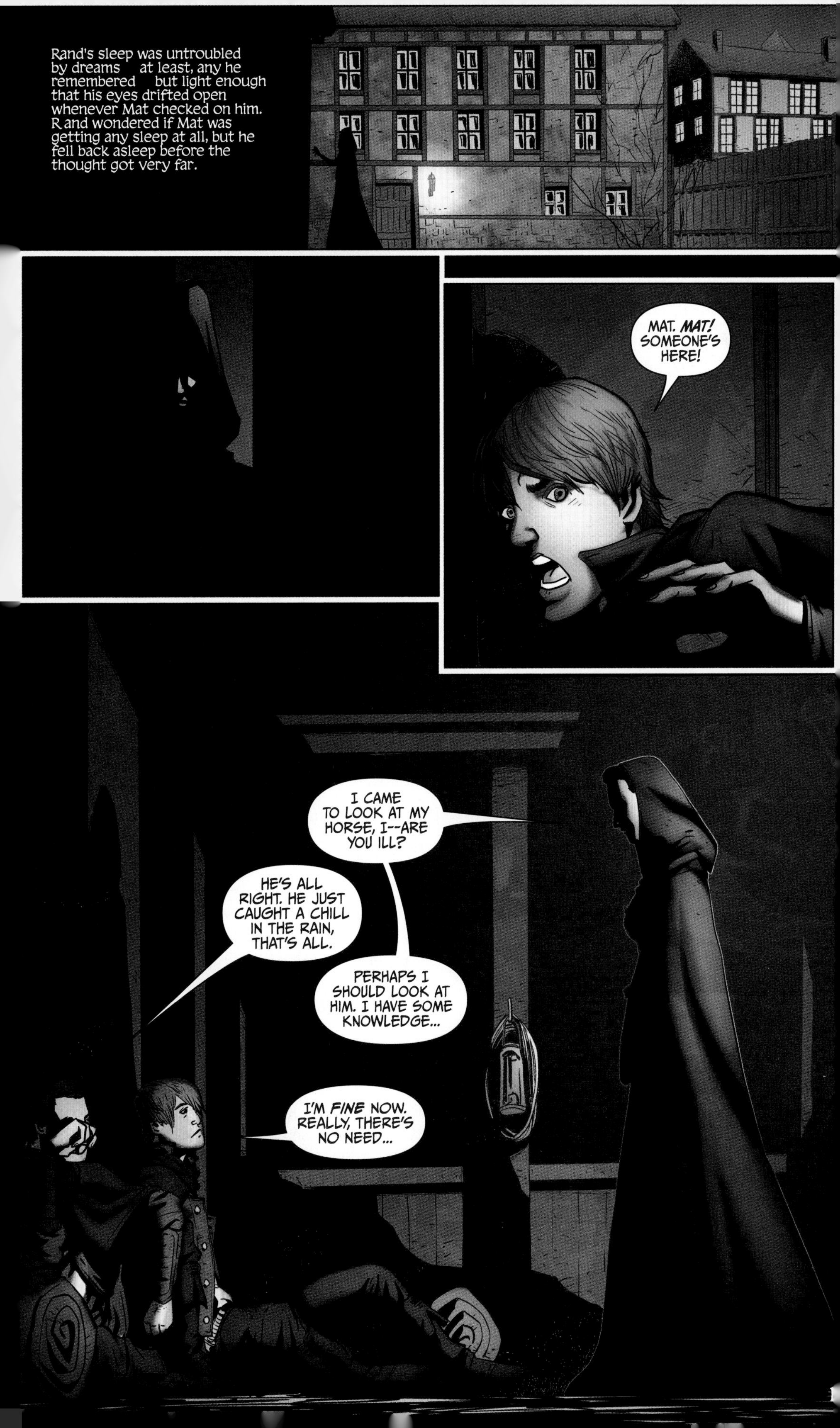
Rand's sleep was untroubled by dreams at least, any he remembered but light enough that his eyes drifted open whenever Mat checked on him. Rand wondered if Mat was getting any sleep at all, but he fell back asleep before the thought got very far.
MAT. *MAT!* SOMEONE'S HERE!
I CAME TO LOOK AT MY HORSE, I--ARE YOU ILL?
HE'S ALL RIGHT. HE JUST CAUGHT A CHILL IN THE RAIN, THAT'S ALL.
PERHAPS I SHOULD LOOK AT HIM. I HAVE SOME KNOWLEDGE...
I'M *FINE* NOW. REALLY, THERE'S NO NEED...

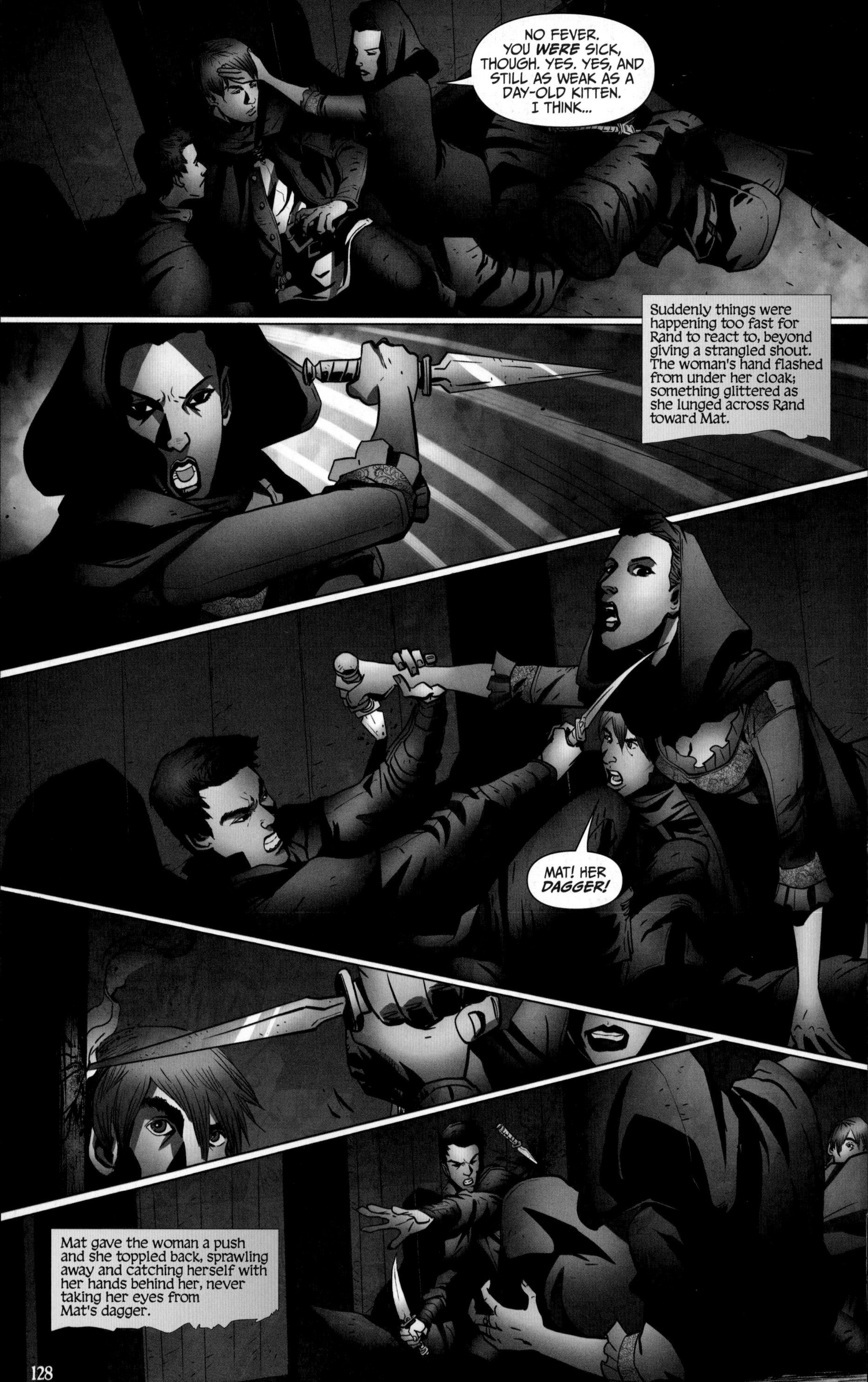
NO FEVER. YOU WERE SICK, THOUGH. YES. YES, AND STILL AS WEAK AS A DAY-OLD KITTEN. I THINK...
Suddenly things were happening too fast for Rand to react to, beyond giving a strangled shout. The woman's hand flashed from under her cloak; something glittered as she lunged across Rand toward Mat.
MAT! HER DAGGER!
Mat gave the woman a push and she toppled back, sprawling away and catching herself with her hands behind her, never taking her eyes from Mat's dagger.

DON'T MOVE.

WATCH HER, RAND.

Rand wasn't sure what he was supposed to do if she tried anything; he certainly could not run after her if she tried to flee.

When Mat pulled her dagger from the wall, the black spot it caused stopped growing, though a faint wisp of smoke still trailed up from it.

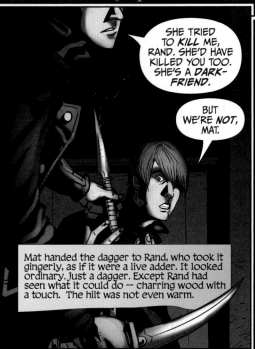

SHE TRIED TO *KILL* ME, RAND. SHE'D HAVE KILLED YOU TOO. SHE'S A *DARK-FRIEND*.

BUT WE'RE *NOT*, MAT.

Mat handed the dagger to Rand, who took it gingerly, as if it were a live adder. It looked ordinary. Just a dagger. Except Rand had seen what it could do -- charring wood with a touch. The hilt was not even warm.

YOU REALLY SHOULD STOP STRUGGLING. IT WOULD BE FOR THE BEST.

YOU WILL HAVE HONORED PLACES IF YOU COME TO THE GREAT LORD OF YOUR OWN FREE WILL, BUT AS LONG AS YOU RUN, THERE WILL BE PURSUIT, AND WHO CAN TELL WHAT WILL HAPPEN THEN?

SO YOU'RE HAVING TROUBLE WITH A COUPLE OF FARMBOYS. MAYBE YOU DARKFRIENDS AREN'T AS DANGEROUS AS I'VE ALWAYS HEARD.

YOU WILL FIND OUT HOW DANGEROUS WE ARE.

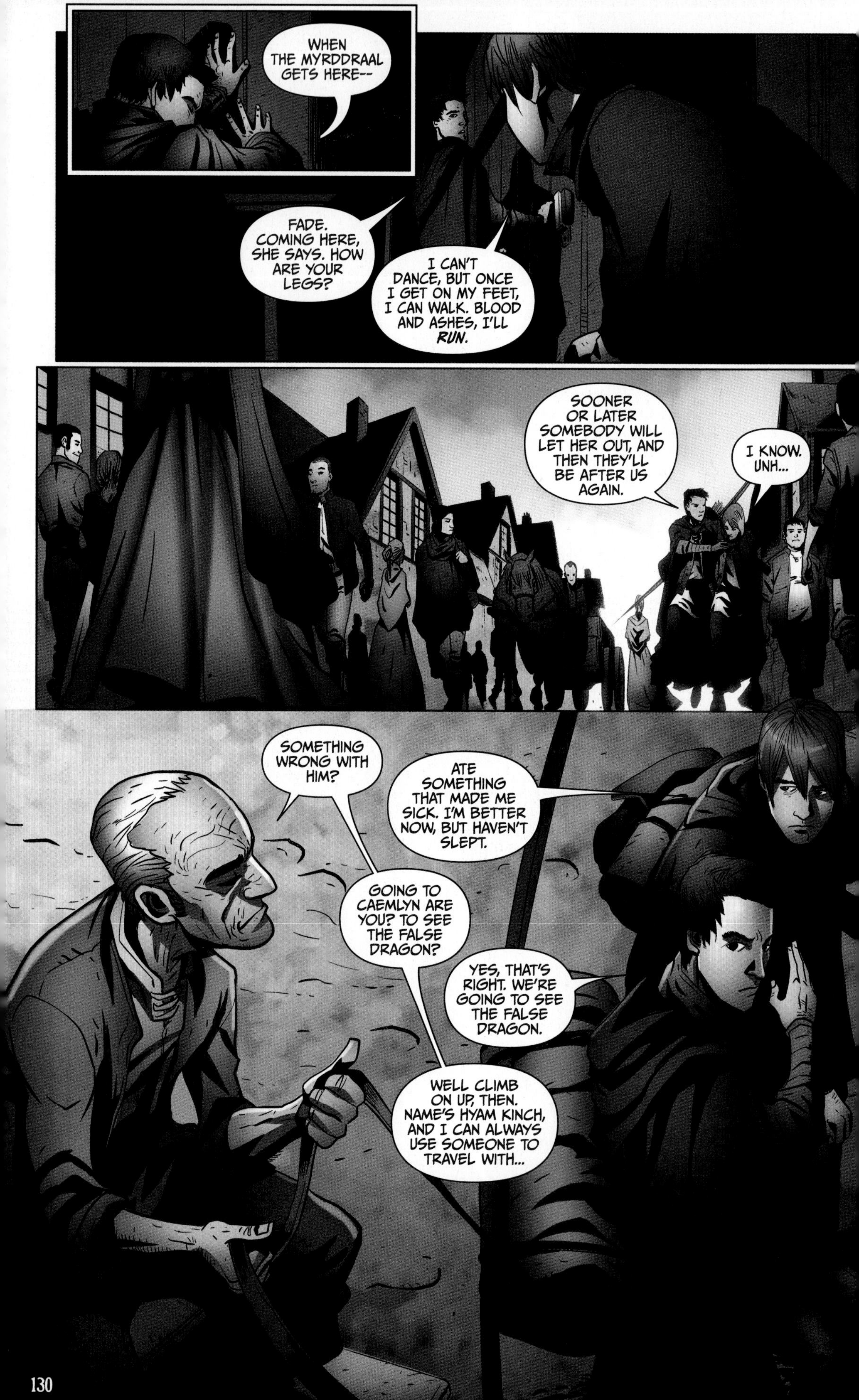

WHEN THE MYRDDRAAL GETS HERE--
FADE. COMING HERE, SHE SAYS. HOW ARE YOUR LEGS?
I CAN'T DANCE, BUT ONCE I GET ON MY FEET, I CAN WALK. BLOOD AND ASHES, I'LL RUN.
SOONER OR LATER SOMEBODY WILL LET HER OUT, AND THEN THEY'LL BE AFTER US AGAIN.
I KNOW. UNH...
SOMETHING WRONG WITH HIM?
ATE SOMETHING THAT MADE ME SICK. I'M BETTER NOW, BUT HAVEN'T SLEPT.
GOING TO CAEMLYN ARE YOU? TO SEE THE FALSE DRAGON?
YES, THAT'S RIGHT. WE'RE GOING TO SEE THE FALSE DRAGON.
WELL CLIMB ON UP, THEN. NAME'S HYAM KINCH, AND I CAN ALWAYS USE SOMEONE TO TRAVEL WITH...

chapter six

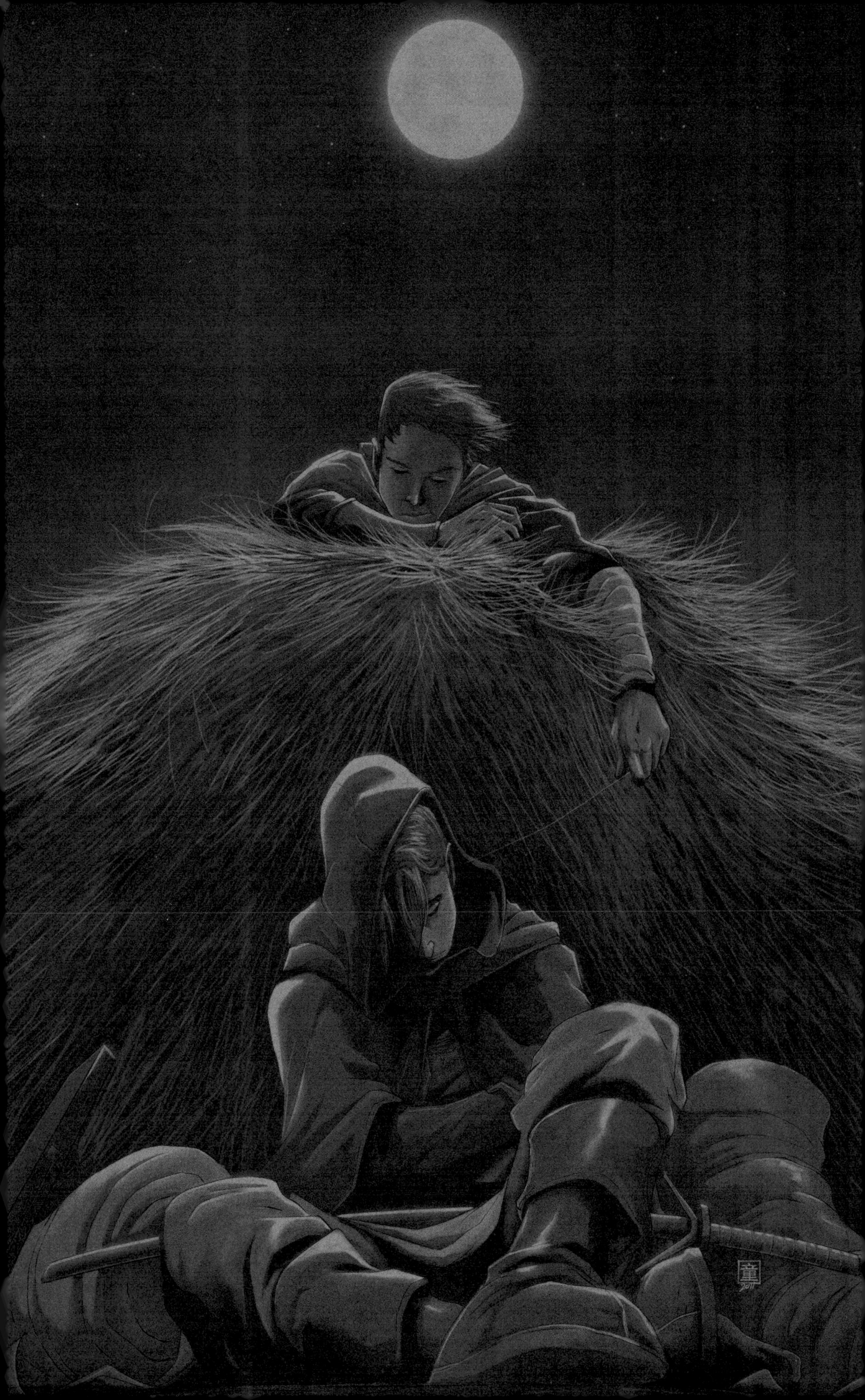

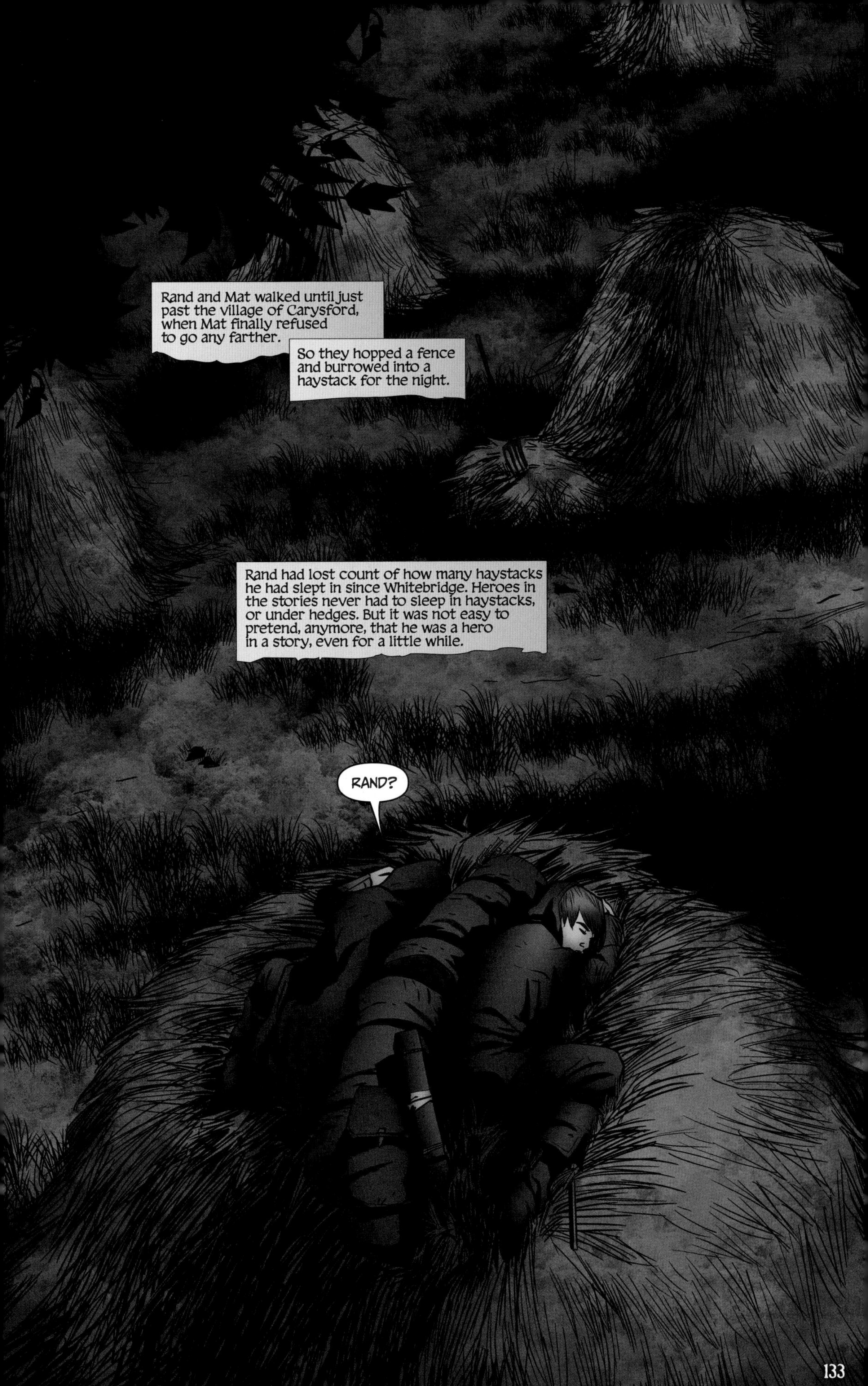
Rand and Mat walked until just past the village of Carysford, when Mat finally refused to go any farther.
So they hopped a fence and burrowed into a haystack for the night.
Rand had lost count of how many haystacks he had slept in since Whitebridge. Heroes in the stories never had to sleep in haystacks, or under hedges. But it was not easy to pretend, anymore, that he was a hero in a story, even for a little while.
RAND?

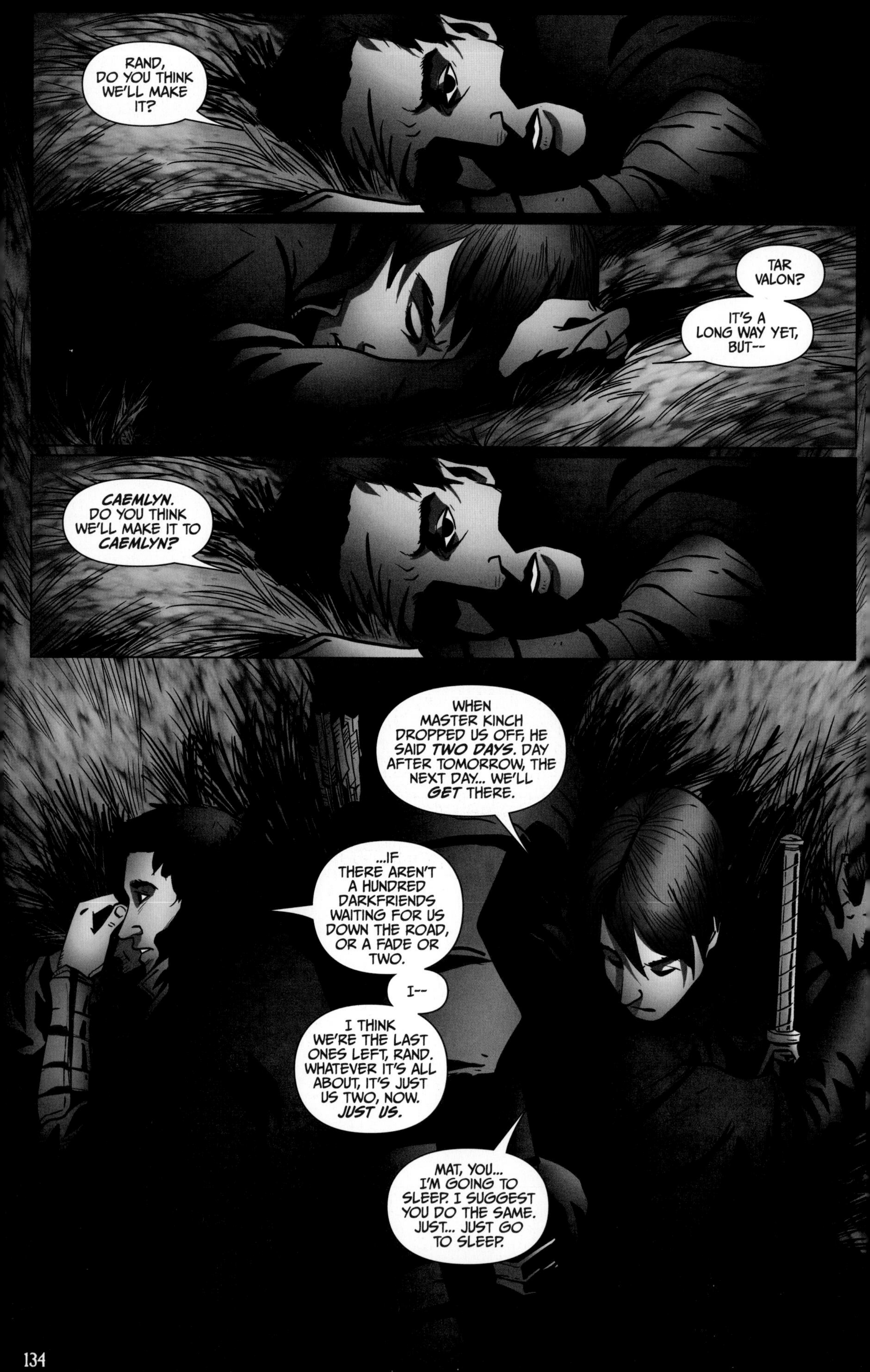
RAND, DO YOU THINK WE'LL MAKE IT?
TAR VALON?
IT'S A LONG WAY YET, BUT--
CAEMLYN. DO YOU THINK WE'LL MAKE IT TO CAEMLYN?
WHEN MASTER KINCH DROPPED US OFF, HE SAID TWO DAYS. DAY AFTER TOMORROW, THE NEXT DAY... WE'LL GET THERE.
...IF THERE AREN'T A HUNDRED DARKFRIENDS WAITING FOR US DOWN THE ROAD, OR A FADE OR TWO.
I--
I THINK WE'RE THE LAST ONES LEFT, RAND. WHATEVER IT'S ALL ABOUT, IT'S JUST US TWO, NOW. JUST US.
MAT, YOU... I'M GOING TO SLEEP. I SUGGEST YOU DO THE SAME. JUST... JUST GO TO SLEEP.

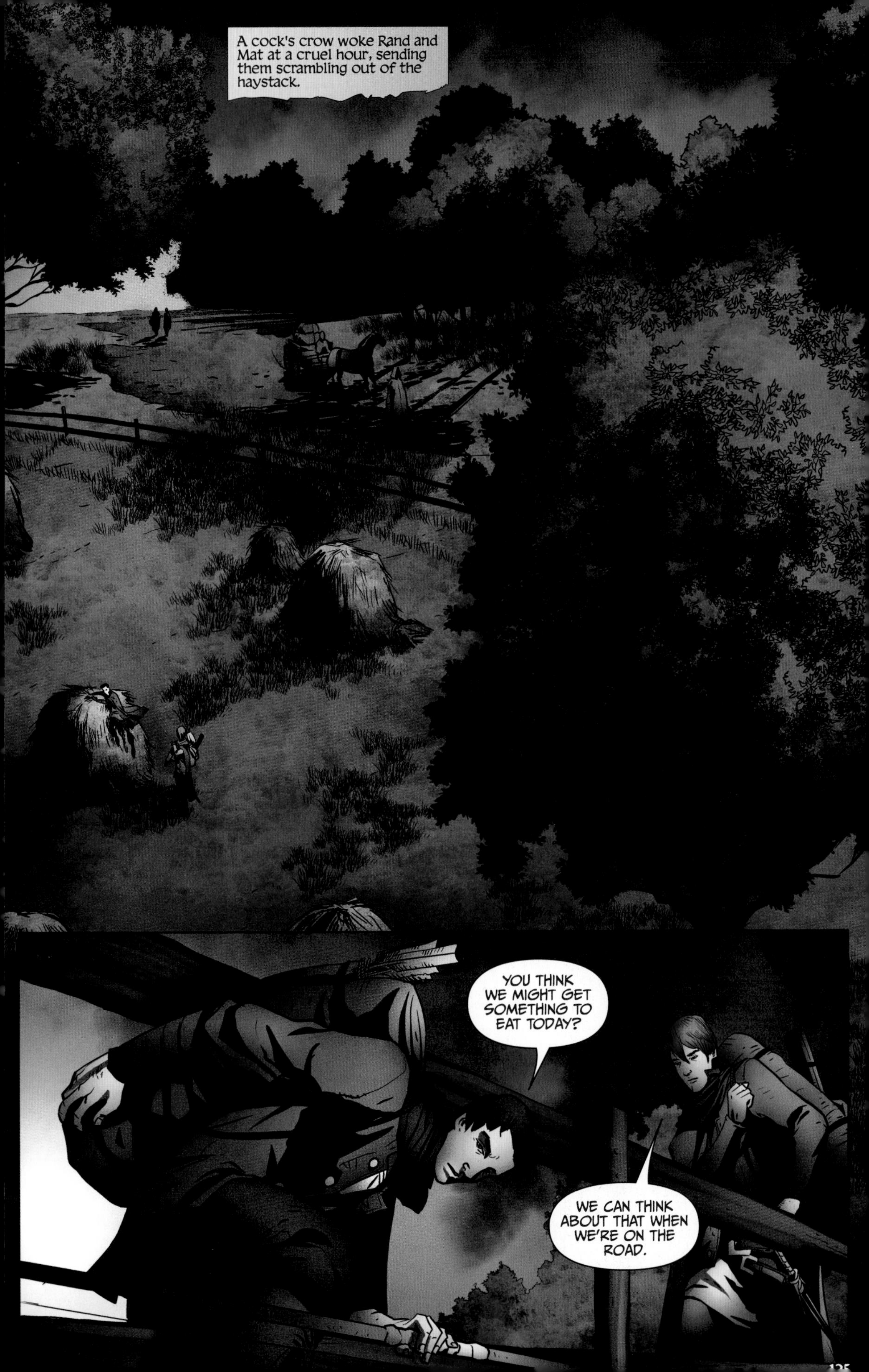
A cock's crow woke Rand and Mat at a cruel hour, sending them scrambling out of the haystack.
YOU THINK WE MIGHT GET SOMETHING TO EAT TODAY?
WE CAN THINK ABOUT THAT WHEN WE'RE ON THE ROAD.

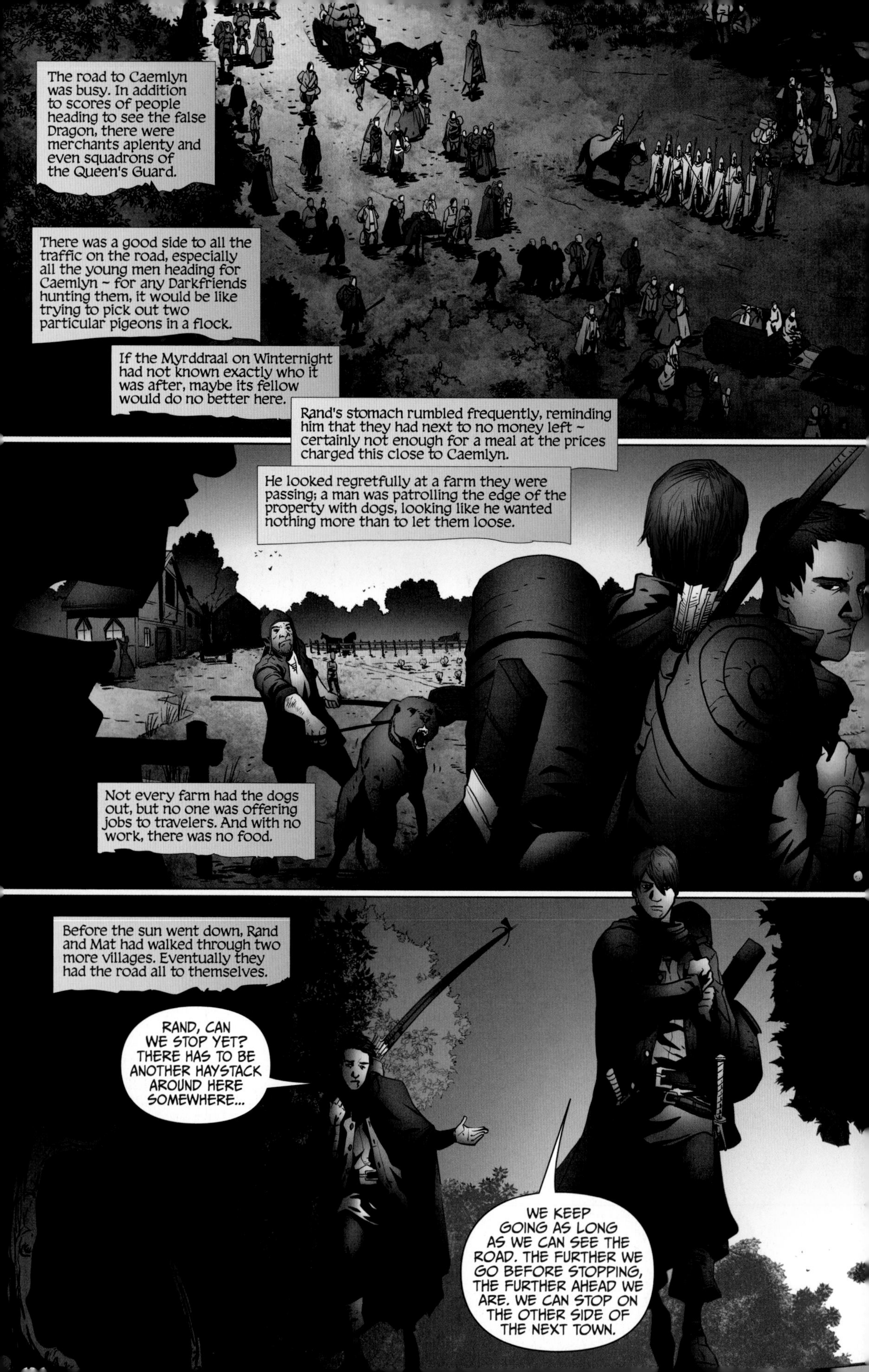
The road to Caemlyn was busy. In addition to scores of people heading to see the false Dragon, there were merchants aplenty and even squadrons of the Queen's Guard.
There was a good side to all the traffic on the road, especially all the young men heading for Caemlyn ~ for any Darkfriends hunting them, it would be like trying to pick out two particular pigeons in a flock.
If the Myrddraal on Winternight had not known exactly who it was after, maybe its fellow would do no better here.
Rand's stomach rumbled frequently, reminding him that they had next to no money left ~ certainly not enough for a meal at the prices charged this close to Caemlyn.
He looked regretfully at a farm they were passing; a man was patrolling the edge of the property with dogs, looking like he wanted nothing more than to let them loose.
Not every farm had the dogs out, but no one was offering jobs to travelers. And with no work, there was no food.
Before the sun went down, Rand and Mat had walked through two more villages. Eventually they had the road all to themselves.
RAND, CAN WE STOP YET? THERE HAS TO BE ANOTHER HAYSTACK AROUND HERE SOMEWHERE...
WE KEEP GOING AS LONG AS WE CAN SEE THE ROAD. THE FURTHER WE GO BEFORE STOPPING, THE FURTHER AHEAD WE ARE. WE CAN STOP ON THE OTHER SIDE OF THE NEXT TOWN.

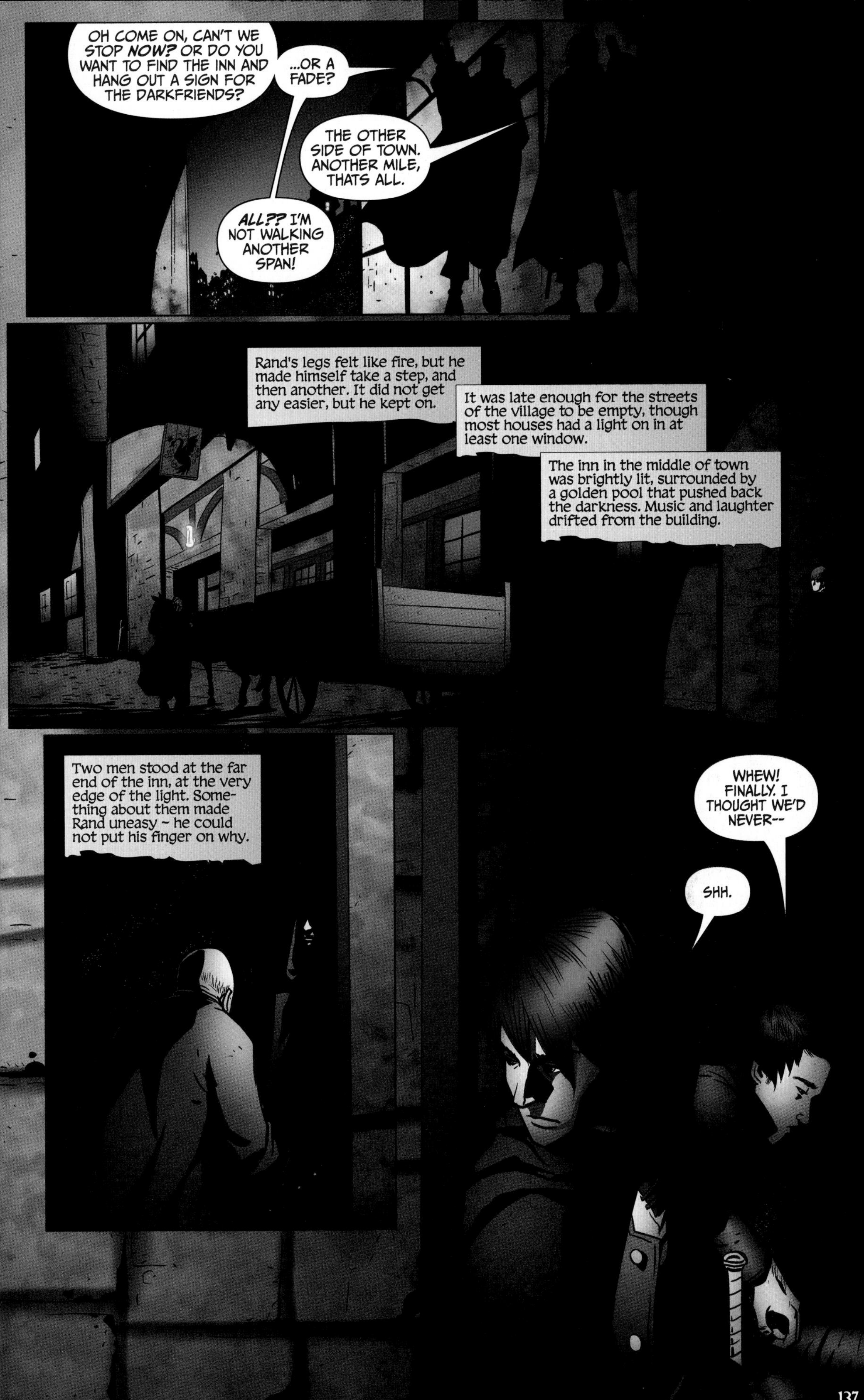

OH COME ON, CAN'T WE STOP NOW? OR DO YOU WANT TO FIND THE INN AND HANG OUT A SIGN FOR THE DARKFRIENDS?
...OR A FADE?
THE OTHER SIDE OF TOWN. ANOTHER MILE, THATS ALL.
ALL?? I'M NOT WALKING ANOTHER SPAN!
Rand's legs felt like fire, but he made himself take a step, and then another. It did not get any easier, but he kept on.
It was late enough for the streets of the village to be empty, though most houses had a light on in at least one window.
The inn in the middle of town was brightly lit, surrounded by a golden pool that pushed back the darkness. Music and laughter drifted from the building.
Two men stood at the far end of the inn, at the very edge of the light. Something about them made Rand uneasy ~ he could not put his finger on why.
WHEW! FINALLY. I THOUGHT WE'D NEVER--
SHH.

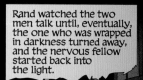

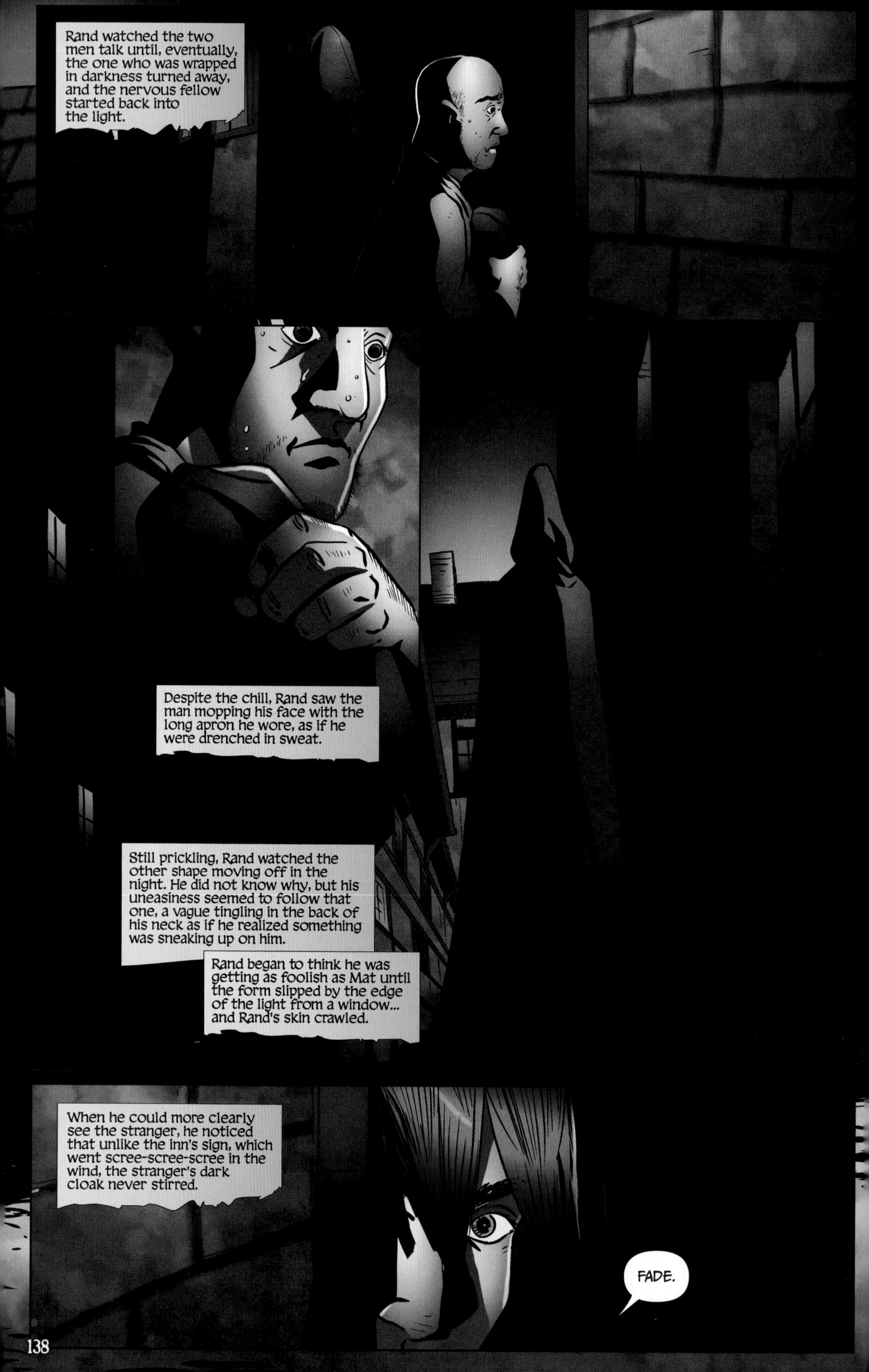

Rand watched the two men talk until, eventually, the one who was wrapped in darkness turned away, and the nervous fellow started back into the light.

Despite the chill, Rand saw the man mopping his face with the long apron he wore, as if he were drenched in sweat.

Still prickling, Rand watched the other shape moving off in the night. He did not know why, but his uneasiness seemed to follow that one, a vague tingling in the back of his neck as if he realized something was sneaking up on him.

Rand began to think he was getting as foolish as Mat until the form slipped by the edge of the light from a window... and Rand's skin crawled.

When he could more clearly see the stranger, he noticed that unlike the inn's sign, which went scree-scree-scree in the wind, the stranger's dark cloak never stirred.

FADE.

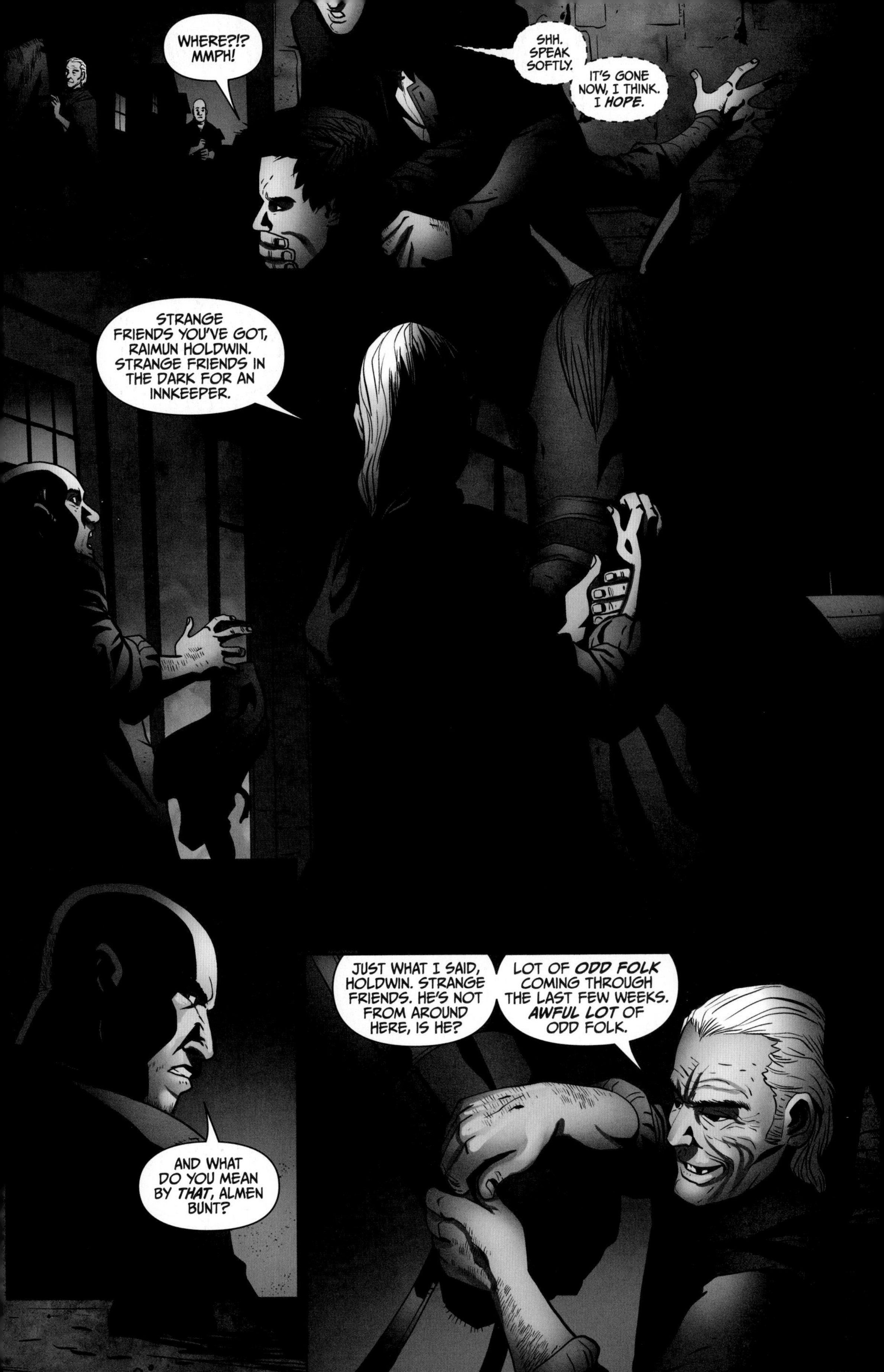
WHERE?!? MMPH!
SHH. SPEAK SOFTLY.
IT'S GONE NOW, I THINK. I *HOPE*.
STRANGE FRIENDS YOU'VE GOT, RAIMUN HOLDWIN. STRANGE FRIENDS IN THE DARK FOR AN INNKEEPER.
AND WHAT DO YOU MEAN BY *THAT*, ALMEN BUNT?
JUST WHAT I SAID, HOLDWIN. STRANGE FRIENDS. HE'S NOT FROM AROUND HERE, IS HE?
LOT OF *ODD FOLK* COMING THROUGH THE LAST FEW WEEKS. *AWFUL LOT* OF ODD FOLK.

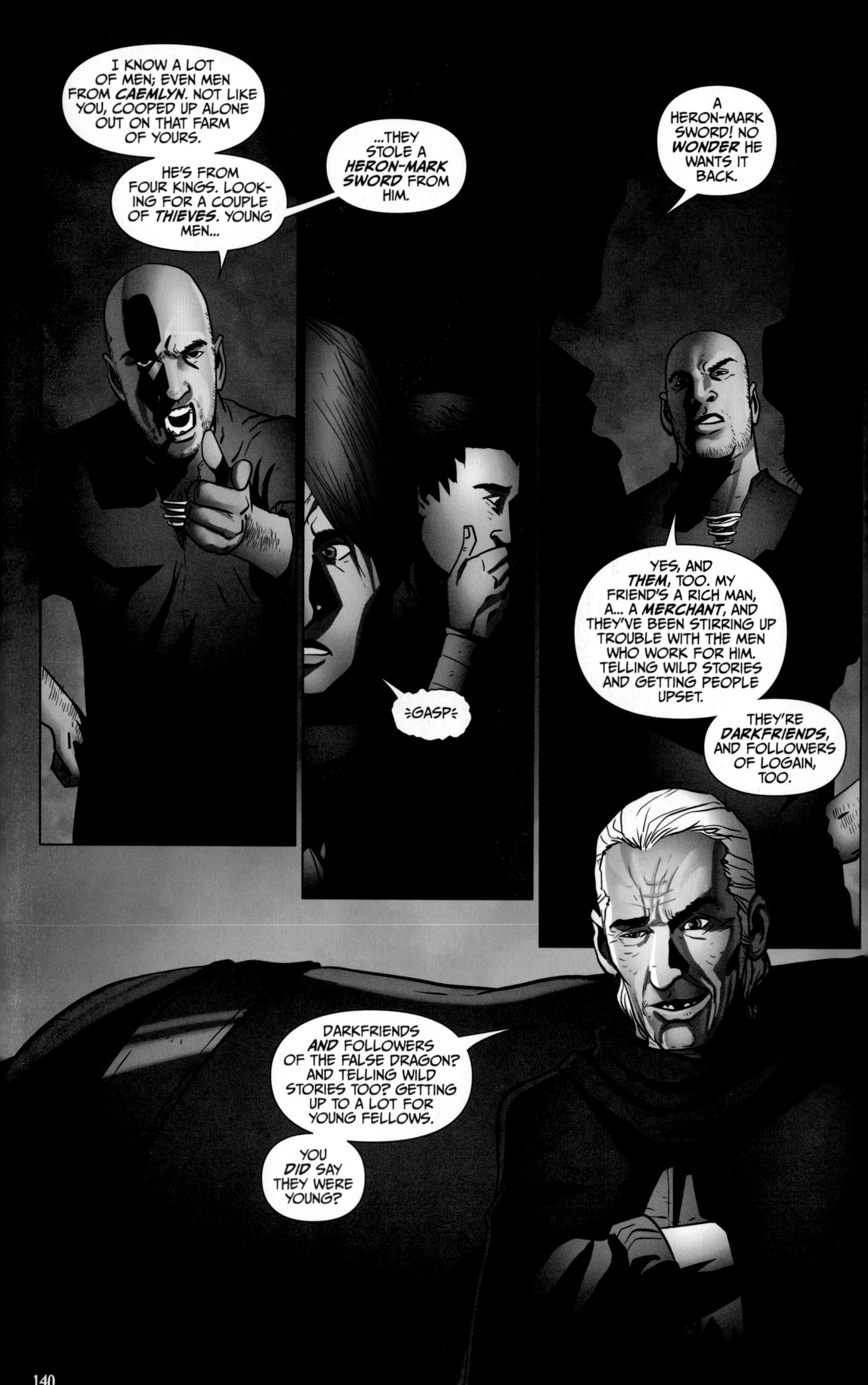
I KNOW A LOT OF MEN; EVEN MEN FROM CAEMLYN. NOT LIKE YOU, COOPED UP ALONE OUT ON THAT FARM OF YOURS.
HE'S FROM FOUR KINGS. LOOKING FOR A COUPLE OF THIEVES. YOUNG MEN...
...THEY STOLE A HERON-MARK SWORD FROM HIM.
GASP
A HERON-MARK SWORD! NO WONDER HE WANTS IT BACK.
YES, AND THEM, TOO. MY FRIEND'S A RICH MAN, A... A MERCHANT, AND THEY'VE BEEN STIRRING UP TROUBLE WITH THE MEN WHO WORK FOR HIM. TELLING WILD STORIES AND GETTING PEOPLE UPSET.
THEY'RE DARKFRIENDS, AND FOLLOWERS OF LOGAIN, TOO.
DARKFRIENDS AND FOLLOWERS OF THE FALSE DRAGON? AND TELLING WILD STORIES TOO? GETTING UP TO A LOT FOR YOUNG FELLOWS.
YOU DID SAY THEY WERE YOUNG?

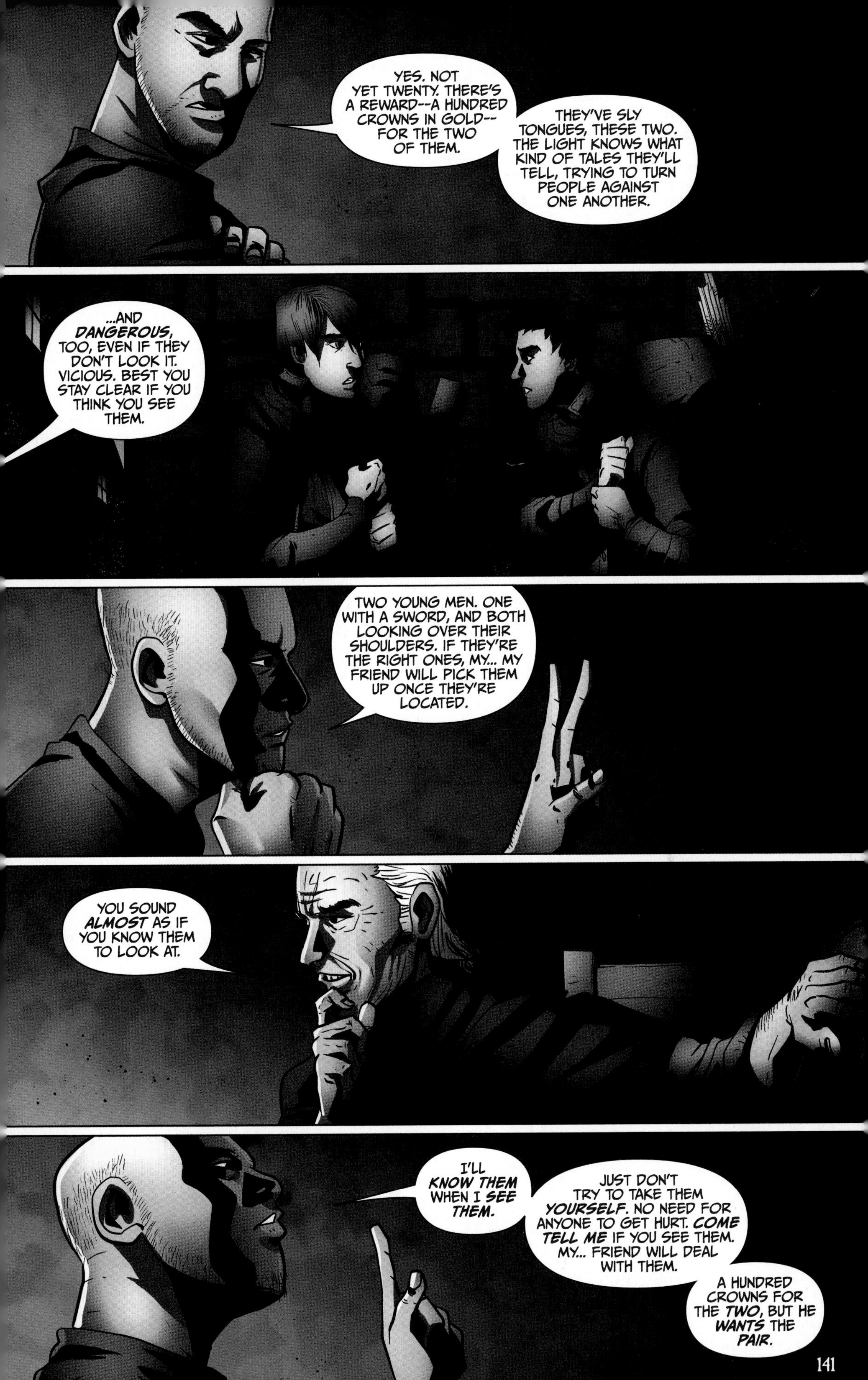

YES. NOT YET TWENTY. THERE'S A REWARD--A HUNDRED CROWNS IN GOLD--FOR THE TWO OF THEM.
THEY'VE SLY TONGUES, THESE TWO. THE LIGHT KNOWS WHAT KIND OF TALES THEY'LL TELL, TRYING TO TURN PEOPLE AGAINST ONE ANOTHER.
...AND *DANGEROUS,* TOO, EVEN IF THEY DON'T LOOK IT. VICIOUS. BEST YOU STAY CLEAR IF YOU THINK YOU SEE THEM.
TWO YOUNG MEN. ONE WITH A SWORD, AND BOTH LOOKING OVER THEIR SHOULDERS. IF THEY'RE THE RIGHT ONES, MY... MY FRIEND WILL PICK THEM UP ONCE THEY'RE LOCATED.
YOU SOUND *ALMOST* AS IF YOU KNOW THEM TO LOOK AT.
I'LL *KNOW THEM* WHEN I *SEE THEM.*
JUST DON'T TRY TO TAKE THEM *YOURSELF*. NO NEED FOR ANYONE TO GET HURT. *COME TELL ME* IF YOU SEE THEM. MY... FRIEND WILL DEAL WITH THEM.
A HUNDRED CROWNS FOR THE *TWO,* BUT HE *WANTS* THE *PAIR.*

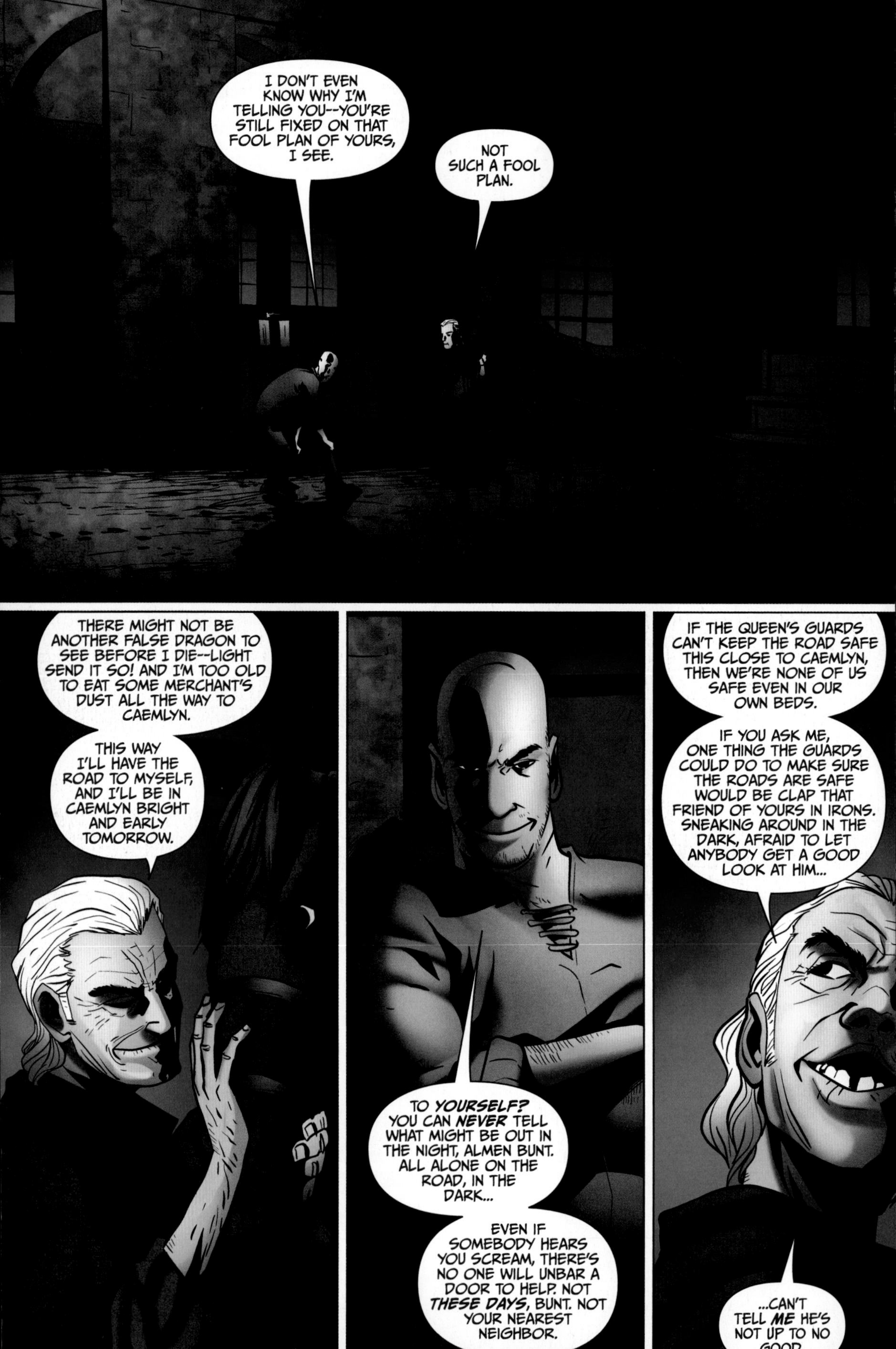
I DON'T EVEN KNOW WHY I'M TELLING YOU--YOU'RE STILL FIXED ON THAT FOOL PLAN OF YOURS, I SEE.
NOT SUCH A FOOL PLAN.
THERE MIGHT NOT BE ANOTHER FALSE DRAGON TO SEE BEFORE I DIE--LIGHT SEND IT SO! AND I'M TOO OLD TO EAT SOME MERCHANT'S DUST ALL THE WAY TO CAEMLYN.
THIS WAY I'LL HAVE THE ROAD TO MYSELF, AND I'LL BE IN CAEMLYN BRIGHT AND EARLY TOMORROW.
TO *YOURSELF?* YOU CAN *NEVER* TELL WHAT MIGHT BE OUT IN THE NIGHT, ALMEN BUNT. ALL ALONE ON THE ROAD, IN THE DARK...
EVEN IF SOMEBODY HEARS YOU SCREAM, THERE'S NO ONE WILL UNBAR A DOOR TO HELP. NOT *THESE DAYS*, BUNT. NOT YOUR NEAREST NEIGHBOR.
IF THE QUEEN'S GUARDS CAN'T KEEP THE ROAD SAFE THIS CLOSE TO CAEMLYN, THEN WE'RE NONE OF US SAFE EVEN IN OUR OWN BEDS.
IF YOU ASK ME, ONE THING THE GUARDS COULD DO TO MAKE SURE THE ROADS ARE SAFE WOULD BE CLAP THAT FRIEND OF YOURS IN IRONS. SNEAKING AROUND IN THE DARK, AFRAID TO LET ANYBODY GET A GOOD LOOK AT HIM...
...CAN'T TELL *ME* HE'S NOT UP TO NO

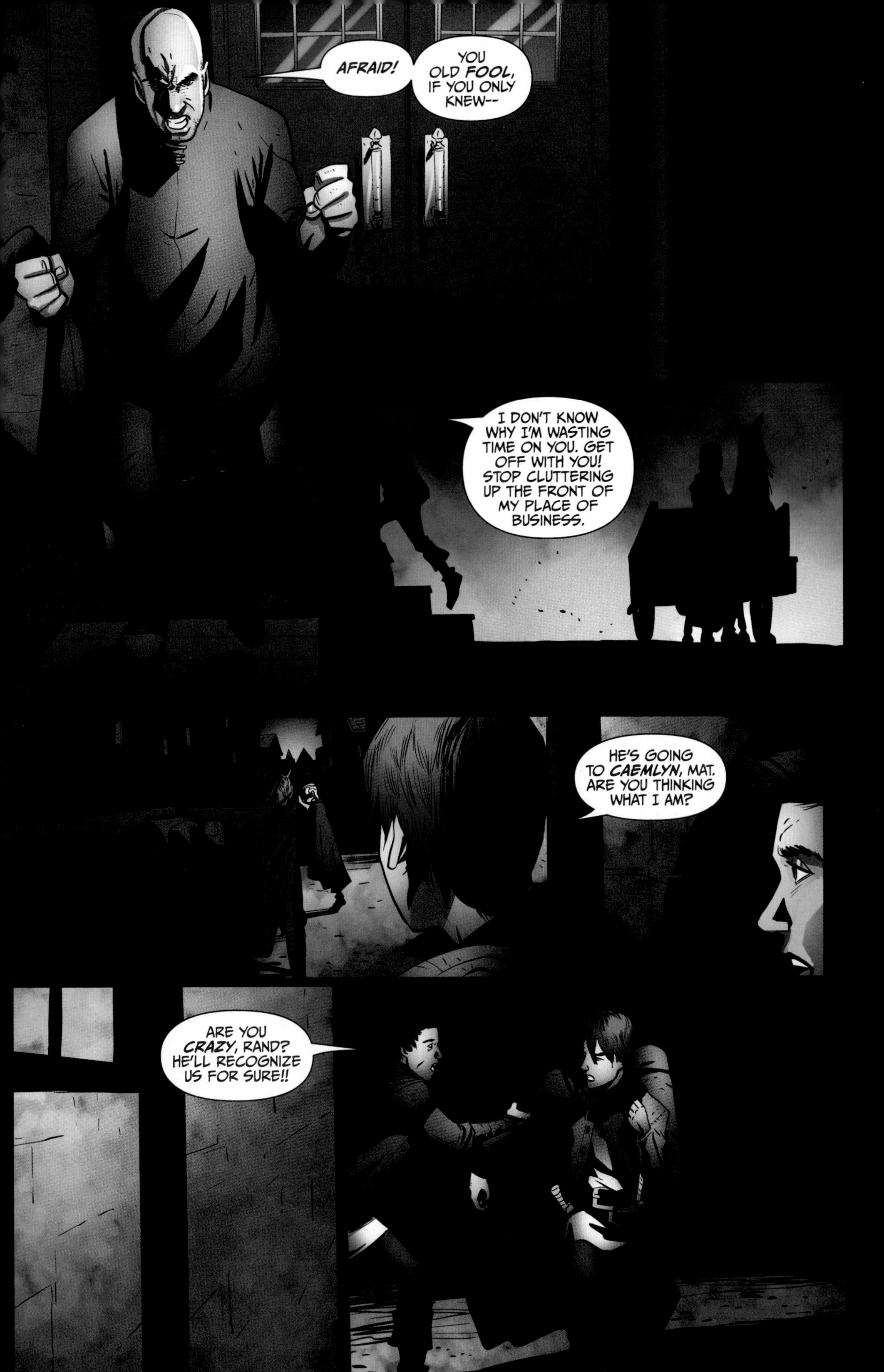
AFRAID!
YOU OLD FOOL, IF YOU ONLY KNEW--
I DON'T KNOW WHY I'M WASTING TIME ON YOU. GET OFF WITH YOU! STOP CLUTTERING UP THE FRONT OF MY PLACE OF BUSINESS.
HE'S GOING TO CAEMLYN, MAT. ARE YOU THINKING WHAT I AM?
ARE YOU CRAZY, RAND? HE'LL RECOGNIZE US FOR SURE!!

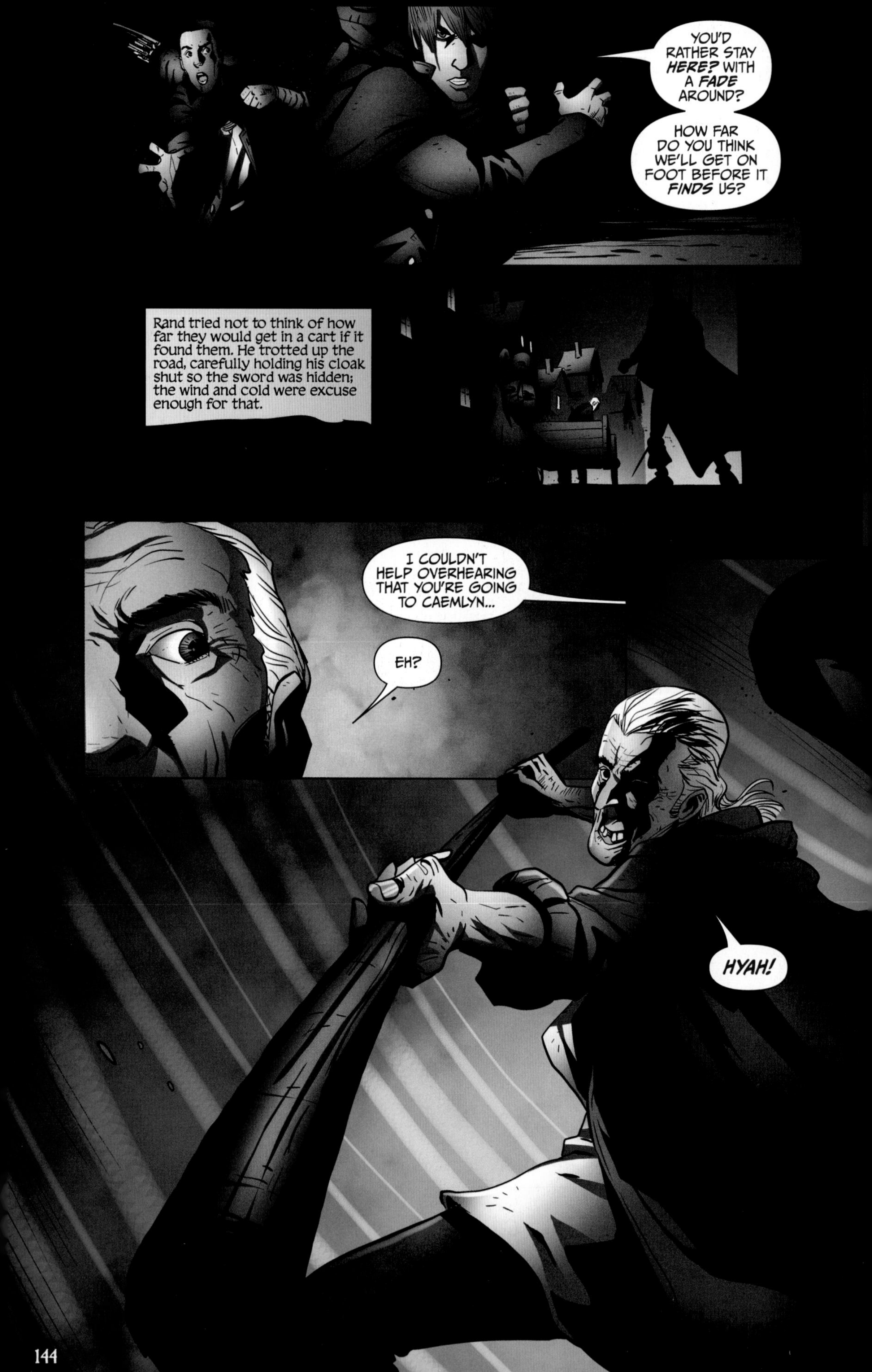
YOU'D RATHER STAY HERE? WITH A FADE AROUND?
HOW FAR DO YOU THINK WE'LL GET ON FOOT BEFORE IT FINDS US?
Rand tried not to think of how far they would get in a cart if it found them. He trotted up the road, carefully holding his cloak shut so the sword was hidden; the wind and cold were excuse enough for that.
I COULDN'T HELP OVERHEARING THAT YOU'RE GOING TO CAEMLYN...
EH?
HYAH!

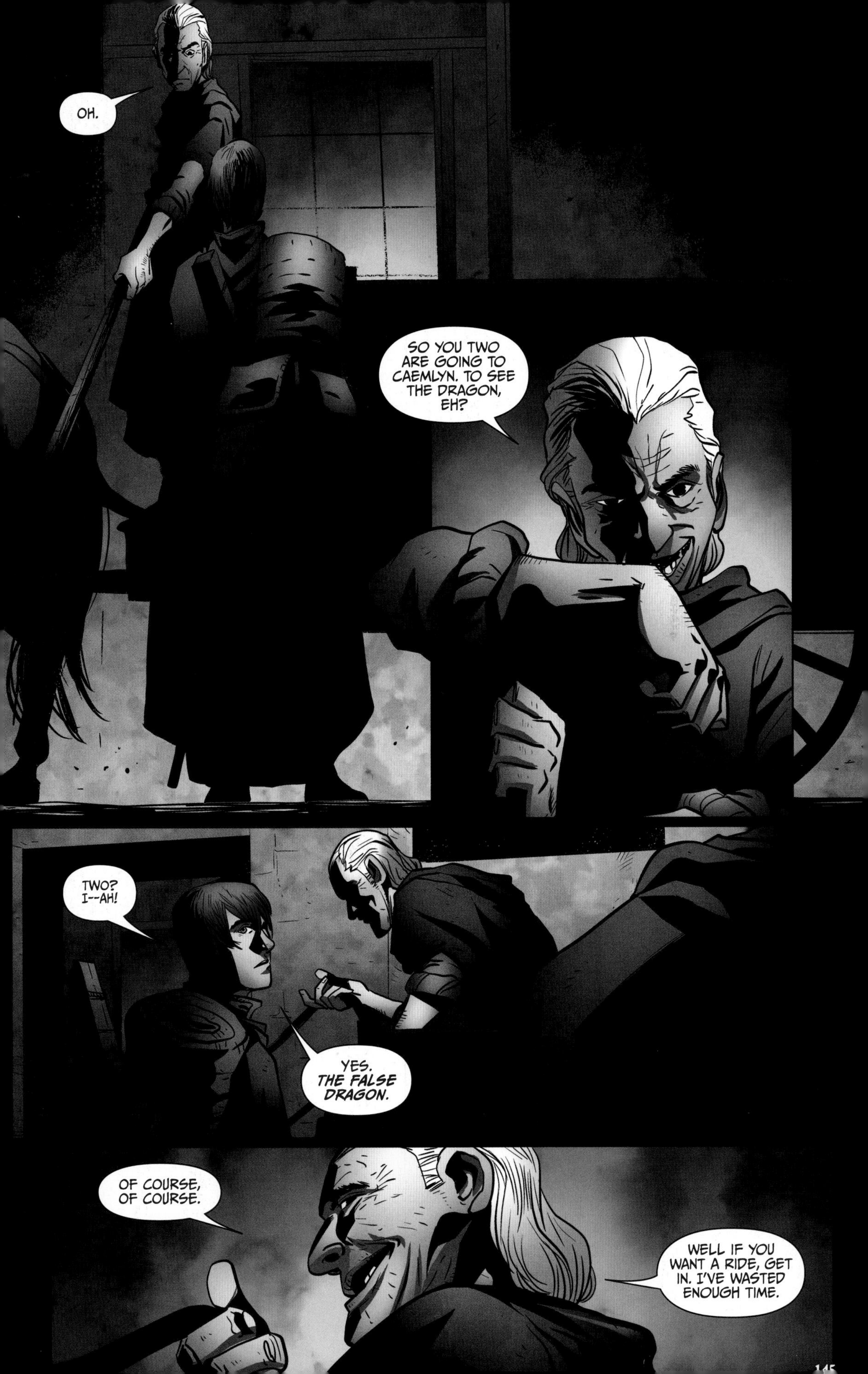
OH.
SO YOU TWO ARE GOING TO CAEMLYN. TO SEE THE DRAGON, EH?
TWO? I--AH!
YES. THE FALSE DRAGON.
OF COURSE, OF COURSE.
WELL IF YOU WANT A RIDE, GET IN. I'VE WASTED ENOUGH TIME.

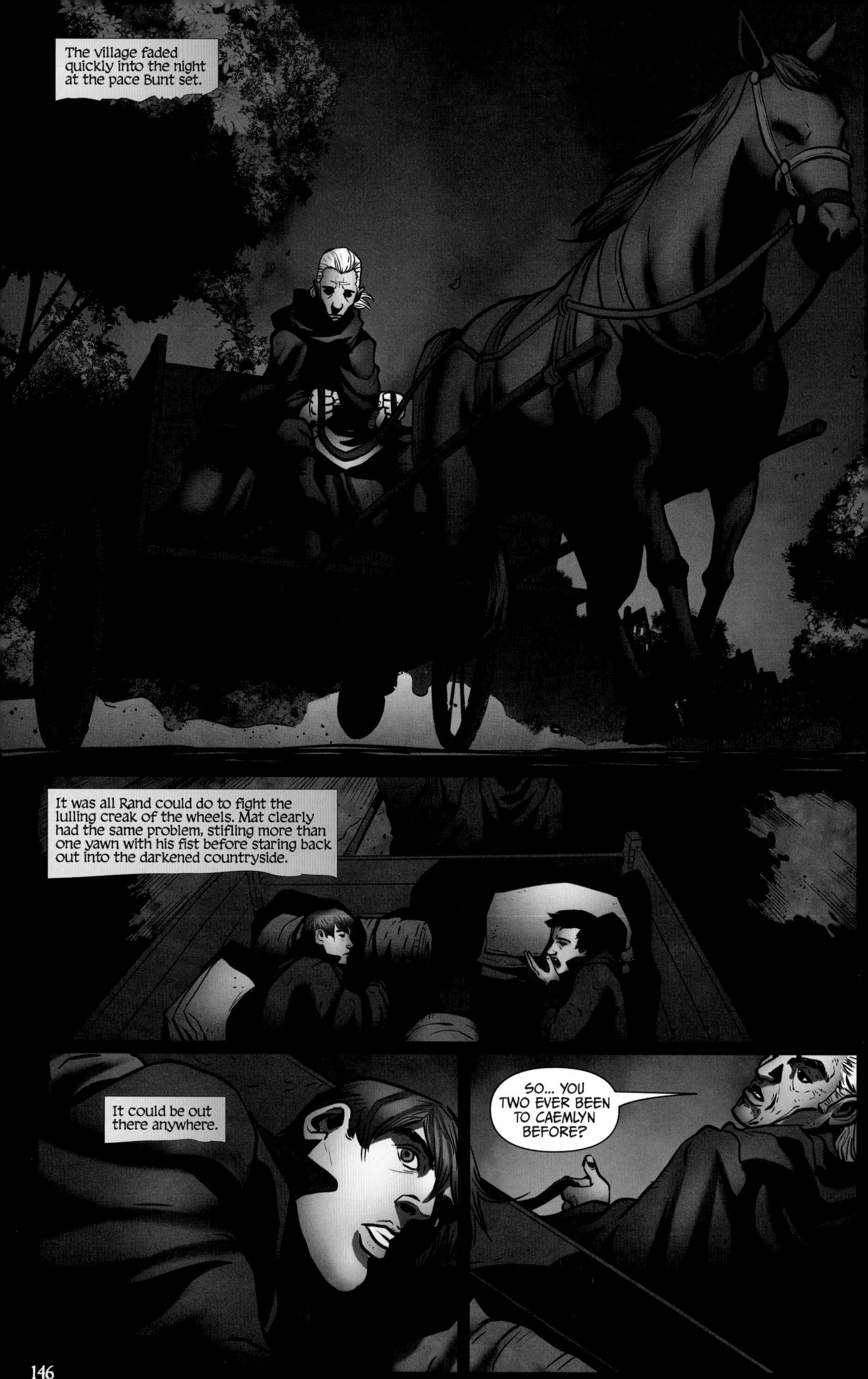
The village faded quickly into the night at the pace Bunt set.
It was all Rand could do to fight the lulling creak of the wheels. Mat clearly had the same problem, stifling more than one yawn with his fist before staring back out into the darkened countryside.
It could be out there anywhere.
SO... YOU TWO EVER BEEN TO CAEMLYN BEFORE?

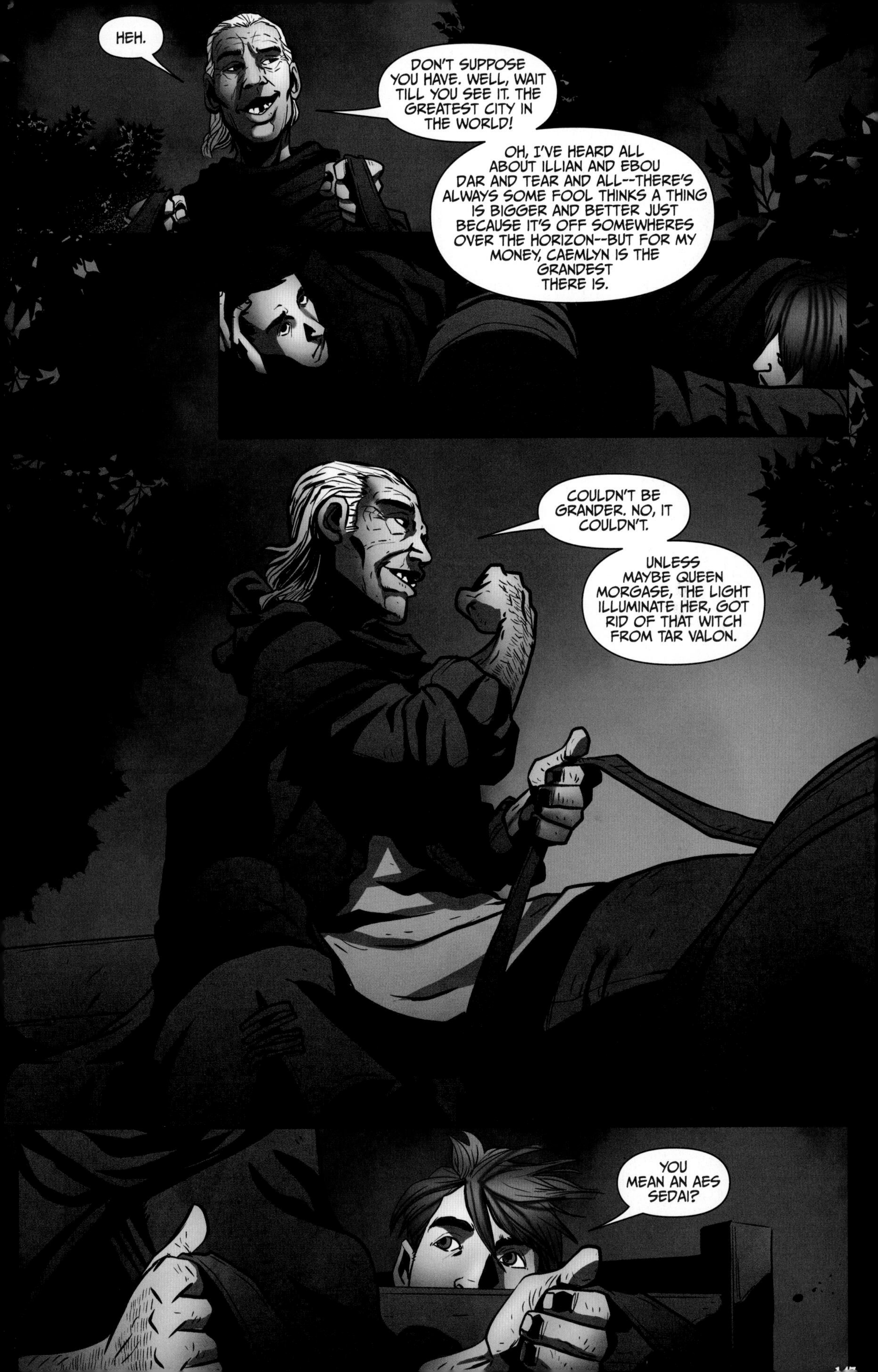
HEH.
DON'T SUPPOSE YOU HAVE. WELL, WAIT TILL YOU SEE IT. THE GREATEST CITY IN THE WORLD!
OH, I'VE HEARD ALL ABOUT ILLIAN AND EBOU DAR AND TEAR AND ALL--THERE'S ALWAYS SOME FOOL THINKS A THING IS BIGGER AND BETTER JUST BECAUSE IT'S OFF SOMEWHERES OVER THE HORIZON--BUT FOR MY MONEY, CAEMLYN IS THE GRANDEST THERE IS.
COULDN'T BE GRANDER. NO, IT COULDN'T.
UNLESS MAYBE QUEEN MORGASE, THE LIGHT ILLUMINATE HER, GOT RID OF THAT WITCH FROM TAR VALON.
YOU MEAN AN AES SEDAI?

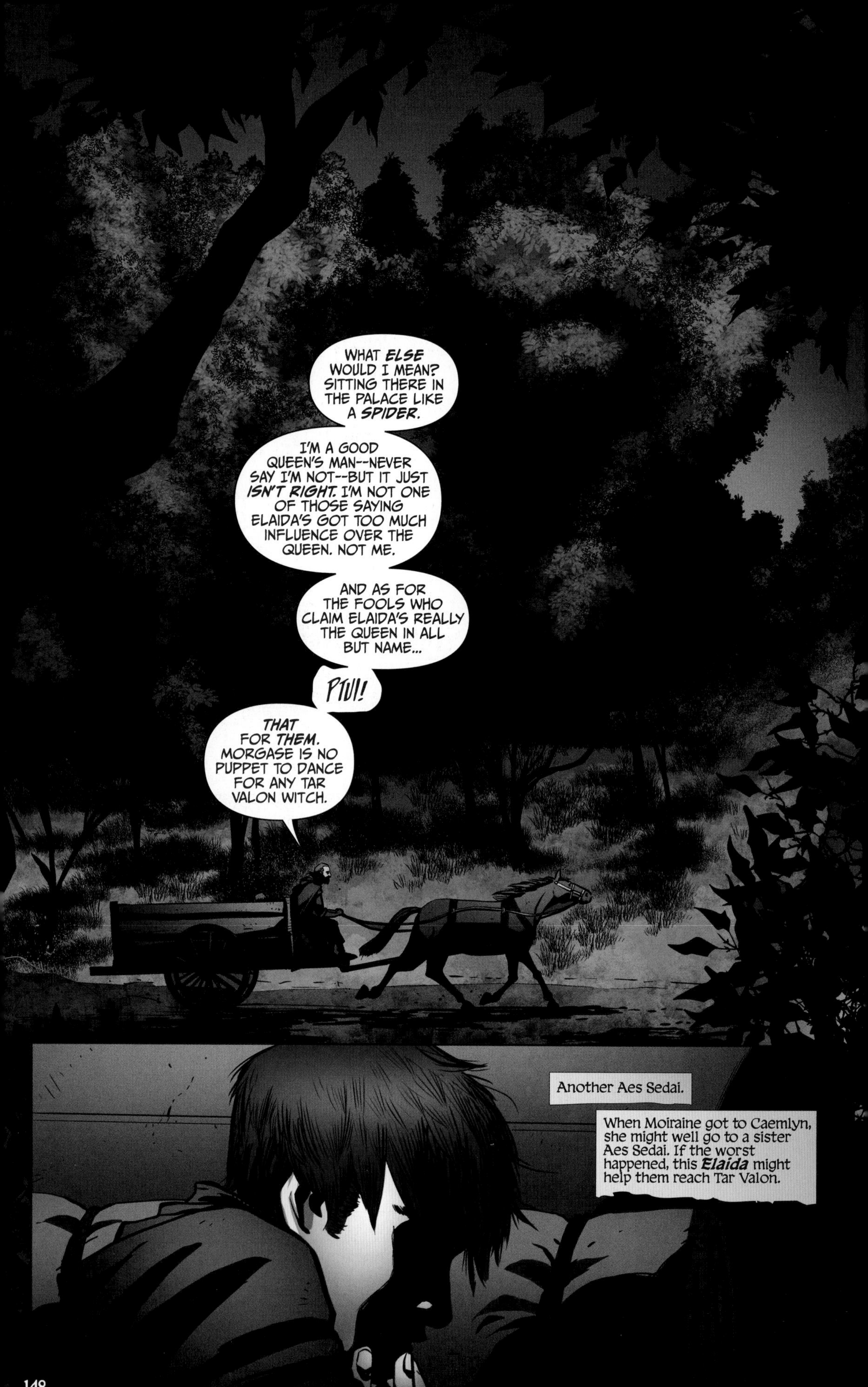
WHAT *ELSE* WOULD I MEAN? SITTING THERE IN THE PALACE LIKE A *SPIDER*.
I'M A GOOD QUEEN'S MAN--NEVER SAY I'M NOT--BUT IT JUST *ISN'T RIGHT.* I'M NOT ONE OF THOSE SAYING ELAIDA'S GOT TOO MUCH INFLUENCE OVER THE QUEEN. NOT ME.
AND AS FOR THE FOOLS WHO CLAIM ELAIDA'S REALLY THE QUEEN IN ALL BUT NAME...
PTUI!
THAT FOR *THEM*. MORGASE IS NO PUPPET TO DANCE FOR ANY TAR VALON WITCH.
Another Aes Sedai.
When Moiraine got to Caemlyn, she might well go to a sister Aes Sedai. If the worst happened, this ***Elaida*** might help them reach Tar Valon.

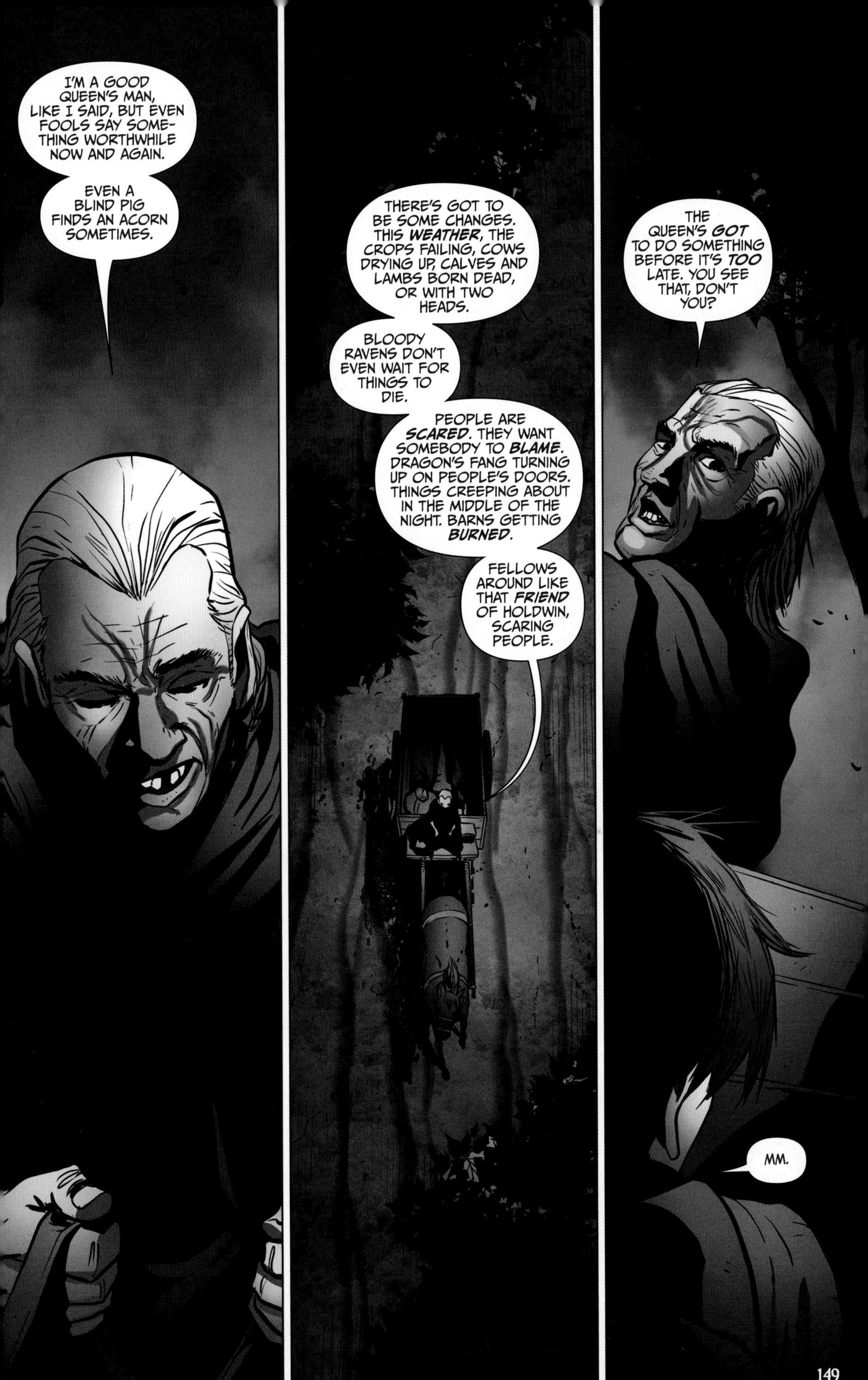
I'M A GOOD QUEEN'S MAN, LIKE I SAID, BUT EVEN FOOLS SAY SOMETHING WORTHWHILE NOW AND AGAIN.
EVEN A BLIND PIG FINDS AN ACORN SOMETIMES.
THERE'S GOT TO BE SOME CHANGES. THIS WEATHER, THE CROPS FAILING, COWS DRYING UP, CALVES AND LAMBS BORN DEAD, OR WITH TWO HEADS.
BLOODY RAVENS DON'T EVEN WAIT FOR THINGS TO DIE.
PEOPLE ARE SCARED. THEY WANT SOMEBODY TO BLAME. DRAGON'S FANG TURNING UP ON PEOPLE'S DOORS. THINGS CREEPING ABOUT IN THE MIDDLE OF THE NIGHT. BARNS GETTING BURNED.
FELLOWS AROUND LIKE THAT FRIEND OF HOLDWIN, SCARING PEOPLE.
THE QUEEN'S GOT TO DO SOMETHING BEFORE IT'S TOO LATE. YOU SEE THAT, DON'T YOU?
MM.

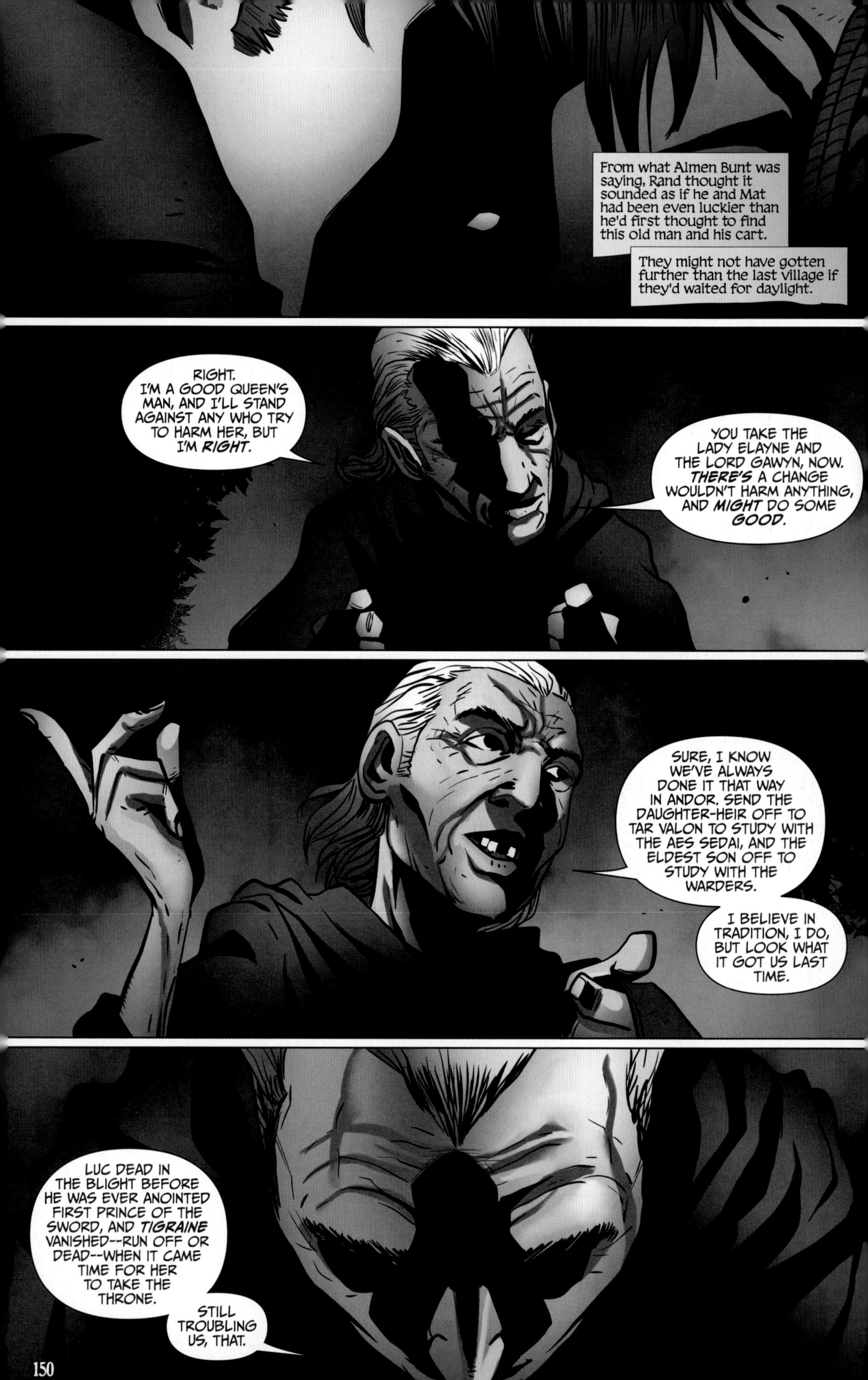
From what Almen Bunt was saying, Rand thought it sounded as if he and Mat had been even luckier than he'd first thought to find this old man and his cart.
They might not have gotten further than the last village if they'd waited for daylight.
RIGHT. I'M A GOOD QUEEN'S MAN, AND I'LL STAND AGAINST ANY WHO TRY TO HARM HER, BUT I'M *RIGHT*.
YOU TAKE THE LADY ELAYNE AND THE LORD GAWYN, NOW. ***THERE'S*** A CHANGE WOULDN'T HARM ANYTHING, AND ***MIGHT*** DO SOME ***GOOD***.
SURE, I KNOW WE'VE ALWAYS DONE IT THAT WAY IN ANDOR. SEND THE DAUGHTER-HEIR OFF TO TAR VALON TO STUDY WITH THE AES SEDAI, AND THE ELDEST SON OFF TO STUDY WITH THE WARDERS.
I BELIEVE IN TRADITION, I DO, BUT LOOK WHAT IT GOT US LAST TIME.
LUC DEAD IN THE BLIGHT BEFORE HE WAS EVER ANOINTED FIRST PRINCE OF THE SWORD, AND *TIGRAINE* VANISHED--RUN OFF OR DEAD--WHEN IT CAME TIME FOR HER TO TAKE THE THRONE.
STILL TROUBLING US, THAT.

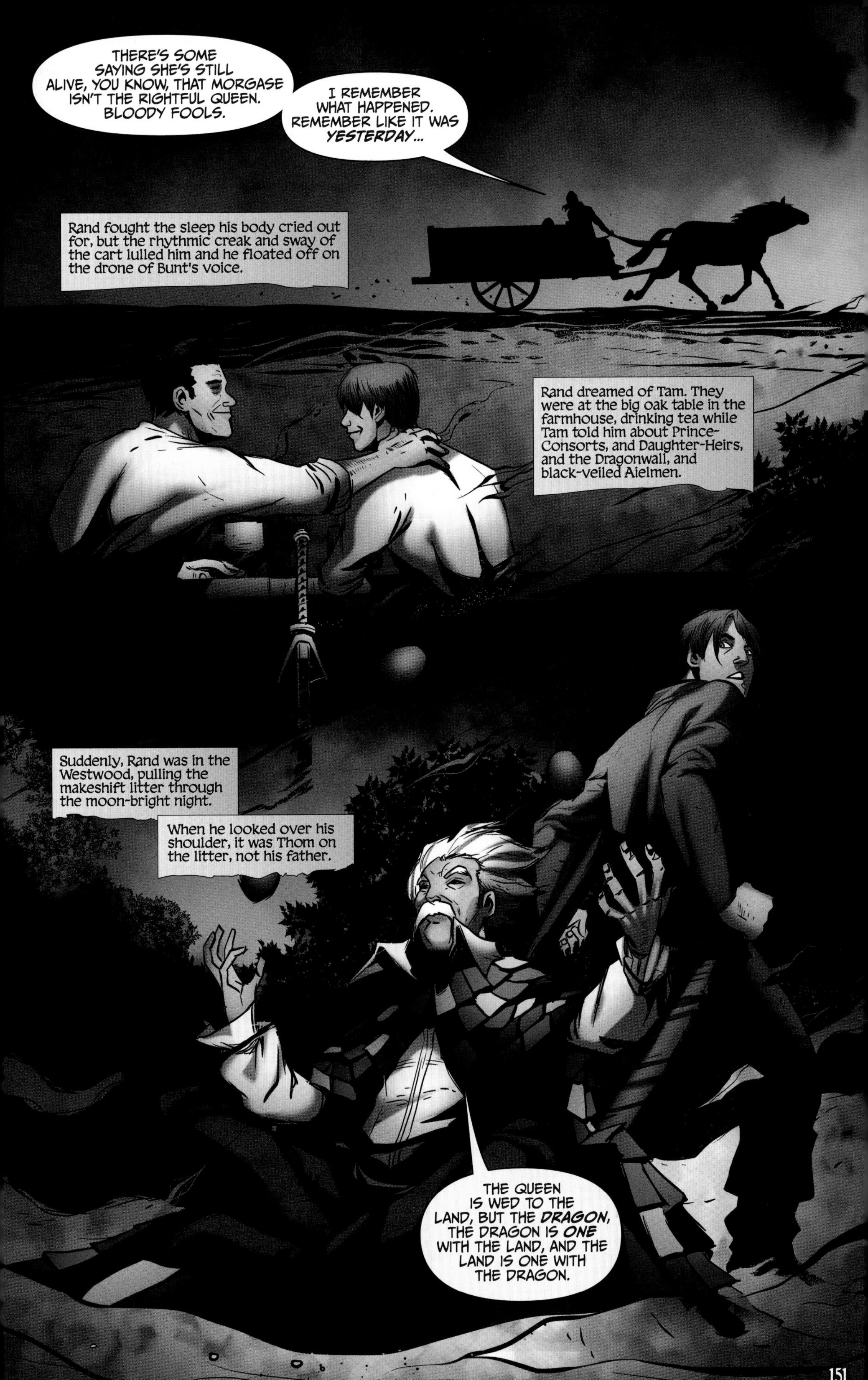
THERE'S SOME SAYING SHE'S STILL ALIVE, YOU KNOW, THAT MORGASE ISN'T THE RIGHTFUL QUEEN. BLOODY FOOLS.
I REMEMBER WHAT HAPPENED. REMEMBER LIKE IT WAS *YESTERDAY...*
Rand fought the sleep his body cried out for, but the rhythmic creak and sway of the cart lulled him and he floated off on the drone of Bunt's voice.
Rand dreamed of Tam. They were at the big oak table in the farmhouse, drinking tea while Tam told him about Prince-Consorts, and Daughter-Heirs, and the Dragonwall, and black-veiled Aielmen.
Suddenly, Rand was in the Westwood, pulling the makeshift litter through the moon-bright night.
When he looked over his shoulder, it was Thom on the litter, not his father.
THE QUEEN IS WED TO THE LAND, BUT THE *DRAGON*, THE DRAGON IS *ONE* WITH THE LAND, AND THE LAND IS ONE WITH THE DRAGON.

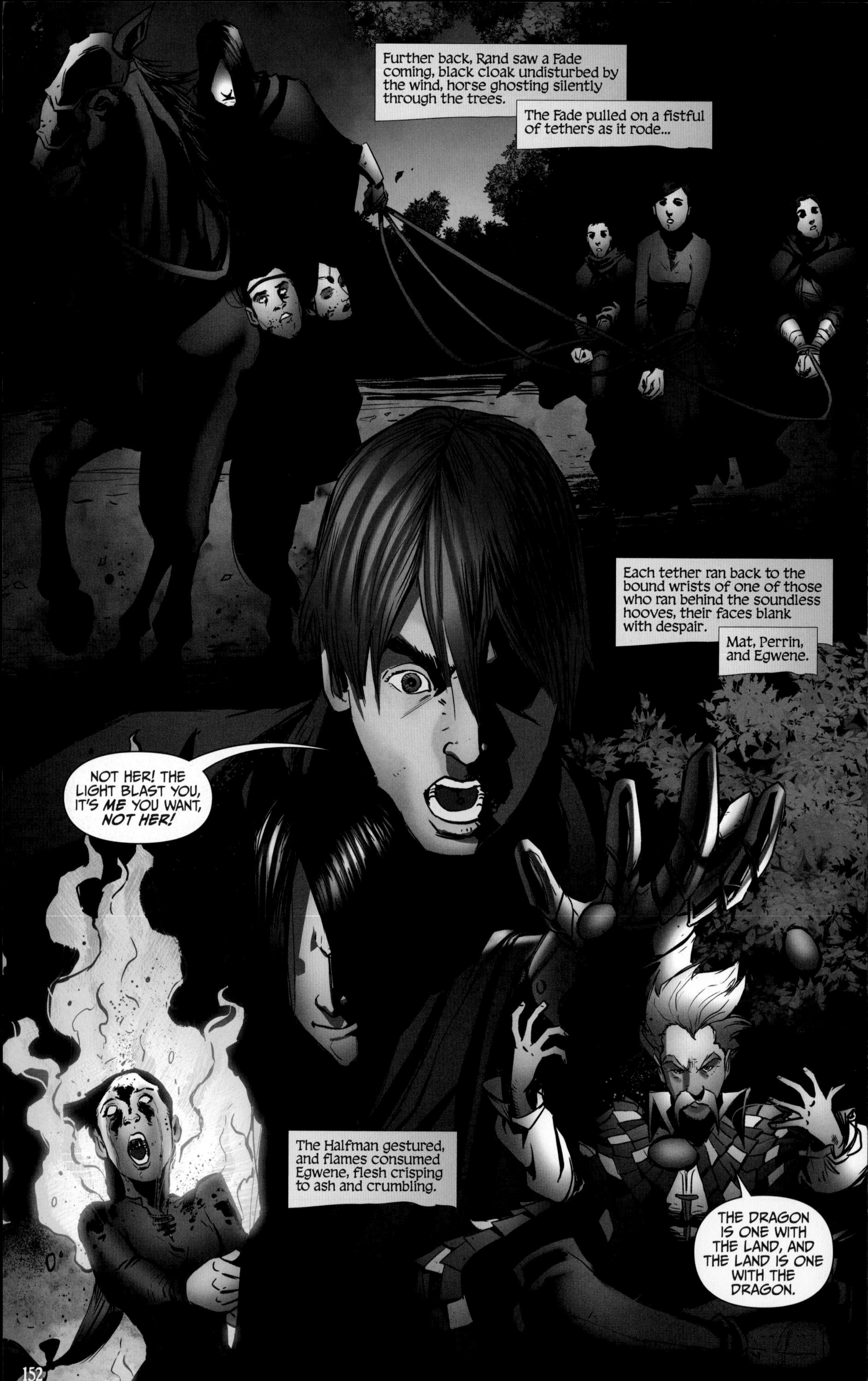
Further back, Rand saw a Fade coming, black cloak undisturbed by the wind, horse ghosting silently through the trees.
The Fade pulled on a fistful of tethers as it rode...
Each tether ran back to the bound wrists of one of those who ran behind the soundless hooves, their faces blank with despair.
Mat, Perrin, and Egwene.
NOT HER! THE LIGHT BLAST YOU, IT'S *ME* YOU WANT, *NOT HER!*
The Halfman gestured, and flames consumed Egwene, flesh crisping to ash and crumbling.
THE DRAGON IS ONE WITH THE LAND, AND THE LAND IS ONE WITH THE DRAGON.

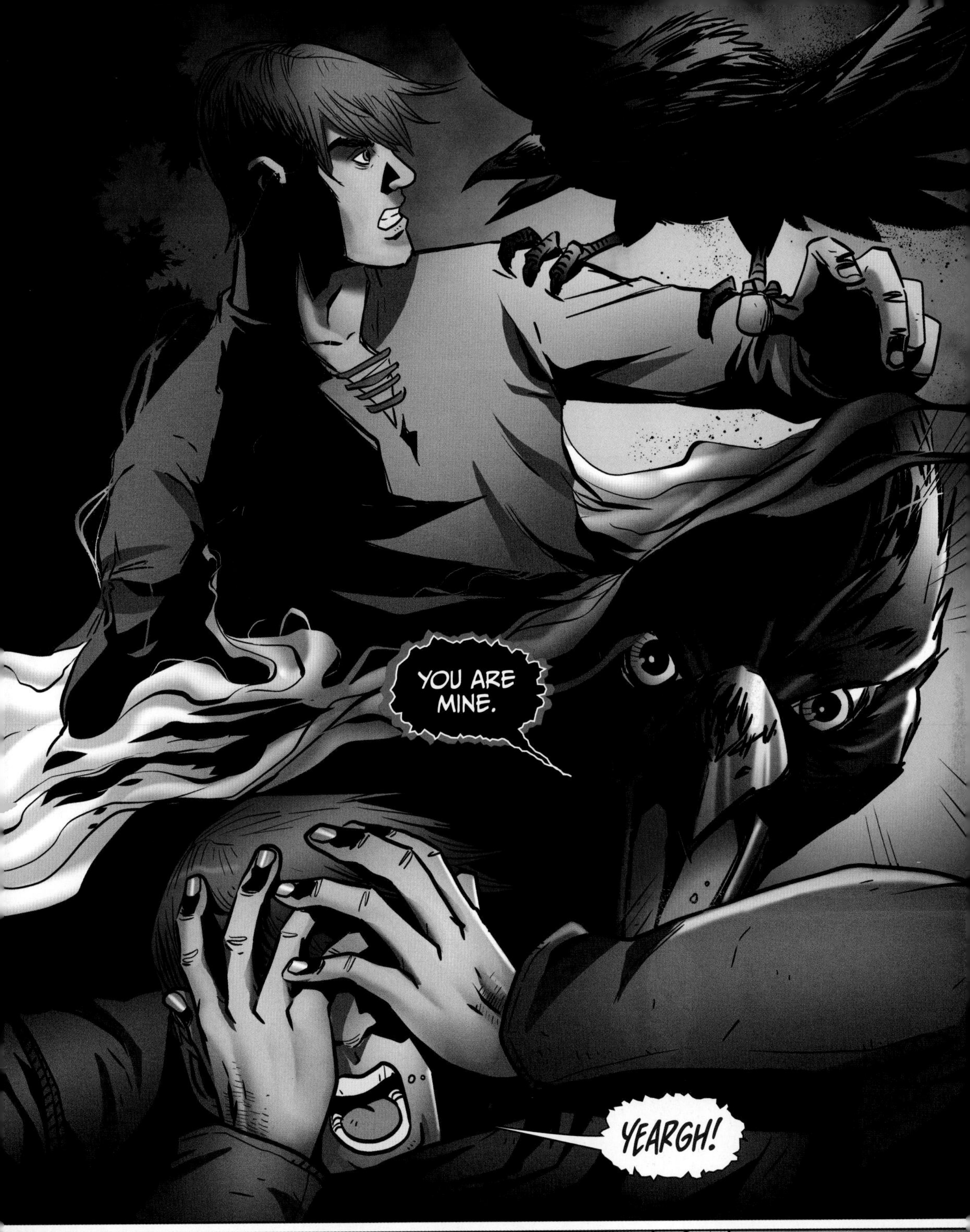
YOU ARE MINE.
YEARGH!

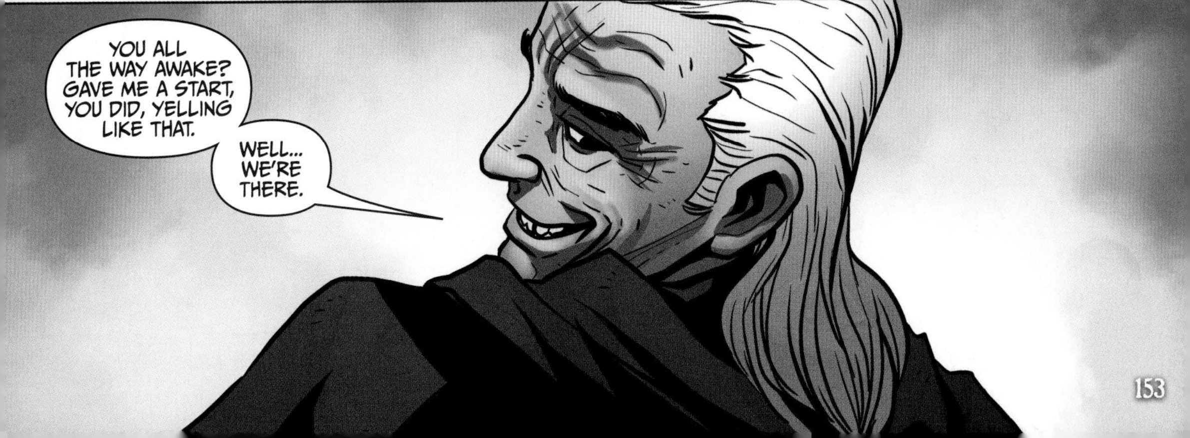
YOU ALL THE WAY AWAKE? GAVE ME A START, YOU DID, YELLING LIKE THAT.
WELL... WE'RE THERE.

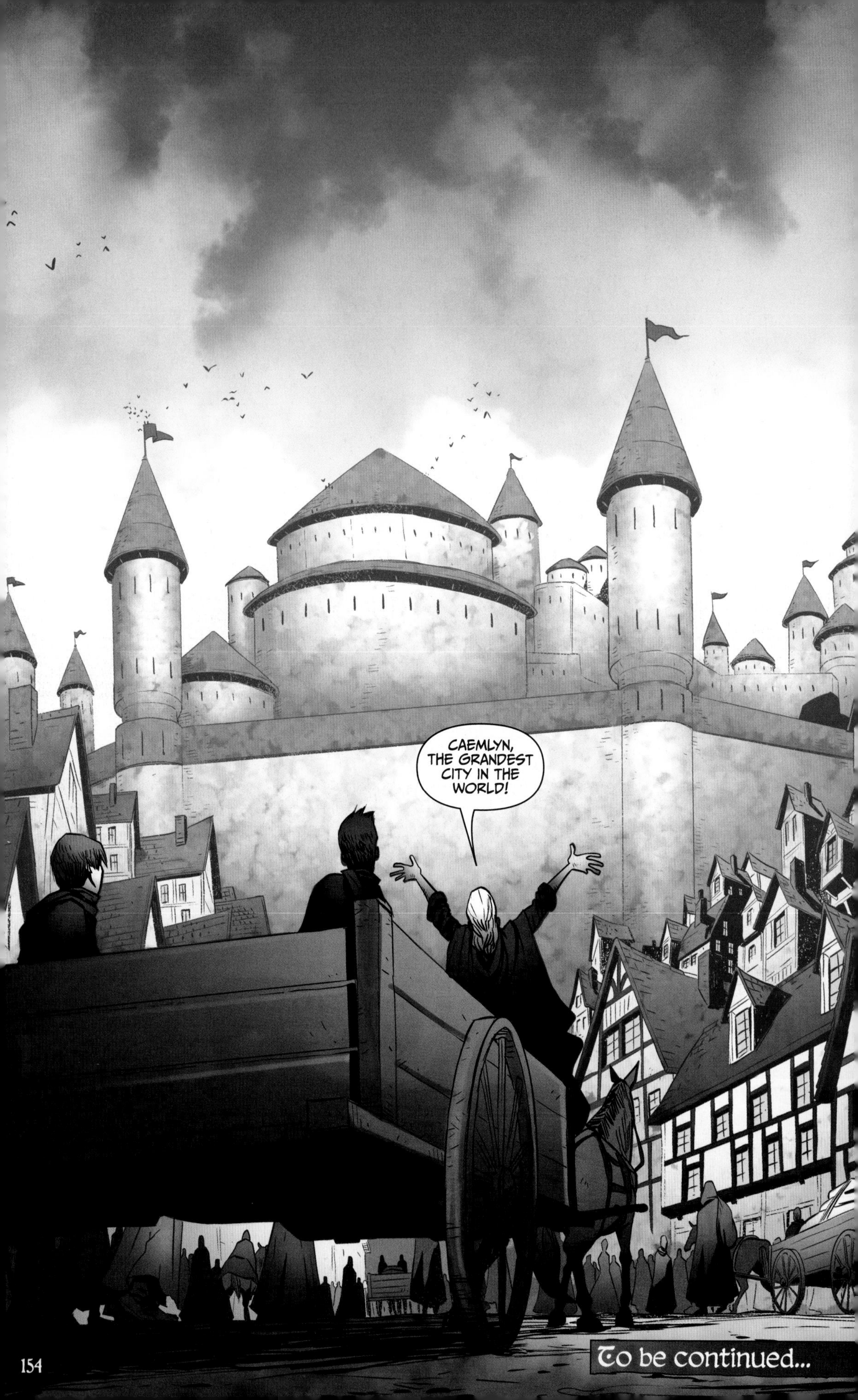
CAEMLYN, THE GRANDEST CITY IN THE WORLD!
To be continued...

cover gallery

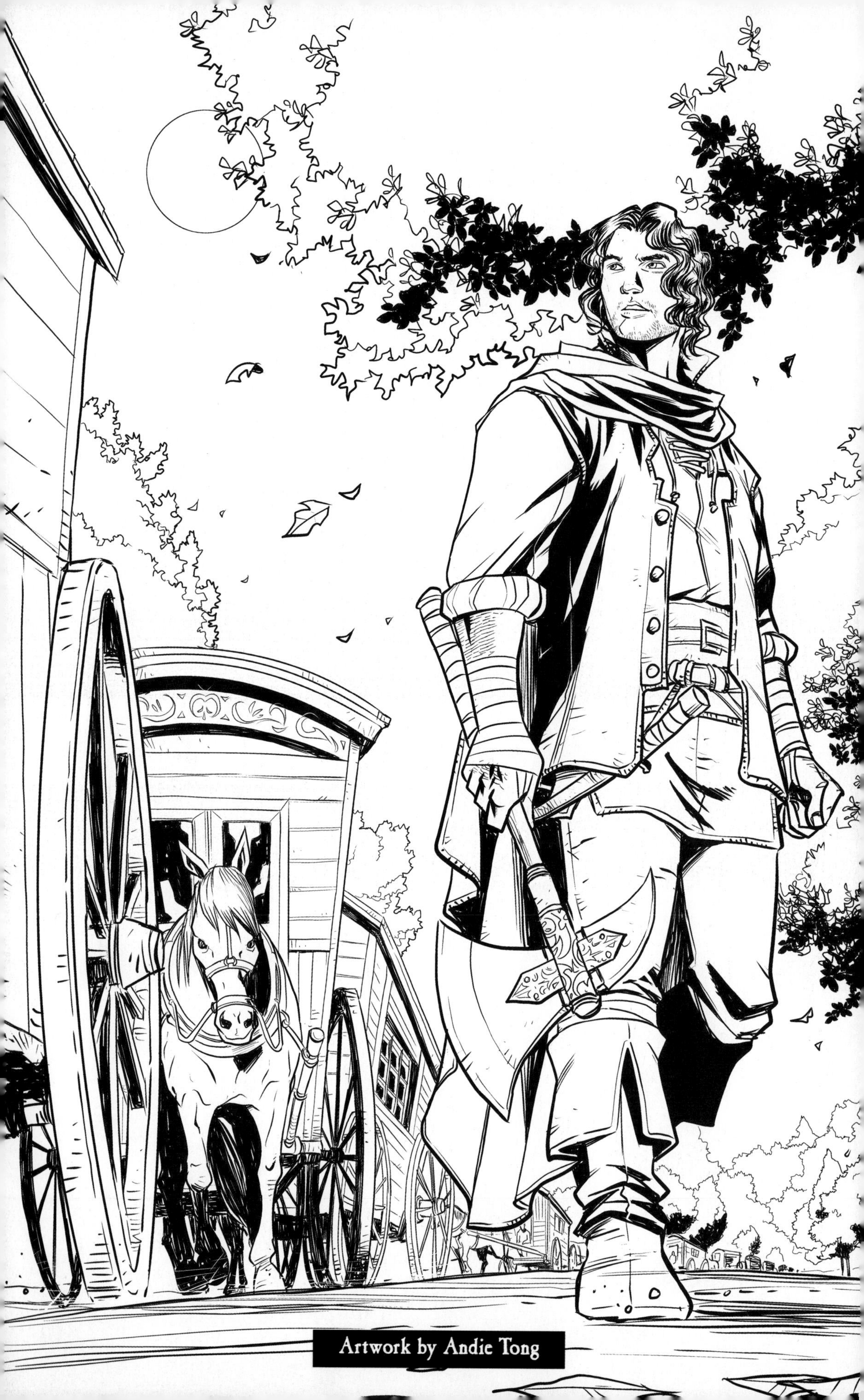

Artwork by Andie Tong

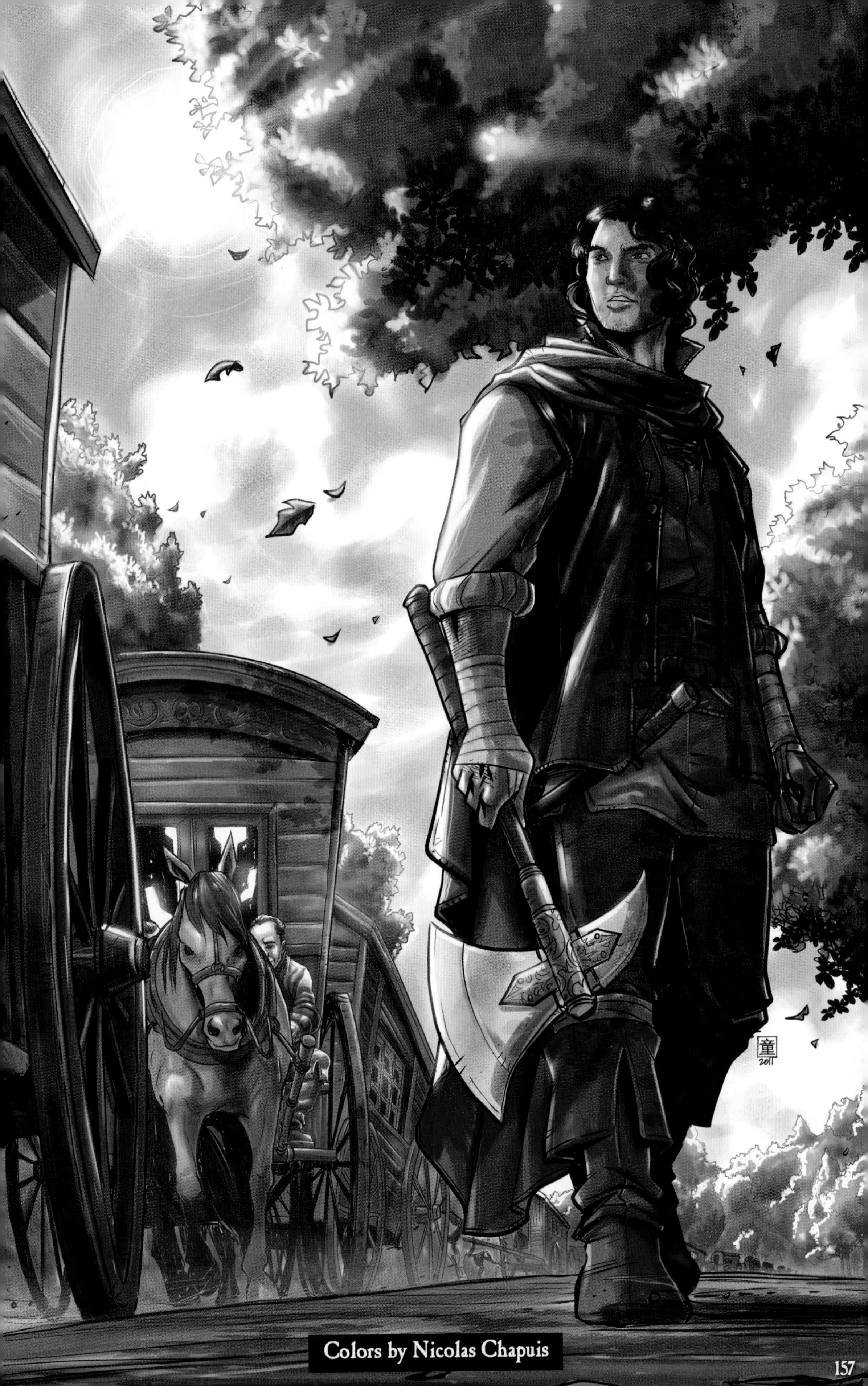

Colors by Nicolas Chapuis

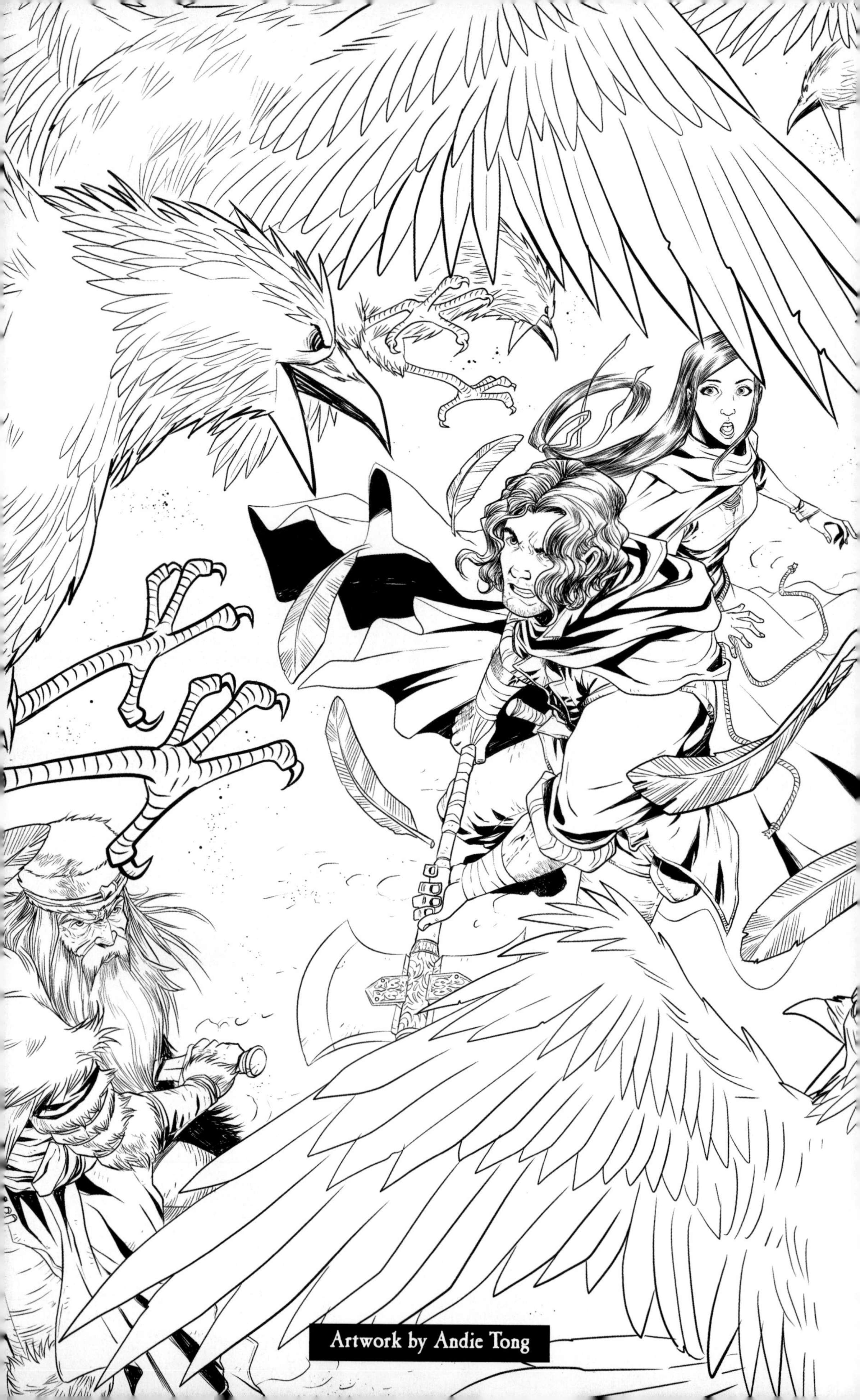

Artwork by Andie Tong

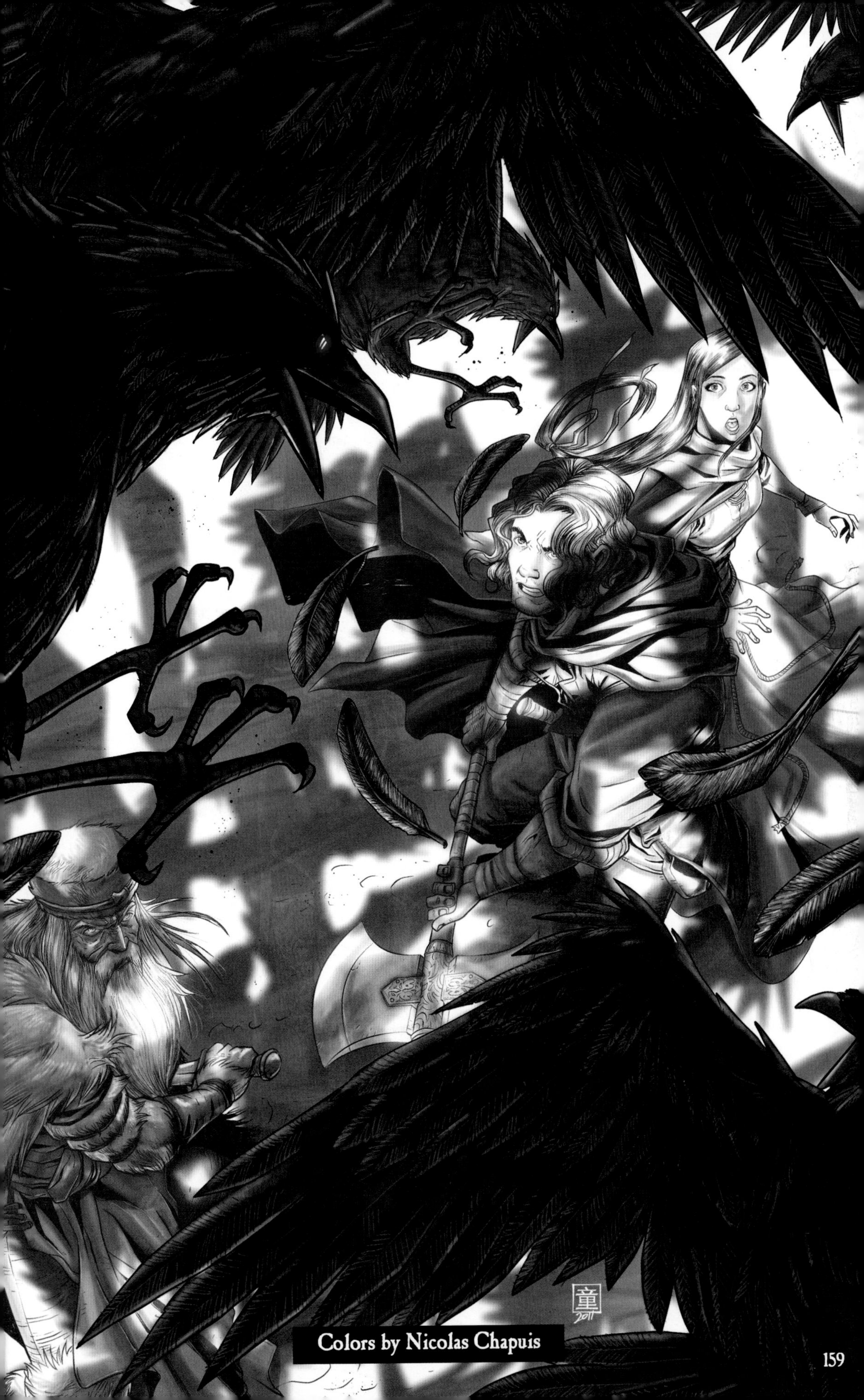

Colors by Nicolas Chapuis

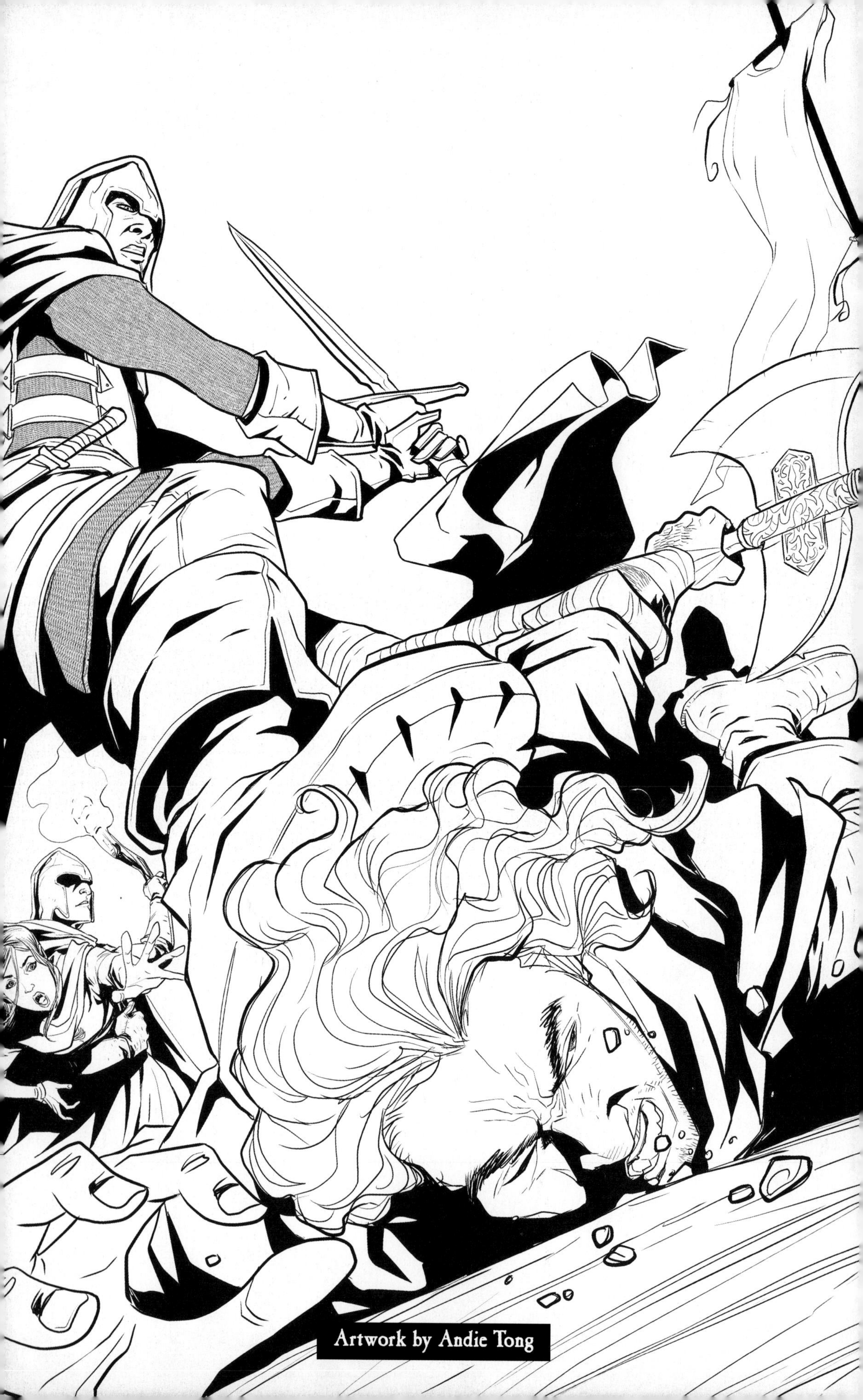

Artwork by Andie Tong

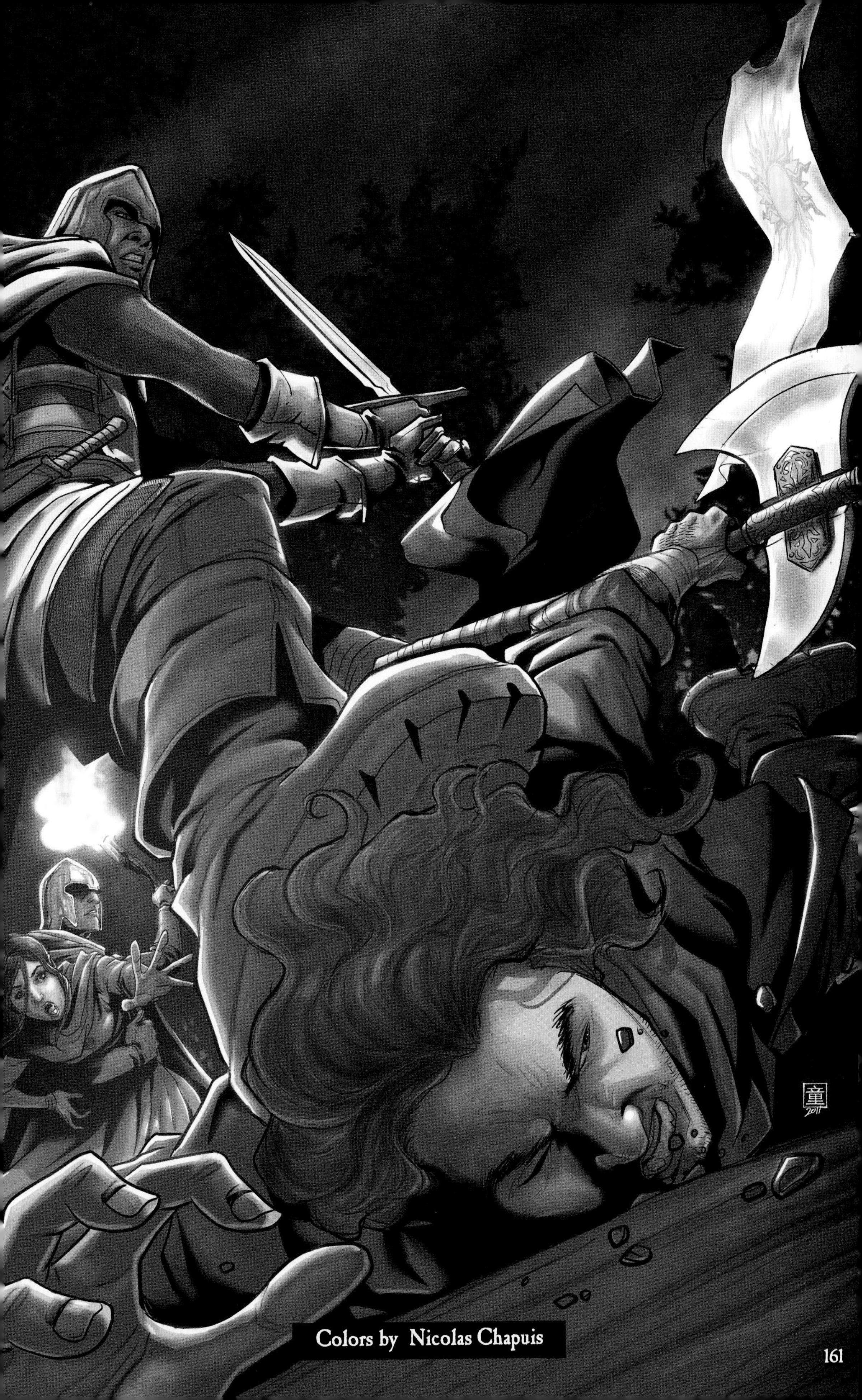

Colors by Nicolas Chapuis

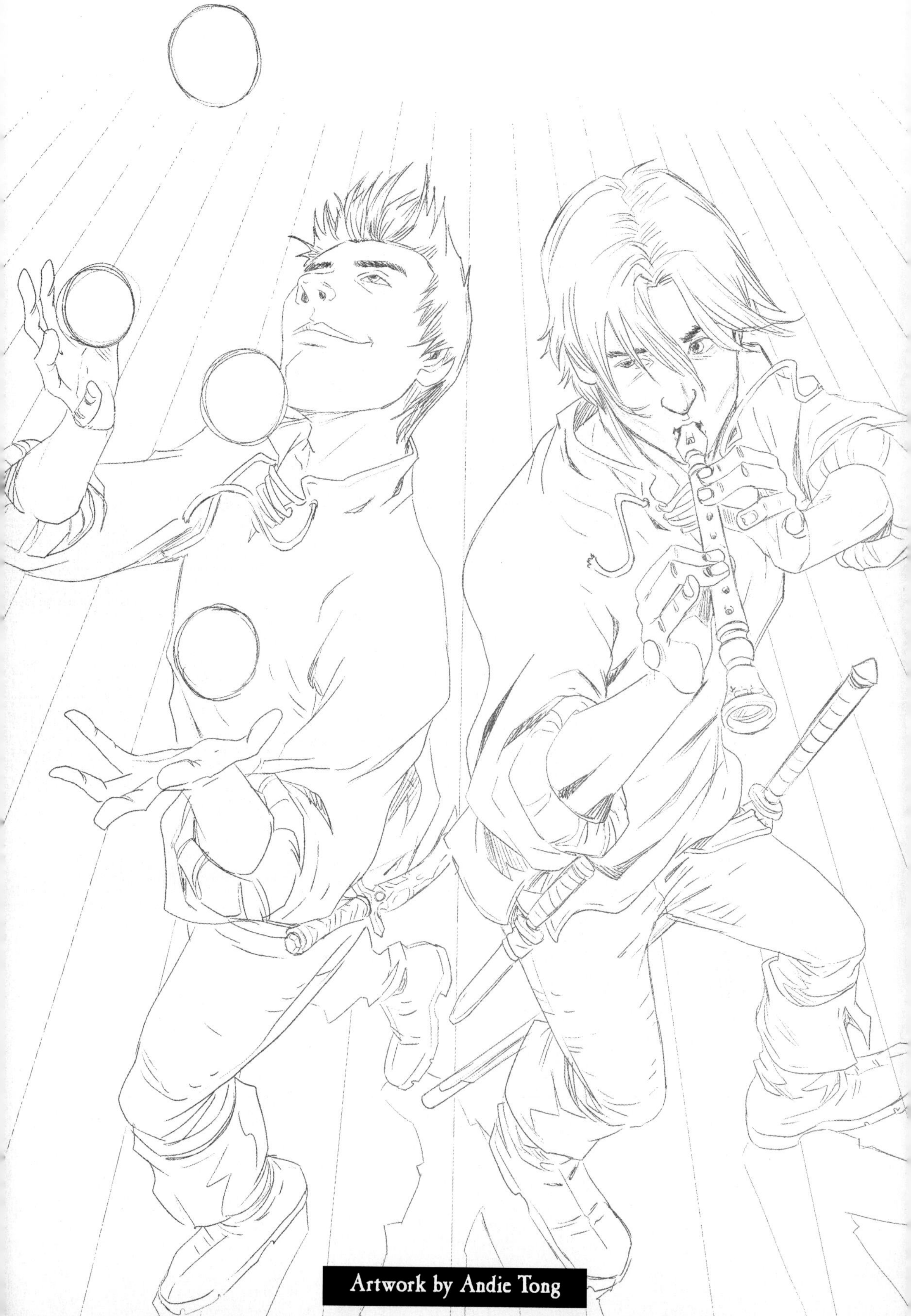

Artwork by Andie Tong

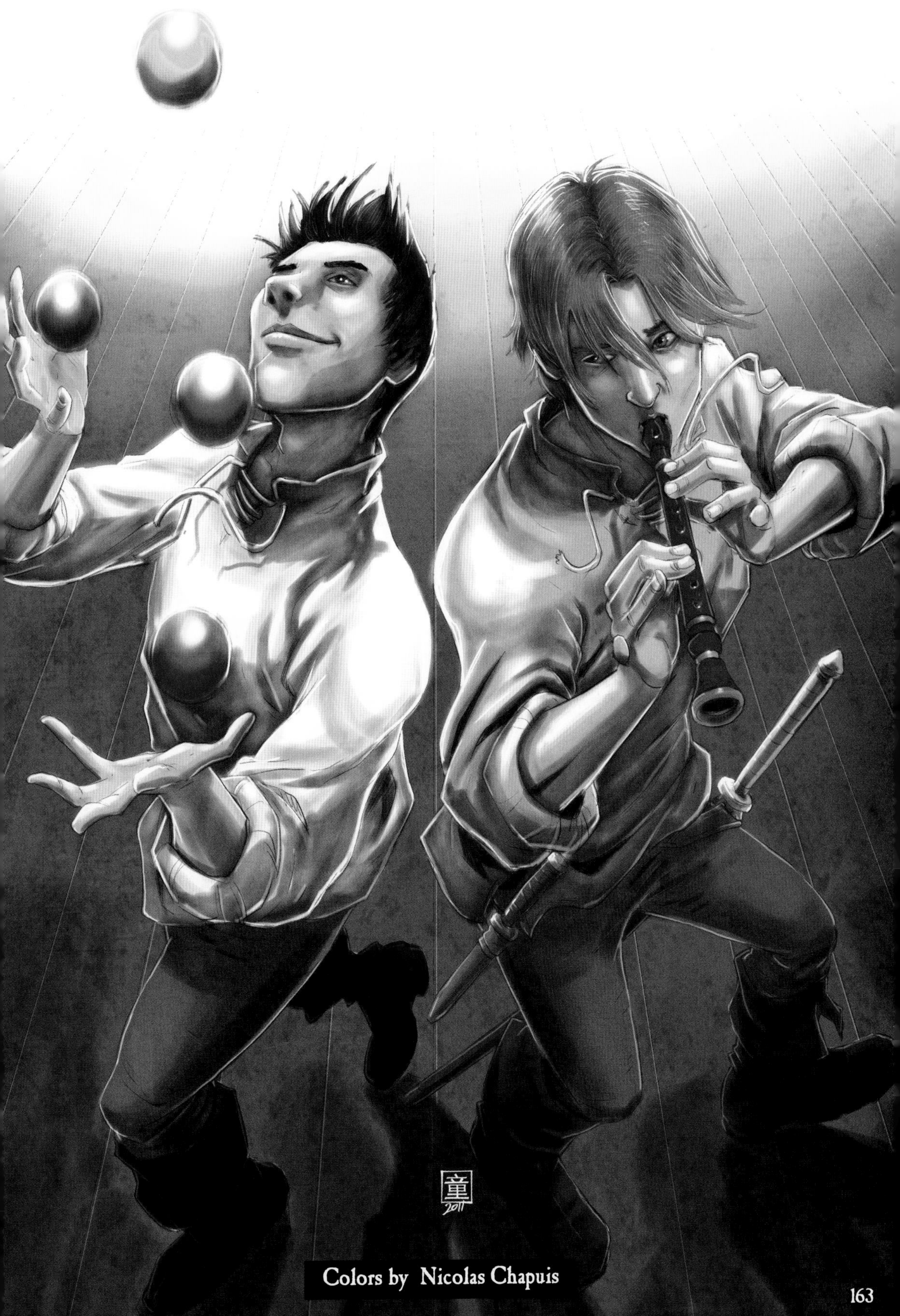

Colors by Nicolas Chapuis

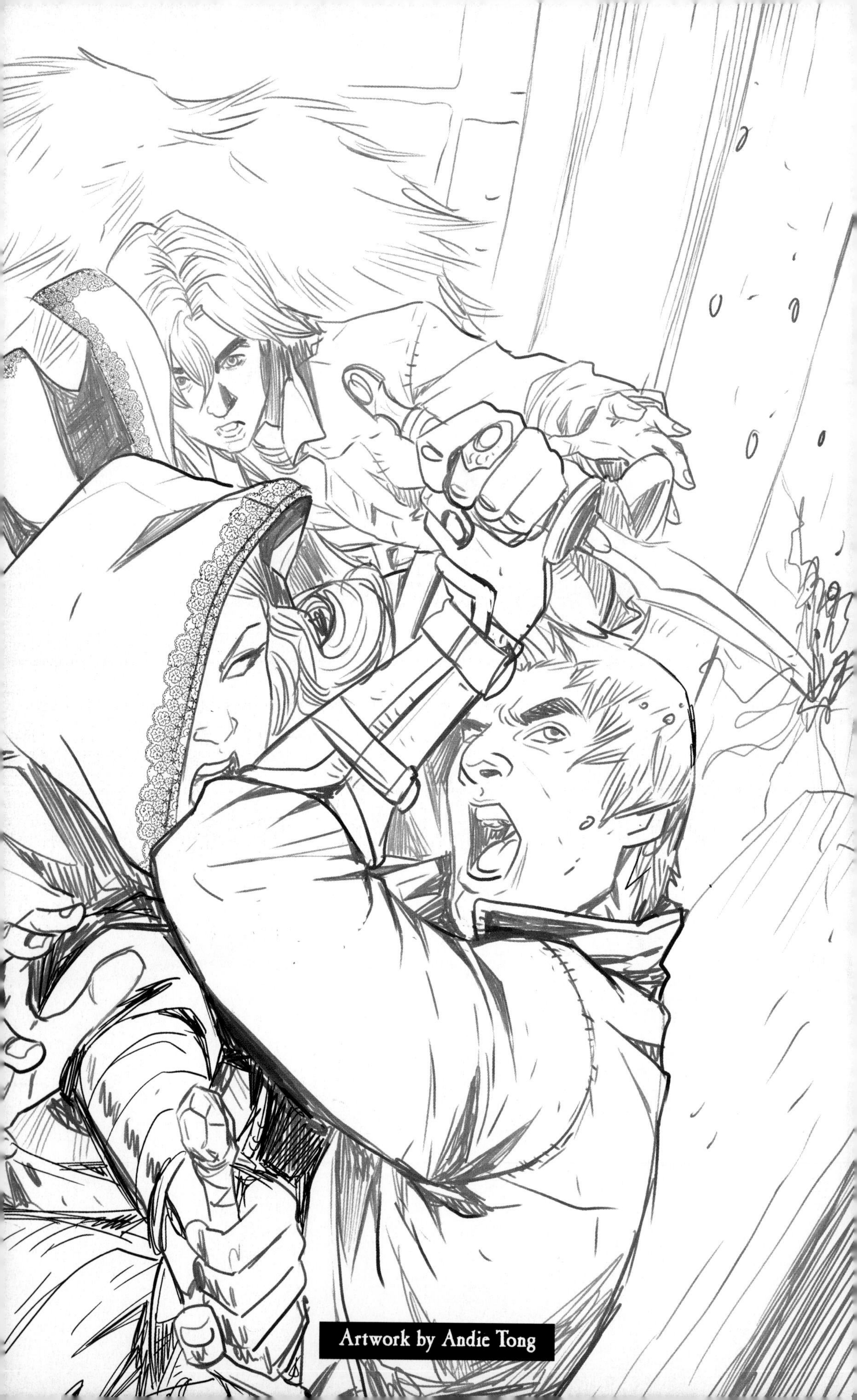

Artwork by Andie Tong

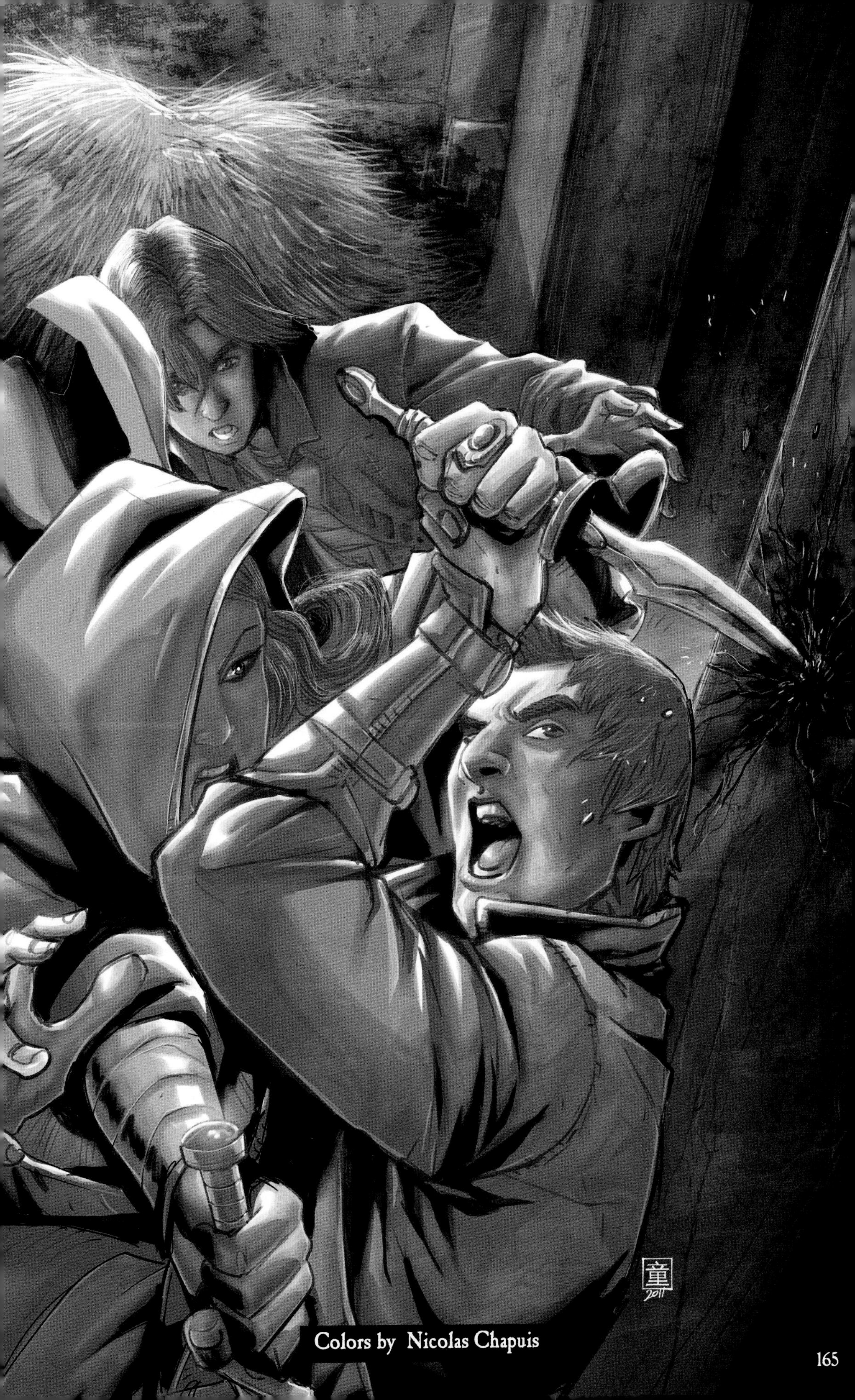

Colors by Nicolas Chapuis

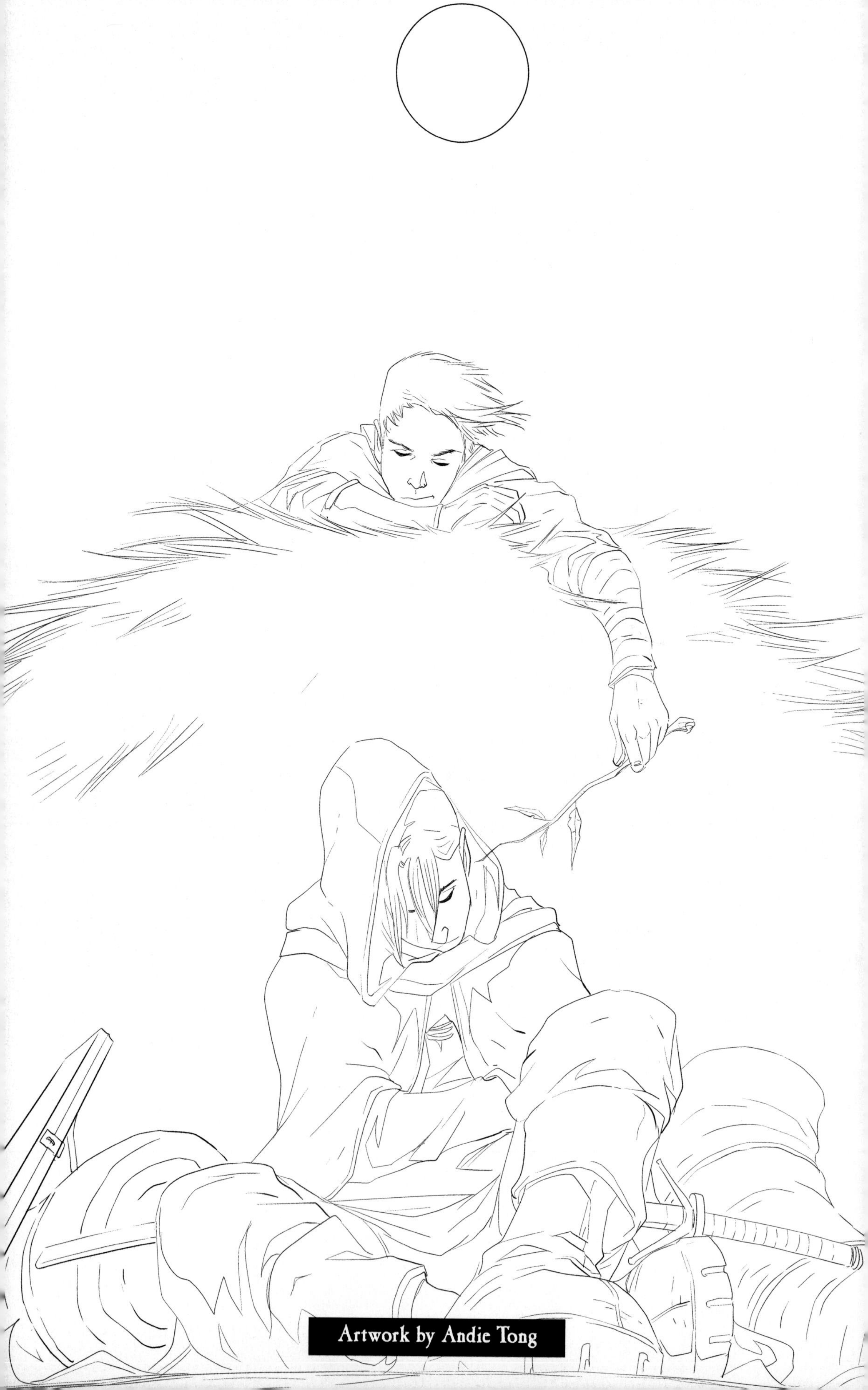

Artwork by Andie Tong

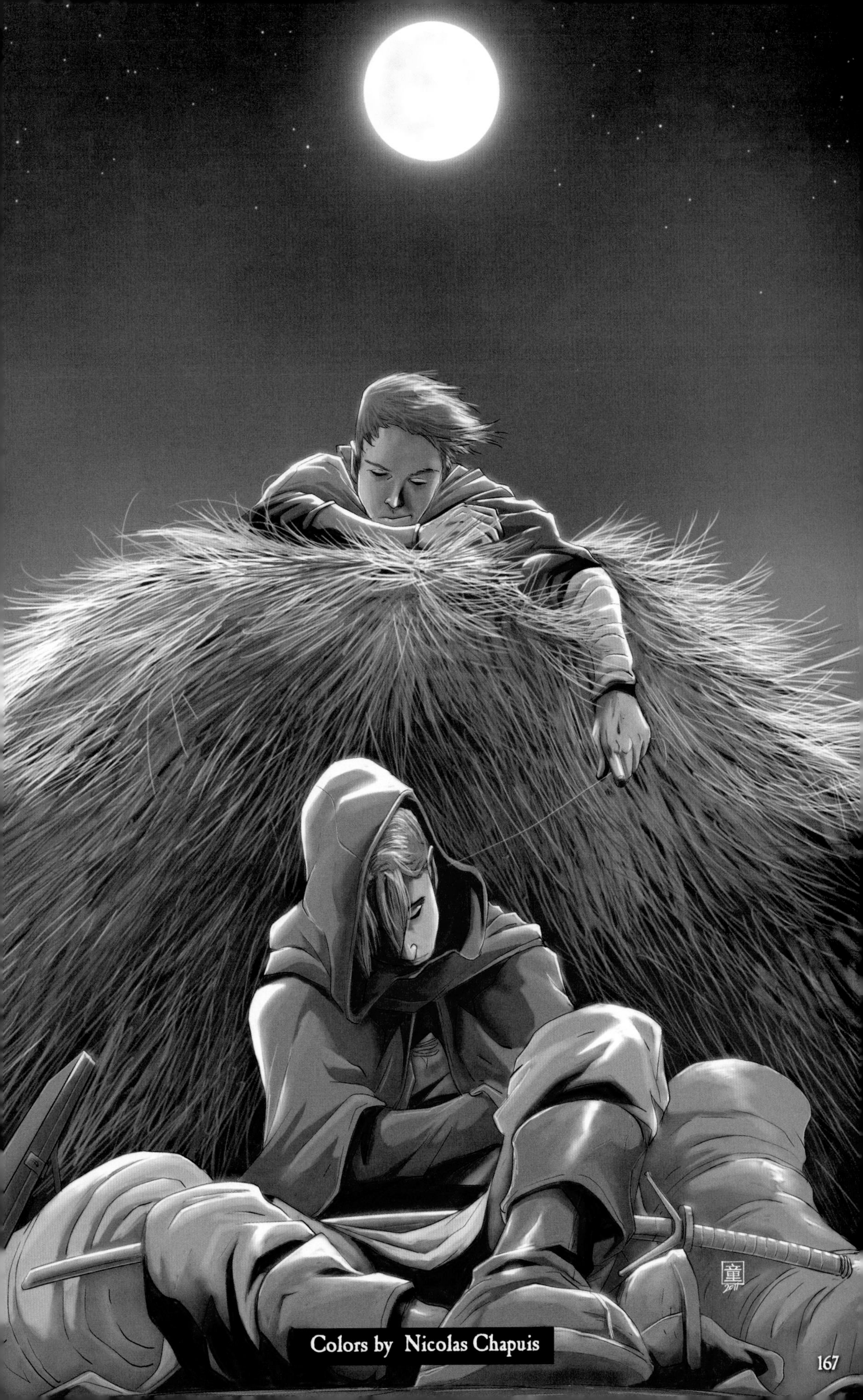

Colors by Nicolas Chapuis

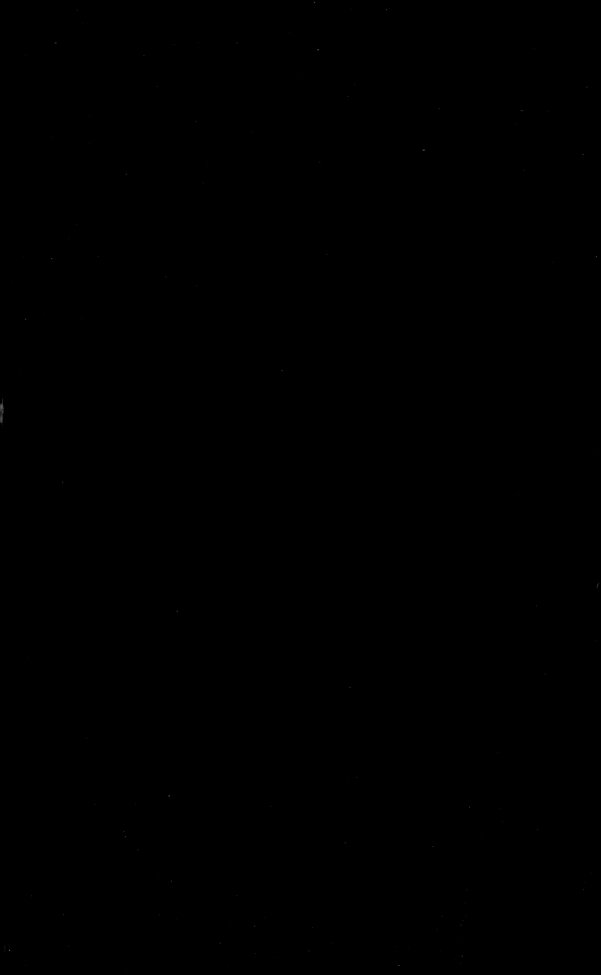

biographies

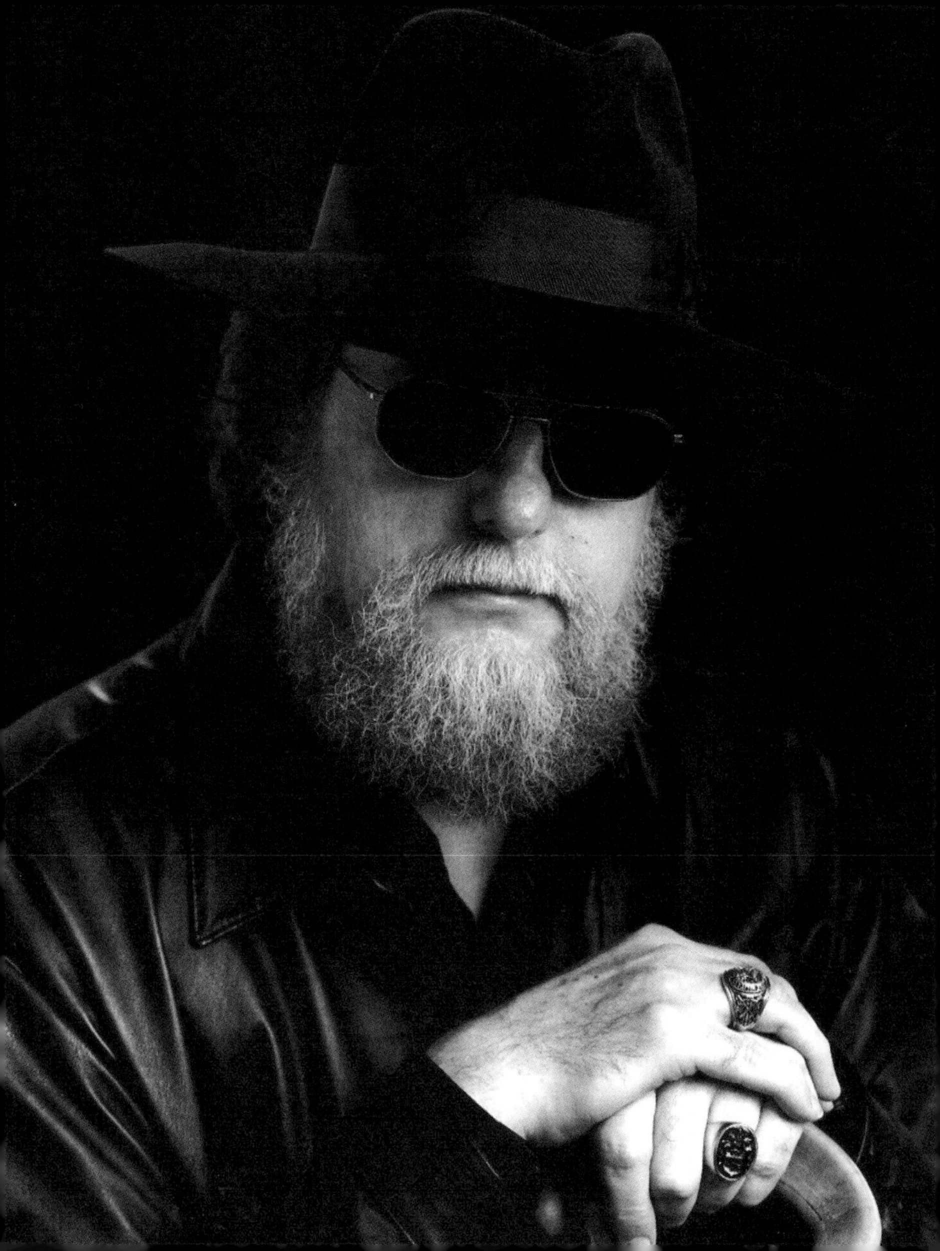

ROBERT JORDAN

Mr. Jordan was born in 1948 in Charleston, South Carolina. He taught himself to read when he was four with the incidental aid of a twelve-years-older brother, and was tackling Mark Twain and Jules Verne by five. He was a graduate of The Citadel, the Military College of South Carolina, with a degree in physics. He served two tours in Vietnam with the U. S. Army; among his decorations are the Distinguished Flying Cross with bronze oak leaf cluster, the Bronze Star with "V" and bronze oak leaf cluster, and two Vietnamese Gallantry Crosses with palm. A history buff, he also wrote dance and theater criticism and enjoyed the outdoor sports of hunting, fishing, and sailing, and the indoor sports of poker, chess, pool, and pipe collecting. He began writing in 1977 and went on to write The Wheel of Time®, one of the most important and bestselling series in the history of fantasy publishing with more than 14 million copies sold in North America, and countless more sold abroad. Robert Jordan died on September 16, 2007, after a courageous battle with the rare blood disease amyloidosis.

CHUCK DIXON

Mr. Dixon has worked for every major comic book publisher as a professional comic book writer. His credits include *The Hobbit* graphic novel, *The Punisher*, *Birds of Prey*, *Batman*, *Catwoman*, *Green Arrow*, *Green Lantern*, *Star Wars*, *Simpsons* comics, and the comic adaptation of *Dean Koontz's Frankenstein*.

Chuck currently resides in Florida.

ANDIE TONG

Mr. Tong started off as a multimedia designer in 1997 and eventually migrated full time to comics in 2006. Since then he has worked on titles such as *Tron: Betrayal*, *Spectacular Spider-Man UK*, *Batman Strikes*, *Smallville*, *TMNT*, *Masters of the Universe*, and *Starship Troopers*, working for companies such as Disney, Marvel, DC, Panini, Darkhorse, as well as commercial illustration for Nike, Universal, CBS, Mattel, and Hasbro. When he gets the chance, Andie concept designs for various companies and also juggles illustration duties on a range of children's picture storybooks for HarperCollins.

Mr. Tong currently resides in Singapore.

NICOLAS CHAPUIS

Mr. Chapuis was born in 1985 and decided to freelance as a comic book colorist after earning a degree in graphic design. His work includes *Robert Jordan's The Wheel of Time*, *Jonathan Stroud's Bartimaeus: The Amulet of Samarkand*, and *Richard Starking's Elephantmen*.

BILL TORTOLINI

Already an accomplished art director and graphic designer, Mr. Tortolini began lettering comics more than a decade ago and has worked with many of the comic book industry's top creators and publishers.

Current and past projects include: *Stephen King's Talisman*, *Anita Blake: Vampire Hunter*, *Army of Darkness*, *Random Acts of Violence*, *Wolverine*, *Back to Brooklyn*, *The Hedge Knight*, *Archie Comics*, *Riftwar*, *Battlestar Galactica*, *The Warriors*, *The Wheel of Time*, *The Dresden Files*, *Transformers*, *Star Trek: The Next Generation*, *G.I. Joe*, *The Last Resort*, and many others.

Mr. Tortolini resides in Billerica, Massachusetts, with his wife and three children, and his loyal dog Oliver.

Artwork by Andie Tong